South-East Asian Social Science Monographs

Non-Government Organizations and Democratic Participation in Indonesia

Non-Government Organizations and Democratic Participation in Indonesia

Philip J. Eldridge

BIBLIOTHÈQUES

uOttawa

LIBRARIES

KUALA LUMPUR

OXFORD UNIVERSITY PRESS

OXFORD SINGAPORE NEW YORK

1995

Oxford University Press

Oxford New York
Athens Auckland Bangkok Bombay
Calcutta Cape Town Dar es Salaam Delhi
Florence Hong Kong Istanbul Karachi
Madras Madrid Melbourne Mexico City
Nairobi Paris Shah Alam Singapore
Taipei Tokyo Toronto

and associated companies in
Berlin Ibadan

Oxford is a trade mark of Oxford University Press

Published in the United States
by Oxford University Press, New York

© Oxford University Press 1995
First published 1995

British Library Cataloguing in Publication Data
Data available

Library of Congress Cataloging-in-Publication Data
Eldridge, Philip J. (Philip John)
Non-government organizations and democratic participation in
Indonesia/Philip J. Eldridge.
p. cm. — (South-East Asian social science monographs)
Includes bibliographical references (p.) and index.
ISBN 967 65 3091 3:
1. Non-governmental organizations—Indonesia. 2. Indonesia—
Politics and government—1966– I. Title. II. Series: South-East
Asian social science monographs.
JQ762.E44 1995
323'. 042'09598—dc20
95-3588
CIP

Typeset by Indah Photosetting Centre Sdn. Bhd., Malaysia
Printed by Kyodo Printing Co. (S) Pte. Ltd., Singapore
Published by the South-East Asian Publishing Unit,
a division of Penerbit Fajar Bakti Sdn. Bhd.,
under licence from Oxford University Press,
4 Jalan U1/15, Seksyen U1, 40000 Shah Alam,
Selangor Darul Ehsan, Malaysia

Preface and Acknowledgements

THIS book represents a personal voyage of discovery as well as an academic endeavour, as my own outlook has changed a good deal over the ten years during which this work has been undertaken. The research process, which began in January 1983, has been somewhat interrupted. The basic manuscript was completed in December 1993, though occasional brief reference to more recent events has been interspersed in subsequent editing.

The origins of this work can, in part, be traced back to earlier research relating to the Australian aid programme in Indonesia in the 1970s, during the course of which I was first exposed to the work of non-government organizations (NGOs). Working mainly through OXFAM, and Community Aid Abroad which at that time supported an extensive range of local groups in Indonesia, I became aware of the dynamics of pioneering self-reliant development at village level. I also came to appreciate the complexities of multiple-level networking and communications entailed in such work, together with the range of support and advocacy roles undertaken by both national and overseas NGOs.

This earlier study took place at a time when the orthodox paradigm of development was coming under heavy fire. Criticism took both reformist and radical forms. Reformist analysis resulted in various reformulations in terms of growth with equity and basic human needs, while radical critiques were reflected in neo-Marxist or dependency theories. Over time, NGO praxis has incorporated both schools of thought, although direct field experience has remained their primary source of creativity. Nevertheless, I was rather more sceptical of the extent to which NGOs could have any serious impact on macro-level politics and decision-making. In a word, I considered them fairly apolitical but was interested in their potential for pioneering alternative models at a micro level, particularly in operationalizing basic human needs models of development.

Some explanation is perhaps required of references to India at various points in the text. The transition from development to politics, in my view of NGOs, occurred during 1983 when I enjoyed several months intensive field-level exposure to their work, first in India, then later in Indonesia. In India, at that time, there had been a substantial exodus from political parties, as part of a mood of growing scepticism about the capacity of political parties to reach out to the poor in specific ways relevant to their needs. However, Indian NGOs (or social action groups as they are often called) have demonstrated a remarkable capacity to link political and developmental spheres in mobilizing disadvantaged groups, both to take their own independent action and to make demands on the state and political process.

While I was not surprised to find such levels of popular awareness and mobilization in India, I was moderately surprised to find them not too far below the surface in Indonesia also. The two countries are, of course, considerably different in culture and social structure, and in their institutions. One relevant difference is that Indonesian NGOs have not yet had to work out a philosophy and operating style to deal with political parties. These are effectively moribund in Indonesia but are active and competitive at all levels in India, where they pose many problems for NGOs, in addition to those which they face in both countries in structuring relations with government agencies.

Despite these differences, many common themes, values, and aspirations and styles of organization, networking, and coalition-building are apparent. Above all, the theme of democratic participation links NGO approaches in both countries. As the study will show in the case of Indonesia, this concept is often confused and ambiguous in its formulation, while articulation of goals can be both utopian and pragmatic. Yet, although their achievements have been mixed, the discourse which NGOs have generated can most usefully be seen as part of an emerging and lively counter-culture in both countries.

Writing about non-government organizations has many pitfalls. (My methodology is explained in the Introduction.) The diversity of the NGO scene in Indonesia is extensive. Consequently, I make no claims to comprehensiveness. I am aware of many groups, including newer groups which are already making a significant impact. However, I have written, so far as possible, only about networks and organizations with which I have at some point made direct contact, supplementing these accounts from documentary sources. Even then, it has only been possible to look at a small proportion of their programmes. No judgements about the worth of anyone's work are therefore implied by their absence from this account. Further, in addition to the constant turnover of organizations and actors, philosophies and agendas are subject to continuing redefinition. Consequently, the conceptual map which underpins this analysis may well be in need of revision by the time the book appears, though hopefully readers will find the framework capable of adaptation to changing circumstances.

I have found a tendency to either over- or underestimate the importance of NGOs in both developmental and political contexts. This book naturally takes pains to explain and justify why I see them, together with other non-state actors, as contributing significantly towards the processes of democratization and the strengthening of civil society in Indonesia. Some readers may nevertheless experience difficulty in accepting that NGOs can play significant political or even developmental, as distinct from welfare and charity, roles. One reason may be that non-state groups have been marginalized in the perceptions of those who see governments and business as prime agents of societal change. Awareness that NGOs can and do play a multiplicity of roles, which involve them in complex forms of public advocacy, has grown slowly. On the other hand, once this point has been grasped, expectations may develop that NGOs are on the verge of achieving some major political transformation. These, no doubt, represent displaced hopes by those who would like to see NGOs as substitute political parties. While neither extreme is realistic, hopefully much middle ground of solid achievement and future potential will be indicated in this study.

Acknowledgements are always hazardous, as many who have provided information and insights, and in other ways helped to make this work convivial, can easily be forgotten. Those omitted will hopefully show forebearance. I wish, in any case, to express heartfelt gratitude to many people too numerous to mention individually, in organizations referred to in the text, together with local people and officials who gave generously of their time to yet another curious foreigner and who, in virtually all cases, manifested great openness. If anything written in this book can, in some way, support those less advantaged in Indonesia whom non-government organizations and other social activists seek to empower, this would be the best possible form of repayment.

Those among the NGO community who have especially assisted me in developing my ideas over more than one visit include the late Mary Johnson; Sutrisno Kusomohadi; Lukas Hendrata; Adi Sasono; Achmad Rofie; Fauzi Abdullah; Mulya Lubis; Heri Ahmadi; Abdul Hakim Nusantara; Kacono; Anton Sujarwo; Bambang Ismawan; Aswab Mahasin; Fr. Mangunwijaya; the late Kyai Hamam Ja'afar; Fr. Suasso; Fr. de Blot; Darwis Khudori; Mochtar Abbas; H. J. Princen; Hardaputantro; Fr. Chris Melchers; Joachim Dwi Heru; Idaman; Toto Raharjo; Abbas Ghazaly; Erna Witular; Agus Purnomo; Jajat Suhaja; Dindin Moelyani; Imam Yudotomo; Indhro Tjahjono; Hira Jhamtani; Heri Ahmadi; Pat Walsh; Toni Pangen; Peter Britton, and Julie Larsen.

Thanks are due to the Institute for Rural and Regional Studies, Gadjah Mada University, Yogyakarta, which provided me with an institutional base at various stages. Academic colleagues in Indonesia who have provided insights and encouragement at various stages include Prof. Hasan Poerbo; Prof. Otto Soemarwoto; Prof. Mubyarto; Prof. Koesnadi Hardjasoemantri; Loekman Sutrisno; Dorojatun Kuncoro Yakti; Arief Budiman; Dawam Raharjo, and Juni Thamrin. Other academic colleagues to whom I owe gratitude include Benjamin White; Bill Liddle; Anton Lucas; Jim and Barbara Schiller; Betty and Herb Feith; the late David Penny; James Scott; Lance Castles, and Juliet Hunt. Particular thanks are due to Susan Blackburn, who commented on the chapter concerning women's mobilization; David Bourchier, who commented on labour, human rights, and general political aspects, and Gerry van Klinken, who gave detailed and meticulous commentary on the whole manuscript.

Financial support is acknowledged at various stages from the Australian Research Council and the University of Tasmania. Thanks are due to colleagues in the Political Science Department for continuing financial, logistical, and moral support. Secretarial and computing assistance from Beverley Brill and Rosemary Smuts is acknowledged, as is research assistance from Liz Clark, Indra Kuruppu, Rick Snell, Jill White, Axel Bosslemann, and Sharon Bessell. Indexing was undertaken by Clodagh Jones.

Friends whose hospitality and other kinds of support have been appreciated include Anne and Jonathan Parapak in Jakarta; Ian and May Cairns, Dibyo and Mina Prabowo, Fong and Yohan Senduk in Yogyakarta; Amalia Baswati and Sjafra Dwipa in Bandung; Francoise and Lester Levinson in Melbourne.

Finally, and specially deserving of acknowledgement, is my family, who have shared some of the field visits and adventure, but have more often accepted with love an absent or preoccupied father and husband. Additionally, my wife Margaret has provided special expertise in the proofreading of many drafts.

Nevertheless, responsibility for interpretations, errors, and omissions remains entirely my own.

University of Tasmania   Philip Eldridge
Hobart
October 1994

Contents

Plates

Abbreviations and Acronyms

ABRI	Angkatan Bersenjata Republik Indonesia (Armed Forces of the Republic of Indonesia)
ACPO	Asian Committee for People's Organizations
APHD	Asian Partnership for Human Development
BAKIN	Badan Koordinasi Intelijens Negara (State Intelligence Co-ordinating Board)
BAKORSTANASDA	Badan Koordinasi Stabilitas Daerah (Regional Stability Co-ordinating Board)
BANGDES	Pembangunan Desa (Rural Development Arm of the Department of Home Affairs—Departemen Dalam Negeri)
BAPEDAL	Badan Pengendalian Dampak Lingkungan Hidup (Environmental Impact Monitoring Board)
BAPPEDA	Badan Perencanaan Pembangunan Daerah (Regional Development Planning Board)
BAPPEMKA	Badan Perencanaan Pembangunan Kabupaten (District Development Planning Board)
BAPPENAS	Badan Perencanaan Pembangunan Nasional (National Development Planning Board)
BIMAS	Bimbingan Massal (Mass Guidance—improved rice varieties programme)
BINEKSOS	Perhimpunan Indonesia untuk Pembinaan Pengetahuan Ekonomi dan Sosial (Indonesian Association for the Promotion of Economic and Social Knowledge)
BINGO	Big NGO
BKKBN	Badan Koordinasi Keluarga Berencana Nasional (National Family Planning Co-ordinating Board)
BKKP	Badan Kesejahteraan Karyawan Pendidikan (Education Staff Credit Co-operative and Welfare Body) (Cibadak)
BKSP	Biro Konsultasi Simpan Pinjam (Savings and Loans Consultative Bureau)
BK3D	Badan Koordinasi Koperasi Kredit Daerah

	(Regional Credit Co-operative Co-ordinating Board)
BK3I	Badan Koordinasi Koperasi Kredit Indonesia (Indonesian Credit Co-operative Co-ordinating Board)
BK3S	Badan Koordinasi Kegiatan Kesejahteraan Sosial (Social Welfare Co-ordinating Board)
BKWK	Badan Kontak Wanita Koperasi (Contact Board for Women's Co-operatives)
BPPT	Badan Penkajian dan Penerapan Teknologi (Board for Applied Technology Research)
BS	Bina Swadaya (Fostering Self-reliance)
BUKOPIN	Bank Umum Koperasi Indonesia (Indonesian Co-operative Bank)
CCA	Christian Conference of Asia
CEBEMO	Katholieke Organisatie voor Ontwikelingssa-menwerking Nederland (Netherlands Catholic Organization for Development Co-operation)
CGI	Consultative Group for Indonesia (Replaced IGGI in 1992)
CHIPPS	Comprehensive Health Improvement Pro-gramme Province Specific
CIDA	Canadian International Development Asso-ciation
CJEP	Central Java Enterprise Programme
CUCO	Credit Union Co-ordinating Organization
DEKOPIN	Dewan Koperasi Indonesia (Indonesian Council of Co-operatives)
DEPKES	Departemen Kesehatan (Department of Health)
DEPKOP	Departemen Koperasi (Department of Co-operatives)
DEPSOS	Departemen Sosial (Department of Social Affairs)
DGI	Dewan Gereja-Gereja Indonesia (Indonesian Council of Churches) (Renamed PGI—Persekutuan Gereja-Gereja di Indonesia in 1984)
DIY	Daerah Istimewa Yogyakarta (Yogyakarta Special Region)
DML	Dana Mitra Lingkungan (Friends of the Environment Fund)
DNIKS	Dewan Nasional Indonesia untuk Kesejah-teraan Sosial (Indonesian Council for Social Welfare)
DPR	Dewan Perwakilan Rakyat (People's Representative Assembly)

DPRD	Dewan Perwakilan Rakyat Daerah (People's Regional Representative Assembly)
EIA	Environmental Impact Analysis
FAHAMI	Forum Agama-Agama untuk Hak Asasi Manusia (Indonesian Inter-Religion Forum for Human Rights)
FBH	Federasi Bantuan Hukum (Legal Aid Federation)
FDPY	Forum Diskusi Perempuan Yogyakarta (Yogyakarta Women's Discussion Forum)
FEER	Far Eastern Economic Review
FISKA	Forum Indonesia untuk Swadaya Kependudukan (Indonesian Forum for Self-reliant Population Control)
FKMY	Forum Komunikasi Mahasiswa Yogyakarta (Yogyakarta Students' Communication Forum)
FNS	Friedrich Neumann Stiftung (Germany)
FORSOL	Forum Solidaritas untuk Buruh (Solidarity Forum for Labour)
FPY	Forum Perempuan Yogyakarta (Yogyakarta Women's Forum)
FSBI	Federasi Serikat Buruh Indonesia (Federation of Indonesian Trade Unions)
GATE	German Appropriate Technology Exchange
GOLKAR	Golongan Karya (Functional Groups)
GONGO	Government Organized Non-Government Organization
GTZ	German Technische Suzammen Arbeit (German Technical Co-operation Agency)
HBKP	Huria Batak Keristen Protestan (Batak Protestant Christian Church)
HKTI	Himpunan Kerukunan Tani Indonesia (Indonesian Farmers' Association)
ICA	International Co-operatives Association
ICCO	Internationaal Christelijk Consortium voor Ontwikkelingssamenwerking (International Christian Consortium for Development Co-operation)
ICFTU	International Congress of Free Trade Unions
IGGI	Inter-Governmental Group for Indonesia (Reformed as CGI in 1992)
IKADIN	Ikatan Advokat Indonesia (Indonesian Lawyers' Association)
IKK	Ikatan Kader-Kader (Association of Cadres)
ILO	International Labour Organization (affiliate of the United Nations)
IMF	International Monetary Fund

IN-DEMO	Indonesian NGOs for Democracy
INDHRRA	Indonesian Secretariat for the Development of Human Resources in Rural Areas
INDOC	Indonesian Documentation and Information Centre (Leiden)
INFID	International NGO Forum for Indonesian Development
INFIGHT	Indonesian Front for the Defence of Human Rights
INGI	International NGO Forum on Indonesia
INPRES	Instruksi Presiden (Presidential Instruction— Rural Development Programme)
INSAN	Informasi dan Studi untuk Hak Asasi Manusia (Human Rights Information and Study Network)
IPB	Institut Pertanian Bogor (Bogor Agricultural Institute)
IPI	Ikatan Pemulung Indonesia (Indonesian Scavengers' Association)
IRJA	Irian Jaya
ITB	Institut Teknologi Bandung (Bandung Institute of Technology)
ITP	Ikatan Tani Pancasila (Panca Sila Farmers' Association)
KLH	Departemen Kependudukan dan Lingkungan Hidup (Department of Population and Environment)
KNPI	Komite Nasional Pemuda Indonesia (Indonesian National Youth Committee)
KOWANI	Korps Wanita Indonesia (Indonesian Women's Corps)
KPPKLY	Koperasi Persatuan Pedagang Kaki Lima Yogyakarta (Association of Yogyakarta Street Trading Co-operatives)
KSBH	Kelompok Studi untuk Bantuan Hukum (Legal Aid Study Group)
KSP	Kelompok Solidaritas Perempuan (Women's Solidarity Group)
KSPPM	Kelompok Studi Pengembangan Prakarsa Masyarakat (Study Group for the Development of People's Initiative)
K-13	Kelompok Tigabelas (Group of Thirteen national-level NGOs)
KUBE	Kelompok Usaha Bersama Ekonomi (informal, co-operative small enterprise group)
KUD	Koperasi Unit Desa (Village Co-operative Unit)
LBH	Lembaga Bantuan Hukum (Legal Aid Institute)

LBHY	Lembaga Bantuan Hukum Yogyakarta (Yogyakarta Legal Aid Institute)
LEMHAMNAS	Lembaga Hankam Nasional (National Defence Institute)
LINGO	Little NGO
LKBHWK	Lembaga Konsultasi Bantuan Hukum Wanita dan Keluarga (Legal Aid Consultative Institute for Women and Families)
LKMD	Lembaga Ketahanan Masyarakat Desa (Village Community Resilience Institution)
LMD	Lembaga Musyawarah Desa (Village Consultative Institution)
LPHAM	Lembaga Pembela Hak-Hak Asasi Manusia (Institute for Defence of Human Rights)
LPPS	Lembaga Penelitian dan Pembangunan Sosial (Institute for Social Research and Development)
LPSM	Lembaga Pengembangan Swadaya Masyarakat (Institute for Developing Community Self-reliance)
LP3ES	Lembaga Penelitian, Pendidikan, dan Penerangan Ekonomi dan Sosial (Social and Economic Research, Education, and Information Institute)
LPTP	Lembaga Pengembangan Teknologi Pedesaan (Rural Technology Development Institute)
LSD	Lembaga Sosial Desa (Village Community Institution)
LSM	Lembaga Swadaya Masyarakat (Self-reliant Community Institution)
LSP	Lembaga Studi Pembangunan (Institute of Development Studies)
LWR	Lembaga Wanita dan Remaja (Institute for Women and Teenagers—SPSI)
MAWI	Majelis Agung Wali-Gereja Indonesia (Indonesian (Catholic) Bishops' Council)
MENDAGRI	Menteri Dalam Negeri (Minister for Home Affairs)
MPR	Majelis Pemusyawaratan Rakyat (People's Deliberative Assembly)
NGO	Non-Government Organization
NOVIB	Nederlandse Organisatie voor Internationale Bijstand (Netherlands Organization for International Development Co-operation)
NU	Nahdlatul Ulama (Religious Teachers' Association)
ORMAS	Undang Undang Organisasi Kemasyarakatan (1985 Law on Social Organizations)

ORNOP — Organisasi Non-Pemerintah (Non-Government Organization)

OXFAM — Oxford Committee for Famine Relief (UK)

PDF — Participatory Development Forum

PEKERTI — Pengembangan Kerajinan Rakyat Indonesia (Association for Developing Indonesian People's Handicrafts)

PELKESI — Pelayanan Keristen Kesehatan Seluruh Indonesia (All-Indonesia Christian Health Service)

PERADIN — Persatuan Advokat Indonesia (Indonesian Advocates' Association)

PERDAKHI — Persatuan Karya Dharma Kesehatan Indonesia (Indonesian Association of Voluntary Health Groups)

PGI — Persekutuan Gereja-Gereja Indonesia (Indonesian Communion of Churches) (replaced DGI in 1984)

PIK — Program Industri Kecil (Small Industry Programme)

PKBI — Perkumpulan Keluarga Berencana Indonesia (Indonesian Family Planning Association)

PKI — Partai Komunis Indonesia (Communist Party of Indonesia)

PKK — Pembinaan Kesejahteraan Keluarga (Association for Promoting Family Welfare)

POSYANDU — Pos Pelayanan Terpadu (Integrated Health Service Post)

PPERT — Proyek Peningkatan Ekonomi Rumah Tangga (Household Income Project) (Klaten)

PPLH/ITB — Pusat Penelitian Lingkungan Hidup/Institut Teknologi Bandung (Environmental Research Centre–Bandung Institute of Technology)

PPP — Partai Persatuan Pembangunan (Development Unity Party)

PROKASIH — Program Kali Bersih (River Cleaning Programme)

PSI — Partai Sosialis Indonesia (Socialist Party of Indonesia)

PT — Pereroan Terbatas (Limited Company)

P3A — Perkumpulan Petani Pemanfaat Air (Farmer Water Users' Association—supported by Bina Swadaya))

P3M — Perkumpulan Pengembangan Pesantren dan Masyarakat (Association for Pesantren and Community Development)

PUPUK	Perkumpulan Untuk Pengembangan Usaha Kecil (Association for Promoting Small Enterprise)
PUSKESMAS	Pusat Kesehatan Masyarakat (Community Health Centre)
PUSKOWANJATI	Pusat Koperasi Wanita Jawa Timur (East Java Women's Co-operatives' Centre)
PWP	Productive Women's Programme (LP3ES Klaten)
RT	Rukun Tetangga (village and neighbourhood/ward)
SBSI	Serikat Buruh Sejahtera Indonesia (Indonesian Workers' Welfare Association)
SEKNEG	Sekretariat Negara (State Secretariat)
SISKAMLING	Sistem Keamanan Lingkungan (Neighbourhood Watch System)
SKEPHI	Jaringan Kerjasama Pelestarian Hutan Indonesia (Indonesian Network for Forest Conservation) (until 1987 Sekretariat Kerjasama Pelestarian Hutan Indonesia—Joint Secretariat for Indonesian Forest Conservation)
SPES	Society for Political and Economic Studies (LP3ES)
SPJB	Serikat Petani Jawa Barat (West Java Farmers' Association)
SPSI	Serikat Pekerja Seluruh Indonesia (All-Indonesia Workers' Union)
UB	*usaha bersama* (informal joint enterprise)
UN	United Nations
UNICEF	United Nations Children's Emergency Fund
UPI	United Press International
USAID	United States Agency for International Development
WALHI	Wahana Lingkungan Hidup Indonesia (Indonesian Environment Network)
YAKKUM	Yayasan Keristen untuk Kesehatan Umum (Christian Foundation for Public Health)
YAPPI	Yayasan Pengembangan Pendidikan Islam (Foundation for the Development of Islamic Education)
Yasanti	Yayasan Anisa Swasti
YBK	Yayasan Bina Karya (Foundation for Labour Advancement)
YBLH	Yayasan Bina Lingkungan Hidup (Institute for Environmental Care)
YBS	Yayasan Bina Sehat (Foundation for Health Promotion)

YDD	Yayasan Dian Desa (Village Light Foundation)
YIS	Yayasan Indonesia Sejahtera (Prosperous Indonesia Foundation)
YLBHI	Yayasan Lembaga Bantuan Hukum Indonesia (Foundation of Indonesian Legal Aid Institutions)
YLKI	Yayasan Lembaga Konsumen Indonesia (Indonesian Foundation of Consumers' Organizations)
YPMD	Yayasan Pengembangan Masyarakat Desa (Rural Community Development Foundation) Irian Jaya
YPPSE	Yayasan Pembangunan dan Pengembangan Sosial Ekonomi (Foundation for Social and Economic Development)
YPSK	Yayasan Proyek Sosial Keluarga (Family Social Service Institute)
YSS	Yayasan Sosial Soegyapranata (Soegyapranata Social Institute)
YSTM	Yayasan Sosial Tani Membangun (Farmers' Social Development Institute)
YTKI	Yayasan Tenaga Kerja Indonesia (Indonesian Labour Institute)
YTRI	Yayasan Teater Rakyat Indonesia (Indonesian People's Theatre Institute)

Glossary

adat	customary law and practice
arisan	traditional lottery and mutual help association
badan	executive body
badan hukum	legal body
bangsa	nation
banjar	hamlet (lowest unit of local administration in Bali)
becak	human-powered tricycle passenger vehicle
Budi Utomo	Javanese spiritual and cultural association
buruh	worker, labourer
dakwah	Islamic missionary activity
Dalam Negeri	(Department of) Home Affairs
Dana Sehat	community health insurance programme
desa	village
dewan	council
golongan karya	functional groups
gotong royong	mutual assistance/co-operation
hak milik	freehold title
kabupaten	district
kampung	(rural or urban) village-type community settlement
kedaulatan rakyat	people's sovereignty
kelompok	group
kemandirian	self-reliance
kesejahteraan sosial	social welfare
ketahanan	resilience
kopdit	credit co-operative (*koperasi kredit*)
koperasi	(officially registered) co-operative
Kring	small 'circle' or 'cell' groups which work together
kyai	head and spiritual leader of a *pesantren*
lembaga	institution
lingkungan hidup	environment
lurah	village head (Java)
masyarakat	community
Mbangun Deso (Javanese)	village development programme
mitra	friend
mufakat	consensus

musyawarah	deliberation
negara	state
negara hukum	rule of law
organisasi	
kemasyarakatan	social organization
organisasi massa	mass organization
paguyuban	traditional association
pahlawan	hero or heroine
Panca Sila	Indonesia's official ideology of 'Five Principles'
pekerja	employee or worker
pembangunan	development
pembantu	
(rumah tangga)	domestic servant
pembinaan	guidance, support
pemerintah	government
pengembangan	development
pengurus	convenor or manager
perempuan	woman
perkumpulan	club or association ('chapter' within BK3I)
pesantren	traditional Islamic educational institution
pondok	kampung-style boarding-houses
pra koperasi	pre-co-operative
rakyat kecil	little people (also *wong cilik* in Javanese)
rupiah (Rp)	Indonesian unit of currency
santri	male student or graduate of a *pesantren*
santriwati	female student or graduate of a *pesantren*
simpan pinjam	savings and loan schemes
subag	traditional Balinese irrigation system
swadaya	self-reliance
swakarya	self-development
swasembada	self-sufficiency
Syariah	Islamic law
tahun	year
tanggung renteng	loan support or guarantee
tapol	political prisoner (*tahanan politik*)
tokoh	notable or influential person
usaha bersama	informal joint enterprise
ustadz	religious teacher
wanita	woman
warung	roadside stall
yayasan	foundation

Note on Indonesian and Other Non-English Terms and Spelling

READERS may find some difficulty with the large number of Indonesian terms, titles, abbreviations, and acronyms. Such problems are, to some extent, inevitable given the nature of this work, which entails referring to many institutions and agencies, both government and non-government. In seeking to address this situation, it has sometimes been found necessary to sacrifice consistency for the sake of clarity in specific contexts.

As a general rule, names of organizations, agencies, programmes, and projects are translated into English on the first occasion they appear in each chapter, with the Indonesian name and abbreviation or commonly used acronym given in parentheses. In most cases, the English translation is given precedence in order to convey the purpose and function of the organization. Otherwise, the Indonesian name only is given. Abbreviations and acronyms are omitted where the name only appears once. They are also omitted in subheadings and in the Contents, where the name of the organization is given in either English or Indonesian, according to the above principles. Abbreviations or acronyms are used in the normal way in the rest of the chapter, though with occasional interspersing of the full organizational name in either English or Indonesian in longer chapters, or when the institution in question is referred to many times.

Other Indonesian terms appear in parentheses beside their English translation in cases where it is considered necessary to give Indonesian readers and other specialists specific points of reference. A list of Abbreviations and Acronyms and a Glossary are provided.

Indonesian spelling of some words was officially changed in the early 1970s. Inconsistencies can occur due to different dates in cited sources or to the retention of old spelling by some users, particularly in relation to proper names. In this book, new spelling has been used, except in cases where old spelling predominates in references cited, or where it is used in quotations. Thus, 'y' is substituted for 'j'; 'j' for 'dj'; 'c' for 'tj'; and 'u' for 'oe'.

Notes on Transliteration and Other Non-English Terms and Spelling

Introduction

The Significance of Non-Government Organizations in the Indonesian Context

THERE has been growing awareness of the importance of non-government organizations (NGOs) in Indonesia in recent years. Such interest appears to be motivated by two broad sets of concerns. The first relates to a search for more equitable and participatory models of social and economic development of a kind which would give greater emphasis to people's own definition of their needs and enhance their capacity for self-management. The second focuses on NGOs as catalysts for promoting democratic values and processes within Indonesia's wider society and polity.

Social and developmental programmes have represented the core of NGO activity during the past two to three decades. Most NGOs feel less comfortable with any kind of action which can be labelled 'political' in any direct sense and, as we shall see, are at pains to define their role in non-political terms. Such a stance is not merely prudential but in many respects reflects their core values and practices. Nevertheless, this study will show that the political impact of Indonesian NGOs has been quite extensive.

The emphasis of NGOs on popular participation has provided the basic link between their developmental and political fields of action. For example, local groups which have developed a capacity to manage their own local programmes tend also to acquire skills and confidence in negotiating with outsiders, including state agencies. NGOs have acted as agents of change and intermediaries in this process. By extension, local organizations and groups which they have fostered often go on to demand legal rights and services to which they feel entitled. On the wider national stage, NGOs which began by promoting developmental and policy goals derived from their specific field experience have increasingly sought to articulate democratic and participatory aspirations and values as norms for the conduct of public life. The process has also worked in reverse, as those initially concerned with legal and human rights have sought to reach out to a wider range of people by supporting local social and economic struggles.

The absence of political parties with any real degree of independence has left an obvious vacuum in Indonesian politics. However, it would be wrong to see NGOs as the only independent voices in contemporary Indonesia. Students and intellectuals as well as educational and religious organizations have played important critical and mobilizing roles throughout this century, at least, and have been no less active during the New Order period (Aspinall, 1993; Uhlin, 1993). In the most recent period, new organizations, such as the Forum for Democracy and the League for the Restoration of Democracy, have been established with the specific aim of promoting democratic values and practice. Such groups draw on many streams of social and cultural energy, including ideas generated by NGOs. Nevertheless, NGOs appear to have developed organizational and ideological resilience especially appropriate to the context of New Order Indonesia. Their ongoing participation in most fields of social and developmental work has enabled them to operate flexibly across a broad canvas and to develop strong lines of communication within both governmental and societal structures, while still retaining a high level of institutional autonomy. Nevertheless, in addressing matters directly concerned with the power structure and ideology of the Indonesian state, NGOs have, with some significant exceptions, remained part of the more general 'culture of silence' which has pervaded Indonesian society since the upheavals of 1965–6, which resulted in mass killings and reprisals against the organized left followed by systematic depoliticization of Indonesian society.

Signs of change started to appear around the middle to late 1980s. Since then, various student and other informally organized networks have initiated more open confrontation with the government and have developed more direct links with workers and peasants. In the process, such groups have challenged established NGOs to adopt a more radical stance. This has been matched by some corresponding movement among NGOs, notably those operating in the labour, legal rights, and environmental spheres. Networking processes among NGOs have, to some extent, drawn in others whose work is usually more oriented towards social and economic activities.

Despite these trends, the centre of gravity of most NGOs remains in the micro-developmental rather than macro-political arena. Effective operation in both spheres will require a far wider range of organizations and socio-political formations than currently exists in Indonesia. Absence of freedom to organize has tended to feed exaggerated expectations that NGOs will undertake a task of political as well as societal transformation. An important objective of this study, therefore, will be to identify more precisely their ideological and organizational capacity to contribute towards such a task.

Objectives, Scope, and Methodology

Within the broad context stated above, this study will seek to draw out the core values and aspirations of NGOs in relation to democratic participation. These will be tested in relation to (i) the NGOs' operational links and styles of working with local groups and (ii) their interactions with government agencies and political processes generally. NGOs are defined, for the purposes of this analysis, as non-party and non-profit organizations, although co-operative enterprises which share profits among their members are included. While the major focus will be on organizations promoting the interests of the poor and disadvantaged, several which pursue more general public interest objectives will feature prominently. Organizations with a purely charitable or welfare orientation are excluded, as are cultural and recreational associations of the non-poor. Educational and religious foundations are only discussed in so far as they are involved in supporting developmental or advocacy activities relevant to the objectives of this study. It should be noted, nevertheless, that some educational institutions have contributed significantly to developing an understanding of democratic values in Indonesia, as well as supporting participatory programmes in the field.

This study does not aspire to offer comprehensive coverage of Indonesian NGOs, which must now be numbered in the thousands rather than the hundreds, by whatever definitions are employed. More modestly, the intention is to draw on the experience of a cross-section of organizations encountered in the course of fieldwork in order to illuminate more general themes. Emphasis is on the contemporary (post-1980) context, though reference is also made to earlier experience, particularly in relation to the early New Order (1966–80) period. Direct fieldwork has only been undertaken in West and Central Java, though documentary and interview sources have been drawn on in relation to other parts of Indonesia. Interviews have been conducted with NGO leaders, staff, and local fieldworkers, among local groups which they support, government and international aid agencies, students, intellectuals, and professionals in Jakarta and provincial centres and indeed, both formally and informally, with anyone with relevant information.

The choice of organizations for study was based initially on my access to and knowledge of existing groups. Several had been encountered in earlier studies during the 1970s and these provided a natural entry point. From there I progressively sought a wider coverage of fields of activity and approaches. My own understanding, both of the range of issues entailed and conceptual approaches to encapsulate these, has thus evolved gradually alongside the NGOs' own growing awareness of issues, their entry into new spheres of action, and the development of appropriate strategies. Standard sampling techniques would have been unlikely to prove effective in such a rapidly changing environment. It must also be acknowledged, in retrospect, that both my methodology and concerns as a political scientist to identify points of interaction with state structures and political processes may have led to a relative neglect of smaller independent NGOs. Even so, several such organizations appear in this account. I have also met with numerous small groups linked to or supported by larger organizations and so am not unaware of the ethos and contexts in which they operate.

When fieldwork for this project began in 1983, the overall number of NGOs appeared limited, based on information from the Indonesian Secretariat for the Development of Human Resources in Rural Areas (INDHRRA), subsequently renamed Bina Desa. Bina Desa's 1981 Catalogue identified 152 foundations (*yayasan*) and institutions (*lembaga*) throughout Indonesia plus 40–50 contacts for smaller groups (Bina Desa, 1981). Some of those listed turned out to be government-sponsored organizations but the large majority fitted with the first model proposed in Chapter 2 in terms of their emphasis on development, style of relations with the government, and approach to popular mobilization.[1] Based on my experience in India,[2] I also sought to identify those NGOs oriented towards popular forms of advocacy and with a more critical social and political outlook. These had slowly emerged in Indonesia during the 1970s and were beginning to make an impact by the time my fieldwork there began. Most of these newer groups seemed to fall into a second category, in that they sought both to mobilize independent local groups while engaging in active critical collaboration with government agencies. However, I gradually became aware of a third stream concerned to raise social and political awareness but to minimize contact with the government. The fourth model, indicated in Chapter 2, was added to account for the emergence, around the late 1980s, of new radical groups, with which I made direct contact in 1991.

Field research was conducted during four visits between 1983 and 1992, supplemented by a continuing flow of documentary material. As not all groups could be visited on each occasion, coverage of many has been uneven. Nevertheless, many were visited at least three times. It has thus been possible to observe their evolution over a fairly extensive period. Obviously, the personnel, structures, and direction of individual NGOs can change quite rapidly, and specific information will have become outdated by the time it emerges from the press. However, data gathered will remain valuable to the extent that it illustrates themes and arguments within given contexts relevant to the overall study.

Fieldwork was based on a checklist of questions relating to each organization's history, context, and rationale for establishment, goals and aspirations, activities, organization, links with groups at grass-roots level, involvement of women, interactions with government agencies, external links and networks, and sources of finance. This approach has made it possible to build up a fairly substantial picture of the orientation and style of operation of NGOs. Inevitably, there has been some unevenness both in the collection of information from NGOs and the material presented in the text. This is partly because insufficient time was available to cover every aspect with every NGO or local group surveyed. In most cases, some aspects appeared more interesting and salient in drawing out more special characteristics of the organizations in terms of their approach to popular participation, mobilization, and interaction with governmental and political processes, which represent the core concerns of this study.

The approaches of NGOs and other social activist groups towards these issues are categorized in terms of the four models stated in Chapter 2. These models represent ideal types rather than rigid categories into which every organization can be fitted. Their value should essentially be seen in heuristic terms, designed to clarify patterns of orientation and action. In order to avoid distortion, a number of individual organizations which appear to fit one or more of the models are discussed in considerable depth. While the account may appear discursive in places, such a risk seems worthwhile in order to convey the contextual richness and complexity within which Indonesian non-government organizations operate.

Perceptions of Non-Government Organization Roles

A common image of NGOs has associated them with either charitable and humanitarian work or very small-scale local developmental projects. NGOs have emphasized the micro-scale nature of their work as one of their greatest strengths. What, therefore, in terms of the title of this book, is the justification for claiming any wider societal or political impact from their activities? In the case of Indonesia, heavy centralization of power during the New Order period and the growing sophistication of the state apparatus's capacity to repress, co-opt, or neutralize dissident opinion and non-official political activity of all kinds, have raised understandable doubts as to whether NGOs can achieve *any* significant impact on Indonesia's overall direction. At the same time, the public profile adopted by most NGOs emphasizes their non-political character. While such a stance can be seen as necessary and expedient in the Indonesian context, it also reflects deeply rooted values and concepts of state and community which permeate the discourse of the NGO movement in Indonesia as well as many other countries, both Third World and Western.

Budiman (1988) has argued that NGOs have become a legitimate channel for social and political participation, otherwise blocked by the government, but that very few of them have actually formulated any political ideas. Here, appearances can be deceptive, particularly as NGOs are prone to extolling action in preference to theory. It is more important to look at the overall impact of NGO activities on the agenda of Indonesian public life and the balance of forces between the Indonesian government and other societal groups. Such impact may be indirect and long term as well as direct and immediate. It is therefore misleading to see only actions designed to win governmental power as political. To the extent that NGOs enhance capacity for self-management among less-advantaged groups, thereby enabling them to deal with government agencies and other interests on more equal terms, they are serving in an important way to strengthen civil society *vis-à-vis* the state.

While many NGOs have an impact on the state by influencing policy formation and public opinion in various fields, most are careful to distinguish such efforts from formal participation in party and electoral processes, which they would see as conflicting in both a practical and ideological sense with their fundamental goal of building strong and autonomous community structures. They display a similar uncertainty in integrating macro- and micro-levels of action, whether in dealing with government agencies or in coalition-building among themselves. However, some progress has been achieved on this front in recent years, particularly among larger NGOs oriented towards public interest and advocacy in fields such as environmental protection and legal and labour rights, for whom monitoring the role of state agencies constitutes a primary activity.

Liddle (1987: 127–46) has referred to a 'populist ideological tradition' which 'Marxists and the more hard-nosed brand of interest and resource balancing political economists are prone to dismiss ... as mere surface expressions of deeper structural forces' and claims that 'there is much more beneath-the-surface political activity in the New Order than the standard model of military and bureaucratic authoritarianism leads us to expect'. In many ways, NGOs can be seen as forming part of that populist tradition which can too easily be marginalized in mainstream paradigms of contemporary Indonesia. Liddle further concludes from his study of rice and sugar growers that official behaviour towards non-government groups has been changed by perceptions of their growing strength and convergence of interests in relation to a range of policy matters. MacIntyre (1990) has indicated similar tendencies in his study of business groups. Although NGOs cannot be seen as interest groups in quite the same way, this study will provide support to justify similar conclusions in relation to them. In a broader sense, it will lend weight to pluralistic as against monolithic explanations of Indonesian politics and society, which have tended to dominate both scholarly and popular analysis of Suharto's New Order. Nevertheless, popular organizations of the kind discussed in this book continue to face dangers of absorption into dominant corporatist structures and other sophisticated threats to their autonomy.

The strength of non-government organizations lies in the range of roles which they play (Drabek, 1987; Korten, 1990; Edwards and Hulme, 1992). While their grass-roots strength is based on flexible adaptation to local contexts, the diversity of organizational forms which they have proved capable of adopting has enabled them to retain a measure of autonomy from bureaucratic control. Proliferation of numerous small group formations has created space for new kinds of popular organization. In turn, the government moves periodically, when sufficiently disturbed, to close loopholes, thus obliging the versatile NGO community to think up further new strategies. In shaping their response, NGOs draw advantage from the government's uncertainty in its overall stance towards them, while developing significant levels of co-operation in specific contexts.

Chapter Outline

Chapter 1 is concerned with core concepts and values which predominate among Indonesian NGOs, beginning with an explanation of current terminology. The definition of basic terms turns out to be quite a complex exercise, given both the special characteristics of the Indonesian scene and the fact that, in any social context, terminology and ideology tend to be closely related. Such discussion needs to be set against a changing social and political context, generational differences, and consequent new challenges confronting NGOs.

Notions of 'self-reliance' and 'participation' are central to NGO values, both of which are open to several levels of interpretation. On balance, the normative framework within which NGOs operate favours group relative to individual decision-making. In practice, self-reliance and participation are operationalized at two distinct levels. The first is concerned with the internal dynamics of NGOs and associated base-level groups. The second concerns external relations, particularly with government agencies. Although this work will focus strongly on NGO–government relations, the influence and authenticity of groups in addressing the wider society is determined to a significant degree by the example they set in their own internal relationships and their effectiveness in mobilizing popular participation among their immediate reference or target groups. Issues relating to participation within local organizations and relations between NGOs and base-level groups are consequently given a good deal of weight in case-studies provided in later chapters.

The second part of Chapter 1 focuses on competing understandings of democracy and expressions of democratic values in Indonesia and ways in which these are reflected in the ideology of NGOs. This discussion leads to a questioning of the assumption that Indonesian NGOs are naturally oriented towards supporting greater political democratization, as expressing their stated core values. During 1993, there was evidence of a stronger trend in this direction, as discussed in the Conclusion. Nevertheless, viewed against a longer historical perspective, it is argued that NGO ideas on democracy reflect the diversity of understandings within the wider society, which in turn are mediated through cultural and historical experience. Many, perhaps most NGOs, appear far more concerned with local problem-solving than with wider political reform. Further, a distinction can be drawn between the majority, whose macro perspective has evolved gradually from their field experience, and those whose search for the grass roots derives from a background of political activism, as with the 1966 and 1974 to 1978 generations of student leaders and, in a somewhat new form, the present generation of radicals. Nevertheless, demands for popular rights of association and self-management provide an emerging point of convergence among NGOs from diverse backgrounds.

Patterns of interaction with the Indonesian government and political process are explored in Chapter 2. The first section provides various local examples, including a fairly detailed account of co-operation between several NGOs and the district government in Banjarnegara, Central Java. In the second part of the chapter, three paradigms are proposed as a framework for understanding patterns of accommodation and conflict between NGOs and the Indonesian government, together with the NGOs' approach to popular mobilization. These have, in turn, been challenged by a new paradigm of militant radical activism. The first category of organizations, in terms of this framework, concentrates on building community participation and self-reliance at local levels. Such NGOs also co-operate with the government in non-political ways in policy development and programme implementation. The second model describes a more proactive approach which both seeks to influence government policy and, at the same time, nurture aspirations of building up grass-roots groups into mass movements. The third type minimizes interaction with government agencies, concentrating on building and empowering local groups to operate independently. In practice, most organizations manifest mixed characteristics, combining elements of these 'ideal-type' categorizations. Despite substantial differences in values and strategy evident within each model, all three are based, for reasons of both principle and prudence, on avoiding direct confrontation with the government.

A network of radical groups has emerged since the mid-1980s to challenge this broad consensus. These, mostly young radicals, have vigorously, often stridently criticized established NGOs for their failure to mobilize the people to fight for structural change in the political system. NGOs, for their part, have always been ambivalent about their aims in this regard. Despite some sweeping rhetoric about social transformation and democratization, local group formation and problem-solving have always been to the forefront of their concerns. Consequently, they charge the radicals with using local people as tools in their wider agenda, with not following through work at village level, and with failing to understand the long-term effort required to achieve change.

Nevertheless, the new radical groups have successfully demonstrated that a measure of confrontation with the Indonesian government is both possible and may sometimes prove effective. Such a course clearly entails a high element of risk. Yet, despite many reported acts of retaliation, including violence, against activists, the state apparatus has so far proved either unwilling or unable to repress the diversity of struggles and protests in any consistent way, as could generally be assumed for most of the earlier New Order period. Also, despite much mutual antagonism and the flow of rhetoric about social transformation and democratization, there are signs that the new radicals are achieving a tacit division of labour and an understanding with at least some elements among established NGOs.

It may be questioned how far these new groups can appropriately be called NGOs, in so far as they tend to use local struggles primarily as vehicles to change state structures rather than promoting self-reliant groups capable of determining their own priorities. From here it is a short step to seeing the capture of state power as a prerequisite for achieving social and economic change. These are common characteristics, both of conventional political parties in countries where these are allowed to function, and of revolutionary movements in general. While in many respects Indonesia's new radicals seem to resemble pre-party formations, some also display characteristics of established NGOs in their earlier, more idealistic phase, such as an emphasis on informality, a rejection of formal power structures, and a preference for direct action.

Chapter 3 looks in detail at the legal and funding contexts within which Indonesian NGOs operate. Legal constraints substantially influence how NGOs articulate their aims and shape their activities and organization. Such constraints may well be having a negative impact on internal democratic processes and accountability to base-level groups, as NGOs become ever more versatile in evading controls through informal arrangements. By way of balance, while dependence on foreign funds produces other distortions, it also provides strategic leverage in relations with the government. However, recent state retaliation against some high-profile Indonesian NGOs by banning the receipt of Dutch government and associated non-government aid indicates that such leverage needs to be exercised with discretion. Potential alternative income sources are also explored in this chapter, though for the most part these have been relatively little developed by Indonesian NGOs.

The themes explored in these three chapters are drawn out in subsequent studies of key organizations and fields of action. The latter include health, community development, appropriate technology, agriculture, rural banking, credit unions and small co-operative enterprises, labour associations, legal and human rights, the role of women, consumer rights, and the environment. While analysis is broadly related to the above three paradigms and the radical challenge to these, other more diffuse material is included in order to minimize selective abstraction from the groups' total activities and experience.

Chapters 4 and 5 look in some detail at several major NGOs as well as several smaller groups which they have fostered. These NGOs operate broadly within the framework of the first two models in their general stance *vis-à-vis* the government and their strategies of popular mobilization. Chapter 6 is concerned with legal and human rights groups. It also discusses some recent developments in the area of labour organization. Chapter 7 focuses on issues and actions in the environmental field. Chapter 8 draws together some issues relating to the mobilization of women mentioned in earlier chapters, with accounts of selected women's organizations. Chapter 9 draws out some explicitly religious and cultural contexts of Christian and Islamic-linked NGO activity, including a detailed discussion of Islamic schools (*pesantren*). However, no attempt has been made in either this or other chapters to artificially segregate religious from non-religious groups.

Various approaches to networking between NGOs are explored in Chapter 10, which examines both the internal organization and the potential impact of networking in the wider societal and political contexts. NGO networks can be broadly classified as sectoral, in the sense of concentrating on specific fields of operation, or geographical, namely, local, regional, national, and international. The sectoral networks discussed cover the fields of health and welfare, consumer rights, and credit co-operatives. Other networks, for example in the legal rights and environmental fields, are considered in earlier chapters. Geographical networks are explored both at the national level and at a regional level with studies of Yogyakarta and Central and West Java. Questions concerning both kinds of networks include (i) their relations with the Indonesian government, particularly strategies for avoiding co-option; (ii) their impact on the balance of power between small and large, local and national-level NGOs; (iii) the problem of who, if anyone, has the right to represent the NGO community, and under what conditions, and (iv) their relations with foreign funding agencies.

It is concluded that networking has become increasingly important, since NGOs cannot avoid dealing with government agencies in relation both to policy matters affecting their own interests and those of their members, and matters of more general public concern. Significant problems of communication, internal bureaucracy, and the establishment of common goals have been encountered in this context. However, mobilization around particular issues on an *ad hoc* basis has proved relatively successful. Conflict between large and small NGOs, which became intense around 1988–90, appears to have diminished due to greater dialogue and more co-operative strategies. Finally, the emergence of the International NGO Forum on Indonesia (INGI) has given a far sharper cutting edge to NGO coalition-building, carrying the NGO community more deeply into the political arena.

The Conclusion attempts to explore future scenarios as well as drawing together main themes. It opens with a statement signed by a cross-section of radical and mainstream non-government organizations and networks in June 1993 (IN-DEMO, 1993). This Joint Declaration on Human Rights asserted the indivisibility of civil, political, social, cultural, and economic rights and demanded that political parties be allowed to operate freely. The last demand projects a more radical stance *vis-à-vis* the political system and an understanding of democratic participation, which goes well beyond the norms prevailing among the majority of NGOs for most of the period covered in this survey, and which seems designed to carry them into quite new spheres of operation. However, it is suggested that there are grounds for caution in assessing the depth of support for this apparent new direction and the potential, both for division among NGOs and retaliation by the government, if it is not grounded in more comprehensive strategies for change. The statement has nevertheless raised the issue of democratization to the forefront of NGO agendas.

Discussion then returns to questions about NGO core values relating to self-reliance and democratic participation, particularly their capacity to link political and developmental spheres of action. It is argued that NGOs need to integrate activities in both spheres if they are to be effective in either. In that context, it is argued that the contribution of NGOs in pioneering innovative and participatory strategies in the fields of social and economic development will continue to provide the basis for their own survival as well as for any leverage they may be able to exert over either the Indonesian government or overseas agencies. Somewhat mixed evidence on this score, drawn out in the earlier case-studies, is further distilled in the next section of the Conclusion, where it is argued that, without support from the people they claim to serve, any influence which NGOs may enjoy at higher levels will soon evaporate. Here they must walk a tightrope between co-operating with the government in order to gain services and resources on behalf of the local people, without becoming identified with the government in popular eyes. This can lead them into frustrating roles of 'critical collaboration' or 'loyal opposition'.

While many examples are cited in the study where NGOs have influenced official policy and practice, this has not yet led to any significant weakening of dominant paradigms or to NGOs playing any decisive role in shaping Indonesia's developmental agenda and strategies. The need for wider coalition-building and some form of entry into the political sphere is consequently receiving greater attention. In any case, strong forces are likely to propel at least a proportion of NGOs into more direct participation in the political arena, in turn raising questions as to whether NGOs should support or even assist in forming political parties. However, it is argued that, once a system of competitive politics is allowed to operate freely, basic differences between the two types of organization will become apparent. In the absence of a free and open political system, false expectations have been created that NGOs can—or should—play a substitute role for parties. Such misperceptions have negatively affected their relations with both radical activists and more conservative elements. Clarity as to the respective roles of parties and NGOs is a prerequisite for any kind of socially beneficial division of labour.

The book concludes with an assessment of the potential impact of various kinds of macro-level political and economic change on opportunities and constraints confronting NGOs. While these may well entail some difficult choices and trade-offs for them, explanations which deny NGOs any initiative and see them as solely dependent on space opened up within larger structures, are likely to prove as inadequate in the future as in the past.

1. See pp. 35–43 for a discussion of the four models used as a frame of reference throughout the work.

2. Theoretical and methodological concerns at the outset of this work can be gleaned from Eldridge (1985: 401–34).

1
Self-reliance, Participation, and Democracy: Core Concepts and Values of Indonesian Non-Government Organizations

PARTICIPATION and democratization are closely linked in Western political thought. To these must be added the concept of 'self-reliance' which recurs constantly in non-government organization (NGO) discourse and which has specific cultural and historical connotations in the Indonesian context. Yet, while participation and self-reliance represent core values espoused by virtually all Indonesian NGOs, their commitment to democracy, even at a rhetorical level, is more ambivalent. 'Democracy' also carries a number of competing meanings drawn from historical experience,[1] some of which recall negative memories for many Indonesians. Thus the association between democracy and politics potentially challenges the NGOs' strongly asserted non-political identity. At the same time, a radical wave of new groups has emerged since the mid-1980s to challenge the established NGOs, demanding that they adopt a more political stance. This, in turn, has encouraged a more positive assertion of democratic values by at least some NGOs. It is hoped that closer examination of the concepts of self-reliance, participation, and democracy in this chapter will assist both in clarifying the core goals and values of NGOs and may provide an entry point for understanding their outlook towards relations with the government and interaction with the political process.

Definitions and Background

Terminology and ideology are never far apart in social and political discourse. In Indonesia, the choice of terminology has been particularly influenced by relations between NGOs and the Indonesian government.

Indonesian NGOs are commonly referred to as self-reliant community institutions (Lembaga Swadaya Masyarakat—LSM) and institutions for developing community self-reliance (Lembaga Pengembangan Swadaya

Masyarakat—LPSM). NGOs and LSM/LPSM, although not totally equi-valent, are used more or less interchangeably throughout this study. In principle, LSMs are primary groups of poor people or local groups which work directly with them, whereas LPSMs are larger, usually city-based groups which support or assist the development of smaller groups.[2] This somewhat arbitrary distinction seems, in practice, to be determined by size.

According to Dawam Rahardjo (c.1990), the origins of LSM/LPSMs in Indonesia can be traced from traditional co-operative associations and arrangements such as *paguyuban* and *gotong royong*. Thus the Association for the Indonesian Nation (Persatuan Bangsa Indonesia), led by Fr. Sutomo in the 1930s, grew into the Farmers' Association (Rukun Tani) which included a vigorous farmers' co-operative move-ment. Labour movements within the Islamic Union (Sarekat Islam)[3] established credit banks. Budi Utomo[4] and Sarekat Islam both initiated education programmes, scholarships, and co-operatives. The establish-ment of such organizations without government aid, says Rahardjo, was an important achievement in the context of the national struggle. LSM/LPSMs would seem to represent a new imported form of organi-zation more appropriate to modern-style development, which has facili-tated the inflow of outside funds to fields of activity neglected in official programmes.

It appears that the LSM/LPSM terminology was first proposed by Sarino Mangunpranoto, an influential person within the Taman Siswa movement and former Minister of Education and Culture (Rahardjo, c.1990). Taman Siswa, founded in 1921 in Yogyakarta by Ki Hadjar Dewantoro, aimed to develop 'an educational system based upon a real-istic synthesis of Indonesian and Western culture which would train Indonesian youth in self-reliance and ... (practical skills)' (Kahin, 1952: 88). Taman Siswa's publications indicate that its basic ideology and practice are firmly rooted in the principles of Indonesia's official ideo-logy, the Five Principles (Panca Sila).[5] Against that background, Mangunpranoto proposed that the whole idea of a self-reliant commun-ity institution could expect to enjoy more historical and cultural reson-ance than the imported term, NGO, or its literal Indonesian equivalent, Organisasi Non-Pemerintah (ORNOP). In the context of discussion in this study as to how far the roles of LSM/LPSMs can be defined as political or non-political, it is interesting to note that Taman Siswa banned the teaching of politics, while its teachers were debarred from membership of political parties. Even so, many of its graduates became active as leaders and participants in the Indonesian nationalist move-ment (Kahin, 1952: 88).

A more cynical view is that the switch from non-government to self-reliance (*swadaya*), some time around 1983, represented a convenient rhetorical shift, motivated by political necessity and designed to avoid the appearance of confrontation with the Indonesian government. NGOs at the time claimed that they had received strong advice, notably from Prof. Emil Salim, Minister for Population and Environment from

1978 to 1993, who was generally regarded as sympathetic to them, that non-government was being widely perceived in government circles and in more conservative sections of the urban middle class as denoting anti-government.[6] However, despite its political advantages, it has been pointed out that the LSM/LPSM terminology allows the government to label as LSM/LPSMs various institutions 'which have been set up by government regulation, whose leadership and membership selection procedures and ... task-description [are] closely defined by those regulations, and which according to most other criteria could not be seen as "non-governmental"' (B. White, 1989: 3).

There is an obvious contradiction between notions of self-reliance and the fact that most LPSMs receive foreign aid. They also increasingly act as channels for distributing such funds to smaller LSMs. Superficial rhetorical convergence with aid donors in support of self-reliance disguises the far greater emphasis given to individual self-reliance in Western middle-class compared with dominant Indonesian values, which place greater stress on community and reciprocity. In that context, it can be argued that unwillingness to pay taxes to support public welfare programmes for disadvantaged groups in Western societies is also projected into reluctance to finance the development of basic infrastructure and services through public spending in the rural Third World. Reliance on local resources can thus seem an attractive low-cost means of overcoming poverty, bolstered by a measure of 'Small is Beautiful'-style romanticism and utopianism.[7] It should also be noted that notions of self-reliance can serve to evade questions of redistribution. While it is not suggested that this is the conscious intention of most Western NGOs, the tendency of much of their rhetoric to delegitimize state attempts to play any significant role in development, points logically to a policy of government non-intervention, which seems designed to leave the balance of private economic power and wealth untouched.[8]

Maintenance of non-government identity nevertheless remains an important priority for NGO/LSM/LPSMs, howsoever described. The term non-government organization (NGO) persists in international usage, and also to some extent in Indonesia. An underlying question here, which the issue of terminology reflects, centres on the nature of relations between the state and civil society. Clearly the notion of state is broader than the specific apparatus of government (Cotton, 1991; Hewison, Robison, and Rodan, 1993: 4–5), but Indonesian terminology tends to blur relevant distinctions. Significant terms refer to nation (*bangsa*), state (*negara*), and government (*pemerintah*). In broad terms, *bangsa* represents the concept of the nation as an integrated community, while *negara* embraces all the institutional structures and processes of the Indonesian state. At neither of these levels, according to official ideology at least, is there scope for any group of citizens to opt out or separate themselves. Only at the third, governmental level is there, even in principle, any acknowledgement of the right of groups in civil society to establish organizations distinct from those of the governmental apparatus.

Even here boundaries can be murky, with numerous semi-government agencies, government-initiated, or government-supported organizations, such as the Village Co-operative Unit (Koperasi Unit Desa—KUD), the Village Community Resilience Institution (Lembaga Ketahanan Masyarakat Desa—LKMD), the Association for Promoting Family Welfare (Pembinaan Kesejahteraan Keluarga—PKK) which controls women's organizations at village level, and the Indonesian Labour Foundation (Yayasan Tenaga Kerja Indonesia—YTKI). YTKI was established in 1969 by the Department of Manpower, with the Minister and several organizations linked to the government-sponsored network of Functional Groups (Golongan Karya—GOLKAR),[9] such as the All-Indonesia Workers' Union (Serikat Pekerja Seluruh Indonesia—SPSI), the Indonesian National Youth Committee (Komite Nasional Pemuda Indonesia—KNPI), and the Indonesian Women's Corps (Korps Wanita Indonesia—KOWANI) represented on the Board of Management. Kothari's term of GONGO (Government Organized Non-Government Organization), coined in the Indian context, could appropriately be applied to such organizations (Kothari, 1988: 84–6).

The two major Islamic organizations, Nahdlatul Ulama (NU) and Muhammadiyah, which have played extensive religious, cultural, educational, as well as socio-political roles throughout this century, are currently categorized as mass organizations under the 1985 Law on Social Organizations (Undang Undang Organisasi Kemasyarakatan—ORMAS).[10] In some respects, they seem more like LSM/LPSMs, since they support many local and sub-units assisting people's self-reliance. In any case, there are numerous informal structures at local and sub-regional levels linking the formal agencies of government with the general society. The real issue for LSM/LPSMs thus appears to be one of relative rather than absolute autonomy. In practice, they have succeeded in carving out a good deal of space for independent self-management, while importing their own goals and meanings into official programmes and ideology, with the aim of encouraging more informal and participatory styles of implementation.

Relations between small and large NGOs will be discussed at greater length later, in relation to networking and other contexts. This issue further confuses terminology, given the predilection of Indonesians for acronyms, which in this case is reflected in rhetorical battles between big NGOs (BINGOs) and little NGOs (LINGOs). Historically, it is worth noting that nearly all BINGOs, or at least those which were initiated independently from the government, began as LINGOs. The LINGO/BINGO dichotomy is reflected in the equally subjective distinction between LSMs and LPSMs, perceptions of which are influenced a good deal by organizational size. However, the addition of the term *pengembangan* suggests that LPSMs are also responsible for developing their younger, weaker brother and sister LSMs. In reality, as we shall see, the relationship is a good deal less idyllic, due to an imbalance in resources, and the influence of BINGOs with higher levels of government and foreign funding agencies, resulting in tendencies towards relations of dominance and dependence.

Scaling up from micro to macro spheres of action is a problem for NGOs everywhere, however radical or conservative, political or non-political their outlook (Korten, 1987: 145–60). In that context, Rahardjo (c.1990) sees consciousness-raising concerning legal and political rights and strengthening civil society as key tasks facing Indonesian LSM/ LPSMs. Achieving these goals entails placing priority on developing the resources of poor people and preventing the destruction of their environment. However, the voluntary sector's limited resources result in a paradox which Rahardjo (c.1990: 10) describes as one of 'full commitment with limited involvement'. Groups commonly attempt to resolve this dilemma by taking up small-scale, pilot programmes, but this leads to a perception that they can make only a very limited impact on the overall task of social transformation. Clearly, the larger goal can only be achieved if such locally piloted ideas are taken up in the wider society. Linking these two arenas of action requires some understanding of how LSM/LPSMs conceive and apply the idea of participation.

Participation

Despite their wide variety in background, outlook, organization, and practice, NGOs share a broadly common core of goals and values directed towards promoting socially just development, human rights, and popular empowerment. From their field experience they have developed critiques of dominant development models and sought to pioneer alternatives. Their rhetoric sharply contrasts the top–down approaches of official programmes with the bottom–up nature of their own efforts, which they claim centre on people as subjects rather than objects. Their strategies for change are similarly local in orientation, stressing self-reliant organization and action.

Many of these ideals are incorporated into the single notion of 'participation'. This, in turn, has close affinities with self-reliance, which carries similar cultural and historical connotations in the Indonesian context. More specifically, participation represents aspirations to play more substantial roles in the overall development process, based on claims that NGOs have special skills in mobilizing popular participation, compared with government agencies or political parties.[11] Such claims have been officially legitimized by the declaration of the People's Deliberative Assembly (Majelis Pemusyawaratan Rakyat—MPR), officially the nation's supreme deliberative body, that participation is essential to national development.[12]

The term 'participation' tends to be used in fairly bland and open-ended ways in NGO discourse, though in reality, the formulation of definitions and indicators is quite complex. To overcome vagueness and ambivalence, Uphoff et al (1979) have attempted to break the concept down into checklists as to who participates in decisions at various stages of the project or programme cycle—conception, design, implementation, distribution of benefits, and post-evaluation. Such tools can facilitate assessment of how various kinds of organizational structure can facilitate or exclude participation. More radical interpretations have been proposed by Freire (1970; 1972) and others, who have sought to develop philosophies and strategies aiming to empower poor people as subjects rather than objects. Crucial to Freire's approach is the idea that the definition of people's needs, the identification and analysis of their problems, and the solutions to these problems should be determined by the people themselves through a process of 'action and reflection'. The overt use of Freire's ideas is not politically feasible in the Indonesian context, although they influence the informal culture of many groups. Finally, there is some interest in participatory as against more traditional modes of academic research, though implementing such ideas does not appear to have progressed far beyond normative and rhetorical stages (LP3ES, 1987a: 2–9).

LSM/LPSMs operate either directly as primary or grass-roots organizations or as support or intermediary organizations at varying degrees of physical, social, and organizational distance from the local scene. As a rule of thumb in Indonesia, LPSMs fall into the intermediary category. LSMs may be of both kinds, though in either case they will be smaller, nearer to or at the grass roots compared with LPSMs. One salient test of the LSM/LPSM claim to promoting participation and self-reliance is the extent to which their efforts lead to the formation of organizations which are controlled and managed by the people who constitute their target or reference groups. One frequently finds that, while some measure of participation may be achieved in relation to individual projects, structures which link base-level groups to each other in ways which enable them to deal directly with government agencies, banks, lawyers, or funding agencies, independently from intermediary agencies, are generally slow to emerge.

Many voluntary activists are becoming more sensitive to these aspects and have sought to develop popular leadership capable of undertaking such wider roles. Obstacles to this process include (i) problems of internal communication and factional rivalries between local groups; (ii) structures of accountability oriented towards external organizations providing financial and other forms of support; (iii) limited local understanding, confidence, and skills in handling dealings outside the immediate local context, and (iv) hierarchical patterns of NGO organization which maintain dependence of client groups. High levels of informality, which LSM/LPSMs feel obliged to adopt in shaping their organizational structures for purposes of survival, are also a factor in holding back the emergence of accountable democratic structures at lower levels, in so far as these reinforce dependence on the good offices of progressive and influential persons (*tokoh*).

While many technical and organizational difficulties may be adduced, in any true understanding, participation means a shift in decision-making power from more powerful to poor, disadvantaged, and less influential groups. Those who hold such power, whether at village, regional, national, or international levels, are naturally reluctant to concede it (B. White, 1989: 8–12). Hence, the dimension of struggle cannot be indefinitely excluded. Yet, here too, radical groups do not necessarily act as agents for empowerment of grass-roots organizations managed by poor people themselves, but rather to impose external agendas and to use them as 'cannon fodder' in wider struggles. In the process, specific local goals can easily be sacrificed for the sake of strategic necessity.

The claims of LSM/LPSMs that they are more effective than government agencies, political parties, or trade unions in fostering popular participation among disadvantaged groups form an important element in promoting and legitimizing their role. Such claims should not be accepted in any blanket way, as their performance varies widely. Mary Johnson (1990: 72–92), who worked for twenty years as a volunteer with an NGO based in the Solo area of Central Java, has painted a vivid picture of NGO life-cycles, developed from a model pioneered by the Canadian-based Manitoba Institute of Management. This sees NGOs moving from infancy, through youth and marriage to maturity and, not infrequently, 'from rags to riches' as their legal and financial security becomes assured through foreign funding and government contacts. At this point, they may take on characteristics of Javanese-style hierarchy and overburdened bureaucracy.

At each stage of growth, NGOs are in danger of losing idealism and contacts with people at the grass roots. One common result is 'divorce', in the form of loss of staff and support, followed by the establishment of new, small NGOs which begin the cycle over again. However, in contrast to the human condition, as portrayed in Shakespeare's 'Seven Ages of Man', decay and death are not inevitable for NGOs. According to Johnson (1990: 85), several organizations have sought to 'offset the dangers of losing grassroots links by expanding their networks with small NGOs and with community cadre'. While not regaining the original elixir of youth '[they] have succeeded, to varying degrees, in reviving some of the enthusiasm and climate of the earlier stage of Maturity'.

Criticisms of organizational size can easily overlook the obvious point that success in any kind of human enterprise usually leads to growth. Successful pioneering work in one or two villages can quickly lead to requests from several others in the neighbourhood. As word spreads, interest is manifested from further afield. Training programmes which disseminate local experience expand their clientele, including government personnel. Whatever the initial entry point, whether health, appropriate technology, water supply, or income-generation programmes, one programme usually leads to another, since development is an integrated and multifaceted process. This confronts NGOs with a choice of diversifying staff expertise, bringing in outsiders on a contract basis, or devising other strategies to link local skills with relevant outside sources of knowledge. In any case, there is no way of avoiding the problems of organizational complexity associated with multiplication of tasks and matching demands with resources. Creative responses are needed in order to maintain overall coherence in vision and strategy, efficient management, and devolution of power to local self-managing groups.

Similar problems are encountered as NGOs feel a need to develop networking arrangements. The rationale for networking has been well expressed by Soecipto Wirosardjono (cited in Johnson, 1990: 82), who has observed that:

... at the level of life and experience which has now been reached by NGOs in Indonesia, it is fitting that they move beyond a welfare or humanistic approach in the narrow sense ... or even the immersion in projects.... [Their] experiences ... in organising activities on a pilot scale in a village, sub-district or even district, [have] provided ... valuable lessons ... [enabling] NGOs to enter a new struggle by developing a role in national development. At this stage ... they need to consciously relate their whole program and all their activities to the vision of a transformation of society, aiming at the just and prosperous order visualised in the constitution.

However, Johnson (1990: 82) expresses doubts whether most Indonesian NGOs have either the capacity or inclination to promote change on a national scale, as most prefer to work with a limited number of small communities to improve their standard of life and dignity. In that context, they 'have been described as "social craftsmen", implying that their work demands great effort and a high level of concentration to achieve even minimal changes in a very confined area'. Johnson further argues that many innovations in reaching 'the poorest of the poor' have been achieved in this way. This view has also been endorsed by former Minister for Home Affairs, Soepardjo Roestam (cited in Johnson, 1990: 82).

As will be discussed in later chapters, it can prove hard to reconcile networking processes with principles of accountability to local groups and respect for their autonomy. Constraints on emerging networks in dealing with the Indonesian government have added to these difficulties. At this stage, it is important to recognize that the problem of scaling up now confronted by Indonesian LSM/LPSMs highlights issues relating both to their own internal values and practices and to the process of democratizing Indonesian government and society more generally.

Competing Definitions of Democracy in the Indonesian Context

Thus far, discussion has centred on themes which can be understood as broadly related to democratic participation among LSM/LPSMs and the base-level groups with which they are associated. This section will seek to understand their conceptions of and aspirations for achieving democracy in a broader political and societal context. Inferences here will draw a good deal on extrapolation of NGO goals and strategies in developing their relations with the Indonesian government and in popular mobilization. These are conceptualized in Chapter 2 and drawn out in various contexts in subsequent chapters.

Korten (1987: 147) has argued that, far from being a luxury that developing nations could ill afford, 'democratization—defined in terms of broadly distributed control over political and economic assets, and the open flow of information—may for many nations offer their only hope for equitable and sustainable progress'. Such processes require 'the development of the complex mosaic of independent yet inter-linked local organisations through which people define and pursue their individual and collective interests within a guiding framework of national policy. These organisations must in turn be supported by institutional structures and policies that create the necessary social and political space for them to function in their members' interests.' In this context, he claims that both national governments and supporting foreign aid agencies are looking for organizations capable of reaching and mobilizing the poor in ways which will bring practical gains in overcoming poverty without creating political disorder.

It thus appears that NGOs are increasingly perceived in international circles as potential institution builders for achieving 'sustainable democratization' as well as 'sustainable development'. Clearly, both concepts are subject to different, often competing interpretations. It is possible to distinguish three broad understandings of democracy in the contemporary Indonesian context.

The first type is 'representative' or 'constitutional' democracy along Western lines, based on open and competitive elections, resulting in a choice of representatives who are, in principle at least, accountable to the people. Representatives are most effectively influenced through the formation of interest groups. In countries like India (Kothari, 1984; Eldridge, 1985; Fernandes, 1985) and the Philippines (Macuja, 1992), where such systems operate, it is necessary for NGOs to compete for the attention of elected representatives with other interest groups, which may well have greater resources and access to decision-makers. The potential of NGOs to trade votes for services is, in part, hampered by their underlying non-political ideology and praxis. This can cause them to gain the worst of all worlds, since such scruples tend not to be understood by politicians, who often see them as potential rivals. In that context, the Indian experience indicates extensive conflict between the expectations of politicians of uncritical support in return for patronage and protection, and the attempts of NGOs to build self-reliant organization and strength capable of demanding services and implementation of laws, intended to benefit the poor, as a right rather than a favour.

Mechanisms for ensuring representatives' accountability to and communication with the masses tend to be deficient even in advanced Western democracies, resulting in a widespread sense of alienation. Nevertheless, evolution in a liberal democratic direction holds growing appeal for significant sections of the Indonesian middle class, as lack of choice in political representation, freedom of speech, and association become increasingly irksome in numerous business, professional, intellectual, and cultural contexts. By contrast, the mass of workers and peasants are more concerned with economic security and subsistence. Although many have come to see freedom to organize as instrumental to these goals, they are likely to find the costs and benefits of a more open and competitive representative process harder to anticipate. In seeking to represent them, LSM/LPSMs tend to stress social and economic needs and express ambivalence towards Western-style political reform.

LSM/LPSMs also tend to feel uncomfortable with the individualistic emphasis which they see as inherent in liberal democratic ideology. In so far as liberal democracy conflicts with the more group- and community-based outlook to which they mostly aspire, they tend to seek an understanding of democratic participation more in accord with their core values. Finally, as we have seen in relation to their change of generic name from NGO to LSM/LPSM, the lack of cultural legitimacy of political models which can in any way be labelled 'liberal' or 'Western' reinforces all but the boldest of LSM/LPSMs' sense of caution and apprehension towards them.

For all these reasons, LSM/LPSMs have mostly preferred to operate within a second ideological framework, that of a Panca Sila understanding of democracy, and to seek accommodations and interpretations favourable to their own outlook. This stance has proved more difficult to sustain in recent years, in a climate of mounting criticism by students, intellectuals, and many other activists of the monopolization and centralization of power by the Suharto government. The NGO community generally identifies with such criticism. However, rather than take up demands for sweeping structural change, most prefer to concentrate their energies on working for more open and participatory interpretations of Panca Sila within their own sphere of operation. Processes of deliberation and consensus, which have historically formed the core of Panca Sila concepts of decision-making, fit well with their own rhetoric and, to a considerable extent, day-to-day practice. Equally, freedom of expression can be accommodated by Panca Sila to the extent that the ultimate goal is to achieve solutions for the whole group rather than for a few individuals. Despite abuses by both present and former governments, the ideals of working together (*gotong royong*) in pursuit of agreed purposes appear to retain a good deal of cultural resonance with many Indonesians at all levels.[13] Such ideals are broadly reflected in the aspirations, if not always the practice, of most NGOs. Despite important differences in analysis, ethos, and style of operation, this also appears to be true of many newer, more radical groups.

The third tradition of democracy in Indonesia has been broadly expressed in terms of social revolutionary aspirations towards 'people's sovereignty' (*kedaulatan rakyat*). Historically, the slogan of people's sovereignty has tended to be associated with the Left. It was interpreted in quite opposite ways by Mohammed Hatta and Tan Malaka during the period immediately after the proclamation of Indonesian national independence in August 1945 (Anderson, 1972). Whereas Hatta saw popular sovereignty in terms of government accountability through elected legislatures, Malaka and his supporters among radical youth stressed direct mass action. Significant rebellions based on mass mobilization outside the nationalist mainstream emerged in some regions.[14]

Parallel, albeit minority counter-traditions to liberal and social democracy are also to be found in Western countries among various anarcho-syndicalist, environmental, and other community-based groups, expressed in demands for direct or participatory action and decision-making. The continuing influence of Gandhian ideas among many social activists in India indicates that the values of direct participation need not necessarily be associated with violence (Ostergaard, 1985). It should also be recalled that direct democracy was the norm among the city-states of ancient Greece, from which Western democracy itself derives much of its intellectual origins (Sartori, 1965: 250–68).

Some elements of this third tradition have rubbed off on today's radical activist groups in Indonesia, and even on elements among mainstream LSM/LPSMs. Values emphasizing mass action for social justice and an ethos of face-to-face decision-making have obvious appeal in many local struggle contexts. They are also reflected in traditions of voluntary action which see diffusion of decision-making beyond the formal processes of politics and administration as essential to any effective development of popular participation. In Indonesia, such ideals are not entirely utopian, in so far as they partly reflect people's experience. Although formal village structures have increasingly become extensions of the government, a case can be made that traditional village institutions have historically contained both participatory as well as hierarchical elements.[15] To some extent it appears that many NGO and radical activists seek to articulate idealized contemporary variants of these much threatened, but by no means dead, traditions. On the whole, however, revolutionary traditions prior to the twentieth century appear relatively weak, although rural Java, at least, has an earlier tradition of rebellion (Sartono, 1973).

LSM/LPSMs draw on all three traditions of democratic participation in shaping both their critique of dominant power structures and their agenda for change. While they appear more comfortable and familiar with the second or third traditions, all three are used eclectically in various struggles by various groups, since each contains some potential counter-cultural challenge to dominant corporate statist ideology. Unfortunately, the reiteration of vague slogans about 'participation', 'people's power', 'bottom–up' decision-making, and so forth serves to compress discussion of their meaning in ways which take no account of these three competing frameworks for understanding democratic participation.

One emerging point of convergence between radicals and mainstream LSM/LPSMs can be found in growing demands for the 'right to organize'. This can be identified as a key theme within all three major traditions of democracy in Indonesia, although it is not readily associated with Panca Sila democracy under Suharto's New Order. However, demands for change are now being vigorously expressed in terms of Article 28 of Indonesia's 1945 Constitution, which affirms freedom of speech and association. Such demands cannot be easily brushed aside, given the government's insistence that the 1945 Constitution and Panca Sila provide the basic legal foundation for the Indonesian state. Article 28 guarantees freedom of association, speech, and assembly, though without spelling out such rights in any detail.

Historically, inclusion of Article 28 in the 1945 Constitution represented a compromise within the Indonesian Independence Preparatory Committee between its chairman, Supomo, who favoured an 'integralistic' political structure, and Mohammed Hatta, who urged that the state should not be allowed to accumulate excessive powers *vis-à-vis* its citizens (Bourchier, 1995). The implication of Supomo's position is that the close family affinity between ruler and ruled precludes any notion of conflicting rights or interests between citizens and the state. During the 1980s, Supomo's ideas were included in official Panca Sila education courses, though without his endorsement of totalitarian ideology which he had associated with German national socialism and imperial Japan. The government's contemporary interpretation of 'integralism' asserts that the spirit underlying the 1945 Constitution overrides narrow and legalistic interpretations of particular clauses which might point in a different direction (Bourchier, 1995).

Government attempts to interpret Indonesian history in this way have brought about a corresponding revival of interest in Hatta's ideas. This has been supported by research by Simunjuntak (1992) and others, indicating that Supomo's views were, in fact, rejected in the final form of the 1945 Constitution. Further, so the critics of integralism assert, attempts to claim an indigenous basis for such a political theory rest on a highly selective view of Indonesian history and culture, which are equally open to participatory and pluralist interpretations.

Bourchier (1995) has argued that the revival of integralist ideas during the 1980s was indicative of efforts by the government to counter a growing wave of legal and constitutionally based assertion of popular rights by human rights groups, NGOs, and dissenting groups such as the Petition of Fifty.[16] This petition had been signed in 1980 by a group of well-known former military, politicians, and intellectuals. Objections to the government's assumed right to monopolize interpretation of the five principles enshrined in Indonesia's official ideology of Panca Sila lay at the heart of their protest. The group has stayed together as a loose reformist network, advocating legal and political change, although their profile has not been so high with the emergence of many more groups calling for reform since the late 1980s. This latter trend has been partly encouraged by policies of economic liberalization adopted since around 1985–6,[17] which has led to calls for corresponding deregulation in the political sphere. The emerging Indonesian middle class has been portrayed as a catalyst for reform in both contexts, although both the strength of such a nexus and the nature and orientation of this middle class has been subject to vigorous debate (Robison, 1986; Tanter and Young, 1990; Lane, 1991).

Despite the growing strength of legal and ideological challenges, collectivist notions of the state as a large family continue to prevail over those stressing individual, voluntarist, and associational perspectives in determining public and political discourse. While appearances can be deceptive, and despite notable exceptions, it is hard to see Indonesian NGOs posing any systematic challenge to this dominant orthodoxy. They may even be reinforcing it with demands to be included in more regular and extensive ways in structures of national decision-making. The Indonesian government may well accommodate such demands in some measure, as part of a more general process of promoting openness. The overall effect could be to legitimize corporatist structures, balanced by some strengthening of trends towards pluralism within established frameworks.[18]

While the pragmatism of LSM/LPSMs is understandable, given the context within which they operate, their bland acceptance of official ideological frameworks carries potential dangers. For example, implementation of Article 28 of the 1945 Constitution is not easily achievable within a political and constitutional framework which systematically overrides the rule of law. Equally, the reliance of NGOs on verbal gymnastics to survive the 1985 Law on Social Organizations, as discussed in Chapter 3, appears unsustainable in the longer term, although their resourcefulness in this and other contexts has been noteworthy.

While ideals of decision-making through deliberation (*musyawarah*) and consensus (*mufakat*) fit well with the ethos of much LSM/LPSM discourse and action, attempts to operationalize these principles beyond relatively small face-to-face communities have never been satisfactorily undertaken in Indonesia. Therefore, some rule of law is needed to achieve a fair overall balance between individuals and society. Parallel concerns apply to interpretations of democracy stressing mass-based decision-making, which would upset this balance from the opposite direction. Such forms of decision-making are likely, in practice, to be dominated by small minorities of those sufficiently active and strategically placed to organize meetings. Rhetoric against liberal or bourgeois democracy, and associated legal and constitutional constraints, serve to conceal the potentially oligarchic nature of such an outlook.

Emerging Agendas for Non-Government Organizations

To place this somewhat esoteric discussion within a contemporary context, a rapidly changing political and social environment is beginning to shift the parameters of discourse within the Indonesian NGO community. Accumulated field experience and awareness of the needs of local people have increasingly drawn LSM/LPSMs into undertaking policy advice and advocacy roles. However, for the most part, they have lacked the inclination or capacity to promote any kind of overall political change. This situation is beginning to change as more LSM/LPSMs urge reforms in law and administration guaranteeing greater freedom to individuals and organizations. Such demands have, to some extent, been legitimized by official slogans calling for greater openness, although the government's intention is most probably to confine change in this regard to the sphere of economic liberalization.

As will be discussed in the next chapter, a new wave of activist groups has emerged since the mid-1980s, mostly based on student forums or study groups, which have formed coalitions with farmers, the landless, workers, urban squatters, women's groups, and others to take up specific grievances. Such groups have expressed impatience with the apparent unwillingness of established LSM/LPSMs to pursue such struggles or, when they do, to pursue them with a sufficient degree of militancy. For their part, LSM/LPSMs see serious problems in adopting any direct confrontational approach towards the authorities. In any case, their basic goals are directed towards building up the capacity of local groups for self-management. As this process is seen as entailing many years of grass-roots work, established LSM/LPSMs tend to doubt the long-term staying power of the radicals. From the perspective of local people, struggles for subsistence provide the focus for all their energies compared with political change, which is perceived as a remote and only dimly understood goal.

As in earlier periods of Indonesian history, such differences reflect, to some extent, generational conflict, which in this context can be seen as helping to renew the NGO movement. In so far as the past provides a guide to the future, it is likely that some of today's radicals will set up their own NGOs, while retaining their interest in and connections with the macro political scene. Quite possibly, they may seek to resolve contradictions in their present stance within a framework broadly similar to that of social action groups which have emerged in India over the past 20–5 years (Sethi, 1984: 305–16; Eldridge, 1985). Though critical of the community-cum-social work emphasis of older-style NGOs, most Indian social action groups also strive to maintain autonomy from political parties. In many ways, such groups have developed their own variant of 'anti-state' ideology, which is a long-standing characteristic of the voluntary action scene in India. Social and structural transformation, according to this perspective, is to be achieved through popular mobilization and direct action on a mass scale rather than through intermediary parliamentary representatives.

The relevance of the Indian social action group model will remain unclear until a more open political system emerges in Indonesia. The lack of such openness has probably aggravated misunderstanding of both the actual and the potential roles of non-government organizations relative to political parties and the state. The primary concern of parties and party-related groups is with capturing and retaining state power through electoral or other, possibly violent or extra-legal, means. By contrast, NGOs and social action groups, although they interact with the state in many contexts, concentrate on promoting independent social organization and action in a direct sense. Nor do such groups see control of the state apparatus as a prerequisite for achieving social change.

As Indonesia enters a stage of wider social and political mobilization, these two distinct approaches can easily become confused. Whichever approach is adopted, scaling up from micro to macro arenas of action is a slow and complex process. Effective understanding of what is entailed requires a capacity to grasp both dimensions simultaneously. Commuting in this study between macro and micro contexts will hopefully be seen as contributing to such an understanding.

1. See Feith (1962) for a comprehensive account of the period of parliamentary democracy in Indonesia from 1950 to 1959. For more recent perspectives, see Bourchier and Legge (1994).

2. Such support roles are implied in the term *pengembangan*.

3. Sarekat Dagang Islam (Union of Islamic Traders), founded in 1911, became Sarekat Islam (Islamic Union) in 1912. While there had been other forerunners with more limited goals, Sarekat Islam was the first broad-based popular movement to promote Indonesian political advancement and later independence.

4. Budi Utomo, a movement for spiritual and intellectual enlightenment founded in 1908, focused primarily on developing a better understanding of Javanese culture.

5. See Soeratman (1982) and Majelis Luhur Persatuan Tamansiswa (1982). The five principles of Panca Sila (Belief in One Almighty God, national unity, humanitarianism, democracy, and social justice) were originally enunciated by former President Sukarno in a speech on 1 June 1945 (Kahin, 1952: 122–7).

6. See LP3ES (1983) for an extensive discussion of these issues, especially the paper by Ismid Hadad (pp. 3–25) and the 'Dialogue' (pp. 65–9) between Emil Salim, then Minister for Population and Environment, and Erna Witular, at that time Executive Secretary of the Indonesian Environmental Association (Wahana Lingkungan Hidup Indonesia—WALHI).

7. See Lipton (1977: 130–8) for a trenchant attack on such schools of thought.

8. See Kothari (1988: 72–87) for a more dramatic version of this proposition. Kothari sees World Bank attempts to promote NGOs as a means to bypass structures of government and political accountability generally, ultimately designed to open up Third World hinterlands to foreign capital.

9. See Reeve (1985) for an explanation of the role of GOLKAR, an association of officially sponsored functional groups, which also dominates national elections.

10. The meaning of ORMAS is disputed and is used with reference to both mass organizations (*organisasi massa*) and social organizations (*organisasi kemasyarakatan*).

11. See Korten (1987: 145–60) for a general discussion of this proposition.

12. MPR No. IV (1978), cited in Wiryosaputro and Muharram (1989: 1–2).

13. This impression derives from the extent to which such values and terms emerged in impromptu fashion in conversations with villagers and other reference people.

14. See, for example, Lucas (1990).

15. C. Warren (1990: 1) has claimed that 'village institutions in Bali where traditional forms of organisation such as the *banjar* (hamlet) operating within the administrative village (*desa*) have proved valuable in engaging precisely the self-help participation which has enhanced the effectiveness and reduced costs to the state of implementing its rural development policies'. This case is probably weaker in the case of Java, given its traditional hierarchical structures. Nevertheless, Tjondronegoro (1984: 236) sees sub-village units there as a primary locus of strong community ties and collective action with 'elements of "primitive democracy" and mutual help practices ... still functioning effectively'. Schulte-Nordholt (1985: 7) has also affirmed the representative character of the Rukun Tetangga (neighbourhood/ward level) leadership in Java and its role in ensuring expression of popular interests within the LSD (Village Community Institution).

16. See Bourchier (1987: 7–10) for background and details concerning the Petition of Fifty.

17. The rationale and context for these policy changes is discussed in Robison (1986: 16–51). See also Hill (1992: 17–42, especially pp. 31–4) for more recent discussion.

18. See MacIntyre (1990: 258–62) for a more general statement of this argument.

2

NGO–Government Relations and Approaches to Popular Mobilization

This chapter will continue exploring the outlook of non-government organizations (NGOs) on democratic participation in the context of their relations with the Indonesian government and general approach to popular mobilization. Their stance on these issues is categorized in the latter part of the chapter in terms of three models, alongside a fourth applied to emerging radical groups. The earlier part deals with the general context of NGO–government relations, followed by examples of interactions with regional and local authorities, including an account of the experience of NGOs in working with district authorities in Banjarnegara, Central Java, in fields relating to health and community development.

Non-Government Organizations' Relations with the Government: General Issues

This and subsequent chapters have drawn somewhat freely on five typologies of relationship between governments and NGOs proposed by Riker (1990: 18). These are (i) benign neglect linked to acceptance of autonomy; (ii) active promotion and facilitation of their activities; (iii) collaboration and co-operation; (iv) co-option and absorption, and (v) containment and dissolution. NGO–government relations in Indonesia range across this spectrum, though a normal distribution curve would probably show a concentration around the third and fourth types. Dissolution has occurred rarely although, at the opposite extreme, this study will indicate instances where groups have more or less attained a desired state of benign neglect. Riker's comment that governments may be expected to exercise less rigorous scrutiny over areas of activity considered relatively neutral, such as health or animal husbandry, than in sensitive areas, such as land or human rights, is certainly borne out by case-studies in subsequent chapters.

Riker (1990: 20–1) further proposes that four key dimensions shape the political space between governments and NGOs. These constitute: (i) principles and ideology, in which governments seek compatibility, if not conformity, by NGOs; (ii) financial resources; (iii) organization, including management of technical and human resources, and (iv) participation in policy debates and input into policy-making. The first aspect is discussed in this chapter, following exploration of more general ideological contexts in Chapter 1. The other three are explored in later chapters.

According to MacIntyre (1990: 6–21), most foreign and domestic observers see Indonesia's state structures as relatively impervious to challenges from outside. However, differences can be identified between commentators such as Jackson (1978) and Crouch (1979; 1986), who see the Indonesian political process primarily as a competition within a relatively closed circle for the spoils of office; Emmerson (1983), who acknowledges a measure of pluralism in policy-making within the bureaucracy, and Liddle (1987), who sees a capacity within state structures to incorporate the concerns of outside actors in some significant measure. King (1982) applies the New Order government's own theory of the state—best known in Western political theory as 'corporatism'—to contend that societal interests are systematically organized as functional groups (*golongan karya*) in a manner which ensures their ultimate subordination to and dependence on the Indonesian government apparatus. MacIntyre applies a similar analysis to the Indonesian business community, while indicating that the balance of forces may, to some extent, be changing in the direction of greater autonomy for non-state actors. Robison (1986) focuses on the emergence of a new class of entrepreneurs from within the bureaucracy who have built up their position through close links with Western and Japanese business interests but have later come to behave increasingly like conventional capitalists.

Not surprisingly, a study of this nature will find more in common with those perspectives which acknowledge some degree of autonomy, or at least influence, for non-government actors. Certainly, there has been wide agreement that until the late 1980s, at least, such actors have operated within a highly regulated environment in which power has been tightly concentrated. Yet, even in the early New Order period, when the official theory of the 'floating mass' severely limited political participation in the conventional sense, significant independent group formation sponsored by NGOs was occurring in a variety of micro contexts. This was made possible by defining such activity as developmental rather than political.

There were also many examples during the 1970s of relatively independent, small-scale organizations and programmes operating with tolerance, if not active co-operation, from local and provincial authorities. Such activities can be seen against a general background during that time of widespread questioning of goals and outcomes from dominant developmental models, which emphasized economic growth and saw the state and private corporations as the main initiators of development. Such questioning was couched in relatively mild terms, while the search for alternatives, though persistent, was conducted in a generally non-confrontational manner. As a result of this patient strategy, the NGO community was able to open up sufficient social and bureaucratic space to survive the more repressive period of the early and middle New Order. In recent years, growing divergence of outlook within the élite appears to reflect trends towards greater pluralism, both within the state and society more generally. Such developments have created a sufficiently favourable climate for a new wave of self-reliant community institutions (Lembaga Swadaya Masyarakat—LSM), institutions for developing community self-reliance (Lembaga Pengembangan Swadaya Masyarakat—LPSM), and other groups seeking change to emerge.

It cannot be assumed that such developments necessarily imply a uni-linear evolution towards liberal-pluralist democracy in Indonesia. While issues of political openness, popular participation, and representation are much to the fore in current discourse, sharp tensions are evident between pluralist and corporatist models of representation. King's understanding of this antithesis is described by MacIntyre (1990: 13) in the following terms:

The societal, or liberal, variant ... found in democratic systems ... involves a more cooperative arrangement between the state and organised interests in society, with the latter being autonomous from and even penetrating the former to a considerable degree. Under state, or authoritarian corporatism, the state is in a much stronger position, controlling and penetrating the various dependent interest associations. One is a system of political representation in which the state seeks to include or involve various societal groups in policy-making, while, conversely, the other is characterised by political exclusion.

While the Indonesian government appears anxious to regulate and, where necessary, repress NGOs which become too assertive, the NGOs have mostly been able to counter such intentions by the variety of services they have provided. They have also been able to exert influence on the government through the support they receive from overseas interests. Thus, too heavy-handed treatment of local organizations could meet with financial sanctions from at least some Western countries in a mood to deny support for policies which receive adverse reports from trusted community, environment, church, and other counterpart groups. Private funding agencies in donor countries are often co-financed by their own governments, many of which also channel assistance to official development programmes and have persuaded their governments to make assistance conditional on developing a community component in such programmes. Overall, this situation has structured a form of co-existence between conflict and co-operation in the relations of NGOs with their governments in many countries, irrespective of their different stages of economic development and widely contrasting political systems.

The World Bank has also made overtures to NGOs, declaring itself to be open to their ideas and criticisms (Qureshi, 1988: 30–6). There is some evidence of an active lobby group within the Bank which has had some impact, notably within the environmental field. However, both the size and complexity of the organization, and its legal obligation to work through government channels, may be expected to dilute and delay any too radical shifts in direction (Van de Laar, 1980). The World Bank has further indicated that it needs feedback on the impact of policy at grass-roots level, claiming that accurate and quick reporting by NGOs can offset the slowness and astigmatism of bureaucracies. In that context, a former deputy director has urged that NGOs should not underestimate their potential to influence Bank policy-making nor its willingness or capacity to oppose rich, urban-based interest groups (Qureshi, 1988: 30–6).

Third World governments have been moderately responsive to such pressures, due partly to financial tightness caused by widespread eco-nomic recession during the late 1980s and early 1990s and partly to pressures for structural adjustment and liberalization of their economies by international lending and financial agencies. In Indonesia, falling domestic revenues due to declining international oil prices since the mid-1980s render the apparently low-cost alternative offered by LSM/LPSMs relatively attractive. More fundamentally, there has been a growing realization within the Indonesian government that its own agen-cies cannot achieve effective outreach or mobilize sufficient community support on their own to implement official programmes aimed at the urban and rural poor, without some assistance.

LSM/LPSMs naturally have reservations towards such an instru-mental view of their role. Some respond by minimizing official contacts, while others perceive opportunities and needs that they are better placed to supply. Overall, the view has been gaining ground, both in NGO and government circles, that NGOs must help find solutions as well as criti-cize. As will be discussed in Chapter 7, Emil Salim, whose role in per-suading non-government organizations to change their generic name to self-reliant community institutions (LSM/LPSMs) was noted in the pre-vious chapter, was active in pressing such arguments in his dealings with environmental organizations.

By way of example, some NGOs operating in the urban informal sec-tor have found it necessary to participate in joint management agencies with the government and private developers in order to gain some con-sideration for their clients. They see subsequent protests, once plans are in place, as doomed to failure. The experience of organizations dis-cussed in Chapters 4 and 5 covering fields such as health, water supply, credit co-operatives, rural enterprises, and the urban informal sector fur-ther illustrates both pressures and opportunities for co-operating with the government in developmental programmes. In general, many official programmes at village level can be seen as empty boxes, which are avail-able to be filled by local groups with appropriate human resources and skills.

Some commentators go further in seeing the government versus non-government formulation of issues as representing a false dichotomy standing in the way of co-operation between progressive elements both inside and outside government in opening up opportunities for change (Byesouth, 1986: 211–26). Anecdotal evidence of such informal co-operation is offered in later chapters in fields such as environment, labour, women workers, the urban informal sector, rural co-operatives, and credit unions. Informal ex-alumni networks operating among former student activists from the 1970s generation, many of whom now hold positions in government or business, have been influential in the evolution of a number of important national-level NGOs. This has also occurred at regional and local levels.

Seen in this light, the Indonesian government apparatus is a good deal less monolithic than commonly depicted by its critics both inside and outside Indonesia, while boundaries between formal institutions and general community life are extremely blurred, particularly at village level. Nevertheless, the government/non-government distinction cannot be so easily discarded, since institutions in any society pursue their own logic despite co-operation between individuals across boundaries. The problem for LSM/LPSMs has been to define their roles in ways which allow them to co-operate with government agencies, where this seems likely to benefit the people they seek to serve, while preserving their independent existence and bargaining power. In this regard, they still face real dilemmas. Despite the opening up of opportunities for NGOs, numerous official and semi-official structures prevent them from realizing their full potential. Consequently, most LSM/LPSMs continue to see core values of democratic participation as most likely to be promoted through direct building of popular strength, independent from the state and political process which are seen as ultimately hostile to such values. At a practical level, however, they feel torn between pressing the state to serve the people and building parallel and autonomous systems.[1] Either way, any excessively moral or ideological claims can detract from effective pursuit of incremental gains for poor clients and members.

Interaction with Local Authorities

Discussion of LSM/LPSM–government relations is mostly conducted in broad national terms. Yet, major interaction occurs predominantly at local and sub-provincial levels. While structures at these levels are essentially similar in form across the country, their mode of operation can vary a good deal, depending on the nature of local society, economy, leadership, and structures of community organization. These can differ from village to village as well as from region to region, although the bureaucratization of village administration during the past two decades (C. Warren, 1990) imposes significant constraints on non-government initiatives.

In 1971, the Department of Home Affairs (Departemen Dalam Negeri) established its own community development arm called Pembangunan Desa (BANGDES), which assumed formal control of all community development activity in rural areas. The approach of BANGDES is very much one of imposing goals, targets, and largely empty structures, such as the Village Community Resilience Institution

(Lembaga Ketahanan Masyarakat Desa—LKMD). LKMDs must be established in each village and assume responsibility for mobilizing and directing community energies and initiatives. All community development programmes are supposed to fit into the LKMD structure. This is divided into 15–20 sections, each under the village head's authority. As LKMDs often appear to be non-operational, new programmes, whether official or non-official, are in practice negotiated directly between relevant parties.

Other para-government structures, such as the Association for Promoting Family Welfare (Pembinaan Kesejahteraan Keluarga—PKK) and the Village Co-operative Unit (Koperasi Unit Desa—KUD), can also significantly hinder the growth of independent group formation. Even when informal co-operatives (*usaha bersama*—UB) nutrition, family planning, or *arisan* groups[2] are established, they often seem to be led by village or sub-village officials or their wives. However, village school teachers often play significant roles in promoting new initiatives, as they have both the status and knowledge capable of linking community needs with government structures.

Tensions between LSM/LPSMs and BANGDES have declined somewhat since the 1970s, due to the more sympathetic outlook of recent Ministers of Home Affairs. However, the pervasive presence of BANGDES and its surveillance of LSM/LPSMs continue to prove irksome to NGOs, who in any case consider that BANGDES officials lack relevant expertise and experience. At a day-to-day level, relations are governed by pragmatism, depending on specific interest configurations between local officials, village hierarchies, and community groups. In that context, larger LPSMs have the advantage of cultivating a wide range of contacts across government agencies, and are sometimes able to exert leverage on the local scene via officials at higher levels.

In recent years, provincial (Badan Perencanaan Pembangunan Daerah—BAPPEDA) and district (Badan Perencanaan Pembangunan Kabupaten—BAPPEMKA) development planning boards have developed closer working relations with NGO networks.[3] This is convenient to both parties since BAPPEDA lacks effective structures below the district level. The attitudes of the provincial governor and senior provincial officials and military at equivalent command levels, which control the operations of both BAPPEDA and BANGDES within each province, are crucial in this context.

One example where local authorities are reported to have obstructed independent community effort has been in Gunung Kidul, a dry, hilly, and traditionally poor sub-region south of Yogyakarta. Efforts to form local LSMs, particularly in the poorest pockets south of the district capital, Wonosari, have mostly proved unsuccessful. One explanation is that the natural community leaders had associations with the former Communist Party of Indonesia (Partai Komunis Indonesia—PKI) in the pre-1965 period and have been effectively crushed. Periodic visits from charismatic leaders from outside the district, such as Fr. Mangunwijaya, based in Yogyakarta, or the late Kyai Hamam Ja'afar, head of Pesantren

Pabelan near Magelang, have not been able to compensate for this lack of local leadership.

The government has not been inactive in this region. However, informal sources have suggested that officials extract some 20–30 per cent of over Rp100 million poured into Gunung Kidul every dry season from government, voluntary, and private sources, in addition to normal government programmes. Poverty of officials at local and sub-local levels appears to be a significant cause. In any case, corruption appears to have rendered programmes of all kinds ineffective. Problems in this area seem sufficiently intractable to require a major combined effort by both government agencies and LSM/LPSMs. For example, the water problem in Gunung Kidul requires wide-scale electrification to pump underground water, but this can only be possible with a major shake-up of the local bureaucracy, accompanied by extensive social mobilization. Only very conventional LSMs are now reported to be working in Gunung Kidul, none of which are willing to confront the local government power structure.

In Pabelan, some 30 kilometres north of Yogyakarta, the local Islamic boarding-school (*pesantren*) has acted as a centre for raising social awareness, both among its own students and the local community. In 1980, Mochtar Abbas, a former student of the school, with active support from the *pesantren* hierarchy, successfully contested the election for village head against the local nominee from the government-sponsored network of Functional Groups (Golongan Karya—GOLKAR). According to his own account, he received excellent service from higher authorities; for example, four new primary schools were established without any corrupt demands being made. However, such impact was purely localized to Pabelan village, without any parallel effort in neighbouring villages. The motivation for special treatment given to Pabelan, therefore, appears to have been one of fear by local and regional authorities of outside contacts enjoyed by Abbas and the *pesantren*.

The experience of the Social and Economic Development Foundation (Yayasan Pembangunan dan Pengembangan Sosial Ekonomi—YPPSE) at Banjarnegara, Central Java, offers a more positive example of LSM/LPSM co-operation with district and local authorities. It also gives insights into the implications for NGOs of working with the government in the field of community development and on problems in building relations between village-based cadres and local authorities.[4]

YPPSE developed from a social and economic development committee brought together in 1974 through the initiative of a former district head, Drs Suwaji. At the end of his term, the arrangement was institutionalized by the establishment of YPPSE. The acknowledged driving force behind both committee structures has been the head of Banjarnegara District Health Services, Dr Arif Haliman. Major participating NGOs have been Yayasan Indonesia Sejahtera (YIS), which had been involved in community health, nutrition, and small-scale development programmes in Banjarnegara since the late 1960s,[5] Yayasan Dian Desa, Bina Swadaya, and OXFAM. These organizations later either withdrew or only supported selected programmes. Consequently, YPPSE has sought to establish itself as a non-government organization in its own right. OXFAM has continued to see value in YPPSE's work and maintained its support.

Though YPPSE is legally independent, close integration with government agencies gives it the appearance of a Government Organized Non-Government Organization (GONGO). Dr Haliman was appointed chairman of YPPSE, the chairman of the local GOLKAR organization became the vice-chairman, a retired regional development officer was appointed secretary, and a retired sub-district head became liaison officer with government departments and participating NGOs. During Drs Suwaji's time, the division of roles between the then Panitia Pengembangan Sosial Ekonomi board members had been reasonably clear, with NGOs channelling private external resources and training cadres, and government departments managing official programmes. The establishment of YPPSE shifted the balance of initiative towards regional technical and service department heads. To place these arrangements in perspective, Dr Haliman has displayed a strong, long-term commitment to community participation and has personally trained many groups of cadres. He expresses impatience with definitional problems as to whether YPPSE can be regarded as an NGO or not, urging that only results achieved among the people are of any significance.

In 1987, OXFAM sponsored an evaluation designed to upgrade the quality of joint planning and community consultation through the *Kring* system.[6] This system had been devised by YPPSE, with substantial input from YIS, in order to co-ordinate community input at village and neighbourhood/ward (Rukun Tetangga—RT) level as a basis for shaping sub-district level planning and allocation of resources. The evolution of this programme has tended to give the Health Department (Departemen Kesehatan—DEPKES) a dominant role in *Kring*, as in YPPSE as a whole. By 1985, the *Kring* system covered 134 villages in twelve clusters (OXFAM, 1987). Meetings were being held quarterly among a cluster of villages, with each playing host on a rotation basis. Participants evaluated each other's programmes and performance, and shared experiences and problems. Administrative heads or deputies attended these meetings, together with appropriate technical experts. YPPSE assisted in preparing material and follow-up activities.[7]

Comments on this programme by Dr Haliman indicate that administrative heads themselves operate under constraints imposed by pressures to implement programmes passed down from national and provincial levels:

The health programs which we've developed in Banjarnegara were a model for POSYANDU,[8] but it is implemented in a different way from our activities. We stress community design, development and implementation of programs, which gives caders an important role to play ... responding to felt needs in each community. POSYANDU is implemented in a top–down way ... it's the same program everywhere, regardless of what the community thinks is important or wants ... community priorities ... [often differ] from what we health professionals think are important. Our experience is that if felt needs aren't addressed first, the community won't support a program. Everyone will complain [of lack of] time to participate [YPPSE, 1986: 41].

Concrete successes include a relatively more active LKMD structure; training of some 4,500 cadres in basic survey and monitoring techniques; more even distribution of health and other basic services to include the poorer hilly region in the northern half of the district, and exposure of administrative staff to the needs of the poorest groups through more regular visits to remote areas. The *Kring* system has also shown the potential to break down rigidities in sectoral planning and so encourage a more integrated approach—a constant theme in the comparative literature on Third World rural development. Significant reductions in infant mortality rates have been recorded.[9] There is visible evidence of reafforestation around Karangkobar. Erosion was reduced by deep terracing and other improved land-use practices which resulted in a greater variety in crops and house-garden production.[10] Increased labour demand has been reported for terracing work. Other activities, such as tree planting, are claimed to have lifted wages in areas covered by YPPSE programmes.[11]

Despite obviously close relations between YPPSE and the district government, the above account provides reasonable evidence that official programmes have been reshaped to reach out to wider segments of the rural population than would have been the case through standard official programmes. Some long-term observers of the Banjarnegara experience believe that, despite uneven implementation, both the spirit and practical experience of community participation are sufficiently widespread to render the reintroduction of top–down planning, normal in neighbouring districts and in most other parts of Indonesia, no longer acceptable in Banjarnegara. If so, this would suggest that the mere fact of LSM/LPSMs seeking to channel popular participation through official structures and programmes does not in itself automatically signify their co-option by those structures.

The dangers of government agencies using *Kring* or similar systems as convenient vehicles to co-ordinate and gain acceptance for predetermined plans must nevertheless be acknowledged, especially where community participation is limited, information and planning skills are inadequate, and village proposals are dependent on outside funding (YPPSE, 1986: 20–1). However, it is also important to recognize the scope for informality and innovation within official structures, which initiatives such as those at Banjarnegara open up. Finally, the case of YPPSE Banjarnegara, together with other examples in this section, indicate that key personalities can make a major impact in the local context.

Orientations Towards Popular Mobilization and Relations with the Government: Four Paradigms

Three broad frameworks can be identified as shaping the relations of LSM/LPSMs with the Indonesian government, their approaches to popular mobilization, and the political process,[12] all of which indicate their desire to avoid overt conflict. However, this notion must be qualified to the extent that LSM/LPSMs undertake advocacy roles which, particularly in the case of groups pursuing the second model, sometimes take the form of 'critical collaboration'. LSM/LPSMs also differ a good deal in the extent to which they co-operate or limit their interactions with the Indonesian government. More recently, a fourth stream has emerged of younger groups, which are active in mobilizing peasants and workers around local struggles and are not afraid to challenge the authorities. As will be discussed, there is some question as to how far groups in this latter stream can appropriately be described as NGOs. While they bear some similarities to social action groups in India, the primarily political nature of their objectives can also give them the appearance of quasi-party formations.

The matrix below attempts to encapsulate the three NGO paradigms, together with the approach of the new radicals.

Orientation	Three NGO Models			New Radicals
	1	2	3	4
Stance v. Official Development Programmes	Co-operate; foster community participation	Critical collaboration	Avoid involvement	Oppose
Orientation v. State Structures	Accommodate	Reform	Maintain distance	Oppose
Concept of Democracy	Participatory problem-solving	Balance economic and political rights	Grass-roots initiative	Direct decision-making
Popular Mobilization	Small-group formation	Economic programmes; promote awareness	Empower small groups	Mass action and demon-strations

The first category of groups follows a two-pronged approach of (i) pursuing small-scale programmes directly at village level, specifically targeted towards disadvantaged groups which are encouraged to manage their affairs on a self-reliant basis, and (ii) seeking to build enhanced community participation into official development programmes. In both contexts, negotiations are conducted as appropriate to each situation, taking pains to cultivate smooth working relations with relevant officials and agencies. Overall, the stance of LSM/LPSMs in this stream could be described as one of 'High-level Co-operation–Grass-roots Development'.

NGOs in this category show no interest in changing or intervening in the political process as such, although they are active in promoting their core values of self-reliance, grass-roots participation, and so forth. Efforts at reform are confined to influencing the policy of those government agencies operating in areas relevant to their own field experience. This kind of approach is seen as the most effective means of preserving both their own autonomy and that of associated local groups. This non-political approach is designed not only to safeguard their own freedom of operation from government interference, but also to give confidence to the people that they are neither an agent of the government nor biased in favour of any political or religious group. In any case, the values of conflict-avoidance are deeply rooted in many of Indonesia's various cultural systems, most notably among the Javanese (Geertz, 1960).

While this first stream includes several of the larger LPSMs, many among them originated as small, locally based groups. As they have spread both geographically and across sectors, and taken on more training, consultancy, and intermediary roles, their managerial structures have inevitably become larger and more complex. To some extent, their growth has been unplanned, and they consequently tend to feel uncomfortable with many of their new roles. Most are nevertheless conscious of the need both to maintain effective grass-roots links and avoid co-option by the government.

The second stream of NGOs is more explicitly critical of New Order development philosophy and practice. While promoting consciousness-raising and the capacity for self-management among specific target groups, they seek legal status and protection for them against local officials and other influential people through contacts forged at higher levels of government. They are also active in local group formation. However, whereas the first stream of NGOs essentially sees this as an end in itself, those pursuing the second model see both benefits to local groups but also as a support base for advocacy efforts at higher political and policy-making levels. This approach could be described as one of 'High-level Politics–Grass-roots Mobilization'.

NGOs in this category initially expressed aversion to participating in official development programmes but now co-operate extensively in fields such as urban informal sector development, water supply, and environmental management. Some key organizations in this second category are led by former student activists from the 1960s and 1970s who have built up strong informal networks, which are to a considerable extent linked with broader Islamic networks. They also have some contacts and influence within the military and bureaucracy, and closely monitor political developments in Jakarta.

The focus of action by groups in the third category is at the local rather than national level, with more emphasis on building awareness of rights than on efforts to change policy. Rather than acting as intermediaries vis-à-vis the authorities, they seek to build up confidence and skills among the people to enable them to conduct their own negotiations. Social and political change is seen as ultimately less dependent on persuasion and policy reform by the government than on strong self-reliant groups, in the belief that eventually a strong, though informally structured popular movement, will emerge. Emphasizing face-to-face dealings rather than formal organization, such groups also tend to minimize involvement in large-scale networking arrangements. While they seek legal and bureaucratic niches within which to operate, only the minimum necessary contact is sought with government agencies. A convenient description of this approach is 'Empowerment from Below'.

Almost by definition, this third approach is found among smaller, more informally organized groups. For this reason, such groups are harder to identify and their extent harder to gauge. Some examples are provided in later chapters. As this approach is difficult to sustain over an extended period, groups which pursue it tend to be squeezed between the two larger, more successful categories of LSM/LPSM and the radicals. However, their influence is probably more widespread in expressing aspirations with which many began in their earlier days. Ideals expressed in the third model, therefore, still have resonance within the NGO community. Even though they are now considered by the mainstream of established LSM/LPSMs, to be too impractical and simplistic, they probably continue to exert some kind of conscience-keeping influence. Such influence is perhaps stronger among LPSMs in the first category than in the second, as the former were originally more oriented towards limiting their involvement with the government, and are more naturally inclined towards a non-political stance.

While these three models may prove useful in identifying divergent outlooks among LSM/LPSMs, it is important not to overlook their many points of convergence. Despite differences in ideology, approach, cultural and religious background, organization, and personalities, the great majority of LSM/LPSMs share several basic goals in common, namely, (i) an orientation towards strengthening community groups as the basis for a healthy society and as a counterweight to government power; (ii) a creative search for new strategies to confront changing social needs and emerging structures of disadvantage and powerlessness, and (iii) a strong commitment to ideals of popular participation in defining and implementing programmes. Such broad commonality of ideals, in the author's view, makes it still meaningful to talk of an Indonesian NGO community, which enjoys a good deal of mutual exchange and support, transcending the above three, essentially heuristic models.

Radical Critics of Non-Government Organizations

This broad convergence has been explicitly challenged in recent years by the emergence of new groups and movements with aggressive and youthful leaders, who criticize established NGOs for what they see as their failure to mobilize workers and peasants or to develop any effective theoretical framework or strategies for change. In particular, they deplore the conflict-avoidance strategies outlined earlier.

From a theoretical perspective, many of Indonesia's young radicals seem, in one sense, to be pursuing a dependency (neo-Marxist) rather than Marxist style of analysis,[13] in which the World Bank and multinational companies dominated by the USA represent the chief sources of exploitation and oppression of Indonesian workers and peasants through their support for the Suharto 'fascist' state. They are correspondingly hostile to the liberal capitalist model of development proposed for Indonesia. Their attitude to political democratization is more ambivalent. On the one hand, stress is placed on rights to organize and the creation of greater democratic space. On the other hand, such demands are apparently dissociated from values of liberal democracy, which is seen as a political project of international capitalism.

In tactical terms, current radical analysis focuses on contradictions within the élite and the emerging urban middle class, even claiming tacit support from groups within the Indonesian Armed Forces (Angkatan Bersenjata Republik Indonesia—ABRI) and the professional and business classes which, for their own reasons, want to see the abolition or, at least, a drastic reduction of the dual civilian and military role of ABRI and a general civilianization of government structures. Similarly, the 'rule of law' demanded by many business people, professionals, and intellectuals is also favoured by radicals as providing a more secure legal base for political activity. Intellectuals, allowing for individual exceptions, are seen by radicals as essentially unreliable supporters of popular struggle, since they lack a mass base, and consequently depend on the regime for their subsistence.

From around 1986 onwards, radical groups began allying themselves with small NGOs in various mobilizations critical of big NGOs, setting up a series of workshops for small LSMs.[14] These culminated in a meeting at Baturaden on 19 December 1990 at which a scathing motion of no confidence in LPSMs and the NGO community generally was drafted (Baturaden Statement, 1990). The gist of this statement was that NGOs, which had been highly critical of orthodox development models in the early 1970s, appeared to have lost their vision and sense of mission to pioneer alternative models of development and to build an opposing movement to represent the poor. Since their own programmes now differed little from the official programmes they once criticized, they now found themselves, in effect, implementing agencies for government programmes. This had, in turn, led to hierarchy, bureaucracy, centralization, and élitism in their own organizations, together with the greedy adoption of all the professional management norms from the world of industry. It was felt that unless this situation was reversed, LSM/LPSMs would end up as hostile to the people. Six corrective steps were proposed so that they could again become instruments of struggle on the people's behalf, namely:

(i) Being bold and open in self-analysis and correction. Re-assessing their role in the overall present and future social context.

(ii) Taking account of the hegemonic structure of international capitalism in relation to the Third World.

(iii) Establishing democratic and just internal structures in order not to become agents of such hegemony.

(iv) Making people the dominant actors. Taking decisions on a collective basis, with a clear system of public accountability.

(v) Pursuing their functions transparently as an instrument of a people's movement. Disseminating information and political education based on principles of non-violence and solidarity both among themselves and in their relations with the people. Concentrating on activities which emphasized advocacy and people's organization rather than on short-term projects which stifled popular struggle.

(vi) Reassessing relations with funding agencies, which were found to be a major factor in distorting their vision and mission. Relying more on their own resources. Being more critical in choosing partners from among foreign funding agencies, and in checking out their background and political orientation.

Many NGOs naturally reacted with some impatience to such broad-brush criticisms, couched in sweeping, quasi-Marxist language, and seemingly well calculated to paralyse most of their day-to-day programmes pending some definitive global analysis of Indonesia's problems. Despite its call for a change of heart, the Baturaden Statement and similar commentary conveyed an attitude of indiscriminate disdain towards all LSM/LPSMs, and so served to alienate the radical movement from the mainstream of the NGO community.

In terms of practical achievement, the new radicals have demonstrated that it is possible to publicly protest against the Indonesian state, certainly not without a measure of violence by way of response, but as yet without any totally crushing repression by the authorities. In the context of this discussion, however, the new pattern of activism appears to represent more a resurgence of mass-based political action than a new stream of LSM/LPSMs. Certainly, that seems to be the radicals' intention, although they have adopted some strategies and organizational forms of the NGO movement in emphasizing face-to-face decision-making and minimizing formal structures.

The fact that LSM/LPSMs represent such a prime target of criticism suggests that the new radicals may see at least some elements from various NGO paradigms as having potential to achieve change. The accusation of 'lost vision' in the Baturaden Statement is probably directed particularly at the previous generation of students responsible for initiating key LPSMs in the second stream (discussed in Chapter 5), who have also showed interest in neo-Marxist (dependency) analyses of Indonesian political economy in the context of global imperialism. While most radicals are drawn from the younger student study groups and networks, a key figure in their formation has been Indro Tjahjono, a former student activist from the Bandung Institute of Technology in the mid-1970s. Tjahjono was gaoled along with other activists at that time, but became increasingly alienated from them in terms of both political direction and strategy.

Accusations that most NGOs have lost their vision seem to be based on an incorrect premise that this vision was originally one of mass action to achieve political change. It also perhaps reflects a hope that they will fill the vacuum left by the emasculation of popularly based political parties by the New Order state. Tensions can also arise from efforts by radicals to politicize local land, environment, and labour campaigns as part of their wider agenda, to the extent that these are conducted in ways which come into conflict with the specifically local, survival-oriented focus of most peasant and worker struggles. Traditional NGO approaches may well prove more durable in that regard.

Issues underlying the conflict between NGOs and the radical student movement were illustrated in a sharp exchange between Aditjondro (1990) and Budiman (1990a) arising from the Kedung Ombo struggle. This centred on a dam project near Solo in Central Java, which would cause the displacement of several thousand villagers.[15] Aditjondro has a substantial background in NGO work in Irian Jaya, but has also been a sharp critic of NGOs. He charged that the student movement had claimed victory prematurely in relation to Kedung Ombo and was more concerned with dramatizing political struggle than resolving, in any systematic way, the problems of people displaced by the dam project and numerous other less publicized cases resulting from dominant paradigms of development pursued in Indonesia. He saw a wide chasm between student activists and a few legal-minded NGOs, on the one hand, who took up the cause of victims without questioning the policies which made them victims, and, on the other, NGOs which do have an alternative concept of development but lack the aggression to publicly articulate it. Aditjondro asked how this chasm could be bridged in order to produce an effective and broad-based 'counter-hegemonic' movement in Indonesia.

Budiman saw Aditjondro's attitude towards students as being too cynical. He argued that they had been motivated by concern for the fate of the local people, mixed with admiration for their perseverance. Although the Kedung Ombo people's problems remained unsolved, radical activists had played a crucial role in bringing them to public attention. Conflict had arisen from differences in perspective. According to Budiman, NGOs mostly saw students as stirring up issues, before moving on to fan the flames of controversy elsewhere, leaving NGOs behind to defuse the situation and reconstruct. For their part, students perceived NGOs as timid, compromising, and concerned for their immediate comforts and long-term career prospects, while 'playing the game' according to rules laid down by the government.

Even so, Budiman saw the LSM and student movements as complementary. While the latter were primarily political mass movements, they differed from formally structured mass movements in being more spontaneous and temporary in nature. By contrast, NGOs had regular staff, extensive resources, and links. Obviously, they were in a better position to take a long-term view. In the case of Kedung Ombo, legal strategies had been exhausted in efforts to gain just compensation for the people. Progressive escalation of demonstrations, initially blocked by the military, persuaded Home Minister Rudini to look into the Kedung Ombo people's problems. The attitude of the press changed, and eventually some concessions were forthcoming from the government, though not before President Suharto had labelled the Kedung Ombo people as ex-communists. With the situation stabilized, the students returned to their studies, leaving the way clear for NGOs to undertake numerous tasks of reconstruction and consolidation, such as helping the people to obtain certificates of landownership. In a word, Budiman considered that both 'explosives experts', capable of removing obstacles, as well as groups or institutions, which could undertake reconstruction over the long term, were needed. Unfortunately, the distinct nature of these tasks and the relative capacity of different groups to perform them have been little understood, aggravated by a continuing 'cold war' between NGOs and student activists.[16]

In a further reply, Aditjondro (1991) offered to produce documentary evidence to support his claim that student activists had essentially become involved in grass-roots action as a form of experiment to concretize ideas arising from their political discussion groups. Despite their move into local struggles, their outlook remained élitist in that they saw themselves at the vanguard of forming public opinion and political bargaining, rather than supporting organizations formed by workers and farmers. In reality, Aditjondro insisted, a wide variety of groups working with people in articulating their rights have been effectively performing political education tasks. He equally rejected any too sharp distinction between NGOs and student groups, while many opportunities existed for co-operation and mutual learning. In practice, many student groups have set up structures not unlike those of NGOs for their practical community work.

Competition to claim credit for actions such as Kedung Ombo has also hindered co-operation. One observer has questioned the realism of expecting relatively marginalized, small, and locally oriented LSMs to spearhead a counter-hegemonic movement for alternative development against the government (Riwanto, c.1991). Clearly, 'difference in outlook and approach caused by ... differences in generation between activists, primordial networks, orientations, approach and strategy, intensity of links with donor institutions or personal aspects', illustrated in the foregoing exchange, are too deeply rooted to be quickly overcome (Thamrin, 1989: 27).

More recently, Aditjondro and Budiman appear to have found a significant measure of convergence in efforts to forge a counter-hegemonic movement. To that end, some 30–40 NGO representatives engaged in dialogue with intellectuals at a series of workshops in 1993 to discuss a study of their general outlook and values (Billah, Busyari, and Ali, 1993). This study had concluded that NGOs lacked vision, tended to be project-oriented, and were little concerned with ideals of democratization. Even more seriously, no paradigmatic differences were observed between NGOs and government, and no proof was given that NGOs were more participatory in their styles of operation. Some participants objected to the study, saying that it was biased towards NGOs' vision and ignored their achievements. They also warned against the futile adoption of radical and childish postures which had little relevance to Indonesian realities.

Of greater theoretical interest, for the purposes of this study, was the Gramscian framework in which the study and discussion were couched (Bobbio, 1979). Thus, Aditjondro saw LSMs as part of the state's effort to hegemonize civil society, citing as evidence their focus on development and lack of concern for the transformation of state and society. He further cited the replacement of the term 'non-government organizations' (NGO) with 'lembaga swadaya masyarakat' (LSM) in 1983 as a form of linguistic colonization, and as evidence that NGO/LSMs had internalized both the values and language of the state (INDECO DE UNIE, 1993; Laporan, 1993: 1–6).

While there is an obvious inter-penetration between institutions of state and civil society, this kind of interpretation appears to stretch the meaning of 'state' to include any kind of formal organization which might co-operate with government agencies for any purpose. Aditjondro's use of Gramsci appears to place him as equally in danger of internalizing official ideology as the NGOs whom he accuses. His explanation of changes in terminology among NGO/LSMs is also too mono-causal, as it ignores questions of historical and cultural legitimacy which influenced their thinking, alongside more pragmatic, political considerations. However, as Gramsci saw dominant groups exercising cultural and ideological hegemony over both state and civil society (Budiman, 1990b: 4–5), NGO/LSMs could hardly hope to escape this theoretical onslaught. One is led to wonder, if this formulation is accepted, whether incorporation into the state will render them weaker or stronger. Moreover, undifferentiated rejection of developmentalism, implied in such use of Gramsci, gives local groups little guidance in selecting programmes, while imposing unreasonably stark choices between developmental and political activity.

The three patterns of NGO interaction with the government and political process in Indonesia outlined in this chapter, and criticisms of them by radical groups, will be illustrated in later chapters by case-studies of organizations in several fields. These studies will also seek to draw out broader issues relating to democratic participation arising from the aims, organization, and practice of these groups. It should be noted, however, that although dominant characteristics of most organizations tend to identify them with one of these four paradigms, groups commonly combine elements to produce their own syntheses. Models should therefore be seen more as ideal-types rather than rigid categories. In another sense, they represent a dialogue between alternatives that takes place in one form or another within, as well as between, organizations.

Before moving on to case-studies, however, it is necessary to look in more detail at the overall context within which LSM/LPSMs operate in Indonesia, particularly in relation to legal and funding aspects.

1. See Crick (1992), who defines politics in terms of the pursuit of realizable and nego-tiable objectives, as distinct from totalistic visions for the transformation of society.

2. *Arisan* are traditional social-cum-lottery clubs in Java. NGOs have found they can be adapted to numerous social and developmental purposes, such as co-operative small enter-prises, house-building and repairs, infant nutrition supplement, the purchase of buffaloes or the hire of otherwise expensive household equipment (e.g. dinner services) for special occasions.

3. See pp. 145–6, 202–6 for a discussion of LSM/LPSM networking in Central Java and the Yogyakarta Special Region (Daerah Istimewa Yogyakarta—DIY).

4. See Eldridge (1990b: 20–4) for a more detailed account of YPPSE's evolution.

5. In 1974, YIS split from the Solo-based Christian Foundation for Public Health (Yayasan Keristen untuk Kesehatan Umum—YAKKUM) which had been founded by Dr Gunawan in the 1950s.

6. The *Kring* (consultative group or circle) system was initiated in Banjarnegara in 1979, when a serious outbreak of malaria brought village and neighbourhood leaders and health cadres from some fifteen villages together with relevant district and sub-district officials to plan necessary control programmes (OXFAM, 1987).

7. YIS sources, February 1991.

8. The government aims to establish an Integrated Health Service Post (Pos Pelayanan Terpadu—POSYANDU) in several villages. See also pp. 59–60 for more detailed discus-sion of POSYANDU.

9. Dr Haliman claimed a reduction in infant mortality rates from 179 to 60 per thou-sand between 1971 and 1974 (YPPSE, 1986: 41). National rates were 138 and 97 re-spectively (World Bank, 1986: 232, Table 27). Indonesia's infant mortality rate subsequently fell to 61 per thousand in 1990 (World Bank, 1992: 272, Table 28), indicat-ing that Banjarnegara had reached the Indonesian 1990 average sixteen years earlier.

10. Based on comparative observations from two visits in 1979 and 1983.

11. OXFAM sources.

12. See Eldridge (1990a) for an earlier formulation of these models, which did not take account of the emergence of more radical movements.

13. For classic statements of these opposed positions, see Frank (1971), W. Warren (1980), and Robison (1986) for an account (nearer to Warren than to Frank in outlook) of capitalist development under the New Order. For an overview of relevant theory, see Higgott (1983: 45–73).

14. See, for example, Kelompok Pinggiran (1988).

15. See pp. 122–4 for a detailed discussion of Kedung Ombo.

16. See Akhmad (1989) for further discussion of differences between NGOs and rad-icals.

3
Legal and Funding Contexts

THIS chapter looks at the broad regulatory context within which non-government organizations (NGOs) operate. Fundamental interest here centres on the institutional and social space which self-reliant community institutions (Lembaga Swadaya Masyarakat—LSM) and institutions for developing community self-reliance (Lembaga Pengembangan Swadaya Masyarakat—LPSM) can open up in pursuing their basic objectives. This is defined both by the law itself and by the emphasis placed by government agencies in interpreting and implementing it. Strategies adopted by non-government groups can influence both aspects. Legal and funding contexts are linked in that financial transfers, particularly from overseas, are subject to regulation. Broader political and international contexts of overseas funding are explored in later chapters, particularly Chapters 6 and 10. This chapter is more concerned with drawing out operational issues in the domestic context.

In a dynamic sense, financial resources strengthen both the overall capabilities of LSM/LPSMs and the leverage which they can exert. Such leverage has been used to minimize the impact of relatively harsh regulatory structures. However, overdependence on foreign funds can weaken the legitimacy of NGOs and render them vulnerable to counter-attack by the government. It can also have negative consequences for their internal organization and operating style. Alternative funding strategies are explored in the later part of the chapter, together with approaches designed to overcome specific problems caused by foreign aid. Indonesian NGOs, nevertheless, seem likely to depend on overseas funds for some considerable time.

Legal Space for Non-Government Organizations

Riker (1990: 17) argues that 'unless central governments are particularly weak, they generally possess the capacity to define and condition the dynamics of NGO initiatives for development'. Governments can resist, co-opt, or undercut NGO initiatives by means of policies and legislation, the content of official development programmes, and the institutional channels through which they are pursued. Their outlook towards NGOs is influenced by the latter's resources and administrative capacity to undertake complementary roles. However, Korten (1987) sees the organizational survival of NGOs as ultimately dependent on their capacity to deliver services to the community and only in a secondary sense to the government. While both Riker and Korten acknowledge the importance of foreign donors in this overall equation, for Korten, the development of distinct local organizational skills and identity represents the bottom line. Both analyses suggest that legal-cum-regulatory aspects should be seen as part of a more complex balance of forces between NGOs and the state, in which attempts at regulation commonly signal battles over ideology and legitimation, as well as control over social organization and resources. Certainly, such conclusions are reflected in the Indonesian experience.

Under Sukarno, a fairly relaxed working relationship existed between the government and voluntary organizations within the framework of Village Community Institutions (Lembaga Sosial Desa—LSD). This programme operated under the aegis of the Department of Social Affairs (Departemen Sosial—DEPSOS), with an operational philosophy broadly in line with standard international social work principles and practice, whereby activities and group formation emerge from felt needs and voluntary participation at the grass-roots (Schulte-Nordholt, 1985). DEPSOS gave general moral and institutional support, but for the most part did not intervene at an operational level. While rhetoric commonly outstripped performance and coverage was uneven, some useful results were reported, considering the general instability of the times.

This *laissez-faire* climate came to an end in 1971 when the Department of Home Affairs (Departemen Dalam Negeri) took over community development programmes (Schulte-Nordholt, 1985). The role of DEPSOS was reduced to overseeing welfare programmes, effectively negating earlier bottom–up approaches. Numerous conflicts were reported between LSMs and the new community development arm of the Department of Home Affairs, Pembangunan Desa (BANGDES), during the 1970s. The NGO community has generally taken the view that, with some individual exceptions, BANGDES has limited experience or understanding of community development. This is illustrated by its formulation of self-reliance (*swadaya*) as the highest of three stages of village development, the others being self-sufficiency (*swasembada*) and self-development (*swakarya*). As defined by BANGDES, self-reliance seems to consist of having a long list of facilities in place, with little obvious regard to quality.

The original security motivation for transferring responsibility still dominates, ensuring that NGOs cannot function without at least the tacit approval of provincial and district authorities. They are thus obliged to spend much time in cultivating officials, yet without becoming so close that their operations come under the control of BANGDES. Necessary balance is achieved by selecting localities where the authorities are co-operative and, where they are not, using leverage at higher levels. Further, the more flexible outlook towards NGOs by former Home

Affairs Minister, Soepardjo Roestam, compared with that of his prede-
cessor, Amir Machmud, was largely continued by Soepardjo's successor,
Rudini. To some extent, fear of unfavourable comparison of their performance has acted as an incentive for regional and local authorities to
co-operate with NGOs.

The 1973 Regulations Governing Overseas Technical Co-operation
and Assistance require overseas NGOs to sign agreements covering general objectives and operating procedures with relevant government
departments. All projects must be reported and cleared by a special Co-
ordinating Committee within the Cabinet Secretariat, which in theory
plays a co-ordinating and liaison role in determining which department
will be responsible for various NGO programmes. Overseas NGOs are
also supposed to sign agreements with the Department of Foreign
Affairs prior to undertaking any negotiations within Indonesia.

These regulations, though never revoked, have been widely recognized as unworkable. Historically, they were in large measure a by-
product of conflict between intelligence agencies and between the
Departments of Home and Social Affairs. In practice, overseas NGOs
rely on their Indonesian counterparts at the local level to seek approval
from and report periodically in general terms to the district head, who
in turn gains clearance from and furnishes necessary reports to higher
authorities. As yet, no formal reporting procedures for local NGOs have
been put in place. Overseas NGOs with permanent offices in Indonesia,
such as OXFAM and the Ford Foundation, have found it both necessary and advantageous to sign basic agreements with relevant ministries
and agencies. However, this does not usually entail obtaining prior
approval for each programme, except where counterpart Indonesian
agencies are operating joint programmes with a government department.
Brief annual or six-monthly reports, together with basic financial statements to the Cabinet Secretariat, are usually deemed sufficient.[1]

Some commentators have assumed that the controversial 1985 Law
on Social Organizations (Undang Undang Organisasi Kemasyarakatan—
ORMAS) has seriously, if not fatally, undermined the autonomy of
LSM/LPSMs.[2] This view tends to ignore the prior existence of extensive regulations outlined above. While these related primarily to foreign
assistance, since the majority of LSM/LPSM funds derive from overseas, such regulations represent a potentially decisive measure of internal
control if fully applied. In practice, the situation for foreign funding
agencies does not seem to have changed in any significant way since the
passing of the ORMAS Law. However, Indonesian social organizations
have themselves become subject to significant regulation.

The 1985 Law has not changed the situation whereby registration
with a notary as a foundation (yayasan) is sufficient in order to become
a legal body. Registration as a foundation enables the board of management to define its own composition and set up executive arms (badan)
as convenient. However, it is now necessary for the five principles of
national ideology (Panca Sila) to be written into every organization's
statement of objectives as the sole foundation guiding all their activities.

While this has caused great heart-searching and controversy among mass organizations, particularly Muslim groups, most LSM/LPSMs have persuaded themselves that this requirement will not detract from their basic functions and character. Most appear to believe that Panca Sila is capable of democratic and pluralist interpretations. They are more concerned over clauses in the ORMAS Law and its subsequent elucidation which could lead to significant control, and guidance of their organization and activities.[3] So far, the impact of these clauses has been blunted a good deal by various informal strategies and by changes in Indonesia's economic and diplomatic situation which give LSM/LPSMs more leverage.

To date, LSM/LPSMs have successfully disputed the 1985 Law's application to them, claiming that the ORMAS acronym refers only to mass organizations (*organisasi massa*), such as political parties, student and youth organizations, trade unions, and so forth. In fact, the law uses the term 'social organizations' (*organisasi kemasyarakatan*), which covers a far broader community context. It also refers to 'similarity in activity, profession, function, religion and the belief in the One Almighty God',[4] suggesting a unified organization with branches or units. In practice, the whole NGO sector is extremely heterogeneous, while even the larger LPSMs have no formal membership base. In late 1987, Soepardjo Roestam supported their interpretation on these various points. Probably, the NGOs' relatively smooth acceptance of the Panca Sila as the sole foundation requirement has influenced the government not to press for detailed application of the ORMAS provisions to them.

While the bulk of the LSM/LPSM community has not been very active in this legal chess game, its response to the ORMAS legislation illustrates a tendency to assert interpretations of official ideology according to convenience, while ignoring less favourable interpretations by the authorities. This appears to be part of a more general strategy of conflict-avoidance. While this approach has enabled LSM/LPSMs to survive and even prosper in a generally restrictive political climate, it has also resulted in their accepting and even legitimizing the continuing lack of any firmly based legal guarantees for their own existence. It is not easy for outsiders to be sure how much such behaviour should be viewed in tactical terms and how much as socialized acceptance of official norms.

The ORMAS Law provides for technical guidance by the appropriate government department and for general guidance through the Department of Home Affairs structure. However, precise responsibility is left vague, leaving organizations with a good deal of discretion in selecting sympathizers and protectors from within the bureaucracy. The law further gives the government powers to disband organizations whose activities are considered detrimental to the values of social harmony and national unity enshrined in Panca Sila.[5] However, this only formalizes powers that have always been held at the discretion of the executive in relation to every kind of organization throughout the whole period of the New Order. To survive, LSM/LPSMs negotiate arrangements with particular authorities on an *ad hoc* basis with the minimum possible formality. Though not explicitly stated, it is feared that the government will seek to appoint its own nominees to executive boards under the extensive powers of guidance laid down in the ORMAS Law. In that context, while informality has no doubt helped maintain organizational autonomy, it has also discouraged the evolution of fully democratic and accountable structures, particularly among the larger LPSMs.

Concern that the government will seek to co-opt larger LPSMs under their own umbrella organizations, or amalgamate them in ways which render them more subject to control, reinforces this preference for informality, as later discussion of networking strategies will indicate. Indeed, in encouraging organizations to join together according to similarity of activity and function, the Elucidation of the ORMAS Law offers as examples the Indonesian National Youth Committee (Komite Nasional Pemuda Indonesia—KNPI) and the Indonesian Farmers' Association (Himpunan Kerukunan Tani Indonesia—HKTI), both of which are dominated by the government-sponsored network of Functional Groups (Golongan Karya—GOLKAR). Consequently, LSM/LPSMs have sought to establish their own alternative networks and forums.

In 1990, the government circulated new instructions to provincial and district authorities (MENDAGRI, 1990). These acknowledged the role of LSMs[6] in assisting people's participation and self-reliance, and their status as friends (*mitra*) of the government in achieving these goals. Regional authorities were instructed to make an inventory of all LSMs in their area, including details of their constitution, internal rules, management, membership, and activities. They were also asked to guide them in relation to the regulations in force and to ensure that their activities would be beneficial to the people and assist in the development of a Panca Sila community. The voluntary and non-profit nature of LSMs was stressed, and the authorities advised of the importance of ensuring an atmosphere conducive to enthusiasm and creativity by self-reliant community groups.

The rights of LSMs, according to the 1990 instructions, are (i) to implement programmes in the interest of the community, nation, and state; (ii) to run their affairs in accordance with their own rules and organization, and (iii) to co-operate with third parties both within and outside Indonesia relevant to their field of activities, avoiding connections which could weaken the interests of the state (MENDAGRI, 1990: 8—Lampiran, Section VII). The LSMs' right to receive outside funds, including those from overseas, was affirmed in similar terms (MENDAGRI, 1990: 8–9—Lampiran, Section VIII). Their obligations are (i) to practise and safeguard Panca Sila and the 1945 Constitution; (ii) to preserve national unity; (iii) to not undertake political activities or practices which would confuse their role with that of social-political organizations, and (iv) to report their presence to government authorities appropriate to their level of operation (MENDAGRI, 1990: 8—Lampiran, Section VII). LSMs receiving foreign assistance in any form are to use such assistance to the best of their ability for community and national development, while observing the various regulations in force. These impose only very general reporting requirements on LSMs, except in the case of overseas agencies registered in Indonesia.

The impact of these instructions is hard to gauge. LSM/LPSMs stress that the internal flow of documents within the government should not be seen as regulations with the force of law, and therefore do not see themselves as placed under any obligations by them. It appears that the government consulted with some larger Jakarta-based organizations prior to their being issued, which may have had some influence in softening the harsher ORMAS-type character of the initial draft. Concern remains that frequent reference to guidance (*pembinaan*) will, in practice, be interpreted at lower levels as giving orders and may also lead to greater monitoring and surveillance. More positively, the instructions provide NGOs with a legal umbrella and recognize their legitimate role in development. However, reference to consultation does not amount to specific acknowledgement of the NGOs' potential to provide input into official programmes and overall policy-making (MENDAGRI, 1990: 10—Lampiran, Section XI, sub-section 3).

In practice, the government already has all the necessary powers to obtain full information from NGOs, but its motivation to do so may be stimulated by the requirement contained in these instructions to collect inventories of their capabilities. There is clearly a potential for co-option, if not direct control, in the various forms of consultation and guidance proposed, though this has yet to emerge in any specific form. In that context, LSM programmes are defined as complementary to those of the Village Community Resilience Institution (Lembaga Ketahanan Masyarakat Desa—LKMD), the official umbrella organization for rural development programmes for which village authorities are formally responsible. These institutions are mostly inactive (MENDAGRI, 1990: 11—Lampiran, Section XIII). LSMs have, at times, found it expedient to operate within the LKMD structure, though mostly they remain aloof.

There was some talk during the mid-1992 election campaign of new controls in the form of a Code of Ethics for LSM/LPSMs (YLBHI, 1992: 20–2). This would be similar in some ways to the code of self-censorship applied to journalists in the name of maintaining national stability. In January 1992, Co-ordinating Minister for Political Affairs and Security, Sudomo, considered by many as a strong opponent of NGOs, stated that they must be channelled into a single organization through the ORMAS Law (YLBHI, 1992: 20–2). Interestingly, this proposal implicitly concedes NGO claims that they are currently outside the scope of the ORMAS legislation because they have no membership base.

In this general context, it is important to appreciate that proposals to tighten legal controls canvassed periodically will encounter the difficulty that both NGO and LSM/LPSM terminology is cultural and ideological in nature and lacks any legal identity (FEER, 1994). Most groups either function informally or derive their legal existence from registered *yayasan*. While laws could certainly be introduced to regulate these more tightly, other problems could then arise for the government from the extremely heterogeneous nature of *yayasan*. These provide a loose framework for many kinds of business, military, welfare, and socio-cultural formations, often with significant involvement from members of the political élite. While differential treatment would no doubt be effected through the executive arms of government, this would not represent any essential change from the current situation for LSM/LPSMs, except that changes in the law would also, in theory at least, place them in a position to demand its equal application to foundations of all kinds.

Issues and Alternatives in Funding Non-Government Organizations

As elsewhere in the Third World, the issue of foreign funding has represented a significant source of tension, both within the NGO community and more widely in Indonesia. This was illustrated in May 1992, when the government aimed a potentially very damaging blow at the NGOs collectively by banning all aid from the Dutch government. This was interpreted to include aid from Dutch NGOs, most of whom receive part of their funds from their government. Church-based groups were particularly concerned, while some key human rights groups and the International NGO Forum on Indonesia (INGI) network, which receive substantial funds from Dutch sources, were forced to rethink their approach. Though various ways around this ban have been found,[7] the Indonesian government was signalling its willingness to counter-attack any coalition of foreign donors and Indonesian NGOs seeking to exert leverage against it by means of aid.

In ideological terms, the receipt of overseas assistance represents a prima-facie diminution of self-reliance, whether at national or community levels. However, it carries certain strategic and structural advantages over other forms of funding. For example, the key element in non-government programmes is human resources. While LSM/LPSMs rely mainly on voluntary labour at the village level, initiating and sustaining popular mobilization commonly depends on a combination of outside animators, or agents of change, and locally recruited cadres. Cadres generally come together from several villages at regular intervals to receive training and share experience. Work in this field is extremely time-consuming. While the traditional expectation has been that such services will be offered on a voluntary basis, experience across rural Asia suggests strongly that unpaid labour cannot be sustained for any length of time, particularly by poor people on the margin of subsistence. It has therefore been found necessary to pay at least a basic wage, though many other kinds of community support and recognition are also important.[8] While local contributions should be encouraged to the greatest possible extent, foreign funding agencies have been found to be the most reliable vehicles for guaranteeing basic payment for field workers and cadres.

Alternative sources to foreign funding include government funding, private local benefactors, local income-generating programmes, consultancies by larger LPSMs, and support from beneficiary communities. The latter usually takes the form of free physical labour and participation in group decision-making, though it may also include some contribution in kind, if not cash, to the upkeep of local cadres. However, meeting the full cost of such support is usually beyond the capacity of poor communities for whose benefit LSM/LPSM activity is intended. Radical groups, which are hypercritical of dependence on foreign funding, tend not to appreciate this point. Student groups, particularly, are able to support their own organizers, many of whom contribute their labour voluntarily. Similarly, peasant and worker demonstrations do not cost much more than transport to the provincial or capital city, with food and accommodation often supplied by supporters. However, such activity is not equivalent to sustained work in socio-economic development and group formation.

Government funding is available where LSM/LPSMs participate in official programmes, but usually not as a subsidy for their own activities. While a variety of exceptions can be identified in the welfare and health fields, the Indonesian government does not normally finance activities relating to popular mobilization and awareness-building. However, an indirect subsidy may be entailed to the extent that the government provides support for physical and organizational infrastructure of religious institutions. Funding and other support may be available on an *ad hoc* basis from local authorities for training and related purposes. Generally, however, LSM/LPSMs fear that the Indonesian government is more likely to exercise leverage over them through funding support than are foreign funding agencies which, by comparison, operate more at arm's length. Here, however, the government can accuse NGOs of undermining national unity, in so far as they become too critical of its policies on the international stage.

Traditions of private giving of donations in Indonesia are reported by LSM/LPSMs as slow to move beyond the established spheres of religion, charity, and education. Non-government overseas development agencies in Western countries have engaged in programmes of development education over the past one or two decades in order to focus the minds of their citizens on the structural and other causes of poverty, as well as programmes offering immediate relief. While Indonesian LSM/LPSMs engage in many kinds of advocacy and public education, most have not yet linked these activities to local fund-raising.

One exception has been the Indonesian Environment Network (Wahana Lingkungan Hidup Indonesia—WALHI), which established a Friends of the Environment Fund (Dana Mitra Lingkungan—DML) as an independent but closely associated body. DML's board of trustees has included Emil Salim, Minister for Population and Environment from 1978 to 1993. The director of WALHI sits on DML's board of directors *ex officio*. By early 1991, DML was raising approximately Rp110 million annually, representing around 25 per cent of WALHI funds. These were distributed in 1990 to cover selected small-scale projects among NGOs (Rp40 million), the Nature Lovers' Club (Rp40 million), and WALHI overheads (Rp30 million).[9] More ambitious plans to use DML as a vehicle for community education were in train. However, there is an ongoing debate as to how far the acceptance of funds from industry compromises WALHI's capacity to confront vested interests, despite insistence that donations are only to be accepted on a no strings attached basis.

Local income-generation programmes operated by small local groups, either independently or in association with some larger LPSMs, are fairly pervasive in Indonesia, most commonly in the form of informal (*usaha bersama*—UB) or formal co-operative enterprises (*koperasi*), *arisan*, savings and loan groups, and credit unions. Such endeavours are not without problems due to market overcrowding, uncertain demand, and the growing complexity of distribution channels. In the increasingly popular field of handicrafts, for example, Western NGOs are flooding the market with the products of their counterparts in Asia, Africa, and Latin America. In theory, some form of clearing house arrangements could provide a solution, at least within individual producing countries, which are now themselves providing significant markets. Unless local producers are significantly involved in seeking markets, as distinct from assuming this is the task of sponsoring LPSMs, the development of their business skills and ensuing capacity for self-reliance will be impaired. This, in turn, points to the need to develop products for local markets to the greatest extent possible, which local people are more likely to understand, and where they are more likely to perceive new opportunities.

Perhaps the most creative mode of income generation, with the potential to substantially reduce, if not eliminate, the need for outside finance, is the revolving fund. This practice is commonly associated with small, informal co-operatives, which are often built on traditional-style associations such as *arisan*. For example, an NGO provides working capital for one family to purchase a buffalo, which calves and produces milk sufficient to repay the loan and generate income. Funds are then available to purchase a further buffalo or, at some stage, pass on some of the offspring to other families. The cycle is completed in a sequence determined by lottery until all the families in the group have buffaloes to sustain future production as a source of livelihood. This process obviously depends on efficient organization and high levels of mutual support and reciprocity.

Consultancies and training programmes provide a growing source of income, particularly for larger LPSMs, although opportunities are also available for medium-sized groups at regional and sub-regional levels. Usually, however, the ultimate source for such finance is a foreign funding agency in the form of an overseas NGO, the government, or an international or regional agency with the United Nations or World Bank. The Indonesian government also increasingly employs Indonesian NGOs in advisory, training, monitoring, and evaluation roles. However, the government itself commonly draws on foreign aid to finance such activities. Since foreign funding agencies look to them to play similar roles and frequently to administer and advise on the distribution of funds to smaller local groups, LPSMs have found themselves, whether by accident or design, in a highly strategic position in relation to both overseas agencies and the government.

Perceptions of the growing power and influence of the larger, more articulate, and well-connected Jakarta-based LPSMs have also caused strains in their relations with many LSMs at village level, while the issue of channelling foreign aid is part of a far larger problem of relations between big and little NGOs. Pressure on larger NGOs from foreign funding agencies derives from the sudden explosion in the number of LSMs and other small groups requesting assistance. Foreign funding agencies feel unable to administer such requests directly themselves due to many kinds of logistical, cultural, language, and other reasons. They naturally turn to established Indonesian LPSMs which they have known and supported over many years, often from very small beginnings, and in whom they feel confidence.

For their part, Indonesian LPSMs are becoming increasingly unwilling to channel requests from LSMs or to evaluate LSM programmes on behalf of overseas agencies. As a compromise, several LPSMs have organized group-training sessions for LSMs, assisting them to clarify their goals and strategies and to develop skills in putting up project proposals. Even so, the problem remains unresolved in many cases, as overseas NGOs generally refuse to handle requests without some intermediary evaluation and recommendation. In one instance, a successful outcome was achieved by the Klaten affiliate of the Social and Economic Research, Education, and Information Institute (Lembaga Penelitian, Pendidikan, dan Penerangan Ekonomi dan Sosial—LP3ES). LP3ES Klaten submitted a common proposal on behalf of fourteen local LSMs for management training, agreed after joint meetings, to the Swiss Development Corporation, which then sent funds individually to each LSM.

The large versus small NGO issue has been aggravated by radical activists, opposed to foreign assistance on ideological grounds, who often give the appearance of having appointed themselves to speak on behalf of smaller LSMs. A common accusation levelled against older NGOs is that their alleged lack of militancy and capacity for popular mobilization has resulted from dependence on foreign funds. Such critics are, nevertheless, more than willing themselves to accept funds from overseas NGOs whom they consider 'progressive'. In practice, these turn out to include agencies which also support many mainstream Indonesian LSM/LPSMs.

Increasingly, LSM/LPSMs are demanding—and obtaining—a more equal relationship with foreign counterparts. The International NGO Forum on Indonesia (INGI), a forum linking major Indonesian and overseas NGOs,[10] claims that it insists on a relationship based on dialogue and a spirit of mutual solidarity as a precondition for receiving funds. A Commission for Dialogue has been set up for this purpose with the Netherlands Organization for International Development Co-operation (Nederlandse Organisatie voor Internationale Bijstand— NOVIB). However, INGI's central focus on monitoring official aid disbursed through the Inter-Governmental Group for Indonesia (IGGI) consortium[11] has served to highlight the issue of foreign aid. Those opposed to all forms of foreign aid, on principle, see INGI's efforts at reform as helping to legitimize aid.

Some of the larger LPSMs have their own, rather different, concerns towards foreign funding agencies. Yayasan Dian Desa (YDD), a large organization based in Yogyakarta, which specializes in appropriate technology, claims that many overseas agencies interpret self-reliance too narrowly by excluding large programmes which might bring mass benefits. For example, YDD claims that OXFAM will only fund income-generating projects, non-formal education, handicrafts, training, and agriculture, all of which YDD sees as quite secondary to water supply in many areas. That problem can only be solved by substantial investment, even if appropriate technology is applied. OXFAM, together with most other overseas NGOs, responds along the lines that 'large schemes don't reach the people'. YDD sees this as too general an alibi, obviating any serious effort to link large-scale infrastructure projects, whether in improvement, health clinics, or water supply programmes with *kampung* community and participatory structures.[12] To achieve these goals requires a systematic assessment of the respective capabilities, attitudes, and skills of the relevant NGO and government personnel.

The reporting and accounting requirements of donor agencies place an increasingly heavy administrative burden on LPSMs, the majority of which are supported by multiple donors. This burden could be reduced if donors were willing to accept consortium arrangements, contribute an agreed proportion to the recipient NGO's overall budget, receive the same reports, undertake joint evaluations, and so forth. Similar arrangements have been successfully put in place by some NGOs in other countries, but foreign donors appear very reluctant to enter into such arrangements in relation to Indonesia (B. White, 1989: 4). There is a related fear in NGO circles as to whether they will be able to retain their identity and control over their own priorities and agenda in the face of the increasing flow of external funds, or whether, in the words of Adi Sasono, they will become 'public-service contractors'.[13]

Significant barriers remain, both within NGO organizations and in their relations with local groups, which hold back development of any real capacity for grass-roots participation. This situation is aggravated by a sense of insecurity among NGO staff as they perceive their future employment prospects as dependent on the vagaries of foreign funding (Strintzos, 1991: 52, 56). In that context, the often unrealistic demands of foreign funding agencies, driven by pressures from their financial supporters for precise statements of goals, achievements, measures, and time-frames, serve to divert organizational energy and motivation away from spending time with the people. The transfer of decision-making power to poor people in Indonesian slums and villages would seem difficult, if not impossible, to reconcile with such requirements (B. White, 1989: 10–11).

Overall, foreign aid is likely to remain a source of tension among Indonesian NGOs, though debate is a good deal less ferocious on this score than in the Philippines or India. Despite the emergence of alternative sources of finance, it was rare for LPSMs interviewed in this survey to report less than two-thirds of their finance as deriving from foreign funding agencies. LSMs, in turn, depend on support from LPSMs. Thus, while it is important to both its legitimacy and ultimate viability for the NGO community to maximize alternative sources of finance from within Indonesia, foreign assistance is likely to provide the most reliable financial base for LSM/LPSMs for some years to come.

1. See Eldridge (1979: 141–5) for an account of the original context.

2. See, for example, Witjes (1986).

3. Peraturan Pemerintah [Government Regulation] No. 18, April 1986, Republic of Indonesia, cited in Witjes (1986: Appendix II).

4. Ibid., Article 2 (1).

5. Ibid., Article 18–21.

6. The regulations refer to LSMs without mention of LPSMs.

7. These have included the swapping of funding commitments by European NGOs, the redirection of Dutch government funds, and the redesignation of funds to Indonesia as private.

8. See Esman et al. (1980) for a detailed discussion of themes and issues in this context.

9. WALHI sources.

10. See pp. 195–201.

11. See pp. 195–200 for a discussion of IGGI's role. IGGI was replaced in 1992 by the Consortium of Groups for Indonesia (CGI).

12. *Kampung* is a general term for a simply constructed human settlement in either urban or rural neighbourhoods.

13. Cited in B. White (1989: 5). Adi Sasono, founder and chairman of Lembaga Studi Pembangunan, nevertheless expressed optimism, in an interview with the author in January 1991, that there was scope for persuading the Indonesian government to serve NGO purposes, given the former's lack of community skills and contacts in many fields.

4

'High-level Co-operation–Grass-roots Development': Three Case-studies

THIS chapter will look at three large, well-known non-government organizations (NGOs): Yayasan Indonesia Sejahtera (YIS), Yayasan Dian Desa (YDD), and Bina Swadaya (BS). It will be argued that each organization fits broadly within the first paradigm presented in Chapter 2 in terms of patterns of accommodation with the Indonesian government and approaches to mobilizing popular self-management. The main feature of this approach is selective co-operation with relevant authorities, both to gain space for NGO programmes and to bring insights gained from field experience to bear in shaping and implementing public policy. Work among the people is directed towards self-reliant group formation. Local people are encouraged to identify and solve problems themselves, rather than make demands on the government.

All three NGOs have been active in offering policy advice based on their field experience. They have also co-operated with the Indonesian government in designing and implementing official programmes, despite their scepticism about the government's capability and approach. Nevertheless, all three organizations are selective in their co-operation with government agencies, according to how they judge the costs and benefits to the people. Where they are unable to negotiate satisfactory arrangements which offer a reasonable degree of independence, these NGOs would prefer to withdraw and move elsewhere than be drawn into relationships entailing conflict. Critical comment and language are avoided, though constructive suggestions are offered as the opportunity arises. The NGOs concerned insist that this approach is as much in the people's interest as in their own.

In terms of generational and sociological identity, both YIS and BS have their origins in the 1950s, whereas YDD emerged in the late 1960s. They are consequently perceived as established within the overall spectrum of the NGO community. All three have evolved from small beginnings. While they are firmly secular in outlook and practice, each has enjoyed informal links with and support from churches. YDD has had close links with a major state university.

Each of the three organizations has retained its ultimate focus on small groups. This is most pronounced in the case of YIS, which has found the necessity to scale up its work, and the consequent increase in organizational size, more painful than the other two. YDD appears more concerned with material outcomes for the people than with group formation for its own sake. BS is the most positive of the three in its willingness to work with the government. This may well be due to the more political nature of its origins and its closer association with farmers' organizations linked to the government-sponsored network of Functional Groups (Golongan Karya—GOLKAR). However, none has ventured far beyond the arena of bureaucratic politics into more public forms of advocacy or awareness-building.

Yayasan Indonesia Sejahtera

Yayasan Indonesia Sejahtera (YIS)[1] was founded in 1974. Its origins can be traced back to the early 1950s when the (Protestant-linked) Christian Foundation for Public Health (Yayasan Keristen untuk Kesehatan Umum—YAKKUM) was initiated by Dr Nugroho Gunawan, a medical practitioner who developed a strong conviction that conventional medicine treats effects rather than causes. He therefore shifted YAKKUM's efforts increasingly towards agriculture, animal husbandry, improved cultivation of house-gardens, nutrition, village house design, irrigation, drinking water, public health, and education, pioneering participatory approaches in community development in each new context. Several key workers left YAKKUM to found YIS in 1974, partly because they wished to make community participation philosophy more central to their practice, and partly because they wished to stress the secular identity of their work.[2]

YIS has continued to diversify since that time, notably into income-generation programmes, small co-operative enterprises, and savings and loans groups, also joining with other NGOs to play an intermediary role in facilitating bank loans to reach the rural poor. YIS has undertaken a wide range of advisory and consultancy services to the Indonesian government, as well as local and overseas NGOs. Its training services are in constant demand all over Indonesia, from both government agencies and community groups anxious to draw on its experience in many fields. Training is carried out either at YIS's centre in Solo or on site, as appropriate.

YIS builds up local groups based on whatever formal or informal structures are available. It is mobile between locations, depending on the attitudes of local authorities. It has built close working relations with the Departments of Health (Departemen Kesehatan—DEPKES) and Social Affairs (Departemen Sosial—DEPSOS) and with the National Family Planning Co-ordinating Board (Badan Koordinasi Keluarga Berencana Nasional—BKKBN). The intervention, in the early 1970s, of the Department of Home Affairs (Departemen Dalam Negeri) in village-level community development[3] caused problems for YIS, as for many other self-reliant community institutions (Lembaga Swadaya Masyarakat—LSM) and institutions for developing community self-reliance (Lembaga Pengembangan Swadaya Masyarakat—LPSM). However, by cultivating relations with individual district heads and concentrating its efforts in areas where the official environment was sympathetic, YIS steadily overcame bureaucratic obstacles. At one stage during the 1970s, it felt obliged to withdraw from Sragen district near Solo but was made welcome elsewhere, notably in Banjarnegara. While keeping its distance from the Rural Development Arm of the Department of Home Affairs (Pembangunan Desa—BANGDES), it also ran training programmes for administrative staff at district and sub-district level.[4]

Soepardjo Roestam, the Provincial Governor of Central Java during this critical time, subsequently became Minister for Home Affairs and a strong advocate of an expanded developmental role for LSM/LPSMs. As one of a relatively small number of groups pioneering such participatory approaches in any kind of widespread and systematic way in Central Java at that time, YIS may well have had some impact on his thinking.

YIS is best known for its work in the community health field, where it has developed a national and international reputation, though it would acknowledge that some of its better known programmes were pioneered in the Solo area prior to 1974 as part of YAKKUM. These range from a community health insurance and referral programme, baby-weighing linked to supplementary feeding, and the adaptation of traditional social-cum-lottery clubs (*arisan*), to family planning, health, and welfare programmes. YIS has also co-operated with other NGOs in the primary health field in disseminating knowledge of oral rehydration, an internationally recognized means of controlling diarrhoea (Werner, 1980: 182–3).

These programmes were taken up and consolidated by the government into a system of Integrated Health Service Posts (Pos Pelayanan Terpadu—POSYANDU), established in 1984. POSYANDU combines family planning, child-weighing and monitoring, nutrition supplement, and immunization at posts being established in all villages. However, this programme depends heavily for its success on co-operation between DEPKES and BKKBN, which has not proved very strong. YIS has always recruited and developed its own cadres, whereas in POSYANDU they are recruited by the village head. Many fieldworkers complain that POSYANDU is implemented in a too uniform and top–down fashion, ignoring specific local characteristics and community wishes. Motivation is hard to maintain under such conditions.

YIS's original health insurance scheme (Dana Sehat) depended for its success on extensive discussion and agreement by all members of local wards (Rukun Tetangga—RT).[5] Each household agreed to pay a small fixed sum per month. More affluent members of the community often paid a higher amount on a voluntary basis. Contributions covered the costs of extension visits and a package of basic medicines and injections. More serious cases were referred to a hospital. During the 1980s, health services became more cheaply and readily available through Community Health Centres (Pusat Kesehatan Masyarakat—PUSKESMAS) which in Java, at least, are reasonably physically accessible in most areas, though often subject to overcrowding and staff shortages. As a consequence, YIS has largely abandoned Dana Sehat.

Other voluntary organizations, notably the Indonesian Association of Voluntary Health Groups (Persatuan Karya Dharma Kesehatan Indonesia—PERDAKHI), a Catholic network, claim that Dana Sehat, which they operate in the Bandung area, still provides valuable referral services while saving local people transport costs. PERDAKHI also considers that the programme retains significant educational potential. PERDAKHI sees regular follow-up and training as crucial, saying these were allowed to lapse in the Solo area. PERDAKHI health cadres meet regularly each Sunday under the leadership of volunteer doctors. YIS has since worked with the Foundation for Health Promotion (Yayasan Bina Sehat—YBS), Semarang, to develop a new, scaled-up approach, whereby health insurance is combined with a credit package. A proportion of loan repayments is set aside to enlarge health insurance revenue, with cover including hospitalization and related expenses. The programme was given a trial in 1991 in six areas in Java, involving the Directorate-General of Co-operation and the Association of Indonesian Credit Unions.

The presence or absence of community participation, activated by well-trained and motivated voluntary cadres from among the intended beneficiaries, has proved to be a key element in many programmes, such as the design and operation of water supply and sanitation systems, which YIS has evaluated on behalf of the Indonesian government.[6] As a support for POSYANDU, YIS helped to develop strategies for child survival, including monitoring of growth charts developed earlier by YIS and the United Nations Children's Emergency Fund (UNICEF), in which they drew on ten years' experience in training district staff in epidemiology and health management. This led to further co-operation with the government to decentralize health planning through the Comprehensive Health Improvement Programme Province Specific (CHIPPS), which seeks to adapt service delivery to local conditions, rather than impose prepackaged programmes. Some sections of the Health Department proved resistant to such ideas, but YIS worked through the United States Agency for International Development (USAID), which supports training of provincial planning staff, to counter this opposition.

Probably the greatest danger which YIS faces, and of which the older staff, at least, seem well aware, is a loss of direct contact with grass-roots community groups as a result of the organization's growing scope and complexity. This has led to a painful period of internal evaluation in seeking to reconcile financial soundness and effective management with the spirit and practice of closeness to people's felt needs, on which the staff had built their work. One strategy has been to restrict staff size to its existing level of sixty core people to handle training and negotiating roles, and to draw on available expertise from universities and elsewhere to manage new programmes and consultancies on either a contract or voluntary basis. To maintain its own grass-roots contacts and skills, and as a means of exposing younger staff to the realities of rural poverty, YIS has used the neighbouring district of Boyolali for training and motivation of cadres in building up integrated community development programmes.

YIS further believes it can maintain grass-roots links through its programmes for the development of small LSMs in Gunung Kidul (DIY), Magelang, and Temanggung (Central Java). YIS has assisted cadres from these groups, together with others in Central and East Java, to form their own network (Ikatan Kader-Kader—IKK).[7] The members of IKK are linked by a newsletter, and also meet periodically to exchange experience and undertake mutual evaluations of each other's village programmes. Cadres are all volunteers who pursue other employment as farmers, teachers, government officials, or skilled artisans. While the association appears to have engendered a sense of pride and common strength among its members, it is uncertain whether it will act as a vehicle for wider mobilization.

YIS has sought to defuse potential conflict and a sense of rivalry between itself and associated small LSMs by offering technical and management assistance to groups during their early stages and assisting them to seek funds. Training has been linked to a critical evaluation of programmes and strategies, and directed towards formulating specific project proposals. YIS claims that four LSMs in Magelang and Temanggung later undertook their own evaluation of relations with YIS, acknowledging that earlier suspicions and misconceptions were unfounded, and that YIS had, in fact, helped them to become genuinely self-reliant.

With regard to networking, YIS works closely with PERDAKHI and its Protestant counterpart, the All-Indonesia Christian Health Service (Pelyanan Keristen Kesehatan Seluruh Indonesia—PELKESI), which are, in turn, linked with parallel Islamic networks based on the Nahdlatul Ulama and Muhammadiyah through the Religious LSMs Communication Forum (Forum Komunikasi LSM Beragama). This meets annually, bringing together religion-affiliated LSMs operating in the health field. YIS has also joined with Bina Swadaya, the Klaten affiliate of the Social and Economic Research, Education, and Information Institute (Lembaga Penelitian, Pendidikan, dan Penerangan Ekonomi dan Sosial—LP3ES) and Bank Indonesia in a project linking banks with small enterprise groups at village level, aimed at identifying and guaranteeing the creditworthiness of poor people, to whom banks would never consider lending in the normal way. Finally, YIS participates in both Central Java and national NGO forums. As in other fields of work, its emphasis is on problem-solving, while avoiding confrontation with the government.

As a matter of both policy and philosophy, YIS has always adopted a low profile, steadfastly avoiding political controversy in its public communications, and preaching a consistent message about helping poor people to form their own groups and define their own needs and solutions. It has constantly sought new ways to implement these ideas in the face of a government structure operating on hierarchical principles. Its Indonesian and English language newsletters (*Bergetar* and *Vibro*) offer many mildly idealized problem-solving stories from field experience, as well as a range of writings on larger themes such as environment, industrialization, nuclear energy, and consumer rights, and more general issues concerning the dangers of capitalist development and distribution of wealth. Blame is never assigned to any person or group. Only problems and alternative solutions are canvassed. If structural problems are mentioned, they are never confronted with any degree of precision or depth. Yet, the organization can reasonably claim to have had a consistent impact on the design and implementation of policy in its main fields of expertise. Indeed, it has perhaps reached the stage where its contacts with government are so extensive and are supported by so many other local and overseas networks, that it scarcely needs to confront recalcitrant authorities directly in order to achieve results.

YIS appears to be feeling its way in a rapidly changing situation, knowing that it must scale up its activities and operate across a broader political and social canvas, while still maintaining close understanding of issues rooted in villages and poorer urban *kampung*. A younger generation without this background is coming to the fore with the passing of key figures—notably Dr Gunawan, the founder of YAKKUM, Dr Lukas Hendrata, internationally respected among primary health professionals, and the quietly charismatic Mary Johnson, an Australian volunteer social worker who worked with YAKKUM and YIS from 1968 to 1988, then continued in a part-time consultancy role in the community health field until her untimely death in October 1991. A large part of Mary Johnson's influence was based on her steadfast belief in and practice of simple living by the affluent as an essential, practical, yet convivial aspect of the overall fight against poverty.[8] The challenge for YIS in the 1990s is to sharpen its analysis of a rapidly changing political, social, and economic scene at the local, national, and international levels without losing its ideals, roots, and fairly unique style and capacity for facilitating practical problem-solving.

Yayasan Dian Desa

Yayasan Dian Desa's (YDD) development philosophy and approach to relations with the government are broadly similar to that of YIS, although it has adopted a somewhat higher public profile. The founder and director of YDD, or Dian Desa as it is popularly known,[9] Drs Anton Sujarwo, has an academic background in engineering and agricultural technology at Gadjah Mada University, Yogyakarta. He was influenced, as a student, by a Dutch Catholic priest and philosophy lecturer, Fr. de Blot, who in the late 1960s mobilized groups of students to undertake social work among poor families in the city, notably families of political prisoners. The students also discussed broader issues concerning the direction of Indonesia's development under the New Order government, which led to their adopting a 'basic needs' orientation. Sujarwo later gathered a small group around him to study the problem of water supply around Cangkringan village on the higher slopes of Mount Merapi, which overshadows the northern side of Yogyakarta.

YDD was established initially to regularize the project which emerged from this study, and to manage the funds allocated by the World University Service and UNICEF. Cangkringan's technical problems were resolved by the development of a gravity-flow pipe system. Sujarwo appears to have received significant assistance in its design from within Gadjah Mada University. As a result of this project, he was awarded the prestigious Magsaysay prize for a significant innovation in service to the rural poor, thereby establishing his own and YDD's international reputation. He was personally received and congratulated by President Suharto for this achievement.

The Cangkringan project has provided water to several villages high up on the slopes of Mount Merapi, plus four villages under Mount Merbabu. To facilitate the project, informal joint enterprise (*usaha bersama*—UB) groups were established, based on personal choice and affinity. Each member contributed 1000 square metres of land, irrespective of other holdings, and worked during the afternoons on a mutual assistance (*gotong royong*) basis. Village councils also provided land for trial purposes. YDD assisted with revolving funds and technical and marketing advice. Cloves and coffee were developed as cash crops, with some experiments in relation to garlic. Profits have been shared between members, the village government, and YDD on a 50 : 25 : 25 basis. The programme is now effectively self-managing, with YDD maintaining only an informal liaison and advisory role.

Since the late 1970s, YDD has tackled water problems in the chronically dry region of Gunung Kidul, south of Yogyakarta, by training some 600 local cadres to construct rainwater collectors using bamboo and cement at a cost of some US$150 each. Evaporation problems were overcome by means of a manhole-type cover, but still insufficient water is available in the later part of the dry season. Participating villages took responsibility for supporting the cadres. YDD monitors and advises periodically. Despite the establishment of village-level water groups, water is overused when available, while too many families attempt to share too few collectors. YDD sent some cadres from Gunung Kidul to Eastern Nusa Tenggara to share their skills.

YDD has also established a shrimp farming programme in the Jepara region with three other field stations-cum-hatcheries spread along Java's north coast. After demonstrating techniques, farmers are organized into groups, with 8–20 families per group. Each group must appoint one person to work full time. Some twenty groups had been established by 1991. Each group is provided with technical assistance plus non-collateral credit for growing small shrimps from larvae. Shrimp farming projects have, however, been increasingly criticized by environmental groups for destroying mangroves. YDD argues that damage is caused by large tanks of 1000–5000 hectares, whereas its own tanks are only 20–50 hectares in size. Natural gaps caused by siltation are selected for their location.

According to YDD, attempts by the Department of Agriculture, assisted by the World Bank, to foster shrimp farming via its Tank Intensification Project (Proyek Intensifikasi Tambak) were unsuccessful. Despite the Department's initial resistance to NGO participation, YDD has progressively taken over regional management of this programme, working through an interdepartmental committee within the framework of the Pilot Project for Development of Coastal Regions (Pilot Proyek Pengembangan Daerah Pantai).

YDD has made efforts to spread the programme to other regions of Indonesia, training a group associated with Yayasan Mandiri,[10] an appropriate technology group initiated by former student activists from the Bandung Institute of Technology which operates a similar scheme on the north coast of West Java. Shrimp farming proved unsuccessful in South Sulawesi, as the project was contracted to an NGO which turned out to be run by university graduates experimenting in social work, who failed to visit regularly, and whom YDD considered not to be serious. More success was achieved in Eastern Nusa Tenggara, where forty staff were employed in 1991 at regional bases in Kupang and Flores. Irrigation and small-scale agriculture have been established, in addition to shrimp farming, and a new industry using skin from shark residue developed. This provides employment to women, both in Eastern Nusa Tenggara, where skins are collected and washed, and in YDD's processing plant in Yogyakarta, where women in the slums of Yogyakarta are trained to make skins into handbags and other artefacts. YDD hopes that self-confidence gained from the programme will help people in Eastern Nusa Tenggara resist the sale of their land, which is under pressure from many directions. Their land title is based on local customary (*adat*) law and can only be made secure by registering land with the National Land Agency. This is proving to be a long and expensive process.

YDD is controlled by an internal working group, consisting of section heads and the director, with an advisory board of outside experts. The structure of groups with which it works at the base level appears to be less participatory than that of YIS. In the case of Gunung Kidul, cadres trained to make rainwater collectors were under technical supervision from YIS, while their routine functioning and that of the water users' groups were essentially under the control of the village authorities. In the case of shrimp farming, the complexities of managing the hatcheries and market distribution require farmers to follow instructions closely, effectively giving local groups the status of contract employees. The various enterprise centres are linked by microwave radio, facilitating weekly co-ordination of activities. This 'command' structure is balanced by a policy whereby YDD shares profits and losses in all commercial programmes, of which shrimp farming is currently the largest, on a 50 : 50 basis. Yet, despite YDD's efforts to devolve as much day-to-day management to local groups as possible, this example points to the requirement of modern enterprise for specialist management skills, technical supervision, and precise co-ordination. However, there is no evidence to suggest that groups are unhappy with these overall arrangements, as they are probably more interested in any kind of economic activity which will guarantee basic subsistence for their families than with abstract ideas of participation.

Overall, YDD's main motivation has been to find new ways for people to enjoy a decent subsistence. The search for feasible, low-cost alternatives using local resources is instrumental to this, rather than any fad of alternative technology. Developing forward and backward linkages is essential if new enterprises are to survive. Unlike many alternative technology groups with strong ideological motivation, YDD has persisted for over twenty years with a pragmatic, field-based approach. It resists criticism that its size is too large, with a staff of nearly 200, including 40–50 at the Yogyakarta centre. In YDD's view, as new opportunities to meet the needs of the poor open up as a result of initial efforts, the size and complexity of organizational requirements will increase, although a range of choices between centralized or decentralized arrangements may be available.

In the latter context, Sujarwo is sceptical towards NGO conventional wisdom, considering that many foreign funding agencies have not thought through the financial and organizational implications of self-reliance. Even so, the organization attracts substantial overseas support, which still provides some 65–70 per cent of its revenue, despite strong efforts to generate income from consultancies and joint enterprises with local people. Some income is provided by private contributions from senior personnel and local well-wishers. Among the overseas agencies, probably the closest and longest-standing relationship is with OXFAM Indonesia, based at Semarang, which has supported YDD's programmes from its earliest days.

The foundation's relations with other Indonesian NGOs are *ad hoc*, based on likely practical benefits. As a member of the Yogyakarta Regional Forum,[11] Sujarwo considers there is significant potential from networking for mutual learning and sharing experience. However, in practice, the forum reached a high point in the late 1980s, and then 'everyone disappeared'. As an example of relations between big and small NGOs, YDD has been responsible for channelling a block grant by the Swiss Development Corporation to twenty-seven LSMs in Kalimantan, Eastern Nusa Tenggara, and East Java. Those with some performance potential are pre-selected for further training, while those with only impressive proposals are eliminated. Despite this tough approach, Sujarwo insists that he has empathy for small groups seeking funds, having lived through the same experience earlier. Nor does he see small groups as subordinate to YDD despite their obvious dependence on his recommendation in obtaining funds.

YDD has had significant interaction with several government agencies. Apart from the shrimp farming programme, it has operated an experimental agricultural centre at Gedong in the dry, eroded hills above Karangkobar as part of the Foundation for Social and Economic Development (Yayasan Pembangunan dan Pengembangan Sosial Ekonomi—YPPSE) programme at Banjarnegara.[12] This was located 3 kilometres from any roads or other facility, but was ideally suited for local farmers to visit and for extension work to be conducted on their own fields. Many fruit trees and vegetable crops were found to be viable in this previously sparsely cultivated area.[13] YDD later withdrew, ostensibly because their five-year contract had been completed but, in reality, because the local village head appropriated control of the centre.

At one stage, YDD played an advisory role to the Central Java Enterprise Programme (CJEP) and also ran training courses for would-be entrepreneurs for the Provincial Areas Development Programme. YDD considered these had limited value, as the government had the major say in selecting trainees. This programme sought to identify potential new enterprises in the region. YDD felt that it was placed somewhat in the role of token NGO without any real say, and that the programme produced little by way of concrete results. Nevertheless, significant deregulation was recommended by the CJEP as a result of YDD's urging.[14]

YDD gained valuable experience and contacts from its participation in the CJEP, which led to other projects, notably slum studies in the port area of Jakarta (Tanjung Priok) and in Yogyakarta. It also participated in Integrated Urban Development programmes with the Department of Public Works and several international donors in Jakarta, Yogyakarta, Surabaya, and Cirebon. For these, YDD involved students in interviewing some 5,000 families. This programme has attempted to link urban planning to the social and cultural needs of the inhabitants. Although it appears to be outside YDD's immediate field of expertise, YDD claims that the experience will enable it to select and concentrate on specific programmes, such as income-generating activity for women living in slums in Yogyakarta. Like YIS, YDD avoids any sharp conflict with government agencies, though it remains sceptical of their capacity or motivation to achieve practical results on behalf of the poor. Its basic stance is that NGOs should concentrate on finding solutions rather than criticizing.

Bina Swadaya

The origins of Bina Swadaya (BS)[15] can be traced back to the foundation of the Panca Sila Farmers' Association (Ikatan Tani Pancasila—ITP) around 1957. Responsibility for ITP's establishment and operation was undertaken by Bambang Ismawan, long-time executive director of BS, and Fr. Chris Melchers, a Jesuit priest. However, it appears much of the spiritual inspiration behind ITP's foundation was provided by Mgr. Soegyapranata, his secretary Fr. Jan Dijkstra, and Fr. Jan Beek, at that time in charge of Asrama Realino, a Catholic theological institution in Yogyakarta, with a tradition of supporting participatory community work.

ITP appears to have been a product of Catholic Action and designed, in part, to challenge the Indonesian Communist Party (Partai Komunis Indonesia—PKI) in a context in which farmers' organizations were initiated by political parties. ITP aimed instead to bring them together on a non-religious and non-party basis, and to stress farming skills and community organization. On this basis, ITP gained support from President Sukarno's government, which facilitated work at the local level. Some ITP members were appointed to the national and regional assemblies as functional group representatives. ITP was actively involved in the Sukarno government's improved rice varieties programme (BIMAS), which involved joint field research between agricultural students and farmers to develop improved crop varieties.[16] At the time, such co-operation represented a mini social revolution. Students also acted as intermediaries *vis-à-vis* the bureaucracy in articulating farmers' grievances.

ITP's non-political, developmental emphasis seemed well-calculated to appeal to Suharto's New Order government. However, the organization was placed on a blacklist, ostensibly because one of its members had been active in land struggles during Sukarno's later years. ITP was abolished and replaced by a GOLKAR-affiliated organization, the Indonesian Farmers' Association (Himpunan Kerukunan Tani Indonesia—HKTI).[17] Ismawan and Melchers anticipated this development by forming the Farmers' Social Development Institute (Yayasan Sosial Tani Membangun—YSTM). In 1984, YSTM's magazine, *Trubus*, and related publication services, through which technical, economic, managerial, and scientific information was disseminated as a popular extension service to farmers, were separated from YSTM in response to a regulation by the Minister of Information that a publishing organization could not undertake other activities. BS was set up to co-ordinate the two legally distinct organizations. At the same time, Ismawan retained links with the farmers' official mass organization by becoming secretary of HKTI. BS and HKTI operate independently, though HKTI provides a major market outlet for *Trubus*.

Following the establishment of YSTM, Melchers, though still retaining close informal links, set up his own entrepreneurial training organization, Yayasan Purba Danata, based in Semarang.[18]

It will be recalled that the application of dominant American social science paradigms at that time to newly developing countries of the Third World stressed Protestant ethic-style values, in particular the virtues of saving and entrepreneurship (Weber, 1930). Many training programmes throughout Indonesia are still influenced by these ideas, notably those of McClelland (1961), in his emphasis on the 'need for achievement'. Such ideas were influential among Jesuit-inspired institutions in the Third World prior to the radical shift which occurred within the order in the 1970s. Jesuits of Melchers' era thus appear to reflect a mixture of Weber, McClelland, and pre-Freirean Christian humanism.[19] Yayasan Purba Danata, though similar to BS in encouraging mutual support through group formation, has steadily shifted its emphasis towards the individual, both as the major driving force behind business enterprise and because individuals are more likely than groups to break free from pervasive traditional patterns of social obligation.

BS's central thrust is on forming small-scale co-operatives (*usaha bersama*—UB), which are widely recognized as its trade mark. A loophole in the law allows small co-operatives to describe themselves as pre-co-operatives (*pra koperasi*), as yet unready for registration. This approach has become more difficult since 1984, when the government issued an instruction giving a monopoly of all village-level buying and selling of basic agricultural produce to Village Co-operative Units (Koperasi Unit Desa—KUD). In practice, BS claims that the KUD system is held in such low esteem by most farmers, due to widespread mismanagement and corruption, that it is necessary to employ the term *usaha bersama* (co-operative enterprise), which is considered more informal than the official *koperasi* (co-operative), in order to gain their confidence. Local authorities seem generally willing to accept and even encourage such arrangements.

BS has developed intensive training programmes to assist fieldworkers and local leaders to establish informal joint enterprises. These may be either productive, market-oriented, or merely savings and loans (*simpan pinjam*) groups. Group size ranges from twenty to fifty members. While registered co-operatives have access to credit at low rates of interest from the government banking system, UBs must generate their own savings. BS usually channels revolving loans to them as seed capital. Before recognizing groups, BS requires that they must have functioned independently for at least a year, have held regular meetings, and have operated an effective bookkeeping system. There are grounds for doubting the extent to which membership of small groups sponsored by BS derives from the poorest strata. A survey in Yogyakarta found that most UB members already have other jobs as teachers, junior government officials, small traders, or wage labourers for whom UB activities provide supplementary income (Siregar, 1987).

In addition to building self-reliant groups, BS seeks opportunities to influence the direction of government (GOLKAR) front farmers' and fishermen's organizations. For example, farmers' responses have been so negative that the Department of Agriculture has felt it necessary to bypass the government-controlled HKTI by establishing its own system of cadres. BS has channelled loans to several such groups.[20] However, it sees HKTI as being a potentially useful vehicle in handling complaints over the highly sensitive issue of land certificates, as a lobby group in relation to prices and delivery of inputs and services, and as a counter to the KUD system which, despite its formally democratic delegate structure, stands in the way of genuinely participatory and accountable structures.

The number of older-style UBs supported by BS fell dramatically from 591 to 288 between 1981 and 1988,[21] although levels of group activity held up in regions such as Yogyakarta where area leaders were employed on a full-time basis. Emphasis has been shifting to (i) linking local groups with banks, and eventually establishing their own bank and (ii) greater participation in government programmes, though maintaining an emphasis within these programmes on training and small-group formation. BS now urges the need for NGOs to scale up their operations if they are to gain sufficient influence to make a mass impact on poverty, with the costs and benefits of co-operating with the government being assessed pragmatically in each situation.

By the end of 1989, BS claimed to be associated through all programmes, directly or indirectly, with a total of 18,085 self-help groups (Ismawan, 1990: 21). One suspects, however, that growing organizational size and concentration in Jakarta will create their own inexorable pull away from direct field contact, which is likely, in time, to be contracted out to smaller LSMs. In spite of, and possibly because of such growth, BS has probably achieved one of the highest levels of self-sufficiency among Indonesian NGOs, whether large or small. Ismawan claims that 85–90 per cent of organizational income is self-generated through consultancies, the sale of publications, economic programmes, fees for training, and so forth, with only 10–15 per cent coming from foreign funding agencies. This gives BS considerable independence and bargaining power in selecting foreign donors, whose priorities it can nevertheless accommodate with little difficulty, given the diversity of its overall programme. Conversely, this example raises a question as to whether foreign funding, by releasing LSM/LPSMs from the necessity to generate income, reduces the need to create complex organizational structures such as that of BS, thus allowing them to concentrate most energies on direct work at field level. Such a conclusion would depend on an assessment of the quality of the groups supported by BS relative to other groups, which is beyond the scope of this work.

BS has become extensively involved in channelling credit, through various arrangements with the banking system, to individuals and groups whom banks would not normally consider creditworthy. In 1986–7, the West German government financed a major study by Gadjah Mada University in conjunction with Bank Indonesia on behalf of BS (Bank Indonesia et al., 1987). The study covered forty-five sub-districts in Bali, Central Java, Yogyakarta, and North Sumatra, with a view to channelling greater financial assistance to small, self-help groups. The subsequent report envisaged that LPSMs, such as BS, would play key intermediary roles in implementing any such scheme by acting as guarantors in many instances, though potential constraints to their effectiveness caused by the KUD and other bureaucratic agencies were acknowledged.

Subsequently, Bank Indonesia conducted a pilot project in conjunction with YIS, BS, and LP3ES aimed at strengthening self-help groups. It was envisaged that NGOs would facilitate lending by banks by monitoring management and creditworthiness. The three NGOs established a pilot project along these lines involving the German Technical

Co-operation Agency (German Technische Suzammen Arbeit—GTZ), Bank Indonesia, and Bank Rakyat Indonesia. Other private banks were expected to join. By early 1991, over Rp1 billion had been distributed, with 97 per cent of repayments due recovered.

The normal disbursement mechanism under this scheme is for NGOs to distribute funds directly to groups, except in Bali, which has strong local organizations based on the traditional irrigation (*subag*) system, where NGOs recommend groups to banks, which then make direct payments. The project structure consists basically of a national policy-making and operational task force, plus teams at site level. BS field staff report that, in practice, banks are unwilling to visit the field or work in any direct way with clients, thus placing a very heavy burden on NGOs. BS is consequently looking for other approaches and sources of finance, including the possibility of becoming a banker itself. It also obtained funding for eleven self-help groups from USAID for one year on a revolving fund basis at 10 per cent interest.

Experience from such schemes suggests that the problem is not merely one of securing and distributing credit, but also extends to the nature of relations between base-level groups and supporting NGOs. These are likely to change as groups deal more directly with banks and other credit agencies. BS training seeks to empower groups in that direction. The nature of relations between existing informal co-operatives and newly created self-help groups is currently unclear. In several instances, they appear to be one and the same. In 1991, BS channelled funds to twenty-three self-help groups in the Yogyakarta area. Many of these appeared to be groups with established enterprises and organization and, therefore, the capacity to repay. Such groups have been built up through BS's established guidance and training processes, and will soon be able to deal directly with banks. However, this leaves open the question of how new groups will emerge, in the first place, if BS withdraws from this role. Regional field staff are being reduced, with resources being concentrated in Jakarta. In 1991, the Yogyakarta region, traditionally an area of strength for *usaha bersama*, had over ninety groups covered by only two 'motivators' responsible for Klaten and Gunung Kidul respectively. On the other hand, it is planned for regional offices to become more autonomous, even to the extent of negotiating directly for foreign aid, with some assistance from BS's national office.

BS's national leaders see their groups as going through a transition stage, with a general instruction to use their own resources where available or otherwise to invite the participation of banks. The organization is evidently unable or unwilling to channel revolving funds in the traditional way from foreign donors on any large scale, and is in the process of establishing rural banks. The Netherlands Catholic Organization for Development Co-operation (Katholieke Organisatie voor Ontwikelings-samenwerking Nederland—CEBEMO) has provided initial capital for this venture, which will thereafter circulate as revolving loans. Rural banks will undertake group promotion, credit delivery, and technical assistance, with collateral not required from clients. The aim is for each unit to become self-managing and financing. However, questions remain about loan recovery mechanisms, and whether rural banks will be in a position to develop equally strong community norms and sanctions as UBs. Also, the question of bank ownership has yet to be resolved. The capacity of local groups and units to buy shares will depend on their ability to raise sufficient capital. In any case, if units can raise capital from other than bank sources, the relevance of the bank to their needs would then come into question.

The plan to establish rural banks is part of an overall decentralization policy. Banking, consultancy, and group formation, with associated guidance and training, will thus become the 'three wheels' driving BS. This blueprint, if successful, will result in diminishing dependence on foreign aid and, ultimately, financial independence. It is envisaged that by setting up its own bank, BS will improve career prospects for field-workers, whose traditional role has been declining. At least some small co-operative groups will come to own shares. However, the soundness of even such a large, financially experienced NGO as BS owning its own bank is open to question in terms of the relatively limited volume and diversity of sources it could draw on to generate finance, and the consequently limited scope for risk-spreading. Banking is a highly specialized task, which could divert from the major role of NGOs of building and strengthening participatory group formation. While there are examples of successful ventures by NGOs, notably the Self-Employed Women's Association, based in Ahmedabad, India, which has a high degree of participation by its members, such banks could perhaps more accurately be described as savings and loans associations or credit unions.

BS's co-operation with the government includes rural water supply and irrigation, family planning, and smallholder and integrated area development programmes (Eldridge, 1990b: 15–16). Such interventions are intended to enhance participatory group formation among consumers of official programmes. BS is seen within the wider Indonesian NGO community as extremely flexible, to the point of being somewhat soft in its dealings with government agencies, despite its conflicts with some local authorities. One study has suggested that accommodation to government priorities influences BS's choice of programmes and target groups in each locality (Utomo and Thamrin, 1989: 11–12). The same study (p. 14) alleges that the organization has a far too generalized notion of poverty and fails to identify the most disadvantaged groups with any degree of precision. BS, for its part, refuses to categorize groups in terms of wealth or poverty, seeing them as interlocking and needing to co-operate in various contexts. Moreover, leaders of various groups, such as schoolteachers, may come from other than the poorest strata of the village. BS has refused to form all-women's groups for similar reasons, seeing women as an integral part both of families, households, and enterprise groups (Utomo and Thamrin, 1989: 24).

Another unusual initiative involving BS has been the development of credit programmes linked to family planning in conjunction with the

Indonesian Family Planning Association (Perkumpulan Keluarga Berencana Indonesia—PKBI), whereby birth-control acceptors are given advantages in obtaining credit. PKBI plays a broad-based community education role in relation to family planning in co-operation with the National Family Planning Co-ordinating Board (Badan Koordinasi Keluarga Berencana Nasional—BKKBN) and is looking for more innovative and interesting ways of presenting its message. However, conversation with both agencies indicates that neither takes the link between birth-control acceptance and creditworthiness very seriously. The programme is based on the slogan of 'a happy and prosperous small family', with the linked aims of promoting economic development and providing rewards and incentives for maintaining a small family size. BKKBN is responsible for providing most seed capital, with PKBI administering the programme and providing vocational and skills training. The Indonesian Credit Co-operative Co-ordinating Board (Badan Koordinasi Koperasi Kredit Indonesia—BK3I)[22] provides ongoing credit and technical and management assistance, facilitates links with banks, and undertakes monitoring and evaluation. Training is less intensive than for BS's normal *usaha bersama*. The clientele receiving credit under this scheme is more middle class, with group sanctions less stringent as a result. Even so, PKBI claims a debt recovery rate of around 80 per cent.

This brief account has given some indication of the expansion and diversity of BS's programmes, and the growing complexity of its links with government agencies, banks, and foreign funding agencies. Its role in NGO networking, discussed in a later section, is also extensive. In many ways, BS is a big NGO (BINGO) *par excellence*. Unlike YIS, which has experienced real tension, fearing that its involvement in Indonesia-wide programmes is shifting its centre of gravity away from grass-roots groups, BS has made a conscious decision that this is unavoidable. It hopes to overcome this dilemma through strategies of decentralization. In the process of facilitating links between local groups and financial and other institutions, BS seems to have given insufficient consideration to the impact of change, both on the nature of groups and, ultimately, the quality of its grass-roots links.

So far as relations with the government at field level are concerned, it appears that the avoidance of restrictions on its small self-help groups by the KUD has only been achieved by means of co-operation with other government agencies. Nevertheless, BS can, at this stage, claim with some justice that its strategy of informal group formation, within a framework of official protection, has generated economic benefits and a reasonable degree of autonomy for its groups. It must also be acknowledged that its organization and leaders have a long and impressive survival record through various transformations and political upheavals, with a proven ability to adapt creatively to a constantly changing environment.

1. The literal translation of YIS's name is 'Prosperous Indonesia Foundation'.

2. Currently, YIS's only formal church link is via one *ex officio* appointment to its Board of Management by the Indonesian Communion of Churches (Persekutuan Gereja-Gereja Indonesia—PGI).

3. See pp. 46–7.

4. For aspects of YIS's early history, see Eldridge (1979: 128–31, 144–7).

5. A Rukun Tetangga, also known as *kedukuhan* in Java, represents the lowest (neighbourhood) level in Indonesia's structure of local government.

6. See Eldridge (1990b: 17–20) for more detailed information on YIS activities in the health field.

7. According to YIS sources, this idea originated from experience in the *Kring* programme in Banjarnegara. See pp. 34–5 and Eldridge (1990b: 22–3).

8. See YIS (1991) for a tribute to Mary Johnson by Herbert Feith, together with a collection of her writings.

9. Dian Desa means 'village light'.

10. See Sidin (1989) for an overall evaluation of Yayasan Mandiri.

11. See pp. 202–5.

12. See pp. 33–5.

13. Based on a comparison between visits in 1979 and 1983.

14. Based on interviews with YDD and BAPPEDA, Semarang.

15. The literal meaning of Bina Swadaya is 'fostering self-reliance'.

16. According to the late Dr David Penny, an Australian agricultural economist who was associated for many years with both the Agricultural Institute at Bogor and the Agricultural Science Faculty of the University of North Sumatra, this collaboration focused on improving traditional rice varieties. Field trials resulted in a 20 per cent higher yield without any of the disadvantages associated with the subsequent high-yielding varieties. Penny claimed that for a variety of political and cultural reasons, the potential of these improved traditional varieties was never properly evaluated by the government or agricultural science establishment in Indonesia, or their overseas counterparts.

17. HKTI also incorporated a parallel organization of fishermen, which had been established in tandem with the Panca Sila Farmers' Association.

18. Melchers first came from Holland to Indonesia as a student in 1952. According to his own account, he made an in-depth study of the Indonesian and Javanese languages. He eventually wrote a thesis on the use of the passive tense in Javanese, with the idea that the language structure expresses the extent to which Javanese are more acted upon than actors.

19. See p. 173 for reference to the influence of Paolo Freire's ideas on Catholic social mobilization in Indonesia.

20. I visited two of these enterprise groups, supported by BS, in January 1988 in the region south of Wonosari in the Gunung Kidul (Eldridge, 1990b: 17, fn. 30). One group had a letter from Dinas Pertanian enabling them to buy cheap seeds and fertilizer from P.T. Petani, a government-owned corporation. The group in question appeared to be replacing the role of the official Village Co-operative Unit, which had proved unable to deliver to farmers on time.

21. BS sources.

22. See pp. 188–93.

5
'High-level Politics–Grass-roots Mobilization': Two Case-studies

THIS chapter studies two major organizations, each with extensive local networks: the Institute of Development Studies (Lembaga Studi Pembangunan—LSP) and the Social and Economic Research, Education, and Information Institute (Lembaga Penelitian, Pendidikan, dan Penerangan Ekonomi dan Sosial—LP3ES). By contrast with non-government organizations (NGOs) discussed in the previous chapter, these two have developed a stance of critical collaboration towards the government in line with the second model proposed in Chapter 2. This entails a measure of conflict in both general ideological and specific policy contexts. LSP and LP3ES have both sought to penetrate bureaucratic structures and influence policy from within, while at the same time building up base-level groups as self-sustaining, economic units, and informing them of their rights and entitlements. Local groups have, in turn, provided legitimation and support for LSP and LP3ES in their dealings with the government. Both organizations have mostly avoided outright confrontation with the authorities, although this has occurred, for example, in relation to forced removal of petty street traders and urban *kampung* dwellers.

Lembaga Studi Pembangunan

Lembaga Studi Pembangunan (LSP)[1] emerged from a group of ex-students of the 1966 generation, who undertook a two-year study critical of dominant paradigms of development. In line with dependency (neo-Marxist) theory, which influenced much radical thinking about Third World issues during the 1970s, LSP's analysis has highlighted the destructive impact of transnational companies, a growing rich–poor gap, and the marginalization of local skills and enterprise. LSP consequently saw its activities as a form of ongoing action research aimed at evolving an alternative development strategy based on democracy and social justice. LSP's strategic instincts and synthesis of field experience appear more soundly based than its incursions into global theories of development, which have not kept pace with the complexity of debate in this field. This aspect has now become less prominent in LSP's overall profile.

A regular structure was eventually established, and an Informal Sector Newsletter started to disseminate themes and findings more widely. It was decided to work on two fronts: (i) constructing alternative paradigms for Indonesia and more general Third World development and (ii) building grass-roots capacity for self-reliance. LSP saw its role as one of linking mobilization at the grass roots with political and governmental processes at all levels, acting together with local people as catalysts for wider change. This approach can, at times, give LSP's programmes a quality of being used as a 'social laboratory' (Sjaifudian, 1989: 36), which target groups may not always understand or appreciate.

LSP's efforts on the intellectual front have continued in the form of seminars and publications. Although several journals have been discontinued, its newsletter has continued to act as a communication vehicle between LSP's various groups. Its search to link macro political structures with popular mobilization was dramatized in Adi Sasono's 1986 paper on 'Semar Management: Towards Democracy and Social Justice' (Sjaifudian, 1989: 7–8). Semar, in Javanese mythology, was the king's wise adviser. He was also close to the common people. Today's counterparts of Semar seem to be advocating mobilization from below led by wise leaders—or perhaps, more ambitiously, some bottom–up version of the just king.

LSP requires that all its programmes should conform to its 'action model', for which it has specified three conditions: (i) the project has the capacity for self-management, i.e. it has the capacity to negotiate with funding agencies independently from LSP, though not necessarily excluding receipt of foreign funds; (ii) the project should be replicable; (iii) the project is potentially self-sustaining and provides employment and raises productivity. LSP does not support social or infrastructure projects. LSP is thus keen on self-reliant community institutions (Lembaga Swadaya Masyarakat—LSM) and institutions for developing community self-reliance (Lembaga Pengembangan Swadaya Masyarakat—LPSM) gaining financial strength to participate in struggles for political and economic reform. It also sees a role for indigenous and other Indonesian business enterprise in the overall struggle.

LSP presses for the legal registration of groups with the Department of Co-operatives, in sharp contrast with Bina Swadaya's informal cum pre-co-operative enterprise strategy, outlined in Chapter 4, believing that groups will then be in a position to organize openly and demand all the rights and benefits laid down in legislation (DEPKOP, c.1968; DEPKOP, 1983). At the same time, LSP uses its contacts and networks in Jakarta to ensure groups are well treated by regional and local authorities. Both approaches seem to achieve results, the common factor being the strong intermediary role of a prominent LPSM. However, Bina Swadaya's emphasis on informal structures, while intended to give greater autonomy both to local groups and to Bina Swadaya itself, appears to depend on cultivating a close overall relationship with a range of government agencies in order to provide protection against the official government co-operatives bureaucracy. LSP believes that by fulfilling legal obligations, groups can assert rights as well as gain access to benefits.

The programmes instituted by LSP are more urban than rural in orientation, with a special focus on the informal sector.[2] LSP says that while organization and mobilization are more difficult in urban areas, where fewer NGOs are willing to work, there are also greater opportunities for programmes to make a political impact. For example, LSP has helped to establish federations of street trader co-operatives in Jakarta, Bandung, and Yogyakarta, together with housing co-operatives in Bandung and Yogyakarta. In Samarinda and Tegal, LSP became part of a management team to ensure that street traders were given a place within new shopping-centre developments, instead of simply being evicted, as normally happens. This also involved assisting them in adapting to change. LSP argues that it is important for NGOs to help find solutions and not merely to criticize, since once a major development has taken shape, protests are doomed to failure.

LSP is run by a ten-member board of management, with a smaller executive body. It employs only core staff. Most executives have other employment and business interests. The chairman of LSP, Adi Sasono, works with a business called PT Arcelina, where the organization has an office. Apart from secretarial staff, everyone works on a voluntary basis, except when employed on a consultancy. A proportion of such earnings is returned to LSP to build future capital. In this way, LSP has worked towards financial self-reliance, claiming, by 1989, that only 20 per cent of its income came from foreign assistance, compared with around 80 per cent in earlier years (Sjaifudian, 1989: 36). A network of volunteers from previous staff or study groups can be called on for tasks appropriate to their expertise.

LSP seeks to influence both the overall direction of development and specific policy fields where it has direct experience. To this end, it focuses its own efforts on the political system, while actively encouraging the mobilization of groups to improve their immediate economic situation, and to understand and press for their rights. LSP's liaison role between people and government is calculated to enhance its own strategic bargaining role and gain access to high-level government contacts. Thus, Adi Sasono and Dawam Rahardjo, a member of LSP's board of management, have for some years been members of a key government advisory body, the National Defence Institute (Lembaga Hankam Nasional—LEMHAMNAS). In 1989, the Ministers for Housing and Co-operatives were reportedly pro-LSM and close to LSP.[3] LSP leaders claim to be pragmatic about such contacts, seeing their justification as conditional on achieving benefits for local groups.

Any account of LSP would be incomplete without reference to its Islamic links. It co-operates with major Islamic social and educational networks, such as Muhammadiyah and the Indonesian Association for Pesantren and Community Development (Perkumpulan Pengembangan

Pesantren dan Masyarakat—P3M),[4] which has strong informal ties with the Religious Teachers' Association (Nahdlatul Ulama—NU). Though formally secular, part of LSP's motivation is to establish a Muslim presence in the voluntary sector, which it considers has been long dominated by Christian-linked groups. The student networks mentioned earlier, with which LSP has close links, have a predominantly Islamic social base, with a broadly modernist and democratic orientation. In that context, the LP3ES network has been particularly important.[5] LSP has working relations with many NGOs, but is selective and sceptical in its approach towards them (Sjaifudian, 1989: 33). Although it was active in founding the International NGO Forum on Indonesia (INGI),[6] it subsequently withdrew, citing a variety of not very clear reasons, including domination of INGI leadership by foreigners, financial dependence on large donors, and a research direction more concerned with money than assisting target groups (Sjaifudian, 1989: 31). LSP leaders have also suggested that international human rights groups were relatively inactive in protesting about human rights abuses towards Muslim groups, for example, in Aceh, compared with more high-profile situations, such as East Timor.[7]

LSP has made some effort to confront problems facing women. It criticizes official approaches for, on the one hand, acknowledging the role of women in securing the basic needs of families, especially among low-income groups, yet failing to tackle their low educational status. Official training programmes are also seen by LSP as substantially ignoring women's needs. LSP has attempted to fill some of these gaps through nutrition and income-generating handicrafts and waste recycling programmes. However, LSP has not placed any women in executive positions (Sjaifudian, 1989: 21–3).

The organization has been generally true to its word in fostering independent grass-roots groups. Local groups have progressively forged their own operating styles and identities, irrespective of initial strategies and agendas conceived in Jakarta. As they become self-managing and autonomous, LSP plays only informal liaison roles on their behalf in dealing with government officials at the national level, and with foreign donors. Groups in the wider LSP family remain linked for information-sharing purposes. In this way, a sense of solidarity and goodwill is maintained, which allows for differences in outlook and approach. These points can be illustrated by looking at some groups originally sponsored by LSP.

Yogyakarta Street Traders

LSP initially worked through a counterpart students' group at Gadjah Mada University, organized in a foundation called Yayasan Dhwarawati. This represented a younger group, formed mainly in response to 'campus normalization' regulations introduced in 1979, which had effectively outlawed independent political activity by student unions. The formation of co-operatives was considered to be one means of blunting the effect of these regulations. Thus, cheap stationery, books, and other necessities were supplied to students on campus, with study groups conducted off campus for the more politically aware.

Though sharing LSP's populist dependency outlook towards official development strategies, the Dhwarawati group claimed to be less interested in theory than in researching current issues, such as the government's treatment of Acehnese dissidents, the extra-legal killings of alleged criminals by the military, and the conflict in East Timor. They also claimed to be exchanging ideas and experience with similar learning networks elsewhere in Java. Community development centres were formed in seven provinces in order to build links with the people. These were to establish co-operatives, both as sources of livelihood and as vehicles of popular empowerment and struggle. The militant aspect of this agenda was blurred by a complex programme of management training, full of social science jargon and abstractions.

During the early 1980s, Dhwarawati co-operated with local street traders in Yogyakarta in a struggle against local authorities which sought to arbitrarily displace them from sidewalks. They were joined in this struggle by other groups, notably inhabitants of the Gondolayu *kampung* led by Fr. Mangunwijaya, who were threatened with eviction as a result of development programmes.[8] This campaign finally succeeded in 1985, when the city authorities agreed to regularize trading locations for members of officially recognized co-operatives. This led to the formation of the Association of Yogyakarta Street Trading Co-operatives (Koperasi Persatuan Pedagang Kaki Lima Yogyakarta—KPPKLY). Yayasan Dhwarawati subsequently disappeared in the next wave of student politics, enabling street traders to establish control over the new association. While grateful for support in establishing their position in relation to the city authorities, they clearly considered the students' ideas as theoretical and lacking in practical relevance.

By early 1991, KPPKLY had established thirty-two groups with 1,900 members, covering fourteen sub-districts in the city and immediate surroundings. At that stage, about 42 per cent of the members were women. The central body claims that an average of 80 per cent of members attend annual general meetings. Local units have become self-managing with regard to receipt and disbursement of loans, collecting and returning repayments to the KPPKLY central body, to whom they are collectively accountable. The board of management is elected tri-annually. KPPKLY has worked closely with other street trader co-operatives, such as Koperasi Tri Dharma in Jalan Malioboro in the heart of the city. KPPKLY also offers general support to other street trader groups, but finance is available only to members. It is usually easier for co-operative members to obtain a licence and fixed trading location than for individual traders, though any such preferential policy has only informal status.

Interest rates to KPPKLY members fell from 5 per cent per month in 1988 to 1.7 per cent in 1991, without any additional payments being required after the initial entry subscription. These benefits were made possible by a subsidy from Bank Jakarta, which enabled KPPKLY to borrow at 1.25 per cent; this resulted from a personal pilot project by a senior Bank Jakarta official who wished to help weak economic groups. Bank staff have been researching the outcome with a view to replication elsewhere. Apart from economic advantages, KPPKLY considers that business dealings with Bank Jakarta are less bureaucratic than with the Indonesian Co-operative Bank (Bank Umum Koperasi Indonesia—BUKOPIN).

By 1987, KPPKLY had negotiated a share of a new middle-class housing complex south of the city, for which construction was financed by BUKOPIN. The Minister of Co-operatives was persuaded, through LSP's good offices, to reduce the annual interest from 12 to 10 per cent. Even so, only 75 of the 100 houses originally planned could be built, due to an inability to pay by others who had originally intended to buy. In 1991, KPPKLY reported, in an interview with the author, that recovery rates had been excellent, with loanees rarely more than 3–4 days late in payments. Plans for some street traders to set up a local market did not work out as the market potential of 150–200 families turned out to be too small. All street traders commute to their original city trading sites by public transport.

KPPKLY has thus evolved from a relatively small, self-help savings and credit organization, solely concerned with the specific economic problems of street traders, into an association more generally involved with advocacy for the rights and welfare of small street traders. It is also active in promoting standards of behaviour and service, working with the government on issues of safety, cleanliness, and general appearance of the city. KPPKLY also co-operates with the National Family Planning Co-ordinating Board (Badan Koordinasi Keluarga Berencana Nasional—BKKBN) and the Indonesian Family Planning Association (Perkumpulan Keluarga Berencana Indonesia—PKBI) in family planning education.

Yayasan Bina Karya, Bandung

The Foundation for Labour Advancement (Yayasan Bina Karya—YBK)[9] was founded in 1981 by eighteen former textile workers, who had lost their position as labour organizers as part of a general restructuring of the Federation of Indonesian Trade Unions (Federasi Serikat Buruh Indonesia—FSBI) (Sjaifudian and Thamrin, 1989: 6–7).[10] Initially, they established a co-operative to provide a basic income, which failed for lack of management experience. They then decided to form a housing co-operative which would provide a legal environment in which a sense of community and solidarity among workers could be developed, linked to a range of other social and economic activities.

LSP's role from the outset was fairly indirect, though it did play an important liaison function in obtaining initial funding. For a while, it also undertook a technical consultancy designed to reassure its major foreign supporter, the Netherlands Organization for International Development Co-operation (Nederlandse Organisatie voor Internationale Bijstand—

NOVIB). YBK draws on and shares experience with LSP's wider network. LSP's government contacts also appear to have been instrumental in smoothing its path at the local level.

A key organizing role in founding YBK was played by Ir Juni, a former student of the Bandung Institute of Technology, who entered FSBI in 1979 and became head of the education section in the Bandung area. He later left to set up a construction company, PT Bandung Raya, which serves as YBK's city contact location. This office is linked by radio with YBK's secretariat, located at Cimekar village some 15–20 kilometres north-west of the city, off the road to Cirebon.

YBK's overall activities cover labour, housing, income generation, training, and education. A separate housing co-operative and general purpose foundation were set up as legally separate entities, although there has been a close interaction between them, with a substantial overlap of personnel on the boards of management of both. Staff have been primarily recruited from textile factories, where most of the villagers are still employed. A private company, PT Bina Karya, was subsequently established to handle fund-raising. It was also envisaged that this new company would have some involvement in building and subcontracting for YBK programmes, and possibly also operate further afield (Sjaifudian and Thamrin, 1989: 17).

The housing co-operative was founded in 1982. By 1989, 120 houses had been completed at Cimekar, with a further 200 planned or completed at three other sites (Sjaifudian and Thamrin, 1989: 9–10). YBK estimated a 50 per cent saving in costs by building co-operatively. The intention was for all occupants to eventually purchase their houses. However, recovery rates were reported at only around 60 per cent, with many workers experiencing low or irregular wages. In 1991, about 10 per cent of housing co-operative members were non-workers, including junior government officials, teachers, health workers, and even some students and journalists. The housing co-operative, as such, was only operating at Cimekar. In the other three villages, housing was merged with local co-operative units, with YBK only playing a facilitating and liaison role. In Majalaya, as an experiment, the programme was linked to the Village Cooperative Unit (Koperasi Unit Desa—KUD), as YBK considered the village head to be very positive in outlook and the KUD well managed.

Cimekar village has brick-built houses, compared with wood and bamboo at the other sites, where the workers are poorer and have fewer savings. Cimekar also has better overall facilities. A micro-hydro programme was installed, assisted by OXFAM and paid for by an additional monthly charge to co-operative members. The range of other services and enterprises appears comparable across the four villages. While decentralization has counterbalanced Cimekar's original advantage as the location for YBK's secretariat, some widening of the economic gap between villages seems to have occurred as some leaders and founding members of YBK in Cimekar have extended their economic activities to surrounding villages, working through co-operatives, other NGOs, and sometimes in a private capacity.

While YBK did not originally plan to reach out to non-worker families, this has certainly occurred as the organization grew and came into contact with farmers and other LSMs and LPSMs (Sjaifudian and Thamrin, 1989: 20). This has led to a healthy balance between co-operative and private enterprises. Its involvement with village and religious authorities has also brought significant improvements in basic services, such as local roads, clean drinking water, and health education. Sports for young people and entertainment for children are also organized during school holidays. While much of this activity is conducted in the vicinity of the four housing centres, particularly around Cimekar, YBK has been working since around 1990 with a local NGO in Cibuni, near Tasikmalaya, some 80 kilometres from Bandung, on a programme to provide clean drinking water. Young people are trained in organization and maintenance. In early 1991, a micro-hydro scheme was being planned in conjunction with the Village Community Resilience Institution (Lembaga Ketahanan Masyarakat Desa—LKMD), with financial assistance from the United States Agency for International Development (USAID) and the German Technical Co-operation Agency (German Technische Suzammen Arbeit—GTZ). Land had been purchased by workers on a government-owned tea estate. The head of the local estate workers section of the All-Indonesia Workers' Union (Serikat Pekerja Seluruh Indonesia—SPSI) was also the village head. Land was to be split up among workers according to capacity to pay, with funds for the land purchase to be collected through an arisan.[11]

In general, YBK and associated co-operatives appear to have achieved significant participation by workers and others in the communities where they have settled. Close feeling and sentiment, based on a shared history as workers and labour activists, provide a strong unifying bond within YBK, with discussion often said to stretch far into the night. Nevertheless, YBK decided to open their membership to other groups for fear of causing divisions in their neighbourhood, though current or former textile workers have retained a substantial majority. In the case of housing groups, initial contributions came from accumulated savings. Houses were built co-operatively, with discussion among members at each major stage of planning and construction. At Leuwigajah, Rp9 million was collected over nine months from sixty candidate members for land acquisition. Candidate members at Jelekong have frequently given free labour. Repayments are collected at weekends, thus bringing people together naturally for other social and informal purposes. Youth groups organize periodic working parties to clean up the neighbourhood. Neighbourhood watch arrangements are organized on a roster basis.

The embryo labour association initiated by YBK faces a more testing time as the organization becomes larger and more complex. Differences are understood to have arisen between yayasan and co-operative, members and leaders, as YBK leaders increasingly play multiple roles, which can lead to confusion and inadequate performance of some tasks. Such flexibility can be a matter of pride among YBK leaders, who liken themselves to a football team whose members are able and willing to play in all positions.

Women are considered an important target group by YBK. Quite a few women are textile workers, though their employment is irregular. While some have a background of militancy, overall awareness levels are uneven, despite the fact that most wives of workers are themselves former workers. YBK sees a need for all women to be supported in this regard, so that the imbalance in awareness between husbands and wives does not become an obstacle to struggle (Sjaifudian and Thamrin, 1989: 20–1). It was also hoped that, since men work longer factory hours, their wives would have more opportunities for local activities. Women have indeed been more active in enterprises than as workers. However, here also their level of involvement has varied, depending on the availability of other members of the family to look after children. YBK offers some labour training courses for women, but these have lacked continuity (Sjaifudian and Thamrin, 1989: 21). Entrepreneurship training has been provided for the wives of workers, but it has generally proven hard for factory workers, both male and female, to adapt to the quite different outlook and skills required as entrepreneurs. Despite their activism on the economic front, no women had been recruited to YBK staff up to that time (Sjaifudian and Thamrin, 1989: 77).

Despite these limitations, YBK has built up a core of activist women with knowledge of the factory system. Major problems reported to be confronted by women include sexual harassment in the workplace and the denial of leave rights for pregnancy and monthly periods. In one instance, YBK claims that the dismissal of Sri Sulastri, head of the women's section of PT Perintis Textil, was reversed due to its good offices. Sulastri subsequently initiated seminars for women workers, together with a counterpart from PT Naintex. Both have become leaders of YBK's informal women's group.

YBK considers that it has had less impact on labour issues, which provided its initial reason for existence, compared with its success in participatory group formation and in raising workers' living standards through income-generation and other practical programmes. Workers' bargaining power and, consequently, sense of effectiveness is weak. The excess supply of workers, due to urban migration from rural areas, pushes down wages. Apart from government suppression of free trade unions, most workers lack knowledge of the law. The large majority of cases taken up through legal channels are lost, and most of the rest are not won decisively.

Since the official trade union movement monopolizes the running of training courses for workers, it is necessary for YBK to work indirectly through its contacts there. It is also possible to disseminate information and skills through informal means. YBK has been criticized for seeming inactivity on the labour front, though such criticism seems unfair, given the constraints under which it operates. YBK's vigorous efforts to compensate, by concentrating on the economic front, raise more fundamental questions as to whether simultaneous promotion of labour solidarity and entrepreneurial skills and values will not, over time, produce an unsustainable dualism within the organization (Sjaifudian and Thamrin, 1989: 81). There are corresponding doubts whether it is possible for a labour movement to develop the kind of management and professional ethos required by YBK's growing business activities.

The account of YBK so far indicates a significant range of relationships with local government authorities. YBK also actively canvasses votes for the government-sponsored network of Functional Groups (Golongan Karya—GOLKAR) at election time. Government contacts are used judiciously to develop small business opportunities, as well as expand benefits and protection for co-operative members. Nevertheless, it seems clear that reciprocal favours accrue to villages and co-operatives far more than to leaders personally. According to their own account, leaders mostly work voluntarily for YBK, or are paid at nominal rates. They are therefore bound to work as farmers or in small businesses in order to provide a living for themselves and their families. Harsiji, the Foundation's senior chairman at Cimekar village, owned 0.25 hectare in Cilengkrang village, Ujung Benung sub-district, some 8–10 kilometres distant, where he was a member of the official KUD. This KUD advanced credit to farmers for the purchase of Jersey cows and appeared to be flourishing at the time of the author's visit in February 1988.[12] Harsiji considered the KUD to be well managed, as it was supported by an honest village head, and wanted to see a similar arrangement established at Cimekar.

If such extensive cultivation of government contacts appears opportunist, it should be borne in mind that permission to run training courses and other activities at village and neighbourhood level is essential if groups are not to operate as a secret meeting. Like LSP and many other NGOs, YBK lobbies at higher levels if obstructed lower down (Sjaifudian and Thamrin, 1989: 33–4). Local officials may not always realize this, and complain that YBK is casual about procedures, particularly when they are not informed about overseas visitors. On one occasion, neither the district nor village head knew that a Minister was arriving. Since then, YBK has been more careful to keep local authorities informed. However, housing and co-operative members have acted as a spur to their neighbours in improving neighbourhood security, health, and other services and in stimulating their village economies. The presence of YBK co-operatives has also probably speeded up village electrification. YBK has contributed to road repairs, and made its meeting centres available for government and community purposes.

Overall, the image of YBK's former workers has changed dramatically in the eyes of government officials, especially the Department of Manpower (Departemen Tenaga Kerja), from one of lowly *buruh* (labourer) and 'hostile' to one of 'businessman' and 'friendly' (Sjaifudian and Thamrin, 1989: 34–5). As further evidence of its favoured status, YBK has received a letter of authorization from the Ministers for Housing and Co-operatives to act as a general housing contractor. This was obtained despite strong opposition from real estate interests, the National Housing Corporation (Perusahaan Rumah Nasional), and the National Savings Bank (Bank Tabungan Negara) (Sjaifudian and Thamrin, 1989: 35).

YBK has participated formally in NGO networking through the West Java Regional Forum[13] and informally through Yayasan Mandiri's 'Coffee Shop'. This includes six LPSMs brought together at the initiative of a common donor called the German Appropriate Technology Exchange (GATE) (Sjaifudian and Thamrin, 1989: 25). Participants include Yayasan Mandiri, Yayasan Swadaya Muda, another group initiated by former students of the Bandung Institute of Technology, and Kelompok Studi Bantuan Hukum (Legal Aid Study Group) Yogyakarta, which share common interests in alternative technology and legal rights. After some initial enthusiasm, participation in networking appears to have lacked a clear focus and has become a burden to YBK leaders.

YBK has developed a strong profile of its own with foreign funding agencies, substantially superseding the LSP's intermediary role in this regard. In 1985, it won an award from UNICEF for its contribution in creating self-help projects. This led to a YBK leader from Cimekar village being invited to visit New Delhi for a conference co-ordinated by the People's Institute for Development and Training. Visitors and researchers frequently seek to visit YBK, which is widely considered to be a success story. A guest-house has consequently been established in each housing complex.

With regard to finance, YBK obtained and prepared land and built two houses from its own savings. Five were financed by GATE, plus another twenty-four from other agencies and a local private donor. The Dutch agency NOVIB then took over as the major foreign aid provider, and by 1985–6 was providing over 98 per cent of housing finance.[14] Finance took the form of soft loans rather than grants, which were only provided for community development programmes, representing around 20–25 per cent of total NOVIB assistance to YBK.

Plans were agreed through joint discussion between NOVIB, LSP, and YBK. NOVIB sent an evaluation team, but did not impose much by way of conditions. YBK has enjoyed a free hand in day-to-day management, but agrees broad criteria in advance with NOVIB on such matters as the choice of occupants and setting repayment instalments. NOVIB was mainly concerned to satisfy itself as to broad feasibility and benefits to target groups. Physical projects like housing are seen as an entry point towards the broader development of people's capacities. NOVIB eventually felt obliged to stand back, as it saw some of the differences over labour organization, mentioned earlier, emerging within YBK. Apparently, NOVIB felt some guilt for supporting too rapid growth, when the group formation process had not yet matured. LSP's weaning of YBK has also perhaps lacked adequate planning or anticipation of the range of tasks which the latter would have to assume from its own resources (Sjaifudian and Thamrin, 1989: 31–2).

Jakarta

In both Yogyakarta and Jakarta, street traders have proved flexible in adapting to a changing environment. In Jakarta, particularly, the role of informal sector markets has become, to a significant extent, complementary as well as competitive with that of department stores, with street traders handling much of the stores' surplus goods. Middle-class consumers, as well as the poor, use the informal sector, often preferring to trade off lack of service and guarantees for lower prices. However, the position of street traders will not remain viable without (i) policy intervention to regularize their legal position;[15] (ii) support programmes from both government and NGOs to raise the quality of their products and service, to educate street traders about their rights and responsibilities, and to develop their skills and resources, and (iii) self-organization to mobilize street traders' own resources, to identify common interests, and to develop their capacity to negotiate directly with the government, private sector, and other relevant interest groups.

The diffuse nature of the informal sector represents a major difficulty in achieving this last objective. While a common image of street traders is one of illiterate and impoverished migrants from rural areas, in larger cities, particularly, many street traders have quite high levels of education. In 1991, in an interview, the Association of Yogyakarta Street Trading Co-operatives estimated the education profile of its membership as only 5 per cent illiterate, most of whom were very old; 25 per cent primary school, 50 per cent lower secondary school; 15 per cent upper secondary school, and 5 per cent either graduates or drop-outs from university. In Jakarta, one LSP fieldworker with long experience of working with street traders in Jakarta, put the figure for upper secondary completion at 40 per cent, with many intellectuals and graduates also operating as street traders. He also claimed that most street traders in Jakarta are not poor, while only 10–15 per cent are local in origin. A large influx arrived from West Sumatra following the political upheavals there in 1957–8. Many others from throughout Indonesia, who had land and assets in their villages, came for political reasons due to some conflict with local authorities. Nevertheless, there appears to be considerable social stratification among street traders and in the informal sector generally, especially when more lowly placed groups such as *becak* drivers are taken into account. For this reason, there is always a danger of a 'labour aristocracy' emerging within co-operatives, or of their becoming a relatively privileged group collectively, since co-operatives still represent only a minority of informal sector workers.

By 1988, LSP had established thirty-two co-operative enterprise groups in Jakarta covering five areas, including twelve women's groups. However, most of the women's groups tended to be savings and loans (*simpan pinjam*) rather than full enterprise groups. Groups were organized across five areas of the city into informal sector centres. Units had become self-governing, with each centre organizing training, access to markets and credit, and liaising with other area centres. LSP has provided a political umbrella in relation to the registration of co-operatives and other major disputes, for example, over land and evictions.

An Overview of Lembaga Studi Pembangunan

Overall, LSP has been consistent in following through its initial basic insights. Groups in this survey, which it has supported, have developed an independent economic capacity, and have generally proven effective in negotiating with relevant local authorities. LSP's services are still required in dealings with the government at national level and, to some extent, with foreign funding agencies. A family spirit is in evidence between LSP and associated groups. However, independent groups of workers and street traders affiliated to LSP show little interest in its theories or broader vision of political change, being more concerned with immediate survival and with negotiating workable arrangements with the authorities. Nevertheless, a measure of struggle has been inevitable to gain practical benefits for diverse local groups, necessitating greater cohesion and mutual support among them. In that context, LSP's strategy of close interaction with the government at all levels has proved effective in achieving its original goals.

Lembaga Penelitian, Pendidikan, dan Penerangan Ekonomi dan Sosial

Lembaga Penelitian, Pendidikan, dan Penerangan Ekonomi dan Sosial (LP3ES)[16] emerged from a section of the 1966 generation of intellectual and student reformers, though its initial sources of support were more broadly based, both politically and academically. LP3ES was the creation of the Indonesian Association for the Promotion of Economic and Social Knowledge (Perhimpunan Indonesia untuk Pembinaan Pengetahuan Ekonomi dan Sosial—BINEKSOS), which was established in July 1970 with a wide-ranging brief to study social and economic trends in Indonesia and overseas. Its moving spirits included such luminaries as Dr Emil Salim, then deputy chairman of the National Development Planning Board (Badan Perencanaan Pembangunan Nasional—BAPPENAS), Prof. Soemitro Djojohadikusumo, Minister for Trade and later Research, Dr Ali Wardana, and Prof. Selosoemardjan. LP3ES was established in 1971 as the operating arm of BINEKSOS.[17]

Philosophy and Goals

The socio-cultural background of BINEKSOS and LP3ES can be seen as part of the broad tradition of modernist Islam, with some patronage from technocrats associated with the former Socialist Party of Indonesia

(Partai Sosialis Indonesia—PSI). Despite its secular and eclectic outlook, LP3ES's network of both past and present members and associates has extensive links with major facets of Islamic life in Indonesia. However, since modernization and democratization of Islamic institutions have always formed part of its mission, its role in this regard has not been free from controversy.

PSI and Islamic modernists had been the staunchest supporters of constitutional democracy under President Sukarno, and were clearly disappointed when the New Order under President Suharto retained key elements of the constitutional structure established under the previous regime. However, it would be wrong to depict the LP3ES group as merely seeking to replicate Western political and economic models in Indonesia. In any case, a more sobre and critical outlook towards such models soon emerged after the initial honeymoon under the new government, while a younger generation of intellectuals and activists introduced new influences into LP3ES during the 1970s and 1980s. Broadly democratic values have, nevertheless, been part of LP3ES's ethos from the outset, which it has sought to extend by pioneering strategies in a variety of grass-roots developmental contexts, supported by advocacy in government, academic, and professional circles.

While eclectic in drawing on overseas ideas, LP3ES has resisted an uncritical imposition of alien blueprints. Instead, it has sought for development models with a more popular and human face by (i) highlighting the potential for using indigenous skills and resources; (ii) placing greater emphasis on redistribution and targeting towards the basic needs of the masses, and (iii) developing strategies of popular participation for achieving these goals. Much of LP3ES's intellectual work is directed towards a search for more culturally authentic, less socially alienating and unequal modes of development, a more open polity, and a middle path between statist totalitarianism and the ultra individualism associated with the West. This latter theme has widespread currency among groups engaged in developing co-operatives, savings and loans programmes, and credit unions throughout Indonesia.

Organization

Initially, LP3ES's director and deputy director were responsible to the council (*dewan*) of BINEKSOS. The number of part-time and short-contract staff increased during the late 1970s as programmes and consultancies expanded, with new sections created, merged, or abolished accordingly. There is no clear hierarchy below the director, but only a division of functions. This can make for uncertainty as to who is to assume particular tasks. However, programme and section leaders meet in a weekly forum to co-ordinate and monitor operations, thus achieving a measure of informal internal democracy. Staff, former staff, friends, and supporters also meet fairly often for discussion and informal exchange. This forum structure provides the base for electing LP3ES's council, which appoints the director. The process appears to work on the basis of collective deliberation, rather than formal election. A strong tradition of periodically rotating the position of director has been developed—a rare phenomenon in the NGO community.

The quality of management and professionalism does not appear to have suffered, and may well have been enhanced as a consequence of such informal democracy. In any case, LP3ES staff have generally high educational qualifications, while a good deal of attention is paid to staff training. LP3ES conducts its own internal annual evaluations of programmes and staff, distinct from evaluations required by sponsors. Careful field-based research, analysis, and data storage have enabled LP3ES to accumulate a sound information base for decision-making. Conversely, accumulated knowledge across the LP3ES network is available to strengthen new programmes.

Activities

LP3ES's initial work focused on youth unemployment and the socio-economic consequences likely to result from a steeply rising rural workforce. Research and programmes were to be targeted primarily at youth, broadly defined as the 15–35 age-group, broken down into urban *kampung* dwellers, villagers, and the educated middle class, especially those with the potential and motivation to tackle poverty (Thamrin, 1989: 5).

After a few years, LP3ES was forced to move into survival mode by seeking out consultancies which allowed a proportion for administrative overheads to be charged. Research commissioned by the government gave scope for LP3ES input into official research agendas. Intellectual concerns were pursued through commercial publications. More idealistic projects, like student training, youth radio education, and journalism training, which were tried in a perfunctory way for a few years, were discontinued after 1978. Moving to new office premises also consumed significant time and money. As a consequence, not much community outreach occurred from 1976 to 1981. However, a major decision was taken during the survival stage after 1976 to consolidate around two programmes relating to (i) small industry and (ii) traditional Islamic educational institutions (*pesantren*). It was considered that geographical extension, based on a successfully pioneered model, would have more social impact, bring in more income, and give LP3ES a clearer identity. A strategy of networking between fieldworkers and part-timers in various locations strengthened the flow of ideas, sense of solidarity, and support for LP3ES.

Dawam Rahardjo, the director from 1980 to 1986, vigorously promoted the *pesantren* programme and consolidated the small industry programme. LP3ES moved to a more action-oriented stance in its cooperation with the government, signing a contract with the Public Works Department (Departemen Pekerjaan Umum) relating to water supply in seven provinces. LP3ES was made responsible for mobilizing water users' organizations among the target groups, including gaining their willingness to pay the necessary costs.

During the 1980s, LP3ES experienced strong competition from large research institutions and publishing companies. In response, it sought to seek a market for low-cost publications on challenging social themes. Under Aswab Mahasin, the director after 1986, LP3ES re-emphasized its intellectual role. *Prisma*, LP3ES's quarterly journal on social, economic, and political affairs, was further promoted as a significant public forum for exchanging often controversial ideas. An English edition was introduced. Contributions, drawn from within Indonesia and overseas, have maintained a critical, but mostly constructive, focus on trends within the country. LP3ES has also expanded its publication of original books and translations on many topics. While some discussion, especially in English translation, lacks sharpness and precision, a good overall intellectual standard has been maintained, given the restrictions on intellectual exchange on social and political matters which still prevail in Indonesia.

LP3ES's role in promoting dialogue between government and LPSMs concerning rationale and strategies for popular participation in national development was also given sharper focus under Mahasin. LP3ES increasingly offered policy advice, particularly in relation to small industry. Overall, the organization has come to see itself as competitive with commercial consultants in terms of its closer, albeit increasingly indirect links with community groups, cheaper rates, and capacity to integrate micro experience with macro analysis. Accumulated knowledge and experience have given LP3ES increasingly greater scope to negotiate terms of reference with the government.

The Small Industry Programme

The Small Industry Programme (Program Industri Kecil—PIK) began with the establishment of industry centres at Cirebon, for producing rattan furniture, and Klaten, for making clothes and handicrafts. In each centre, LP3ES's basic approach has been to (i) develop people's skills in specific fields; (ii) co-ordinate with government agencies over the delivery of supplies; (iii) invite the private sector to purchase the product, and (iv) gradually broaden the base of community development in the surrounding area, using groups formed in the initial process. Models have been developed in relation to co-operative structures, management, credit, and purchase of materials. From this experience, eight handicraft production centres were established in six provinces. As many foreign donors are willing to support these ventures, new opportunities emerge for export promotion. PIK has given LP3ES pioneer status in this field, leading to requests for collaboration from government, the private sector, and NGOs seeking to expand to other areas.

In an attempt to expand marketing outlets, LP3ES co-operated with other NGOs, notably Bina Swadaya, the Indonesian Council of Churches (Dewan Gereja-Gereja Indonesia—DGI), and the Indonesian (Catholic) Bishops' Conference (Majelis Agung Wali-Gereja Indonesia—MAWI), in founding the Association for Developing Indonesian People's

Handicrafts (Pengembangan Kerajinan Rakyat Indonesia—PEKERTI). LP3ES subsequently withdrew from this association, as it felt unable to take on such a specialized role. PEKERTI itself, after initial success, experienced significant marketing difficulties.

In 1985, a new body, the Association for Promoting Small Enterprise (Perkumpulan Untuk Pengembangan Usaha Kecil—PUPUK) took over much of PIK's work. The rest was devolved to LP3ES Klaten, leaving LP3ES free to concentrate on research, publications, and consultancies. Key individuals in the small industry programme moved to PUPUK, probably with some encouragement from LP3ES's major foreign sponsor, the Friedrich Neumann Stiftung (FNS), but this did not prevent LP3ES involving itself in a joint management team with LSP and the Jakarta city planning authorities for redevelopment of the Kemayoran airport area. Unfortunately, the involvement of NGOs in forming local groups seems to have occurred *after* the government had established a federation of co-operatives.

LP3ES Klaten

LP3ES's programme at Klaten, established in 1978, has included small industries, entrepreneurial training, household economy, and women's programmes (Sutrisno et al., c.1986). Co-operative units were linked in a federation called Bina Usaha, which formed part of LP3ES from 1978 to 1984. In this same period, Bina Usaha went through a semi-autonomous transition period, during which it still received management assistance. Since 1987, Bina Usaha has become completely autonomous, though it still remains informally part of the LP3ES family, enabling it to share information, skills, and experience.

By February 1991, Bina Usaha had established 53 units covering 793 small business people.[18] Only entrepreneurs are allowed to be members. LP3ES claims that democratic structures have been set in place, with annual meetings attended by unit representatives to receive reports and accounts, and to conduct triennial elections to the board of management. Nevertheless, LP3ES's reports have suggested some lack of drive in seeking alternative sources of capital. Bank Indonesia loans facilitated by LP3ES were reported to be encountering resistance, as many people were unwilling to pay 2 per cent per month.[19] Earlier government small credit schemes in this locality were suspended when repayments proved slow. Revolving credit schemes of the kind operated by Bina Swadaya have evidently not been tried. Marketing arrangements also appear weak, in that local traders have been employed without any obvious strategy of collective bargaining.

LP3ES has preferred to support co-operatives, as against individual entrepreneurs, in view of the latter's weak capital base. An Islamic model of profit-sharing is pursued in that LP3ES provides interest-free loans on the basis of sharing both profits and losses. Each individual enterprise takes 60 per cent, LP3ES 20 per cent, and Bina Usaha 20 per cent of profits. LP3ES shares losses on a 50 : 50 basis. However, there is a good deal of confusion as to whether base-level co-operative groups should consist only of poor people,[20] or be drawn from a mix of socio-economic groups. As a compromise, it was determined that 75 per cent would be selected from the poor and 25 per cent from the middle stratum, in the hope that such a mixture of classes would strengthen overall skills and capability (PPERT, 1986: 9–10; Richards, 1986: 4–5).

According to various reports prepared around 1986–7,[21] this theory does not seem to have been borne out in reality. Rather, groups appear to have been formed on the basis of shared ideology and friendship, with cadres chosen from among members. As a result, many groups were not being adequately integrated into the surrounding community environment. Many groups met infrequently, while there has been insufficient supervisory staff with an adequate range of skills to cover the number of people involved. The application of poverty criteria was also reported to be inconsistent. Often poor members did not receive their quota of training or attention, while available loan funds have tended to be used up before poorer groups were ready to benefit from them. Nevertheless, 60–90 per cent of a sample of participants surveyed reported overall benefits from group membership (Sutrisno et al., c.1986: 25). However, the same survey reported (pp. 39–45) wide variations in responses as to whether involvement in LP3ES's programmes had increased incomes and reduced economic burdens on families.

LP3ES has only involved itself in actual group formation to the extent of training and supporting cadres, who are meant to be selected, as far as possible, from poorer households. They are expected to have middle or senior high school qualifications, plus some community work experience. Cadres have frequently encountered negative attitudes from village officials. For example, if groups undertake activities which meet with disapproval, 'past history' can be brought up against them.[22] LP3ES has sought to defuse hostility from the authorities by emphasizing that the programmes are economic rather than ideological. Obstruction has also been experienced from village officials engaged in money-lending, though LP3ES claims that this has now been largely neutralized. LP3ES's intermediary role in obtaining protection from district and sub-district heads is thus crucial. It has also lobbied successfully to register co-operative associations against opposition from the KUD system.

Specific benefits to the poor from such co-operative enterprises may be questioned in relation to the kind of trade-offs experienced in this programme. There is, in any case, some contradiction between seeking to increase individual incomes, and overall improvement to the community as a result of group efforts. The emphasis on groups in preference to individual entrepreneurship has also been questioned. Channelling credit and technical assistance to groups does not always ensure that the necessary skills and outlook will be developed by individual entrepreneurs. Further, NGO staff often lack an understanding of the dynamics of small enterprises, and fail to conduct specific research into the technical, management, and marketing problems which small enterprises face (Strand and Fakih, 1984; Richards, 1986).

LP3ES Klaten has supported an extensive, mainly income-generating programme targeted toward women, the Productive Women's Programme (PWP), which will be discussed in Chapter 8.

The Pesantren Programme

In the mid-1970s, LP3ES sought to use its extensive links with local communities of traditional Islamic schools (*pesantren*) as an entry point for promoting more participatory approaches to social and economic development. Urban activists had, by then, become sharply aware of their lack of links with rural people, which they saw as weakening the support and legitimacy for their struggles to bring change at higher levels of politics and decision-making. They also hoped that mobilizing staff and students to promote change in surrounding communities would encourage the modernization of the *pesantren* themselves.[23]

Pesantren attract students from both urban and rural families from orthodox Islamic backgrounds, as well as others who want a more strongly focused Islamic education for their children. Since *pesantren* are mostly located in villages or small towns, opportunities exist for close interaction between students, teachers, and local people, with the latter often passing on their skills to students. *Pesantren* are led by *kyai*, who are often descended over several generations from the original founder of the institution.[24] *Kyai* have traditionally tended to specialize in some branch of Islamic learning. For the most part, they are held in considerable awe and esteem by both students and local people. *Pesantren* vary in their levels of female participation, and the extent to which female students are integrated or segregated within the institution.

LP3ES's work in *pesantren* has focused on building up skills and motivation among students and teachers to foster social development, both internally and in the surrounding community. Its programme began by training community extension workers at Pesantren Pabelan, near Yogyakarta, in 1977, who would return to their *pesantren* and train others. Several larger *pesantren* in Java, Madura, and Lombok have evolved as key centres for training and development of smaller neighbouring *pesantren*. Specialized courses are offered in line with needs defined by local groups. However, LP3ES acknowledges an initial tendency to predetermine needs and impose programmes, which it sees as an important reason for its lack of success in introducing appropriate technology. For example, exhibitions were arranged at several *pesantren* without offering locally field-tested examples, causing social workers to appear as executors of outside programmes.

As in other programmes, LP3ES uses pilot projects to develop local groups and cadres, which are organized into teams to spread community development ideas and skills in the surrounding area. Cadres are taught the basic research skills of gathering primary and secondary data. Reformers can draw on *pesantren* educational traditions which expect *santri* (male students) and *santriwati* (female students) to develop practically oriented skills in addition to religious education. Students are also allowed considerable scope to organize programmes and determine their own pace of learning. Employment opportunities for *santri* in the urban sector are necessarily limited, as *pesantren* education is not recognized by the authorities. This is partly offset by the establishment of a network of Islamic tertiary institutions. Many *santri*, therefore, expect to seek employment in rural areas and so are glad to develop relevant skills. Community development skills can also offer employment to students from rural backgrounds.

In 1983, *pesantren* participating in LP3ES's original programme set up their own Association for Pesantren and Community Development (Perkumpulan Pengembangan Pesantren dan Masyarakat—P3M). LP3ES and P3M have co-operated closely through training programmes, forums, and the distribution of each other's literature. P3M's *Pesan* magazine links participating *pesantren* with news and views. The rationale for P3M was, at one level, simply a recognition that participating *pesantren* were ready to operate their own network. More basically, it was anticipated that an organization of 'insiders' would be better able to integrate community development work with the life of the *pesantren* itself. While this has proved true, up to a point, underlying tensions between these two objectives have persisted. LP3ES later saw a need to emphasize developmental aspects in a new *pesantren* programme in Sumba and Lombok.

Significant conflicts can arise between *pesantren* and local authorities. Attempts to work within local Village Community Resilience Institution (Lembaga Ketahanan Masyarakat Desa—LKMD) structures have led to conflict in several places. At Cipasung, for example, they led to demands by the village government that it should control programmes on the grounds that it provides funds for many *pesantren* needs, even though the *pesantren* collects funds for such purposes from the villagers. This demand was deflected by the registration of a multi-purpose co-operative. Serious quarrelling also erupted at An-Nuqayah, Madura, after a village head took a prize awarded to the village in a local competition. The *pesantren* decided to avoid involving the government in future programmes (Sulaiman, 1985: 245–63).

At Kajen, where *pesantren* workers were active within the local LKMD structure, village leaders gave lip-service support only to their various project proposals. A delegation was sent to the district authorities at Pati. An investigation was conducted which resulted in the village authorities being forced to support effective functioning of the LKMD (Pesan, 1987a). Roads were subsequently built and the neighbourhood cleaned up, while thirteen savings and credit unions received Rp 50,000 from the village treasury. Later, *pesantren* social workers became members of LKMD boards of management in six villages. A parallel strategy was adopted by women fieldworkers in relation to both the government-sponsored Association for Promoting Family Welfare (Pembinaan Kesejahteraan Keluarga—PKK) and small, informal clubs and associations (*arisan*). More effective results have been claimed in those villages where such strategies were pursued (Pesan, 1987a). Village heads were subsequently more willing to acknowledge the effectiveness of the work of village fieldworkers, and less inclined to perceive *pesantren* activists as a source of political rivalry. They were later invited to extend their work to new villages (Pesan, 1987b).

In a broader context, networking among *kyai* through NU and other associations has enabled the *pesantren* movement to develop stronger dialogue with the government. NU's withdrawal from party politics in 1984, in order to concentrate on social and educational work, was influenced both by tactical considerations, notably the problem of how to respond to the 1985 Law on Social Organizations (Undang Undang Organisasi Kemasyarakatan—ORMAS) legislation, and internal debates concerning the relationship between Islam and the state. However, there has been growing recognition that the involvement of *pesantren* in grass-roots development has the potential to introduce a significantly new dimension in overall relations between Muslim groups and the Indonesian government.

Relations with the Government

LP3ES's relations with the Indonesian government have been extensive over the years, including co-operation with the Departments of Agriculture, Transmigration, Co-operatives, Trade, Manpower, Information, Home Affairs, and Religion, and with the Ministers of People's Housing and National Production. LP3ES has never adopted a stance of open or outright opposition towards the government, or denied the importance of its role in development. In many ways, it has played bureaucratic politics, cultivating an image of professionalism while seeking to influence both the general direction of Indonesian development and specific policies.

Essentially, LP3ES synthesizes lessons from the field, presents these to relevant authorities, and attempts to work out alternative models co-operatively. The quality of its management and research has raised its status in the eyes of the government, which, in turn, has come to recognize the value of LP3ES's community networking. LP3ES has used its good standing to improve the government's perception of the importance of people's participation. This seems to have been achieved without it being classified as an LPSM which needs watching. Its extensive government contacts enabled it to be perceived as neutral during conflicts between the Indonesian government and INGI in 1989 and 1992.[25] On the other hand, LP3ES's growing consultancy and intermediary roles have caused friction with LSM/LPSMs outside its network. Though by no means unique in terms of its extensive contacts and co-operation with the Indonesian government, LP3ES's intellectual approach to research, and discussion of issues, aggravates relations with other NGOs inclined to pursue more direct forms of advocacy, which also tend to see the information which LP3ES disseminates as more theoretical than action-oriented.

Funding

LP3ES's sources of income have become increasingly diversified, although the German foundation, Friedrich Neumann Stiftung (FNS) has, until recently, provided core support. During its early years, FNS gave sufficiently substantial assistance to LP3ES to enable it to concentrate on its work without spending time raising money (Thamrin, 1989: 5). In 1975, however, a timetable was agreed for progressively phasing out FNS aid by 1980. Under this agreement, FNS was not to interfere at an operational level, while LP3ES was free to contact other donors. A subsequent joint evaluation determined that such a phase-out was too drastic. Instead, FNS was to change its role from an institutional sponsor to one of assisting programmes. An independent consultant was appointed to assist LP3ES in developing a survival strategy. This led to a greater emphasis on income-earning activities, including publications and commissioned research for the government. The Small Industry Programme (Program Industri Kecil—PIK) was also seen as a potential source of income to LP3ES. FNS subsequently funded the English language edition of *Prisma*. Finally, the Society for Political and Economic Studies (SPES) was established to conduct more specialized forms of research.

Such efforts succeeded in reducing LP3ES's dependence on foreign aid, which in 1989 was estimated at between 30 and 40 per cent of total revenue.[26] A specific management allocation is received for managing block grants to other NGOs and small groups, so that it is not necessary to deduct from their allocation. Part of this payment is used in helping groups prepare their proposals and fulfil donor conditions, for example, by assisting with auditing and ongoing evaluation. It should be noted in that context that its quality of management and general reputation cause many donors to channel aid to other NGOs and target groups through LP3ES. Even the World Bank has sought to employ them as a channel for soft loans (Thamrin, 1989: 20). The annual block grant disbursed by LP3ES was around Rp15–20 million in 1989 (Thamrin, 1989: 26).

LP3ES was encouraged by foreign funding agencies to establish an NGOs' Consultant Team in order to perform these complex tasks. However, this set off a strongly negative reaction in the NGO community, and may well have provided the catalyst for the no confidence declaration at Baturaden in December 1990,[27] although this obviously reflected a broader spectrum of discontent. LP3ES disseminates publications on the theory and practice of participatory action research among the NGO community.[28] LP3ES's social capacity building is evidenced through its role in establishing three NGO networks—PEKERTI, P3M, and PUPUK—and in handing over responsibility for programmes, which it had initially pioneered, to these new bodies. Links with grass-roots groups are further maintained by sharing profits and losses with small enterprises. Finally, LP3ES was active in obtaining assistance from FNS and NOVIB to put P3M, the new *pesantren* and community development network, on its feet. This did not prove difficult, as the *pesantren* programme attracted substantial foreign funding from the outset.

An Overview of LP3ES Network

LP3ES fits broadly within the second model of 'High-level Politics–Grass-roots Mobilization', though with somewhat more emphasis on the former than the latter compared with LSP. Its rhetoric and styles of advocacy are also somewhat less confrontational and influenced by now dated neo-Marxist development theory. Its high-level contacts and intellectual standing have enabled it to retain a broader influence than most other NGOs, though it has paid some price in the form of suspicion by activists outside its own networks. LP3ES's intellectual impact has probably been greater among the professional middle class, with possibly far-reaching impact in that social group's perceptions of the needs and potential contribution of Indonesia's 'little people' (*rakyat kecil*). LP3ES has also contributed towards theorizing about the role of NGOs, although its impact has probably been greater on non-NGO audiences. The focus of LP3ES's programmes has been on social and economic development, rather than political reform. However, many publications which it sponsors examine basic questions relating to political structures and processes. No doubt its standing in the development sphere and its intellectual reputation allow space for such critical work. Styles of advocacy are similarly indirect, with LP3ES better placed than most to convey new insights to technocrats.

Reports cited indicate that LP3ES programmes have been generally successful in mobilizing participation among beneficiary groups, and in building up independent networks for information-sharing among them. However, women's participation does not seem to feature as a specific issue within the organization, although a limited number of women are in evidence at programme management, field staff, and village cadre levels. The involvement of women in social and income-generation programmes within the small industry and *pesantren* programmes appears to be along conventional lines.

There is little evidence of LP3ES's associated groups being involved in any wider popular mobilization, although a certain amount of general awareness-building and development education has occurred in *pesantren* and among some other groups with which LP3ES has been associated. In some areas, such as Klaten, which still bear many scars from the 1965–6 political upheavals, any large-scale mobilization would almost certainly produce serious clashes with the authorities. This approach has probably done a good deal to rehabilitate, as well as protect, the local population. The Klaten programme thus has some characteristics of the first model of 'High-level Co-operation–Grass-roots Development', rather than the second which characterizes LP3ES overall.

As evidence of the latter, the *pesantren* network can be seen as a form of popular alliance by providing an informal constituency and support base for broader agendas pursued by LP3ES and P3M. Mobilization by *pesantren* cadres in struggles with local government officials has been relatively successful in several instances. However, the realities of alliance-building at higher levels, as well as the effectiveness of local programmes, necessitate good relations with the *kyai*. Here, hierarchical structures within *pesantren* hold back the evolution of autonomous popular organizations at grass-roots level. LP3ES's and P3M's efforts could thus have the unintended effect of reinforcing the *status quo* in terms of the overall balance of forces bearing on the development of *pesantren*.

P3M, together with PEKERTI and PUPUK, offer examples of independent networks emerging from LP3ES's initial spadework in setting up the base from which they were built. At each stage, LP3ES has faced a problem of redefining its own special role. Currently, this takes the form of a shift back to intellectual and publication work. In time, this too may be taken over by its more specialized, now autonomous protégé, the Society for Political and Economic Studies, raising questions as to where LP3ES will derive the authentic field experience which has thus far sustained its wider reputation and influence.

Unlike many NGOs which talk vaguely about 'empowerment', LP3ES has successfully promoted and handed over responsibility for groups to self-managing federations which it has helped to build up. This very success seems to have left it rather footloose, as evidenced by the search for new intermediary and dialogue-promoting roles between the government, NGOs, and grass-roots groups (Thamrin, 1989: 17, 23–4). Although such dialogues could result in considerable social benefits, the example of the ill-fated NGOs' Consultant Team also indicates their capacity to invite suspicion. LP3ES as an institution seems to face choices between enjoying the role of benign patron, while relying on government and foreign funding agencies for its survival, or rejuvenating itself by fostering more small groups and undertaking new field programmes.

1. Translated as Institute for Development Studies. As the subsequent account indicates, LSP has never established a formal research institution and is primarily action-oriented.

2. See LSP (1983) for a general explanation of LSP theory and strategy in this field; see also LSP (1986a) for further details of its operational strategy.

3. See Sjaifudian (1989: 29–30) for a list of government agencies and authorities with which LSP had operational contacts in 1989.

4. See pp. 93, 180–1 for a discussion of P3M.

5. For example, Dawam Rahardjo, formerly chairman of LP3ES and one of its most prolific writers, was a foundation member of LSP's board of management.

6. See pp. 195–201.

7. Interview with LSP leaders in January 1991.

8. See pp. 125–6.

9. Information in this section is drawn from interviews at Cimekar village (1988) and Bandung (1988 and 1991); LSP (1986b and *c*.1987), and Sjaifudian and Thamrin (1989).

10. The workers indicated to the author that they had been dismissed for labour activism

11. Information in this paragraph is based on interviews with YBK in February 1991 and Sjaifudian and Thamrin (1989: 21–4).

12. Net profits of around Rp80,000–100,000 per month (then worth around US$ 50–65) were claimed by KUD members at Cilengkrang.

13. See pp. 144–5, 206–7.

14. LSP sources.

15. See Jellinek (1991) for an account of the destructive effect on street traders of the uncontrolled development of shopping complexes, and negative or indifferent official attitudes towards their fate.

16. The literal translation is 'Social and Economic Research, Education, and Information Institute'. However, as the subsequent account will indicate, LP3ES's role extends across a far broader spectrum of action than research and education.

17. See Thamrin (1989: 4) for details of LP3ES's origins.

18. LP3ES Klaten sources, February 1991.

19. Ibid.

20. Poor groups targeted were defined as those earning less than Rp1,000 per month, lacking in permanent employment, having access to less than 0.25 hectares of land, petty traders, farm labourers, and those living in houses lacking permanent structures, with bamboo walls and earth floors (PPERT, 1986: 8).

21. Sutrisno et al. (c.1986: 39–45), PPERT, and LP3ES Klaten sources.

22. The Klaten and Boyolali areas experienced substantial PKI activity during the late Sukarno years, with consequent heavy reprisals from the military in 1965–6, and in subsequent security crack-downs.

23. More general issues relating to the role of *pesantren* in development, together with religious and structural aspects, will be taken up in Chapter 9.

24. See Dhofier (1982) for detailed studies of *pesantren* and the role of *kyai*.

25. See pp. 198–200.

26. Thamrin (1989: 23, 26) mentions 30 per cent on p. 23 and 40 per cent on p. 26. The latter figure appears swollen, as it includes block grants which LP3ES channels to other NGOs.

27. See Kelompok Pinggiran (1988); Thamrin (1989: 27), and pp. 39–40.

28. The Indonesian Action Research Network publishes the periodical *Alternatif* from LP3ES's Jakarta office.

6
Legal, Human Rights, and Labour Groups

THIS chapter will consider major groups and networks operating in the field of legal and human rights, together with issues relating to labour relations. Reference will also be made to land and environment struggles, though the latter are mostly covered in Chapter 7. National-level analysis will be supported by regional perspectives from West Java and Yogyakarta. The chapter will conclude with some discussion of programmes for the rehabilitation of political prisoners in Yogyakarta and Central Java. These latter programmes operate along more charitable and welfare lines, with few apparent links with the mainstream of legal and human rights organizations, due no doubt to the extremely sensitive environment surrounding former political prisoners.

Most groups and networks working in the human rights field combine elements of the second and third models, proposed in Chapter 2, in shaping their relations with the Indonesian government and approaches to the political process. In recent years, they have been challenged by groups operating from a more radical frame of reference. Nevertheless, despite sharp differences in outlook, there has also been a good deal of mutual support across the field as a whole. Of necessity, all human and legal rights groups operate at the 'sharp end' of the Indonesian state's legal and security apparatus, and have found fewer opportunities than other self-reliant community institutions (Lembaga Swadaya Masyarakat—LSM) and institutions for developing community self-reliance (Lembaga Pengembangan Swadaya Masyarakat—LPSM) to mix legal and political struggle with conventional-style development activity. While a strong nexus has been forged at the radical end of the spectrum between awareness of legal and human rights and developmental perspectives, particularly in relation to land, labour, and environmental issues, legal and human rights education has not yet been effectively integrated into the mainstream of community development and training activities of LSM/LPSMs.

The Foundation of Indonesian Legal Aid Institutions

The best-known organization in the field of legal aid is the Foundation of Indonesian Legal Aid Institutions (Yayasan Lembaga Bantuan Hukum Indonesia—YLBHI). YLBHI originated from the Jakarta-based Legal Aid Institute (Lembaga Bantuan Hukum—LBH), founded in 1971. YLBHI has subsequently linked up with a network of affiliated organizations in many major cities, which, in turn, have fostered local posts in smaller towns and villages. YLBHI has subsequently evolved into an umbrella organization facilitating mutual support, channelling resources, and providing training and other facilities. Affiliated groups operate their own programmes, while YLBHI appoints local directors and plans the overall use of resources. The board of YLBHI, consisting of prominent legal and other personalities, appoints the executive director. Local directors have access to the board, but affiliates, as such, are not represented. As noted earlier, this type of informal, relatively undemocratic structure, is common among LPSMs. YLBHI considers such an arrangement essential in order to avoid co-option by the government, and as providing protection in an uncertain legal and political climate.

LBH began from a very limited concept of legal aid. However, it was never intended that this should constitute the main thrust of its work. Rather, it was to be seen as an entry point into far broader efforts at legal education and awareness-building. Legal aid has, nevertheless, retained a significant place, as it brings contact with a wide cross-section of people and problems, provides legitimacy in relations with the government, and earns income to sustain the Institute's overall work. People are charged according to their means, with better-off clients subsidizing the less affluent.

While political education has never formally been part of LBH's or YLBHI's agenda, most legal rights activists have recognized that the reform of legal processes and structures would be difficult, if not impossible, to achieve without political reform, particularly in relations between the military and civilians, and the executive, legislature, and judiciary. In technical jargon, the issue of litigational versus structural legal aid has been one of the most persistent and difficult to resolve within YLBHI (Lev, 1987: 19). Major differences also persist among those seeking change; between reformists, who emphasize regularization of legal processes, and radicals, who argue that legal equality will remain an impractical ideal unless gross imbalances in wealth and power are corrected. YLBHI has sought to reconcile these two positions by establishing a human rights division, which has undertaken extensive social and economic research, which YLBHI aims to integrate with its legal education and action programmes.[1]

YLBHI's work has attracted fewer patrons and protectors in high places compared with other LPSMs in the second category. Its closest high-level contacts have tended to be with dissenting elements, notably among the Petition of Fifty group. YLBHI received substantial assistance during its formative years from the Jakarta regional government, when Ali Sadikin was Governor. However, this did not inhibit it from supporting struggles against evictions of squatters during his tenure of office. Jakarta authorities continued to provide financial assistance after Sadikin's retirement in 1977, though on a less generous scale, until 1986 when it was cut off.

YLBHI has pursued different strategies in urban compared with rural areas, based on different social contexts and perceived needs. In rural areas, YLBHI sees key concerns as centring on land tenure and the arbitrary behaviour of local police and military authorities. Both urban and rural people suffer loss and disruption as a result of resumption of land by state authorities for public or semi-private purposes (Lucas, 1992: 79–92). Key conflicts in the cities centre on the status of informal sector small traders, labour rights, wages, and conditions.

YLBHI commonly makes contact at village level through informal leaders, many of whom play some guidance role in government programmes. Sympathetic leaders are brought together for courses run by YLBHI affiliates at regional centres. While it could be objected that such persons form part of the village élite, who are therefore locked into political-cum-patronage arrangements with the governmental power structure, village authorities commonly lack the resources and personnel to handle the many programmes imposed on them from higher levels, and are often glad to accept voluntary assistance. Schoolteachers, for example, are extensively involved in such programmes due to their social status and capacity to communicate with different groups.

YLBHI has placed pressure on the government to implement existing labour laws and interpret them consistently. Such efforts are often unsuccessful, but considered useful as a means of public awareness-building. For example, in 1988, the Central Labour Arbitration Committee (Panitia Perselisihan Perburuhan Tingkat Pusat) resolved to ask PT Elbiru to reinstate workers striking over a dismissed labour leader. This decision was overruled by the Minister of Labour, who refused to specify his reasons despite a law which states that the committee's decision can only be overruled for major reasons of public order and national security. YLBHI took the case to court, but their plea was dismissed on grounds of national policy.[2]

Legal certification of ownership rights has gained greater importance throughout Indonesia with the expansion of capitalist development, for example, as a precondition for bank loans. Much land has been held on a traditional basis over many generations, and such demands commonly cause distress and a sense of outrage. Necessary documentation must be obtained from village and sub-district authorities, thus enhancing their power. In any case, records may not be easily available. A possible interim solution being explored is for LPSMs to act as guarantors for bank loans to be channelled to small farmers, thus bypassing demands for such documentation. Such arrangements are linked to the formation of self-help groups (Bank Indonesia et al., 1987; Bank Rakyat Indonesia, 1987).

As in the case of small stallholders and hawkers discussed in the previous chapter, conflict between tricycle passenger vehicle (*becak*) drivers and local authorities is also rife in many cities. For example, plans were announced in 1988 to drastically reduce the number of *becak* in Bandung. Since then, authorities have imposed heavy fines for minor legal infringements, frequently confiscating *becak*. However, public demand for *becak* services is still strong, including demand from middle-class residents, especially women and children. Some non-government organizations (NGOs), notably the Bandung Legal Aid Institute (LBH Bandung), have played an intermediary-cum-advocacy role with the authorities, at the same time educating *becak* drivers to understand and, as far as possible, obey the constantly changing traffic regulations. Additionally, informal co-operative small enterprises, linked to appropriate training programmes, have been formed. However, as elsewhere, organizing *becak* drivers has proved difficult due to the high occupational turnover.

These various examples indicate a shift in emphasis to legal education and empowerment, which has become more explicit since around 1988. YLBHI's current policy focuses on four main areas: (i) conflicts over land and more general arbitrary behaviour by local and military author-ities in rural areas; (ii) labour issues; (iii) environmental destruction entailing loss of people's amenities and livelihood, with an emphasis on applying existing laws and procedures more strictly, and (iv) political prisoners (*tapol*), including those labelled as criminals for engaging in political activities. Specific emphases are decided by local and regional affiliates. As YLBHI is unable to cover all these fields itself, it is neces-sary to develop people's human resources in the legal field. This, too, is a slow process. For example, LBH Bandung has only three staff and an uncertain number of volunteers. The choice of activities tends, con-sequently, to be reactive and *ad hoc*.

YLBHI's goal of changing national policy, the legal environment, and structure, in line with its ideals of a society based on the rule of law (*negara hukum*), aligns it basically with the second model linking a high political profile with grass-roots mobilization. However, YLBHI's associ-ation with many smaller LSMs and informal groups, which limit contact with the state and concentrate on popular empowerment through dis-semination of legal knowledge and skills, indicates openness towards the third model.

YLBHI's stance towards the government appears more oppositionist compared with many NGOs in the second category. Thus, its board of trustees includes prominent legal and human rights campaigners, with the Petition of Fifty group well represented.[3] YLBHI does not operate devel-opmental work of a kind which would bring it into a regular co-operative, problem-solving relationship with the authorities, and which might serve to mediate other areas of conflict. The nature of its work and the realities of Indonesia's institutional structures push it towards the radical end of the NGO spectrum. Even YLBHI's bread-and-butter work in legal aid is seen by its founder, Adnan Buyung Nasution, 'as the cutting edge of a movement to reconstitute the Indonesian state' (Lev, 1987: 20). Thus, legal aid is intended to serve as an entry point to wider legal education, both about existing rights and, because such rights are limited, the need for changes in the law itself. In this regard, YLBHI, along with the Indonesian Advocates' Association (Persatuan Advokat Indonesia—PERADIN), had some influence on the new criminal justice procedures introduced in 1981 (Lev, 1987: 34). YLBHI was active in persuading the government to include habeas corpus provisions into this legislation. While implementation remains a major problem, YLBHI considers that this reform provides it with a legal basis from which to work.

YLBHI's perceived oppositionist stance has evoked various kinds of negative response from the government. Apart from periodic attacks on its financial sources, YLBHI has become concerned with the proliferation of legal aid organizations in recent years, notably within government agencies and para-statal bodies. In late 1990, the government formed the Legal Aid Federation (Federasi Bantuan Hukum—FBH). YLBHI sees this as a potentially damaging political move against it, and has considered possible name changes to make the distinction clear.

As will be discussed in this chapter, local land, labour, and environmental issues have come to represent focal points in struggles for legal rights. In the process, there has been a growing awareness that education on legal rights can be an effective tool in broadening people's understanding of their social and economic struggles. This appears to have shifted YLBHI's overall strategic emphasis towards a belief that individual legal rights can only be realized by the mass of Indonesians within the context of social and economic rights.

Heri Ahmadi, who spent two years in gaol in the late 1970s for his part in student protest movements in Bandung, has dissented from this emerging conventional wisdom.[4] He opposes the view that economic empowerment is a prerequisite for social and political empowerment on the grounds that, in Indonesia, economic as well as all other institutional structures are set up in such a way as to reinforce governmental powers. This has the effect, he argues, of depoliticizing and de-ideologizing every aspect of society. He therefore concludes that human rights activists must place their first priority on asserting the political and legal rights of individuals, rather than seeking to achieve these indirectly through social and economic campaigns.

To this end, Ahmadi took a leading role in establishing the Human Rights Information and Study Network (Informasi dan Studi untuk Hak Asasi Manusia—INSAN) around 1986. INSAN had a loose affiliation with Lembaga Studi Pembangunan. The organization attracted some attention from the security forces during student demonstrations in December 1987. INSAN established a database in order to support legal, human rights, and associated struggles in Indonesia, networking with parallel groups in neighbouring South-East Asian countries. This project appeared to lose momentum after Ahmadi's departure for study in the USA in 1989.

The synthesis between legal, socio-economic, and economic rights appears to have reached a high point in June 1993 with the Joint Declaration on Human Rights signed by 52 NGOs and NGO networks and 109 individual activists. YLBHI played an active role in drafting the statement. It stated, *inter alia*, that 'Human Rights are often formulated in terms of civil and political, social, cultural and economic rights. In reality, there is no dichotomy between these rights. All ... should be viewed as a whole and as being indivisible. Any trade off of such rights ... is unacceptable' (IN-DEMO, 1993: 1). The statement, as will be discussed,[5] was drawn up in the context of a strong attack by several Asian governments on the universal validity of the United Nations Charter on Human Rights, and therefore it represented, in part, a defence against the argument that legal and individual rights could be overridden by state-defined imperatives of economic development. In that context, the NGOs' statement affirmed the individual as the subject rather than object of development.

Signature of this document by both radical and mainstream legal and human rights groups appeared to represent a potential convergence between them, set against the background of conflict described in this chapter. However, such trends may have received a set-back by upheavals within YLBHI during 1993, as NGOs in Bandung, Jakarta, and Yogyakarta, with whom YLBHI has co-operated in various campaigns, demanded democratization of its structures (Thompson, 1993). Specific demands included the direct election of YLBHI's board of trustees, closer links between its members and activists on the ground, and improved networking. They felt that YLBHI's goals should be defined more systematically towards democratizing Indonesian society, than in reacting to events on a case-by-case basis.

While most YLBHI leaders responded positively to such demands, several influential activists, among them H. J. Princen, saw dangers of outside interference, and hinted strongly at the importance of maintaining YLBHI as a foundation rather than a membership-based organization. The use of this tactic as a device to avoid the provisions of the 1985 Law on Social Organizations (Undang Undang Organisasi Kemasyarakatan— ORMAS), and other forms of co-option by the government, has been noted in earlier discussion.[6] On the other hand, YLBHI's dilemma here dramatically illustrates the limitations on internal democratic processes which this approach entails. YLBHI has sought to respond to the various demands by restoring Adnan Buyung Nasution, widely respected by both older and younger activists, as head of its board of trustees, expanding the board, and replacing older members with younger activists from local affiliates (Thompson, 1993: 8–9).

Radical Networks

The LBH network has been complemented and, at times, challenged by a loose network of radical groups and organizations in the legal and human rights field, which have concentrated on mass mobilization and generally adopted a more confrontational stance towards the authorities. Though willing to use legal arguments and precedents as convenient, they see these as secondary to political struggle. However, there is a convergence of views between YLBHI and some radicals in so far as both place importance on international opinion.

The longest established legal and human rights organization in this group is the Institute for Defence of Human Rights (Lembaga Pembela Hak-Hak Asasi Manusia—LPHAM). LPHAM preceded YLBHI, having been founded in April 1966 by Haji Princen.[7] According to Princen, LPHAM was founded as a reaction to the violation of human rights under President Sukarno's Old Order. Buyung Nasution, the first chairman of LBH, was a member of LPHAM. The two organizations have cross-representation on each other's board of trustees. LPHAM, in many ways, plays an intermediary role between YLBHI and emerging, younger radical groups.

LPHAM's relations with YLBHI appear to have been characterized by both friendly disagreement on tactics and, to some extent, philosophy, side by side with co-operation based on an informal division of labour. Thus, YLBHI works painstakingly within the system, taking up legal cases, researching, and citing laws, regulations, and precedents in its presentation of cases. LPHAM, in contrast, speaks out more strongly and openly and, according to its own account, sees international public opinion as its prime audience. In that context, it sees YLBHI's legal spadework as a valuable resource in gaining support, for which it is necessary to demonstrate that all legal avenues within Indonesia have been exhausted. Even in the domestic context, LPHAM sees court cases as valuable in gaining publicity. While the local press may not print full reports, indirect Javanese-style signals will be conveyed. Besides, whether a case is lost or won, the older generation of Indonesian human rights activists, represented by the founders of YLBHI and LPHAM, stoically insist on the necessity of performing one's duty by bringing all facts into the open. Only in this way will it be possible to win the 'verdict of history'.

LPHAM co-operates rather more with younger radicals than YLBHI, though both provide some protection for them. Ultimately, though LPHAM sees political value in using the state's laws against the state, it has little expectation of success through legal means, due to the Indonesian judiciary's lack of independence. Essentially, LPHAM agrees with the radical groups in seeing political struggle as the key to change. LPHAM is in close contact with the Indonesian Front for the Defence of Human Rights (INFIGHT), which emerged during the 1980s. INFIGHT overlaps a good deal in membership and operation with the Indonesian Network for Forest Conservation (Sekretariat Kerjasama Pelestarian Hutan Indonesia—SKEPHI).[8] Both groups have worked closely with students, farmers, workers, women, and other activist groups in various provincial and local struggles.

LPHAM finds broad agreement with the INFIGHT network in opposing foreign aid in all forms. Both have consequently opposed efforts by the International NGO Forum on Indonesia (INGI) to improve aid quality through negotiation with international donors. YLBHI plays a leading role in INGI which, as will be discussed in Chapter 10,[9] has forged increasingly strong co-operation between Indonesian and overseas NGOs. LPHAM's style, however, is less strident than that of other radical groups in its relations with INGI and YLBHI. Rather, it is more along the lines of 'agreeing to disagree'. Moreover, while LPHAM and YLBHI differ on tactics, they are both strongly committed to international standards as laid down in the United Nations Charter of Human Rights, and so in placing a strong emphasis on legal and political rights. INFIGHT is more inclined to stress economic rights and class struggle. It sees legal and political rights more as an instrument of struggle, and has, therefore, not endorsed the UN Charter. In this context, although their views and agendas are no doubt anathema to one another in most respects, it is possible to see a curious convergence between the negative outlook of both the Indonesian government and its radical critics, in their opposition to Western-oriented liberals, who are portrayed as giving higher priority to individual political and legal rights than to social and economic improvement of the masses.

Relations between LPHAM and the INFIGHT–SKEPHI network can be partly understood in terms of generational differences. Thus, LPHAM feels some frustration with what it considers as a lack of organization and the gung-ho styles of decision-making—though, in that context, it should be noted that SKEPHI, in particular, appears well endowed in terms of its computer networking and the quality of its publications. Like more traditional NGOs, radical networks avoid formal membership lists and make decisions through forums open to their sympathizers. While discussion is both intense and extensive, decisions and action plans appear to emerge by consensus, rather than through any formal rules or meeting structures. Indeed, spontaneity is stressed as a prime virtue in contrast to the bureaucracy of established LPSMs.

The INFIGHT–SKEPHI network's orientation towards the political process is unclear. Certainly, they condemn the present political structure, particularly the military's dual-function role, and the suppression of popular organizations, in unambiguous terms. They paint an equally stark picture of the effects of official economic strategy, and what they see as its international support base, in marginalizing and impoverishing the Indonesian masses. However, the alternatives which they advocate are less clear. On the one hand, they take a strong line on the right to organize, vigorously asserting that this right already exists under Article 28 of Indonesia's 1945 Constitution. On the other hand, they express a generally negative outlook towards the values of liberal democracy and constitutional strategies of all kinds. In some ways, younger radicals reflect the third model proposed in Chapter 2, in that they do not seek to co-operate with or influence government policy in any way other than through mass action. Indeed, group formation and mass action seem, at times, to be promoted as ends in themselves without any obvious vision as to how these might ultimately have an impact on the macro political process.

In terms of the earlier discussion of different understandings of democracy, the radicals can be placed as broadly within the tradition of poeple's sovereignty (*kedaulatan rakyat*).[10] While this term has been incorporated into official discourse, linked to popular participation, within the framework of Panca Sila democracy it also carries quite different populist and leftist connotations. Consequently, its unauthorized use as a vehicle for popular mobilization invites classification as 'communist', or some other form of subversive element, by the authorities. Radicals, therefore, see it as more politic to refer to 'human rights' in seeking legitimacy for mass action.

In organizational terms, the new radicals cannot simply be labelled as some kind of pre-party formation, since there has been little evidence of any strategy or coalition-building aimed at gaining political power. Indeed, they manifest some definite distaste for power-seeking. Similarly, since formal organization, rules, and procedures are a necessary part of any constitutionally based system of representative democracy, the radicals' lack of interest in such a reform agenda, in line with their stated preference for spontaneity, should cause no surprise.

Advocates of constitutional reform along Western lines tend to be depicted by radicals as part of the dominant élite. In reality, such reformists have always been a minority in Indonesian politics, and are constantly under attack from both conservative and radical ends of the spectrum. Ironically, there is a convergence, albeit from opposite directions, between radicals and the Indonesian government in objecting to a limited legal and liberal democratic view of human rights, independent from specific social and economic contexts. Nevertheless, several radical groups were associated with the NGOs for Democracy declaration cited above, which asserted the indivisibility of human rights and expressed scepticism towards selective government rhetoric equating dissent with negative cultural influences from the West.

The most important difference between the current wave of radical activists and the mainstream of the LSM/LPSM movement lies in the radicals' willingness to actively confront the authorities. This can be seen in the number of groups willing to make strong public statements and demonstrate in national and provincial capitals, and the range of issues they are willing to take up. While conflicts over land alienation and environmental destruction, and the rights of workers and urban *kampung* dwellers predominate, broader political issues, such as the Gulf War and military killings in East Timor, have also been pursued.

The authorities' response has varied, though in most cases local groups have borne the brunt of harassment, detention, and even torture. At national level, the INFIGHT–SKEPHI group has developed a tactic of informing the media in advance of its intention to hold a demonstration for which, on principle, it refuses to seek permission. Requests to go to a military office are refused if no warrant is produced, as occurred on the occasion of Japanese Prime Minister Kaifu's visit in 1989, when a demonstration was planned. It is believed that this more direct approach provides a greater measure of protection. However, Haji Princen, convenor of LPHAM, and Indro Tjahjono,[11] convenor of the INFIGHT and SKEPHI networks, were both subjected to intensive interrogation following a demonstration in Jakarta protesting against the killings in Dili, on 12 November 1991.

Perhaps the greatest single contribution by the new radicals has been to challenge the conventional wisdom among activists concerned with human rights and people's development that, even though the legal basis of many bans on organization and meeting in Indonesia may be dubious, outright dissent or direct challenge to the government is impossible without support from at least some elements within the military. In the sense of overthrowing the government, this is still undoubtedly the case. However, a range of protest actions on social and economic issues has produced an inconsistent response from the authorities. This suggests that the apparatus of repression is less than monolithic, with specific responses depending on the combination of forces involved in particular disputes, and the style of protest pursued. Radical leaders stress the opportunities opening up as a result of intra-élite conflict. They chide mainstream NGOs for their unwillingness to use these for purposes of mass mobilization, attributing their caution to fear, the desire for institutional survival, a conservative outlook, and the involvement of some NGO leaders in various power plays.

The differences between YLBHI and the radicals may have narrowed since YLBHI adopted a more explicit policy stance around 1988–9, emphasizing its support for struggles over land, labour, environment, and prisoners classified as criminals, but whom YLBHI regards as political cases. Differences over the value of taking cases to court remain, together with suspicion on the part of younger radicals that such action represents a way of avoiding more dangerous forms of confrontation with the authorities. Tensions persist in relation to alleged 'claiming of credit' for popular action by the INFIGHT–SKEPHI group. However, common involvement in various struggles has led to a sharing of information and experience, and seemingly some cautious mutual respect. By contrast, relations between the INFIGHT–SKEPHI group and most Jakarta-based LPSMs are very negative. There are corresponding tensions in the provinces, except in specific local instances where there may be experience of working together. Generally, the NGO community tends to regard the radicals as too strident, sweeping, and dogmatic in their denunciations and prescriptions, while their respective analyses of the nature and purpose of popular group formation remain poles apart.

These various themes, together with patterns of co-operation and conflict among legal and human rights groups, will be illustrated with reference to struggles in the fields of land, labour, and environment, followed by a more local focus on the Yogyakarta region and some regions of Central Java.

Labour Organization and Rights

Relatively little attention has been paid by most NGOs, at least until quite recently, to issues of labour rights and organization compared, for example, with the effort they have put into the informal sector and small co-operatives. Given the growth in Indonesia's labour force relative to employment opportunities (Manning, 1988; 1989), these latter represent one potential strategy for absorbing the surplus labour force. However, poverty and exploitation of both urban and rural workers[12] should also represent a cause for concern in terms of NGOs' proclaimed concern with 'the poorest of the poor'.

In terms of ideological principle, at least, unions can be seen as voluntary, non-profit, and self-help associations which aim to empower people, although, historically, unions in the Third World have tended to be the creation of parties or broader national-cum-social movements. This has been basically true in Indonesia also, although once established, both unions and various groups of workers have manifested significant capacity for independent action.[13] In Indonesia, they have been mostly, though not exclusively, associated with the left parties (Mortimer, 1974). In any country, notions of workers' rights are closely linked to the functioning of business and the state at the macro level. NGOs have consequently found it difficult to accept trade unions as non-political, even in a limited non-party sense. However, there is no reason in either principle or practice why labour associations cannot be created independently from party affiliation.

Most LSM/LPSMs currently see their choice of action as lying between co-operating with a state-controlled monopoly trade union, and creating small informal associations of labourers in the guise of LSMs or co-operative enterprises. While the latter have been created among target groups of workers, they are strictly off-site from factories, and their activities structured to provide either additional or alternative sources of livelihood, as in the case of Yayasan Bina Karya discussed earlier.[14] Low-level co-operation has been established between some officials in the government-sponsored All-Indonesia Workers' Union (Serikat Pekerja Seluruh Indonesia—SPSI), YLBHI, and associated legal rights groups. There have also been attempts by SPSI officials, particularly in the Women's Section,[15] to create NGO-type structures within SPSI in order to escape from their own organizational strait-jacket.

LSM/LPSMs have probably also been slow to accept a role in supporting the development of labour associations because of their focus on rural areas, where most of Indonesia's population and poverty are still located, and which most accounts of Indonesian development see as relatively neglected in official allocations and policy-making. They have, consequently, been slow in coming to terms with rapidly accelerating urbanization and industrialization. The urban programmes of NGOs are still concentrated on small enterprises in the informal sector, plus some public health and education programmes. Nevertheless, as B. White (1989: 12–14) has argued, it is unreasonable to expect that the majority of peasants and workers in any country will become entrepreneurs. Since industrialization trends and policies are established facts, he sees an urgent need for NGOs to address issues relating to the working conditions and employment opportunities of millions of Indonesians.

There has, nevertheless, been evidence of interest in this area by NGOs since the mid-1980s, stimulated by two main factors. First, deregulation policies have brought in a rapid flow of foreign investment, much of it from the newly industrializing economies of East Asia. Many companies pay very low wages and fail to observe even minimum legal conditions for workers. Indonesia's official trade union system has been widely blamed for their non-enforcement. Secondly, the creation of SPSI, following the restructuring of the former Federation of Indonesian Trade Unions (Federasi Serikat Buruh Indonesia—FSBI) in 1985, caused considerable discontent among many existing and former unionists who were left out in the cold (INDOC, 1986: 15–18; INGI, 1991b: 2–4).

The new structure was very much the creation of Security Chief, Admiral Sudomo. As the government has sought increased flows of foreign investment to speed Indonesia's industrialization, so it has been more and more concerned to keep a still tighter rein over labour activity. Though obviously part of the government-sponsored network of Functional Groups (Golongan Karya—GOLKAR), the old FSBI was a federation of industrial unions with a moderate degree of autonomy at enterprise level. It also retained some sense of industrial identity compared with the new corporatist creation. Many positions were eliminated in the more unified and centralized SPSI. The organization of SPSI on the basis of economic sectors rather than industry groupings has made association between factory-based units more difficult.

The term *pekerja*, which replaced *buruh*, can mean either worker or employee. However, *buruh* was felt to have leftist political connotations and to be more specifically associated with 'blue-collar' industrial labour. Sudomo also considered the term *buruh* as implying opposition to the government, more in line with liberal capitalism than Panca Sila democracy.[16] Naturally, this has left some sense of discontent among those concerned to emphasize the needs and identity of industrial workers. Various displaced unionists established labour-oriented LSM/LPSMs, which eventually formed the nucleus for a rebel union called Serikat Buruh Setia Kawan.[17]

During the 1980s, YLBHI sought to exploit a perceived opportunity provided by earlier labour legislation which, while giving FSBI/SPSI the sole right to organize labour, permitted associations to be formed at enterprise level where more than twenty-five workers were employed. In most cases, SPSI, which covers less than 6 per cent of the Indonesian work-force, has not taken up this opportunity (Asia Watch, 1993a). Indeed, the Indonesian government has itself come to admit that there is a problem. In a submission to the Office of the US Trade Representative, the Indonesian government identified the main obstacles to forming more units as 'lack of worker familiarity with trade union practices, employer resistance, employee apathy and employee fear of possible employer retaliation' (US Trade Representative, 1992).

Labour associations initiated by YLBHI were, for a while, able to operate relatively autonomously under the umbrella of SPSI. However, a new regulation in 1986 required that the formation process be overseen by tripartite structures comprising SPSI, government, and employer representatives along lines similar to those functioning at higher levels. YLBHI felt obliged to accept this arrangement, in view of its own stress on the rule of law, but has sought to lengthen the period over which the group is formed. This would provide scope for building a stronger in-formal organization, which could be further strengthened by forming credit unions and informal joint enterprises (*usaha bersama*) outside the workplace.

Where possible, YLBHI and associate groups have been involved in training programmes concerning labour rights and organization-building. However, the SPSI hierarchy insists that the purpose of such courses be spelled out precisely. As notions like 'solidarity', 'consciousness-raising', or 'self-reliance' fit uneasily with official ideology, such courses tend to be one-off affairs and to lack the necessary continuity. YLBHI initially sought to respond by creating small credit, savings, and loans groups, but claims it was unable to gain support from established NGOs. Its strategy consequently shifted towards facilitating informal meetings be-tween local units, in order to strengthen awareness and communication between them.

Such responses are considered totally inadequate by radical groups and, indeed, by many leaders within YLBHI itself. Finally, at a meeting of NGOs convened by YLBHI in Jakarta in August 1990, it was decided to focus on workers' conditions prior to the meeting of the International Congress of Free Trade Unions (ICFTU) in September 1991, and also to hold an opinion poll among workers concerning SPSI prior to their Congress due to be held two months later. Haji Princen subsequently drafted a manifesto, which several organizations signed immediately. Fauzi Abdullah, YLBHI's long-term labour affairs specialist, held back as he felt that more prior awareness and organization-building were necessary at the local level. He also thought that the document might conflict with YLBHI's emphasis on enforcing implementation of labour laws through the court system.

On the basis of this manifesto, a new trade union, called Serikat Buruh Setia Kawan (commonly referred to as Setia Kawan), was estab-lished.[18] The choice of name was significant for two reasons. First, 'Setia Kawan' is an exact translation of 'Solidarity'. Princen asserted that the analogy with Poland precisely fitted Indonesia's situation, since both countries were under a dictatorship and in need of an independent trade union. Secondly, the term *buruh*, as indicated earlier, had been expunged from the official lexicon as having connotations both of leftism and class conflict.

Setia Kawan held its first Congress on 15 December 1990 at which a constitution, by-laws, and a formal organizational structure were established (Setia Kawan, 1990). Princen was elected president and Indro Tjahjono vice-president. Some perfunctory efforts were made to gain government recognition despite Setia Kawan's insistence that this was not legally necessary in terms of Article 28 of the 1945 Constitution, which asserts freedom of association, and Laws 18 of 1956 and 14 of 1969, which guarantee freedom to organize in the labour field. Convention No. 98 of the International Labour Organization (ILO) was also invoked. The general thrust of this Convention is to assert freedom of bargaining and association. Article 2 states, in part, that 'Workers and employers' organisations shall enjoy adequate protection against any acts of interference by each other or each other's agents ... in their establishment, functioning or administration ... acts which are designed to promote the establishment of workers' organisations under the domination of employers or employers' organizations ... shall be deemed to constitute acts of interference within the meaning of this article' (ILO, 1951: 852). Setia Kawan and other independent labour activists have used this article to reinforce their depiction of SPSI as under direct government control, as its leadership is dominated by GOLKAR and military nominees.

Despite these defiant sentiments, Setia Kawan's leaders tried to meet the Minister of Home Affairs in order to register their organization. This request was refused, with the head of the department's social and political section informing Setia Kawan that only SPSI was recognized by the government. Subsequently, the president stated that Setia Kawan was redundant, as SPSI was already fulfilling its role. Setia Kawan duly replied with a letter detailing SPSI's inadequacies.

Interestingly, the government never sought to suppress Setia Kawan in any direct way, despite having declared, for twenty-five years, that only one official union would be tolerated. Setia Kawan's president, Haji Princen, claimed that the new union enjoyed a measure of sympathy from a section of the military, motivated, in part, by their own dissatisfaction with the economic corporate power of some members of President Suharto's family.[19] General Benny Murdani, in particular, is said to have defended the new union's right to exist. Moreover, some influential economists, concerned with excessive concentrations of wealth, have seen more effective labour organization as one means of narrowing the growing rich–poor gap. Finally, Princen's personal credentials as a fighter for Indonesia's independence and as an anti-communist gaoled under both Sukarno and Suharto, who has extensive international links, probably afforded Setia Kawan a measure of protection.

Indonesia's sensitive relations with the ILO and the international trade union movement generally appear to have limited government heavy-handedness towards the emergence of independent unions and greater labour militancy, although the evidence on this point is rather mixed. Indonesia had only finally acceded to the ILO Convention in 1989, so immediate suppression of Setia Kawan could have seriously dented its international image. Acceptance of this Convention also entailed formal acceptance of Indonesian workers' right to strike. However, amended regulations still confront workers with a series of complex and potentially costly steps before they can legally take strike action (Asia Watch, 1992).

Independent labour activists have skilfully exploited their international contacts with overseas labour and human rights groups. This has been reflected in growing pressures from American union networks on the US Congress to link Indonesia's trade access via the General System of Preferences, with adherence to ILO norms. Setia Kawan further sought to exploit the ban imposed by the ILO Convention on employer and state-controlled labour unions. However, the dangers of overplaying the international card on the labour, environment, and human rights fronts became apparent in May 1992, when the Minister for Home Affairs, General Rudini, announced a ban on the receipt of Dutch aid, including non-government assistance co-funded from Dutch government sources. YLBHI and LPHAM are crucially dependent on Dutch funds. After some initial anxiety, funds from Holland continued to arrive. YLBHI pointed out that a Ministerial statement, not reinforced by specific regulations, carries no legal force. Also, purely private donations were not affected.

The Indonesian government appears to have taken seriously moves in the US Congress during 1993 to deny Indonesian exports preferential trade access to US markets. The blocking of some US military aid since the killing of civilians by the Indonesian military in Dili, East Timor, indicates a more general sense of disquiet in Washington concerning Indonesia's human rights record. Teams have been established to represent the Indonesian government's viewpoint and to confront arguments put by Asia Watch and other critics, while pressure has also been placed on employers to accept SPSI units. Much comment in the Indonesian press has been cynical towards US motives, in the light of American trade problems, but also acknowledges that workers' conditions leave much to be desired. At the same time, it has been noted that only US$643 million out of US$4.4 billion worth of exports to the USA in 1992 were attributable to tariff preferences. It has consequently been claimed that Indonesia's dependence on this benefit should not be exaggerated (Media Indonesia, 1993). Suhadi Mangkusuwondo, vice-chairman of the Trade and Management Development Institute, in making the same point, urged that Indonesia prepare to shift more non-oil exports to other countries (UPI, 1993). On the other hand, it can be argued that tariff preferences would hit sectors crucial to Indonesia's expanding export-oriented industrialization strategy, while discouraging potential investors (Lambert, 1993: 29–30).

The government dealt with the challenge from Setia Kawan by taking no action against its leaders, but denying union organizers access to workers at the enterprise level. At one stage, Setia Kawan claimed affiliation of labour associations and labour-oriented LSMs totalling around 60,000 members. A more realistic figure may well have been 5,000–10,000 so far as active membership is concerned, although unorganized labour militancy, evidenced in strikes and other activities, certainly increased since around the time of Setia Kawan's formation. Some demonstrations in Jakarta, for example, by textile and furniture workers and by taxi drivers, were organized in the name of Setia Kawan. However, by mid-1992 it had become inactive as a union, although it was not formally disbanded.

Despite its short-term lack of success, the Setia Kawan experience brought together the major legal and human rights groups. Labour issues were also given a higher international profile through INGI, facilitated by YLBHI's leading role within this network. This experience helped lay the foundation for the establishment, on 25 April 1992, of a new organization, the Indonesian Workers' Welfare Association (Serikat Buruh Sejahtera Indonesia—SBSI). Firm overall membership figures are not available, although SBSI delegates, representing sixty-one out of seventy-seven branches covering eighteen provinces, arrived for a conference called at Cisarua, south of Jakarta, on 29 July 1993 (Asia Watch, 1993c). Permission to hold this conference was refused and delegates were dispersed by the military.

Interestingly, from the standpoint of this study, the government, in justifying this action, claimed that SBSI should be considered a nongovernmental organization dealing with labour affairs, rather than a labour union run by workers (Asia Watch, 1993c). At the time of writing, all but two of SBSI's executives are workers. One of the two is Muchtar Pakpahan, a well-known labour lawyer from North Sumatra, who convened the original national workers meeting at Cipayung, West Java, at which SBSI was established. It would be more realistic to see SBSI as an alliance between workers, supporting NGOs, and other activists. In the short term, at least, faced with new coalitions and a growing wave of direct action by workers independent of formal union structures, the government has responded by tightening regulatory controls, while military dealings with workers appear to have become more violent (Asia Watch, 1993c). Such official reactions probably indicate that both independent labour action and associated LSM/LPSM networking have become more effective.

Joint involvement by YLBHI, LPHAM, and INFIGHT networks in the labour field can be seen in the context of a potential convergence on broader questions of human rights and democratization, indicated in their common support for the joint statement by Indonesian NGOs for Democracy in June 1993 (IN-DEMO, 1993). However, the situation between YLBHI and radical groups in relation to various land and environmental struggles has proved more tense.

Land Struggles

Conflict over land has produced a spate of legal disputes throughout rural Indonesia. YLBHI, SKEPHI, and the Indonesian Environment

Network (Wahana Lingkungan Hidup Indonesia—WALHI), a loose Indonesia-wide federation of over a hundred active environmental groups,[20] supported by numerous local LSMs and student and other activist groups, have reported a stream of cases where local people have been displaced from land which they have cultivated continuously for many years, to make way for various kinds of development programmes (INFIGHT, 1990; YLBHI, 1990). Using their contacts with journalists and editors, these groups can often gain national publicity for local conflicts, particularly when farmers are displaced from productive land to make way for what are, in the eyes of many Indonesians, luxurious and wasteful purposes, such as golf courses (SKEPHI, 1989: 19–23; INFIGHT, 1990: 7). National publicity is often countered by provincial and regional military authorities exerting pressure to prevent critical comment being published in their areas. More mundane problems, such as individual farmers requiring certificates of land title from their village heads in order to secure bank loans, tend to gain less coverage. Here, NGO intervention takes more the form of acting as intermediary-cum-guarantor to banks than engaging in direct confrontation.

A common pattern can be seen as underlying these various cases. First, the legal situation itself is quite confused, both between national and customary (*adat*) law, and between various levels of use and lease, short of freehold (*hak milik*) title. Only the latter gives any security, with the rest subject to manipulation and arbitrary decision-making by authorities at different levels. Frequently, ownership or lease by the Dutch colonial government or Japanese military is cited as evidence of state ownership, even though successive republican governments have legalized, or at least legitimized, cultivation by local people, for example, by receipt of development and land taxes. Secondly, even freehold title can be overturned by compulsory acquisition in the name of national development.

Compensation is determined by committees appointed by the district and provincial authorities, which routinely exclude local owners and leaseholders. Although official procedures require some indeterminate consultation with local people prior to the commencement of a development programme, such consultation is almost always confined to the local authorities. Once levels of compensation have been determined, no negotiation for revision is entertained, except where external assistance for the project may be endangered. Compensation is usually fixed at well below market levels.[21] Sometimes alternative land is offered, though this is usually not comparable in size, fertility, or economic location. Transmigration is often proposed as a solution or threatened as punishment.

Local and area military commands are decisive in determining and enforcing such decisions. Those who resist are routinely labelled as subversive and/or communist, and are detained or harassed. Dissenting government employees are threatened with dismissal. In Pulau Panggung, Lampung, coffee plantations and houses were burned (INFIGHT, 1990: 10–11; SKEPHI, 1991: 10). Not surprisingly, in such an environment, government agencies, private companies, or even educational or religious institutions seeking land for any purpose do not bother to approach landowners, but deal from the outset with local civilian or military authorities.

The Environment

Many NGO reports indicate links between environment and land rights issues (WALHI, 1990a; YLBHI, 1990; SKEPHI, 1991). Attacks on both people's livelihood and the environment itself are commonly justified as serving the greater good of national development. At other times, the people themselves are depicted as threatening the environment, notably in cases where the Forestry Department acquires people's land for purposes of community tree planting, officially defined as social forestry. Critics allege that this term provides cover for more general exploitation (SKEPHI, 1991: 29–32). YLBHI has increasingly co-operated with WALHI in taking up cases at both national and regional levels. SKEPHI and INFIGHT, in alliance with local and outside student groups, have also been active in most of these struggles. Radical and mainstream NGO networks sometimes co-operate, and at other times operate separately in supporting local groups.

In a celebrated case, WALHI and YLBHI took PT Inti Indorayon Utama to court in Jakarta in January 1989 for fouling river and tributaries and causing soil erosion in the upper reaches of the Asahan River, North Sumatra, where the company had leased 150 000 hectares for pulp milling. Local people complained of fish dying, of water for washing and swimming being heavily polluted, and of foul smells. The company's letter of authorization obliged it to avoid pollution by processing waste via an aerated lagoon to a second lagoon of water hyacinths, using goldfish as a test of cleansing before releasing the waste into the river. However, careless construction led to the lagoon being breached, with eyewitness accounts of rubbish being piped directly into the river (YLBHI, 1989a: 34–8; WALHI, 1990b: 3–6).

WALHI took the Ministers for Forestry, Industry, Population and Environment, and the Provincial Governor to court in order to focus on the processes of drawing up and implementing environment-related agreements. It turned out that no proper environmental impact study had been undertaken as required under relevant sections of the 1982 Environment Law.[22] Although the appeal failed, the Jakarta court did not uphold defence calls to reject WALHI as a legitimate plaintiff, thereby opening up more general scope for public interest litigation. YLBHI then took the case to court in Medan. However, four complainants withdrew their accusations, allegedly as a consequence of military pressure. The case was dismissed on the grounds that mediation should have been attempted initially. Local plans to appeal were withdrawn in the face of further threats and intimidation.

Ten women in Sugapa village, North Tapanuli, subsequently retaliated by systematically cutting down some 16,000 trees planted by the com-

pany. They claimed such tree planting ignored local people's cattle graz-
ing rights, as well as disturbing the region's watershed (Asia Watch,
1990). In February 1990, the women were tried and sentenced to six
months gaol. LBH Medan and a local NGO, Study Group for the
Development of People's Initiative (Kelompok Studi Pengembangan
Prakarsa Masyarakat—KSPPM) took up their case. Subsequently, the
regional military command took retaliatory action against KSPPM and
the Batak Protestant Christian Church (Huria Batak Keristen
Protestan—HBKP), from which KSPPM had originated in 1983, several times interrogating both Church and NGO leaders. KSPPM was
banned, by order of the regional commander, for allegedly breaching
ORMAS legislation. Efforts to seek clarification of their status from the
Minister of Home Affairs were unsuccessful.

In November 1992, North Sumatra's Regional Stability Co-ordinating
Board (Badan Koordinasi Stabilitas Daerah—BAKORSTANASDA)
intervened openly in a conflict within the HBKP, issuing a decree
appointing as its own choice for *ephorus* (roughly equivalent to a bishop),
a man whom Asia Watch stated to be a convicted embezzler. In the
ensuing uproar, it was alleged that houses were searched without warrants,
press coverage of the situation was banned, and some sixty people were
detained (Asia Watch, 1993b). A Medan court initially struck down the
military commander's appointee, but subsequently reversed its decision
on grounds which it failed to disclose (Straits Times, 1993).

In that context, it is hard to believe that the regional authorities would
go to such lengths to gain control over a religious body merely for
patron–client, family, and factional reasons, though these were no doubt
present. Rather, it appears that sustained social militancy by elements
within the Church was considered a threat to security. In this whole
saga, legal intervention by WALHI and YLBHI achieved little in concrete terms, apart from publicity, without which the subsequent repression may have gained little outside coverage and the affairs inside the
Church dismissed as simply a local faction fight. In such cases, YLBHI
activists tend to adopt a stoical view that by taking a case to court, it is at
least placed on the record, which in the end may bring larger forces to
bear on the side of justice.

Yogyakarta Groups

The Yogyakarta Legal Aid Institute

YLBHI's regional affiliates are autonomous in management and in
determining local priorities and strategies. Resource allocation is determined nationally on the basis of close consultation between national and
regional directors. Publications and training resources are provided from
Jakarta, though local groups are free to develop their own resources.

While the Yogyakarta Legal Aid Institute (Lembaga Bantuan Hukum
Yogyakarta—LBHY) has broadly followed nationally determined
priorities, as outlined earlier, it has been widely regarded as cautious in

its operating style. Outreach is achieved through contact with local personalities (*tokoh*) and informal groups, known as 'friends of legal aid'. Informal leaders and activists are invited for periodic discussion, seminars, information exchange, and facilitation of small cases. In many respects, the local culture and hierarchical structures are not conducive to confrontational approaches. LBHY has therefore considered a gradualist approach—balancing legal aid, education, and socialization—essential to legitimizing legal rights values among local communities. However, many groups avoid using LBH's name, fearing that any too direct link will attract harsher control and attention from the government. LBHY says there is still a problem of socializing government at both regional and local levels to understand and accept the role of NGOs in social and economic development.

In Yogyakarta, LBHY has worked with WALHI on several cases. These include (i) a leather factory (PT Budi Progo Perkasa), which had caused pollution in the Sleiman area. Co-operation with several LSMs at *kampung* level produced sufficient pressure for the factory to be closed for a while, equipment to be changed, and an *ex gratia* payment made to the people before it was reopened; (ii) chemical pollution of the river by a mushroom factory in Kulon Progo. LBHY trained local contacts to take samples, which were later tested in a laboratory. These showed that pollution could not be unequivocally assigned to the factory, and (iii) a pattern of water use by domestic consumers in fast-growing housing development schemes, which increasingly deprives farmers of their traditional water source. Informal groups were formed, emboldening farmers to take their grievances to local authorities. This culminated in a delegation to the regional parliament, but no clear outcome was achieved.

LBH Yogyakarta has also been involved, together with other groups, in issues relating to compulsory land acquisition for tourist development, notably around the historic temples of Borobudur and Prambanan and in the coastal area of Parang Tritis. According to LBHY, development plans for this area form part of prospective regional plans for continuous development along the South Java coast, stretching from Cilacap to Wonogiri, and ultimately extending into East Java. In all these cases, LBHY aims to empower people to take up issues of adequate compensation and alternative employment. Each group is left to decide whether to adopt a strategy of outright resistance, or to settle for some combination of compensation, resettlement, and retraining. Most seem willing to settle for a path of compromise.

Notable recent cases have included the defence and continuing support for three student activists from Gadjah Mada University charged with, and later convicted of, subversion for selling illegal literature (notably the work of internationally recognized novelist and former political prisoner, Pramoedya Ananta Toer) and organizing discussion groups. YLBHI, LPHAM, and the Indonesian Bar Association lent support to local efforts. The case has also received a good deal of international support and publicity. LBH Yogyakarta highlighted issues relating to academic freedom and creativity, using its networks to maintain contact and keep the issue alive.[23]

The Legal Aid Study Group

The Legal Aid Study Group (Kelompok Studi untuk Bantuan Hukum—KSBH), based in Yogyakarta, represents a good example of the third model proposed in Chapter 2, in terms of its approach to popular empowerment and relations with the authorities. This group emerged around 1980 from an informal study group, which led to various legal education and local action programmes. KSBH appears, however, to have become inactive since around 1992. The group relied on 6–8 core activists, but had limited administrative facilities. YLBHI in Jakarta provided support for publications, but KSBH relied mostly on donations from supporters, with volunteers assisting on an *ad hoc* basis.

KSBH claimed that its approach differed from that of LBHY in stressing empowerment rather than litigation. In that context, it felt a closer affinity with YLBHI. KSBH saw LBHY as being unduly inclined to mediate with the authorities on behalf of clients, whereas its own policy was only to take up individual cases where some strategic advantage was likely to accrue. Thus, KSBH aimed to help people conduct their own negotiations, although it might accompany them in very difficult cases, for example, in the case of a lone resident of Prambanan who resisted eviction pending adequate compensation.

KSBH was active in relation to conflicts over land acquisition around Prambanan and Borobudur for purposes of tourist expansion. In Borobudur, local people resisted the loss of land until forced to accept the situation by direct military coercion.[24] In the case of Prambanan, efforts were concentrated on gaining adequate compensation. Some cases were taken to the courts, supported by a good deal of pressure on selected corrupt village and sub-district officials and police, by local posts set up by KSBH. At the level of public advocacy, KSBH demanded that committees established to determine compensation, should include representatives of those displaced from their land (KSBH, 1987).

At one stage, KSBH had fostered the establishment of seventeen local posts, though only 40–50 per cent could be described as active at any given time. Legal education work was commonly linked to the establishment of informal associations (*arisan*) and joint enterprises (*usaha bersama*). KSBH produced a monthly bulletin, *Nawala*, distributed material on land law and compulsory expropriation, and ran a local theatre group using street theatre, puppets, and other popular dramatic media. Its legal status was based, somewhat precariously, on an understanding with the Department of Social Affairs (Departemen Sosial—DEPSOS), from which it received some minor assistance in the form of office equipment.

KSBH was still supporting 7–8 local posts in 1991 in Boyolali, Prambanan, and Imogiri. KSBH itself had no established presence in these localities, relying on short, informal field visits. Local leaders also travelled to Yogyakarta for workshops and other exchanges. Boyolali experienced considerable political upheaval and much bloodshed during the 1960s, followed by continuing heavy security clamp-downs during the whole period of the New Order. The Kedung Ombo struggle,[25] in which KSBH was involved alongside several other groups, had the dual effect of opening up the area to outside activists and reawakening local capacity to organize and protest. KSBH's legal aid posts in Boyolali, located in the hills outside the area immediately affected by the dam project, played a broadly political educational role.

In the more stable area of Imogiri in Bantul District, south of Yogyakarta, where five legal rights units loosely associated with KSBH were formed, it proved possible to develop a more broad-based approach. This network was initiated following an invitation to a Mr Suharto to attend a training session, on the recommendation of a KSBH contact. Using a handbook on handling land disputes adapted by KSBH, in conjunction with YLBHI, Suharto, who subsequently became its convenor (*pengurus*), built up a local legal rights unit around the issue of forced cultivation of sugar-cane (KSBH, *c.*1981a; *c.*1981b). Since 1981, the district authorities, reminiscent of Dutch colonial rulers, had issued instructions that quotas of sugar-cane were to be delivered in rotation. Farmers estimated that payments would amount to only one-quarter of the income they could obtain from rice cultivation. Some 500 farmers, covering 47 hectares, successfully resisted government demands by a combination of passive resistance and the use of media and political contacts. The local authorities then punished them by not providing letters of authority and certificates necessary to the conduct of their daily life and business.

Another legal rights unit was formed in the area in response to demands for the sale of village land by the village head (*lurah*). The villagers affected believed that the initiative came from an Islamic educational institution, which wanted to construct a secondary agricultural school, though elements of the Indonesian Armed Forces (Angkatan Bersenjata Republik Indonesia—ABRI) may also have been involved.[26] When threatened with PKI identification and transmigration, the villagers, rather than refusing outright, demanded Rp2,000 per square metre as against the Rp500 offered. Pressure on them was subsequently withdrawn. KSBH considers that an important reason for this outcome was that since no national project was involved, higher-level authorities did not exert themselves to support the *lurah*. The National Land Agency, which was responsible for collecting data and recommending compensation prices, took no action.

The Imogiri group also fought the electricity authorities over alleged overcharging for power installation. Each consumer was charged Rp152,000 instead of Rp106,000, which was considered the correct price by the KSBH group. The price is controlled by a government-appointed committee for each newly electrified village, which, in this case, maintained that the price difference was due to the addition of

1 The late Mary Johnson, an Australian community development worker who spent over twenty years with YAKKUM and YIS, discusses plans with a village leader in Central Java, *c.*1971. (Overseas Service Bureau)

2 Fr. Mangunwijaya, a Catholic priest, architect, and social activist, based in Yogyakarta. (Inside Indonesia)

3 A training session for fieldworkers organized by YIS. (YIS)

4 An NGO network planning session. (YIS)

5 Achmad Rofie of LSP with a group leader and scavengers at a Jakarta tip. (Inside Indonesia)

6 A scavenger leaving a Jakarta tip with a heavy load. (Inside Indonesia)

7 The *becak* is a popular and flexible form of urban transport. (Inside Indonesia)

8 *Becak* being forcibly seized by the authorities. (Inside Indonesia)

9 *Kampung* dwellers from Tanah Merah, Jakarta, threatened with displacement, demonstrate in front of the Department of Home Affairs, 27 March 1992. (Inside Indonesia)

10 Displaced farmers uproot sugar cane in Majalengka, West Java. (Inside Indonesia)

11 An INFID meeting in Paris, 1994. The executive director of YLBHI, Buyung Nasution, is in the centre. (Inside Indonesia)

12 Jan Pronk, the Dutch Minister for Overseas Development, meets with INFIGHT and SKEPHI representatives in Jakarta, 1992. (Inside Indonesia)

13 An urban *kampung* on the Ciliwung River, Jakarta. (Inside Indonesia)

14 The PT Inti Indorayan Utama pulp mill outlet to the Asahan River in North Sumatra. (Inside Indonesia)

street lighting. As this was not supplied, the local group organized a demonstration against the committee and took the issue to the press (Berita Nasional, 1990a, b, and c; Kedaulatan Rakyat, 1990). Street lighting was subsequently installed and new consumers in the area were charged the correct price.

The Imogiri legal rights network, set up in 1981, had no formal membership and, until 1987, elected its executive board by consensus, when it was formally registered as an LSM. This contrasts with KSBH itself, which was never registered. Groups in Imogiri later started savings and loans and animal husbandry programmes in order to supplement individual and organizational incomes. KSBH provided working capital and began developing co-operation with Yayasan Mandiri, an alternative technology group in Bandung. A limited attempt to encourage involvement by women in non-economic programmes was initiated by taking up a breach of promise case, on the principle that this was likely to prove both winnable and popular. Such trends indicate a likely evolution of Imogiri legal aid posts along more conventional community development lines. They also provide yet another illustration of the close links, irrespective of the initial point of entry, between issues and fields of action in efforts to overcome poverty and exploitation, legal-cum-political struggles, and programmes of social and economic development.

Suharto describes himself as a small businessman. He has some involvement with the Indonesian Democratic Party (Partai Demokrasi Indonesia), and has apparently gained some personal influence with the authorities. Foster Parents' Plan, which is active in this area, asked him to advise them in selecting families for adoption after some money, intended for community development, was diverted by a *lurah* for village roads. Members of legal aid groups themselves informed the author that they had received benefits from Foster Parents' Plan, including one unit convenor, who received funds for his children's education.

The Yogyakarta Students' Communication Forum

The Yogyakarta Students' Communication Forum (Forum Komunikasi Mahasiswa Yogyakarta—FKMY) is a loose network of students and former students from several institutions of higher education in Yogyakarta city. At the local level, it works closely with the Yogyakarta Women's Discussion Forum (Forum Diskusi Perempuan Yogyakarta—FDPY).[27] Nationally, it shares a broadly similar outlook to the INFIGHT–SKEPHI group, with whom it co-operates closely. It holds negative views on mainstream NGOs generally, including the Yogyakarta Legal Aid Institute (LBHY) in the local context, and remains unconvinced by the more action-oriented policy line of the Foundation of Indonesian Legal Aid Institutions (YLBHI), adopted at the national level since 1989, claiming to see a wide gap between words and actions. In particular, it claims that LBHY withdrew from Kedung Ombo in 1987, causing anger among local people. FKMY pursues a strategy of direct action jointly with local groups in relation to agreed areas of struggle. Demonstrations are often taken up in Jakarta, as FKMY claims that by only demonstrating at district and provincial level, one invites retaliation. There is a better chance of gaining publicity, and consequently protection, by taking an issue direct to the national capital, although demonstrations directed towards the People's Regional Representative Assembly (Dewan Perwakilan Rakyat Daerah—DPRD) may also provide some degree of safety.

Interactions between LBHY, KSBH, and FKMY can be further understood in relation to the Kedung Ombo struggle.

Kedung Ombo

This conflict, centring on the construction of a dam in the Solo region of Central Java, brought together the major actors and issues discussed earlier in this chapter. The conflict was played out at local, provincial, national, and international levels, and involved both overseas NGOs and the World Bank, whose finance had made the project possible in the first place. However, by the time the issue had attracted serious national and international attention, the project was too advanced to stop, so that protests and bargaining were only feasible in relation to compensation and the provision of alternative sources of livelihood. Nevertheless, the issue of whether to stand firm or to bargain for better compensation has continued to divide the local people and the groups supporting them.

During the early stages, outside involvement came mostly from NGOs based in the Yogyakarta–Solo region. Subsequent external involvement led to increased pressures on the local people and the LSM/LPSMs assisting them. LBHY was forced, on the orders of the Yogyakarta police, to postpone indefinitely a workshop on the Kedung Ombo project, involving several academics and WALHI. Many international NGOs, the World Bank, and the district heads of Sragen and Boyolali districts, where the dam is located, had been invited. Thereafter, outside activists were excluded from the thirty-seven affected village areas, although people regularly travelled outside to meet them. At one stage in 1987, LBHY and KSBH temporarily accommodated Kedung Ombo refugees, later persuading them to return home and continue resisting.

Pressure on the people of Kedung Ombo remained immense, including threats of classification as ex-*tapol*, and compulsory indoctrination and 'guidance' (*pembinaan*) sessions. They were also threatened with the prospect of transmigration (Tapol, 1988: 21–2). Even so, by April 1989, only a few hundred families had accepted the government's compensation of Rp750 (US$0.45) per square metre and were ready to move from their home area. The majority, consisting of 3,391 families, refused compensation and moved to higher ground (WALHI, 1990a: 15).

National and international awareness of Kedung Ombo accelerated from around 1987. Student groups visited the area in large numbers, leading to demonstrations and clashes with the military. These visits gained significant media coverage, with films of events around the dam site being passed to INGI, which subsequently showed them at an international meeting in Brussels. In April 1989, farmers from Kedung Ombo were received in the Jakarta office of the World Bank (SKEPHI, 1991: 40–1). INGI made vigorous representations to the Inter-Governmental Group for Indonesia (IGGI) Consortium meeting in Brussels, demanding that further funding be made conditional on adequate compensation and effective supervision of its distribution.[28] The Home Affairs Minister, General Rudini, responded by immediately summoning NGO leaders and reprimanding them for embarrassing Indonesia in the eyes of foreigners. It appears, however, that he was acting on instructions from the State Secretariat (Sekretariat Negara—SEKNEG), and was fairly conciliatory in private, only urging that NGO concerns be expressed directly to the government. Thereafter, while the larger LPSMs adopted a lower profile for a while, the government moved to mollify at least some of the local discontent. President Suharto, nevertheless, formally inaugurated the dam, bringing resistance on the ground to a crisis stage as the flood waters rose.

From this point, differences among the local people and outside groups supporting them began to surface more openly. Villagers were confronted with the choice of accepting government offers of resettlement, compensation, or alternative forest land or resisting outright. The government appears to have embarked on a policy of divide and rule. Eight villages were favoured by the provision of television sets, radios, and access to forest land. However, as official land certificates were not provided, people still lacked security for the longer term. The other twelve villages faced a choice of accepting very limited compensation, or continuing in the area with no legal security. It is alleged that some people who accepted compensation were forced into transmigration after the money had been paid.

The inhabitants of Kedung Pring village, on the margin of the flood waters, chose to stay put and reconstruct their village along lines more suited to a water-based lifestyle. Houses were constructed on the water, and more villagers began to draw a living from fishing. Their continuing occupation is illegal, according to the government. Some accounts have suggested that resistance to any official presence is so strong that women scream whenever government representatives arrive. Villagers have totally refused all offers of compensation, other government assistance, or any alternative resettlement schemes. With assistance, notably from well-known, charismatic activist, Fr. Mangunwijaya from Yogyakarta, the village has sought to manage its own affairs. Mangunwijaya established a non-formal education programme and worked with the people to develop styles of local construction appropriate to their newly flooded habitat. He further mobilized volunteer teachers to teach primary-level children, as parents refused to send them to outside government schools.

The Kedung Pring villagers persisted in taking their case to court, despite knowing they would lose. Their sense of justice had been offended by the government's failure to engage with them in a process of deliberation and negotiation (*musyawarah*). Mangunwijaya believes that had this been done, some compromise might have been reached. Failing that, they preferred the satisfaction of their day in court. They also seem to have been persuaded by Mangunwijaya's argument, which reflects YLBHI and LPHAM's position concerning the importance of placing one's case on the record for the sake of influencing domestic and international opinion over the longer term. Mangunwijaya himself was requested to sign a letter of introduction by the social-political section of the Department of Home Affairs, which had expressed a wish to help. Mangunwijaya also twice refused requests from the State Intelligence Co-ordinating Board (Badan Koordinasi Intelijens Negara—BAKIN) to talk the people of Kedung Pring out of taking court action, quoting speeches by President Suharto insisting that the 1945 Constitution offered the only road for solving problems.

Interest from outside organizations like the Japan Foundation for Human Rights, plus the Kedung Pring villagers' own efforts may discourage the government from moving them. However, Mangunwijaya has come into conflict with radical students who want to involve Kedung Pring villagers in national-level protests and who regard legal-based approaches as futile. This appears to reflect deeper divisions between Mangunwijaya, LBHY, KSBH, and Protestant Church-based groups in Solo, and the Yogyakarta Students' Communication Forum, which has no faith in law as a means of struggle. While making allowances for youthful inexperience, Mangunwijaya expresses concern about the use of people as tools by outsiders. Above all, he has warned against taking up arms which will lead to 'everything being lost'. So far, the Kedung Pring villagers have been persuaded to the view that participating in demonstrations is, in their circumstances, both dangerous and a waste of time, and have preferred to concentrate their energies on standing firm on the ground.

Mangunwijaya considers that the Kedung Ombo experience indicates that something can be achieved in similar circumstances if local people are willing to be bold. He suggests that the approach of the villagers may prove to be replicable, particularly when people feel driven to the point where they consider they have no effective alternative. Kedung Ombo also appears to validate the belief of Sartono (1973), that resistance by rural people against the might of the state cannot succeed without support from outside intellectuals and other influential persons. Even so, it must be acknowledged, despite the diversity and labour intensity of supporting NGOs and other activists on the ground, that specific benefits for the Kedung Ombo people have been fairly limited. Nor has any obvious demonstration effect been achieved in relation to many other similar projects where relatively little NGO and other activist interest has been aroused (Aditjondro, 1990).

Gondolayu

Mangunwijaya's approach is sufficiently unique to merit further examination in relation to another struggle in which he was involved. In 1983, he supported a local initiative in community-building among a semi-permanent riverflat population at Gondolayu in Yogyakarta. Most of these residents were near the bottom of the city's socio-economic ladder. The Gondolayu riverflat community, like many similar neighbourhoods, was not effectively integrated, or even officially recognized as part of the local government structure.[29] Willy Prasetyo, then a young social-political science student and a native of the Gondolayu community, took upon himself the role of intermediary between the police and groups commonly regarded by them as criminals and vagrants.

Mangunwijaya, based in a neighbouring Catholic community, who already enjoyed a national and international reputation as an intellectual and social activist, came to live with the community. He was well received both by Prasetyo and the community due to his simple lifestyle and open, informal approach. Young voluntary workers were, in turn, attracted from neighbouring high schools and the local Catholic theological college. Small-scale community programmes were initiated, emphasizing non-formal education, including arts and drama, among younger groups. A reading-room and meeting-house were established. Mangunwijaya, who also has a background in architecture, initiated various improvements in housing construction and landscaping. However, the process of community-building did not prove easy as, according to Mangunwijaya, apart from suspicion among some city authorities, minor criminal elements were resistant to change which might disturb their own petty exploitation of local residents.

In 1983, the city authorities appointed Prasetyo as head of Terbun Neighbourhood, of which Gondolayu forms a part. He was later promoted to village head. Such recognition, however, did not lead to security of tenure for the residents. Instead, the riverflat residents faced pressures from city authorities and some private interests seeking to acquire their land for a beautification programme. The struggle waged against this proposal gained national, and some international, recognition after Mangunwijaya adopted the quasi-Gandhian tactic of undertaking to fast if the proposal was not withdrawn. The authorities, unable to predict the wider consequences of such an action, gave in. Many social activists in Yogyakarta believe that their retreat on this issue opened the way for more general changes in policy towards the informal sector and other marginalized communities in the city, notably the security given to stallholders and co-operatives after 1985.[30]

Despite this rather striking success, the longer-term outlook for the Gondolayu community is less clear. Mangunwijaya, whose subsequent work took him more outside the city, though maintaining contact, has expressed scepticism. Other groups of young, mostly Church-based volunteers continued support for the various programmes but, by comparison, lacked experience and finely tuned social and political awareness.

Prasetyo's elevation to village head also produced some contradictions. Despite retaining close grass-roots links, he was, to some extent, perceived as having been co-opted into the official structure. On the other hand, his bargaining power with the authorities was based a good deal on the fact that without the efforts at community-building initiated in Gondolayu, no effective structures of local government would have been created. Some officials feared that devolution would weaken their authority, and saw dangers in allowing local leaders to gain too much prestige.

In Mangunwijaya's view, petty criminal elements remained a pervasive influence and a barrier to effective community-building. One result was that control over locally accumulated resources reverted from the people to leaders recognized by the authorities.[31] Such elements, which Mangunwijaya claims include some former junior military personnel, appear to have provided a convenient foil to popular community leaders, who are obliged to play the role of skilful Javanese mediators in order to avoid polarization between the people and the authorities, which any direct challenge to criminal groups could provoke.

The Gondolayu experience broadly followed the third model proposed in Chapter 2, in concentrating energies on building an autonomous popular organization, rather than on co-operating with official programmes or seeking to change government policy or structures. The community itself existed somewhat at the margin of the formal local government structure. However, a major development proposal threatened to bring them into direct confrontation with the city authorities. This was averted through the support of a charismatic local priest and an educated local leader—perhaps an example of the 'Semar management' called for by Adi Sasono?[32]

Unfortunately, the subsequent decline in community-building, when taken together with the somewhat patchy success and apparent demise of KSBH, suggests that the 'autonomous empowerment' approach envisaged in this model is somewhat precarious. It is, nevertheless, widely espoused by smaller LSMs and activist groups, particularly in their formative years. To some extent, it also fits the self-image of many politically oriented new radicals. It can thus perhaps best be understood as some kind of 'idealized other' among the NGO community, rather than as a sustainable strategy over the longer term.

An Overview of Yogyakarta Legal and Human Rights Groups

The following points emerge from a comparison of the major Yogyakarta-based groups discussed in this section which, allowing for special local features, appear to broadly reflect the spectrum of action found elsewhere in Indonesia, particularly in Java:

(i) LBHY is formally registered, while KSBH has pursued a determinedly informal study-cum-action group approach.

(ii) LBHY has moved very slowly from its original legal aid approach, which it has taken great pains to adapt to Yogyakarta's subtly differentiated social environment and culture, which place strong emphasis on social harmony and conflict avoidance, in an overt sense at least (Geertz, 1960; Mulder, 1978; Koentjaraningrat, 1985). Interestingly, KSBH retained the term 'legal aid' in its name, presumably for tactical reasons, but otherwise concentrated on legal education and empowerment. Local units supported by KSBH were initially structured fairly informally, although some have recently evolved in the direction of LSMs, taking up economic programmes as well as legal and land issues.

(iii) The gap in approach between KSBH and LBHY narrowed a good deal from around 1988. Co-operation between them in the Kedung Ombo struggle indicates that some of KSBH's characterization of LBHY's approach to relations with the authorities was oversimplified. LBHY caution can be seen against a background of heavy pressures from military sources in its initial years. LBHY's co-operation in legal education with a local women's organization, Yayasan Anisa Swasti,[33] suggests that it has been breaking new ground.

(iv) The apparent inactivity of KSBH since 1992[34] suggests that informal group structures, almost by definition, lack a capacity for institutional survival. KSBH's determinedly low profile enabled it to survive for over ten years and to pioneer strategies of empowerment in relation to legal rights, particularly in cases of eviction and compensation, in a highly repressive environment. Unfortunately, the generation of students which initiated that group does not seem to have provided for a younger group to take over. Different elements of KSBH's work will no doubt be absorbed by other groups, particularly LBHY. KSBH's impact can perhaps best be judged in the longer term by the effectiveness of the units which it initiated.

(v) FKMY has adopted a distinct position in supporting neither court cases nor economic programmes. Its focus has been entirely political, in the sense of being directed towards state structures. FKMY has used demonstrations, either on-site, as in Kedung Ombo, or in Jakarta, as its major weapon.

(vi) FKMY and its counterparts across Indonesia seem unclear as to their broader political goals, whether these are to confront, restructure, or ignore established structures. FKMY also illustrates the lack of clarity among radical groups generally, despite its stress on rights to organize, as to whether people are to be regarded as subjects in defining their own struggles or objects in a wider political project.

(vii) Mangunwijaya's strategies of popular mobilization and dealing with the authorities, which have combined dialogue, legality, and passive resistance in both Kedung Ombo and Gondolayu, are not easily classifiable in terms of any of the categories proposed earlier.

Former Political Prisoners

No survey of human rights activity in Indonesia would be complete without mention of the efforts of at least some organizations to rehabilitate former political prisoners (ex-*tapol*). Comments are confined to the

Solo–Yogyakarta–Klaten region, and may not be valid for other parts of Indonesia. Most of these efforts were Church-based.[35] Fearing the consequences for ex-*tapol* of overidentification with Christianity, the Churches made strong pleas for cross-religious co-operation. However, the issue either proved too sensitive for Muslim groups to respond, or there was resistance to the reintegration of ex-*tapol* into their communities.

Prior to 1980, by which time the bulk of political prisoners detained following the 1965–6 upheavals had been released, efforts were confined to welfare work among prisoners and their families. Programmes were run from Asrama Realino in Yogyakarta, first by Fr. de Blot and later by Fr. Suasso, both Dutch-born priests from the Jesuit order. De Blot's approach, continued more cautiously by Suasso, consisted of three parts. The first concentrated on supplying prisoners with essentials, such as clothes and blankets. This involved considerable skill and diplomacy to ensure that a reasonable proportion arrived at their intended destination. The suspicions of the military authorities were countered by reference to the third (humanitarian) principle of the Panca Sila. Prison guards, often nearly as deprived as the prisoners, according to de Blot, were allocated a proportion of the supplies. The second part of de Blot's approach was to encourage self-reliance among the prisoners' families by teaching them practical trades, such as sewing, tailoring, weaving, and carpentry. They could then supply a proportion of the prisoners' needs themselves. Thirdly, students were motivated and trained to undertake community work with the families. In this way, both families and students developed new skills, understanding, and mutual support.

Consciousness-raising among students concerning poverty and human rights issues in a relatively informal environment was an important consequence of this last approach. De Blot's programmes proved too radical for the government, the Church hierarchy, or both, and he was asked to leave Indonesia. His work was carried on along more conventional social work lines by Suasso, who also acted as an intermediary *vis-à-vis* Indonesian Catholic and international agencies in relation to several other programmes aimed at political prisoners.

The release of the bulk of former political prisoners from the 1965–6 era, between 1977 and 1979, albeit subject to many restrictions and continuing harassment of various kinds, set off a search for means to rehabilitate them. One relatively successful effort was the establishment, in 1981, of Koperasi Mandiri, Yogyakarta. At its high point, this co-operative network linked forty-two workshops, producing furniture, metal products, and agricultural tools, into a federation. Its policy was to integrate former *tapol* into the work-force so that they constituted no more than 15–20 per cent of any group. Initial capital was provided through a Rp2 million interest-free loan from the Archdiocese of Semarang, of which Rp600,000 had been repaid by July 1983, plus a further Rp1.1 million collected through members' savings. Koperasi Mandiri achieved a combined profit of Rp1 million in 1982. Co-operation was forthcoming from the provincial authorities in the form of a certificate from the Governor allowing Koperasi Mandiri to bid for official tenders. At that stage, negotiations were under way for contracts with various government departments to supply furniture.[36]

The atmosphere appears to have changed from around the time of the 1985 Law on Social Organizations (Undang Undang Organisasi Kemasyarakatan—ORMAS). This resulted in drives to apply the five principles of state ideology (Panca Sila) in all areas of politics and society. Interpretations by many local authorities bore harshly on ex-*tapol*. Consequently, Koperasi Mandiri found contracts harder to obtain, while it appears that the Department of Co-operatives brought pressure on them to reduce the proportion of ex-*tapol*—a policy which was also supported by funding agencies on more general sociological grounds. Economic performance and management declined as a result of these various pressures, and the federation broke up into a few small units which ultimately became unviable.

For several years the Catholic Church at Klaten operated a range of economic and welfare programmes for former prisoners through its Family Social Service Institute (Yayasan Proyek Sosial Keluarga—YPSK). These included animal husbandry, nutrition, sewing, a *becak* drivers' co-operative, savings and loans schemes, and health programmes. Scholarships and hostel accommodation were provided for children of former political prisoners, who often experienced discrimination in their own localities. YPSK was perhaps justifiably criticized for being too paternalistic, and not encouraging greater self-reliance among enterprise groups. However, expectations that they could become entrepreneurs after some brief training and experience took little account of the trauma prisoners had suffered, and continued to suffer, due to their past experiences, continuing harassment, job discrimination by the authorities and, quite frequently, the break-up of their families. Application of self-help criteria by funding agencies seems relatively inflexible. For similar reasons, foreign agencies were willing to support only productive programmes, but not hostels and scholarships for the children of ex-*tapol*. Limited funds for these purposes were raised by Indonesian Catholics through the annual Lenten Fast for Development Action (Aksi Puasa Pembangunan).

An initiative to help both past and present political prisoners and their families was also undertaken by a Protestant pastor, Revd Broto Semedi Wiryotenoyo, who established the Institute for Sheltering Victims of the Social Situation (Yayasan Perlindungan Korban Situasi Sosial) in Salatiga. The organization's name, not surprisingly, angered and embarrassed the authorities, who pressured him to change it. Broto refused, on the grounds that it had been chosen as an expression of Christian faith. The government did not ban the organization, but ordered it to confine its activities to Christians. As it turned out, Muslims would not accept funds for economic programmes, but would accept legal defence services. Programmes for non-Muslims have been mostly of the conventional income-generating kind, based on revolving funds to purchase and breed goats, using seed capital from the International Christian

Consortium for Development Co-operation (Internationaal Christelijk Consortium voor Ontwikkelingssamenwerking—ICCO).

Major human rights organizations and radical activist groups discussed earlier appear to be little, if at all, involved in programmes to rehabilitate ex-*tapol*, which have been predominantly oriented towards income-generation and welfare activities. More radical legal awareness approaches would almost certainly compromise their position disastrously, considering the severe restrictions under which released political prisoners have been placed. These include the need to report regularly to local military authorities, attendance at periodic Panca Sila guidance sessions, and barriers placed on their employment. Both YLBHI and LPHAM have campaigned for the lifting of such restrictions, particularly the notorious 'certificate of non-involvement' in the abortive coup attempt of 30 September 1965, which even the youngest and most distant relatives of ex-*tapol* must still obtain for travel, employment, and other essential purposes.

The missing link in all these approaches is that no way has yet been found of empowering former political prisoners to participate in such campaigns, or even, in most cases, their own social and economic rehabilitation. Though this problem will, no doubt, remain intractable for some time, greater co-operation between church organizations involved with individual ex-prisoners and mainstream human and legal rights organizations appears to be an essential prerequisite for developing effective and coherent strategies for their rehabilitation.

1. In this context, Lev (1987: 21–2) acknowledges the role of T. Mulya Lubis, who succeeded Buyung Nasution as director of LBH in 1980.

2. YLBHI sources.

3. YLBHI's board of trustees in 1991 consisted of Mochtar Lubis, Buyung Nasution, H. J. C. Princen, Harjono Tjitrosubeno (chairman of the Indonesian Lawyers' Association, Ikatan Advocat Indonesia—IKADIN), Ali Sadikin, Bratanata, Aswab Mahasin, and Prof. Tuti Heriati.

4. Personal interview with the author, February 1988.

5. See pp. 212–14.

6. See pp. 47–51.

7. Princen, who came to Indonesia in 1946 as a Dutch military conscript, deserted to the Republican cause. He subsequently took Indonesian citizenship and converted to Islam. He has campaigned persistently on social justice and human rights issues, being imprisoned under both Presidents Sukarno and Suharto; see Princen (1992).

8. See pp. 141–2 for an explanation of SKEPHI's origins.

9. See pp. 195–201.

10. See pp. 21–2.

11. Radical leaders interviewed during the author's field visit in early 1991 were mostly from the 1980s student generation. By contrast, Tjahjono was a leading student activist at Bandung Technology Institute during the 1970s. According to his own account, as a result of more outspoken opposition, he served a longer period in gaol than his fellow students, many of whom subsequently became active in NGOs.

12. See YLBHI (1991a) for a general survey of labour conditions in Indonesia.

13. See Ingleson (1986) for the history of Indonesian trade unions in the earlier part of this century.

14. See pp. 79–85.

15. See pp. 163–5.

16. *Tempo*, 7 December 1985, cited in INDOC (1986: 15).

17. Setia Kawan may most appropriately be translated as Solidarity. See p. 111.

18. The account of Setia Kawan presented here is based on interviews with Haji Princen in January–February 1991 and July 1992; documentation supplied by Setia Kawan concerning its structure and rules, and Bourchier (1992).

19. Based on an interview with Princen in July 1992.

20. In an interview with the author in January 1991, WALHI estimated that 120–150 affiliates were active out of 500–600 listed.

21. Thus, compensation was fixed at Rp730 in Kedung Ombo for land which local people claimed was worth around Rp5,000 at normal market rates in the area (INFIGHT, 1990: 9).

22. The 1986 Elucidation of Article 16 of the Act of the Republic of Indonesia No. 4 of 1982 Concerning Basic Provisions for the Management of the Living Environment required Environmental Impact Analysis (EIA) processes to take into account the social and cultural impact of proposed development programmes. See Koesnadi (1987: 29, 39–40).

23. See Nugroho (1991) for relevant viewpoints from student, professional, and intellectual activists.

24. It appears that a dead body was left outside the house of a local activist leader for a whole day before the authorities took action to dispose of it. Thereafter, all villagers were visited and classified as green, yellow, and red according to the degree to which they were considered co-operative.

25. See pp. 122–4.

26. Based on an interview with KSBH Imogiri network in February 1991.

27. See pp. 166–8.

28. See pp. 198–200.

29. See Guinness (1986: 83–108) for a detailed analysis of government structures at *kampung* and neighbourhood level in Yogyakarta.

30. See p. 78.

31. For example, during Fr. Mangunwijaya's residence in Gondolayu, community funds were held in a locked chest opened only at public meetings.

32. See p. 75.

33. See pp. 160–1 for a more detailed account of Yayasan Anisa Swasti.

34. This does not necessarily extend to autonomous units supported by KSBH, on which the author has no current information.

35. Information in this section relates mostly to Catholic programmes, though the author is also aware of similar support programmes operated by ministers of religion associated with the Duta Wacana Theological College in Yogyakarta.

36. Information in this section was supplied by Fr. Suasso and Koperasi Mandiri.

7

Environmental Action

The Context of Environmental Activism

CONCERN for the environment has stimulated a second wave of activism by non-government organizations (NGOs), as part of a more general movement of dissent towards the New Order's development direction and the search for appropriate alternatives. Earlier expressions of dissent had focused mostly on economic aspects, notably perceived inequities in the distribution of wealth and income, inappropriate targeting of projects towards the modern industrial sector, a lack of linkage with the informal sector, and the marginalization of indigenous skills and enterprise. Over time, the role of political structures in supporting dominant development paradigms has become more widely understood. However, as indicated in earlier chapters, the NGO community is divided as to whether reformist or radical approaches are most likely to achieve change.

In the field of environmental action, although Indonesian NGOs and activists have drawn on the ideas and resources of the environmental movement in the West, their focus has been clearly local. Indonesia has experienced widespread ecological destruction, and even devastation, in many parts of the country through logging, mining, deafforestation, and transmigration. Pressures on ecological balance have been compounded by rapid urbanization, industrialization, and population growth, which have led to serious problems of pollution, deafforestation, flooding, and land degradation.[1]

While some groups were formed in reaction to specific developments, others have been of a more general study-action, hobby, or lobby kind. At the same time, many existing self-reliant community institutions (Lembaga Swadaya Masyarakat—LSM) and institutions for developing community self-reliance (Lembaga Pengembangan Swadaya Masyarakat—LPSM) have incorporated environmental concerns into their programmes. The role of nature clubs and walking and mountaineering groups has also been significant in providing an entry point to more general ecological awareness, particularly among young people, and as agents in community education. However, most nature and hobby groups do not have the necessary capacity or orientation to implement projects themselves (Yunanto, 1989). During the 1980s, most NGO environmental mobilization was in Java, although the most accelerated ecological devastation has occurred outside Java, particularly in Eastern Indonesia. In the most recent period, popular mobilization has been gradually keeping pace in the 'outer islands'.

Ecological values are by no means alien, and arguably complement those cultural values within Indonesian society which emphasize balance, harmony, and integration. Although this traditional ethos has been challenged over the past two or three decades by the values of modernization and development, these are, in many ways, still only skin-deep in the consciousness even of urban Indonesians. A theme repeated by academics and activists most closely involved in this area, in interviews with the author, is that, in contrast with much Western experience, most rural Indonesians, and even urban workers of recent rural background, need little persuasion in principle of the importance of the environment for longer-term survival, in both a personal and community sense. However, as they are in no position to trade off immediate survival against the longer term, energies must be concentrated on working with people to find ecologically sound subsistence strategies.

According to this view, a related battle must also be fought between top–down and participatory approaches to environmental management. The latter would enlist the community, whereas the former runs the risk of placing the weight of blame on local people and ignoring the far greater damage inflicted by outsiders. Indeed, environmental arguments may provide pretexts for excluding local people from land, forests, or fishing areas in order to make way for outside exploitation—an allegation commonly levelled, for example, against social forestry programmes in Indonesia and elsewhere (WALHI, 1990d). Though true, it should be noted that such analyses are people-centred and less concerned with ecological integrity in its own right.

In terms of the four models proposed in Chapter 2, evidence in this chapter will indicate that the emergence of environmental issues has shifted NGOs' centre of gravity towards both critical collaboration and popular empowerment. In some ways, they may also have evoked greater understanding of NGO ideals within the government, which has consequently taken initiatives to recognize their potential contribution. While the more established LPSMs discussed in Chapters 4 and 5 have taken up some of the environmental agenda, the running has mostly been made by newer groups and networks. However, a significant exception has been among legal and human rights groups. As indicated in Chapter 6, both the Foundation of Indonesian Legal Aid Institutions (Yayasan Lembaga Bantuan Hukum Indonesia—YLBHI) and the Indonesian Front for the Defence of Human Rights (INFIGHT) networks have been heavily involved in environmental struggles, linked, as they commonly are, to issues of land tenure and other aspects directly affecting people's livelihood and legal rights.

Comparison in this chapter of approaches by the Indonesian Environment Network (Wahana[2] Lingkungan Hidup Indonesia—WALHI) and the Indonesian Network for Forest Conservation (Sekretariat Kerjasama Pelestarian Hutan Indonesia—SKEPHI) is intended to further draw out differences between reformist and radical outlooks. Some special features of NGO–government relations will be identified in a discussion of Environmental Impact Analyses. In the later part of the chapter, some issues concerning networking, organization, and interaction with the authorities will be explored in specific local and regional contexts relating to (i) regional environmental forums in Central and West Java; (ii) water programmes, and (iii) a case-study of Citanduy, West Java, initiated by the Environmental Research Centre (Pusat Penelitian Lingkungan Hidup—PPLH) at the Bandung Institute of Technology (Institut Teknologi Bandung—ITB).

The Indonesian Environment Network

Momentum for change was given impetus in October 1980, when WALHI was set up as a communications forum on the initiative of ten core groups.[3] Fears of co-option by the government slowed down its organizational development, and membership grew slowly for the first two to three years. By 1983, these had been substantially overcome by the very loose framework adopted. Subsequently, WALHI grew rapidly into a potential unwieldy 'paper tiger', with many groups listed which were not obviously active. WALHI still has no formal membership but, by 1991, over 500 corresponding organizations had been listed, of which 120–30 were considered to be active.[4]

Activities, Organization, and Funding

WALHI's main functions cover training, research, general education, and communication. It arranges forums and dialogue between community organizations, the government, and other interested groups, and participates in and sometimes co-ordinates technical and other working groups in preparing environmental impact statements. Emphasis is placed on encouraging local groups to become involved in their own action research, and to undertake similar advocacy and communication roles, calling on the services of WALHI where necessary (Koesnadi, 1986b: 363–7). WALHI also undertakes education programmes on behalf of the government within the framework of national programmes, such as the National Conservation and Reafforestation Programme (Program Pengendalian Penghijauan Nasional). In that context, provincial and district heads are reported to be pleased for WALHI to undertake responsibility as they do not have to pay, as is the case when programmes are conducted by organizations linked to the government-sponsored network of Functional Groups (Golongan Karya—GOLKAR), such as the Indonesian National Youth Committee (Komite Nasional Pemuda Indonesia—KNPI). Access gained through such programmes has enabled WALHI to promote broader ecological understanding among young people.

WALHI has constantly monitored policy and legislation, undertaking public advocacy in many contexts. As will be discussed, close links have been forged with some senior persons in the government, notably the former Minister for Population and Environment, Prof. Emil Salim. Given Salim's academic as well as ministerial status, WALHI's effectiveness in dealings with the government has depended a good deal on the quality of work undertaken at grass-roots level by its affiliated groups. This has remained a source of some tension, as Salim constantly called on environmentalists to become more professional in their advocacy. While WALHI has encouraged groups to improve the quality of their research and presentation, it has neither the power nor the inclination to direct them, defending their right to express local concerns as they see fit.

WALHI has a governing praesidium of sixteen and a secretariat of thirty-two plus the director, who changes after each national meeting. Active groups are invited to a general meeting every three years to elect a praesidium and appoint a director. Care is taken to achieve socio-cultural and regional balance in membership of the praesidium. As with other LSM/LPSM networks, the lack of formal membership is designed to avoid control or co-option by the government. 'House rules' take the place of a formal constitution. Though less than fully democratic in a legal sense, WALHI's mode of operation seems reasonably representative and participatory, given the logistical and communications problem of maintaining such a large national network. Regional networks are now in place in several provinces.

WALHI has received external funding from the United States Agency for International Development (USAID), the Asia Foundation, and the Canadian International Development Association (CIDA). Most of these external funds are earmarked for specific purposes and channelled directly to individual groups. Unlike many organizations, WALHI claims not to take a percentage for its own administrative costs. Some routine costs are provided by the Indonesian Wildlife Fund. For the rest, an interesting innovation has been introduced to provide funding and general support to WALHI through the establishment of Friends of the Environment Fund (Dana Mitra Lingkungan—DML) as a non-profit organization.[5] This has attracted significant business support through regular subscriptions from both individuals and corporations (Koesnadi, 1986b: 367–70). In 1991, annual subscriptions were Rp50,000 for individuals and Rp250,000 for corporate members. A statement endorsing the importance of the work of LSMs in the environmental field in terms of Panca Sila, and as an essential qualitative component of Indonesia's overall development, was signed on 27 October 1983 by a list of notable persons, including Prof. Emil Salim, Prof. Soemitro Djojohadikusumo, Prof. Koesnadi Hardjasoemantri S.H., Drs Frans Seda, and Ir Erna Witular (Koesnadi, 1986b: 367–70).

DML established its own organizational structure, with Soemitro as chairman, and prominent banking and business figures on its board. It has enjoyed direct lines of communication to the Office of the Minister for Population and Environment, as well as WALHI. The board seeks subscriptions and other forms of support from the general public. In 1987, approximately Rp2.5 million was paid to WALHI and Rp7 million to individual organizations from interest accruing from the trust fund established from such receipts (Koesnadi, 1986b: 367–70).

Questions of conflict of interest have arisen, both in relation to business funding and the measure of protection and support which WALHI enjoys from government sources. However, despite this high-level support and patronage, WALHI is not lacking in independent strength. Its structure has been designed to protect the organization from take-over. Every associated group is legally autonomous, while most activities depend on voluntary co-operation at regional and local level. Key WALHI personnel have their own links with other LSMs and networks. Thus, much that is done with the support of WALHI is not necessarily done in its name.

Relations with the Government

WALHI's relations with the Indonesian government have been close from the outset. The first director was Ir Erna Witular, who subsequently became director of the Indonesian Foundation of Consumers' Organizations (Yayasan Lembaga Konsumen Indonesia—YLKI). Apart from her own personal dynamism, the generally favourable response from the Indonesian government to WALHI was, no doubt, assisted by her husband's membership of the People's Representative Assembly (Dewan Perwakilan Rakyat—DPR) and position as secretary of GOLKAR. The strong support given to the role of community organizations by the Minister of Population and Environment, Prof. Emil Salim, enabled WALHI to satisfy legal requirements by registering with the Department of Population and Environment (Departemen Kependudukan dan Lingkungan Hidup—KLH), leaving the Minister to deal with the Home Affairs Department.

The importance of Salim's support for the environmental cause lay in the high esteem in which he was held in economic and planning circles. His skills as a communicator enabled him to bridge numerous cultural, disciplinary, ideological, and other gaps between environmentalists and technocrats. He also deflected government criticism towards environmental and other NGO activists for criticizing Indonesia in international forums, by personally launching attacks on Western hypocrisy, in demanding protection of rain forests and so forth without addressing the structural imbalances in the world economic system which maintain Third World indebtedness.

Article 19 of the 1982 Environment Law[6] establishes the right of LSM/LPSMs to participate in implementing environmental policy. These are defined as including, among others, professional groups with relevant concerns, hobby groups 'who love nature and are motivated to sustain it', and interest groups 'who are interested in contributing to the development of the living environment. . . . In performing their supporting role, self-reliant community institutions function as a means of involving as many members of the community as possible in the effort to attain the goals of the management of the living environment' (Koesnadi, 1987: 41). Such official recognition of community groups has been substantially attributed to the efforts of Salim, who worked closely with WALHI in drafting the 1982 law.

Despite these apparently close relations, WALHI and the government have come into sharp conflict over major cases, such as Kedung Ombo and the Asahan River, North Sumatra. Nor is WALHI afraid to embarrass the government internationally. For example, *Environesia* published an exchange of correspondence between twelve Indonesian NGO representatives and the president of the World Bank, Barber Conable, which demanded that funding should be withheld until the Indonesian government produced 'proof that large scale resettlement of farmers to the outer Indonesian islands is ecologically sustainable' and evidence of commitment and capacity to ensure 'that settlements will not be permitted to infringe on or adversely affect primary tropical forests, important wetlands, and other key wildland areas', concluding that 'the ... [Bank's] policies on indigenous people will continue to be ineffective and without credibility until there is a systematic involvement of indigenous communities and actual protection and demarcation of tribal lands' (WALHI, 1987: 7–8).

WALHI has come to see its relationship with the government as having evolved from technical and bureaucratic, to political in a wider sense. Initial dealings with the Department of Population and the Environment and the State Secretariat (Sekretariat Negara—SEKNEG) have been expanded to ministries responsible for industry, forestry, and mining. WALHI's loss, along with YLBHI and local groups, of a court case in North Sumatra involving PT Inti Indorayon Utama and several government agencies,[7] nevertheless led to requests from relevant ministries for dialogue—a useful example of the NGOs' bargaining position being improved after action at field level.

Environmental Impact Analyses

Background

Detailed requirements relating to environmental impact analyses, laid down in the 1982 Environment Law and subsequent Regulation No. 29 of 1986, have resulted in regular interaction between the government and WALHI (Koesnadi, 1987: 13). At the same time, the introduction of Environmental Impact Analysis (EIA) processes strengthened the position of the Minister for Population and Environment within the government. A new Environmental Impact Monitoring Board (Badan Pengendalian Dampak Lingkungan Hidup—BAPEDAL) was set up, largely as a result of Salim's initiatives, alongside the National Development Planning Board (Badan Perencanaan Pembangunan Nasional—BAPPENAS), and a parallel board to promote technology research

(Badan Penkajian dan Penerapan Teknologi—BPPT), to oversee the environmental impact of Indonesia's development.

The Politics of Environmental Impact Analyses

EIA aims to assess the impact of proposed projects in advance. How the Suharto government, mostly committed to conventional 'fast track' economic growth, was persuaded to introduce substantial non-economic criteria and across-the-board controls on both public and private sector enterprise remains something of a mystery, especially as many in the government echo common rhetoric in Third World countries depicting environmental controls as a 'Northern luxury'.[8]

One not implausible explanation is that popular cries for comprehensive environmental management relegitimate the role of government, with the potential to counter widespread demands for deregulation and devolution of decision-making (Cribb, 1988). Nor is it clear that demands from NGOs were a decisive factor, since focus on the environment, developed as a consequence of accumulated field experience, did not feature prominently on their agenda until the late 1970s. The major initiative for WALHI's foundation came from leading mainstream NGOs rather than specialist environmental organizations, although they have played a supportive role. Pressure from some foreign donors has also been influential, although most environmental activists consider that the World Bank, which still plays a key role in influencing Indonesia's economic decision-making, has on balance promoted, rather than constrained, anti-environmental policies. Overall, it appears that ecological arguments have proved convincing to a significant minority of intellectuals and planners, who have displayed sufficient energy and professionalism to gain at least passive assent from their colleagues within the policy and decision-making process.

However, in this, as in other fields, consensus on philosophical principles in Indonesia is often negated at the level of implementation, as scrutiny of EIA processes reveals.

Legislation and Procedures

The basic conditions and processes governing EIAs are laid down in the Environmental Act 1982 and the EIA Regulations 1986. New legislation in June 1987 greatly extended the range of projects requiring EIAs, including forestry, hydroelectric, nuclear power, and transmigration sites. Article 27 of the 1986 regulations requires that every project for which an EIA is required must be publicly announced by the local authorities, together with relevant environmental information, the analysis itself, and plans for rehabilitation (Koesnadi, 1986a: 19).

This procedure has the potential to open the way for large-scale NGO participation. However, both standing and non-standing committees established at provincial level to undertake EIAs for new projects are dominated by government personnel (WALHI, 1987: 9–10). NGOs are only represented on non-standing committees, although they may exercise indirect influence through university environmental studies centres, which are recognized in the legislation. Final decisions at both the national and provincial levels rest with standing committees. The public at large enjoys even less chance to participate before the final standing committee decision. NGOs are represented in relation to general policy aspects through WALHI, which is a non-permanent member of the Environmental Impact Commission (Rapat Komisi Amdal). This has a broad brief to assess the social, economic, and environmental appropriateness of projects, in accordance with its guidelines.

The Environmental Impact Commission was very much the creation of Prof. Salim, and it remains to be seen how it will develop with his replacement in the Cabinet appointed in March 1993. In any case, both WALHI and the government have so far been hamstrung by a shortage of human resources. The situation is also confused by the fact that several government departments have set up environmental committees to undertake EIAs in their own areas. These are structured very much on an *ad hoc* basis, with cases of corruption and incompetence being frequently alleged. BAPEDAL has been set up in order to regularize this situation. However, like its National Development Planning Body counterpart, BAPPENAS, BAPEDAL has only advisory powers, with its effectiveness therefore depending on its access to and influence with senior government personnel.

In that context, both the quality and motivation of participating LSMs vary a good deal. Some appointed by government agencies are non-government in name only. WALHI has sought to deal with this situation by demanding that all consultants and groups working for the government on EIA projects be registered with it. Salim and the rural development arm (Pembangunan Desa—BANGDES) of the Department of Home Affairs responded favourably to this proposal, though it has yet to be implemented. In general, there are unresolved problems as to the degree of independence accorded to environmental investigation teams, particularly at sub-provincial levels.

Training Courses: Experience of Environmental Impact Analyses

A major bottleneck in implementing the EIA process is the lack of background knowledge and training of the members of relevant commissions, including most NGO personnel. WALHI has sought to correct this by means of training programmes through its networks and associates. The Department of Population and Environment, together with population and environmental studies centres at various universities, have also sponsored EIA training programmes. A key idea underlying such training is that strategies for research and action in relation to particular projects should evolve from discussion with local people.

WALHI has attempted to go further than formal training courses, and to develop strategies for EIAs and other action in relation to particular projects, based on discussions with local people. One idea for popular empowerment was attempted through the Barefoot EIA Training

Workshop organized by a local environmental study group in Tumou Tou, North Sulawesi, in conjunction with the Irian Jaya Rural Community Development Foundation (Yayasan Pengembangan Masyarakat Desa—YPMD), WALHI, and YLBHI Jakarta (WALHI, 1987: 9–10). Clearly, there will need to be many more such workshops linked to upgrading in skills, research capabilities, and resources, if a critical mass of persons with relevant expertise is to emerge from NGOs and base-level groups. In that context, Prof. Hasan Poerbo, director of PPLH/ITB, sees an urgent need to train development consultants among local leaders in order to help them think and plan strategically.

Effective working of EIA procedures is currently frustrated by, on the one hand, limited human and financial resources, and on the other, by the sweeping nature of legislation which applies EIA processes to virtually every project. In other words, the legislation can easily be dismissed as impractical, and so is widely ignored. Further, the concept of EIA needs to be broadened and built into development processes from the outset. In the case of major developments especially, formal steps to undertake surveys mostly come too late as key decisions are already in place. For example, during 1989–90 some 18 000 hectares (reduced from an original 45 000) were allocated for industrial development in West Java, excluding additional land required for housing and urban amenities. Land had subsequently been acquired without any prior assessment of environmental (or social) implications.[9] Application of EIAs to individual projects can thus have only a very marginal impact.

Evidence of contradictions arising from EIAs was apparent in the case of the Sentani Lake hydroelectric development in Irian Jaya, which entailed collaboration between Acres International (Canada), YPMD, and CIDA. Acres conducted an intensive survey of villagers' opinion to ensure that 'the concerns and aspirations of [the] people were included in their final report'. As a result, Acres proposed an alternative alignment which would 'decrease cropland loss and building displacement, as well as lessen the overall impact of construction on traditional land use, fishing and hunting activities, community health and sanitation, aquatic habitat and water quality' (WALHI, 1987: 11–12). Considerable disruption to the local economy, lifestyle, and environment would still result from the team's recommendations, with part of one river drying up and a significant loss of wildlife habitat. Agriculture and fishing would be correspondingly disrupted. Acres' research team leader, Lynn Smythe, admitted that 'a no-build option was not part of our mandate'. The EIA thus led to only a mitigation of the original proposal, with no guarantee that recommendations would be accepted or precisely implemented. WALHI concluded that at least Acres should be credited with having taken the rare initiative of consulting and working with a local NGO (WALHI, 1987: 11–12).

Progress in this field depends on combining community action with political advocacy. Much also depends on the government's political will in implementing stated policies. With the strengthening and extension of EIA regulations in mid-1987, the Indonesian government showed signs of adopting a firmer line. For example, an order to the Mie Won food processing factory in Surabaya to cease polluting the neighbouring river system was enforced after many years, following direct pressure by the Minister for Population and Environment and the Governor of East Java. Both men threatened to employ sections of the 1982 legislation which would impose imprisonment on the company owners.

Overall, EIAs may be seen as providing a potential entry point for raising awareness of environmental issues, both in government circles and in the general community. But they could equally be used as a vehicle for gaining NGO acquiescence, or at least the watering down of opposition, to already predetermined schemes, in the absence of well-informed and active local groups. Authorities often fail to take initiatives to establish environmental impact surveys, tending to be reactive to NGO protests. A lack of funds and appropriate human resources are also major constraints. NGOs frequently approach the government for finance. Alternatively, they are placed in a situation of having to fund environmental impact surveys resulting from their own protests. As with much else in Indonesia, most finance for EIAs derives from overseas sources.

The Indonesian Network for Forest Conservation

In its original form, this network was set up as the Joint Secretariat for Indonesian Forest Conservation (Sekretariat Kerjasama Pelestarian Hutan Indonesia—SKEPHI) at a workshop attended by fourteen NGOs in August 1982. Initiative for the workshop came from Yayasan Mandiri, a Bandung alternative technology group, which for two years provided the secretariat office, and WALHI. Initially, SKEPHI's role was complementary to that of WALHI, with a concentration on monitoring, information-gathering, and dissemination. At that stage, SKEPHI was seen, and saw itself, as a quasi-NGO playing a specialized service role. However, from around 1985, following training programmes in Kalimantan from which volunteers, who later became key organizers, were recruited, a transformation began which shifted SKEPHI in the direction of becoming a network-cum-movement.

This new direction crystallized at a workshop attended by fifty-six NGOs at Pakenjeng from 18 to 22 August 1987. Participants determined that SKEPHI should change drastically in terms of its vision, organization, and programmes (SKEPHI, c.1990). As indicated earlier, SKEPHI has networked closely with legal, human rights, students', and women's groups which share similar perspectives, participating actively in each other's campaigns and demonstrations. The resulting Pakenjeng Declaration set the tone for SKEPHI analysis, which has sought to link forest exploitation with more general social and economic exploitation, supported by an 'anti-people' political structure.

SKEPHI does not see the problem as one of merely designing better programmes targeted towards the poor, or conservation of the environment. It believes that solutions must be sought through building popular

awareness and mobilization of a kind capable of resisting external interventions and of developing self-managed and sustainable programmes.
Ideas of participatory action research fit easily within such parameters.
In organizational terms, SKEPHI stresses function rather than hierarchy
as its basis for determining roles and relationships internally. Membership is open, with individuals and affiliated groups participating in
campaigns according to their own priorities. In this way, SKEPHI believes
it can avoid what it sees as the rigidity and bureaucracy of established
NGOs. However, not surprisingly, an inner core group, based around
full-time staff and activists directing all or most campaigns, has emerged.
In that context, the research which SKEPHI conducts on many fronts
requires science-based skills. Field-based research, using mostly voluntary labour, is supported by computer networks which enable SKEPHI
to collate local, national, and international information.

SKEPHI's analysis of the Indonesian NGO community is scathing
and strident. Not surprisingly, relations with NGOs other than those
within its own networks are often extremely strained. If SKEPHI is seen
as 'too political' by its opponents, it responds with a counter-accusation
that they, whether intentionally or not, are too much the instruments of
ruling élites. While both sides agree on the need for community organizations which can articulate social interests independently from the state,
SKEPHI argues that NGOs have adapted themselves to the prevailing
order throughout the nationalist and immediate post-independence
periods and the various phases of the New Order. Under Suharto, according to SKEPHI, community structures have become more feudal,
bureaucratic, and engineered. NGOs reflect this in their analysis, organization, and programmes. The true essence of an NGO, SKEPHI
believes, is to 'act as an alternative power with the community as its
main basis, not the state or government' (SKEPHI, c.1990). Adoption
of the dominant modernization and development analysis leads inevitably
to a project and engineering approach to community organizing. Consequently, mainstream NGOs are unable to achieve any significant change
for the poor, and their programmes only take up elements of work left
undone by the government.

In the environmental field, according to SKEPHI, the failure of mainstream NGOs to challenge dominant modernization and development
paradigms has caused them to accept technological fixes such as the
'green revolution', and to adopt conservation and utilization approaches,
whereby remote areas and exotic species are protected and subsequently
exploited for tourist purposes. According to SKEPHI, such models
depict local people as enemies of the environment over whom control
and management must be exercised from above, with NGOs assisting in
their 'education', rather than as the most effective vehicle for discovering
models of ecologically sustainable development. While such arguments
have some merit, it cannot be automatically assumed that there are no
conflicts between the needs of the rural poor and a stable ecology other
than those created by outside interests. In this and other contexts,

SKEPHI has tended to overstate its case by idealizing its own role, polarizing choices, imposing one-dimensional analyses of the Indonesian state, development processes, and community structures, and stereotyping NGOs' roles towards them.

One of the less attractive features of NGOs is their tendency to be ideologically judgemental towards each other, but pragmatic in assessing their own situation. In this regard, SKEPHI displays special zeal in differentiating itself from others, particularly those with whom it interacts most closely in common struggles. Yet, despite its rhetoric, at a practical level SKEPHI shares the problems faced by most NGOs, for example, in relation to funding, building effective base-level organizations, communication, and dealing with the authorities. Nor, in a longer historical perspective, can its goals and methods be seen as unique. SKEPHI has been well-endowed financially from the outset, and receives funds from a similar range of internationally recognized agencies as other mainstream Indonesian NGOs. SKEPHI justifies the receipt of foreign aid in terms of its unconditional nature, and as an expression of solidarity rather than dependence.

SKEPHI–WALHI relations are characterized by ideological, tactical, and, to some extent, personal differences, in the context of SKEPHI's initial foundation by and subsequent breakaway from WALHI. SKEPHI attends WALHI national meetings, but this access is not reciprocated. SKEPHI lacks a formal structure and membership. WALHI considers its own system more democratic, with more respect shown for members' rights. More fundamentally, disagreement over tactics in dealing with the government lies at the heart of other differences. While WALHI gives credit to SKEPHI for its achievements in mobilizing struggle and in bringing many cases to public attention, it also sees a need to offer solutions to the government. Otherwise, conflict will lead to polarization, resulting in further alienation and repression. SKEPHI considers that the Indonesian government's structure, developmental orientation, and international support base make such an approach unrealistic.

SKEPHI's structure as a network-cum-forum contains some implicit contradictions. The nature of a forum is to facilitate and represent the diverse aspirations of affiliated organizations. This requires at least some formal organization, meetings, and procedures, if affiliated groups are not to be used as instruments of centrally determined agendas, or committed to actions or policies without their consent. For these reasons, in WALHI's view, it would be more appropriate for SKEPHI to become an LPSM, if it wishes to adopt a single-minded radical stance. In SKEPHI's view, organizations have a choice whether or not to join its network and, in any case, retain their own freedom of action. Despite these major differences, both SKEPHI and WALHI are present in many common struggles, while many affiliated organizations belong to both networks. They have also undertaken joint research, for example, in relation to biodiversity.

Regional Forums

WALHI's outreach has been steadily extended through regional forums based on provincial or smaller regional groupings. These forums or networks are autonomous, comprising diverse combinations of organizations and groups, based on common locality, outlook, or chance interaction. It is not uncommon to have more than one environmentally oriented forum in a province or sub-region, with many organizations active, or at least listed, in more than one forum. Membership and rules are defined fairly loosely. The involvement of groups in activities mostly depends on how particular developments impinge on them. Forum members are also involved in a range of other issues and programmes apart from the environment. Environmental forums are therefore usually linked with more general NGO regional networks.[10]

WALHI shares the new emphasis emerging within the NGO community on 'advocacy', which has been facilitated through the spread of regional and local networks. WALHI forums are autonomous, but linked at national level through an elected praesidium. Advocacy based on local research is brought together at national level for submission to the national government. Submissions are also channelled to regional and local governments, supported by court cases where necessary. Decentralization has led to local groups being encouraged to undertake their own environmental impact surveys. This trend has sharpened local debate on questions of the proper balance between popular empowerment and science-based professionalism. Notions of advocacy are interpreted in different ways by those stressing popular mobilization, and those who consider that protest must be accompanied by efforts to show the government how to resolve problems. However, the antithesis between the two approaches is somewhat less sharp at regional than at national level. Rather than establishing opposing regional forums, these differences tend to be articulated as a continuum of views within networks and organizations.

In West Java, for example, the Bandung Legal Aid Institute (Lembaga Bantuan Hukum—LBH), an active member of WALHI's regional forum, takes a somewhat more radical stance than either the WALHI network or its own national affiliate body, with regard to land and labour disputes. LBH also operates its own network, which takes up a number of environmental struggles. However, the two networks regularly exchange information. Yayasan Mandiri, which was founded by former Bandung Technology Institute student activists of the 1970s generation, is more inclined towards a professional approach, in line with the Social and Economic Research, Education, and Information Institute (Lembaga Penelitian, Pendidikan, dan Penerangan Ekonomi dan Sosial—LP3ES), with which it has close informal ties. However, the majority of WALHI's 65–70 member organizations concentrate on local issues, either from a community development or nature lovers' standpoint, and only attend meetings they consider directly relevant to their situation. This gap between WALHI Jakarta's emphasis on advocacy, and local LSMs' orientation towards local activity, could possibly be resolved by appropriate training and promoting general environmental knowledge as a basis for building the motivation and skills to conduct local surveys.

In November 1990, the West Java regional co-ordinator was requested to prepare plans for such a programme, but the necessary organizational infrastructure at regional level has remained weak. Six sub-regional groupings, which meet twice yearly, also appear to lack the capacity for co-ordinated local outreach. Resources are similarly stretched, requiring groups and the network to find and, in effect, risk their own funds. These may later be partially reimbursed by WALHI Jakarta, though this is not guaranteed. Support for the regional secretariat was cut off in early 1990, causing tensions between Jakarta and Bandung. Relations were aggravated by disputes about the distribution of funds raised by Dana Mitra Lingkungan for hobby groups, and allegations that WALHI Jakarta had claimed credit for actions which the regional forum considered to have resulted from its own initiatives. Farmers' struggles against the proposed golf course in Cibadas and Sagurling dam, where many fish were killed by pollution, were cited as examples. The West Java Forum claimed in the latter instance that, following media coverage which they initiated, the government proved more willing to negotiate with themselves and YLBHI.

WALHI regional networks appear stronger in Central Java, where environmental issues have provided a significant focus for more general networking, and where strong sub-regional networks are emerging. WALHI's Central Java Praesidium links convenors (*pengurus*) from four residencies, namely, Solo–Boyolali–Sragen–Sukoharjo–Wonogiri; Pati–Semarang; Kebumen–Purwokerto–Cilacap, and the Tegal–Pekalongan north coastal area. Each residency contains a regional forum, with responsibility for linking together LSM/LPSMs concerned for the environment with other student and nature lovers' groups and individuals. Regional forums meet at least twice a year to discuss both current and anticipated future issues, and to formulate strategies. These are passed down to working groups which undertake responsibility for co-ordinating local action. In 1991, the forum based in Solo comprised forty-three LSMs, twelve nature groups, plus students linked into the Student Nature Lovers' (Mahasiswa Pecinta Alam) network. The various working groups were co-ordinated by the regional forum's secretariat, based in Solo at the office of the Rural Technology Development Institute (Lembaga Pengembangan Teknologi Pedesaan—LPTP). LPTP is a major LPSM, which assists many LSMs with training, advice, and facilities.

Issues taken up by WALHI networks in Central Java have included (i) the pollution of river water by PT Semarang Diamond Chemicals in the Dukuh Tapak area of Semarang. Fifteen LSMs joined with local people in launching a Gandhian-style, non-violent boycott against the company, which finally resulted in a negotiated settlement of the dispute (WALHI, 1991: 11–12; YLBHI, 1991c: 254–6; WALHI, 1993: 13–14); (ii) monitoring potential nuclear power development, and (iii) Kedung

Ombo.[11] In this case, no real NGO consensus proved possible, with agreement only for each group to pursue its own approach, and (iv) the Solo River, where industrial pollution has grown in a context where there are no proper plans for land use (WALHI, 1989). A connection has been made between LPTP, local LSMs, working groups, and the government agency responsible for cleaning up the river.[12] Differences emerged between the LSM networks and this agency, which has seen its task as being confined to cleaning up the river, rather than tackling the basic causes of pollution.[13]

At this stage, it is too early to judge the eventual strength of regional environmental forums. However, the strategy of linking area forums and working groups, pursued with a good deal of success in Central Java but more haphazardly in West Java, appears to offer a sound model, at least in principle, for developing a critical mass of local leadership and popular-based action. Effective communication and co-operation between WALHI national, regional, and local leadership are also essential.

Water Management

Most NGOs working in rural areas, whether environmental specialists or not, encounter problems of water shortage, as has already been illustrated in the case of Yayasan Dian Desa.[14] Experience suggests that effective and equitable management of water, as a scarce commodity in most areas during Indonesia's dry season, is best achieved through co-operatively organized water users' associations. As water systems and flows need to be integrated across an extended area, local groups need to be consolidated into wider associations or federations. Co-operative networks of water users have a long-standing history in some parts of Indonesia, notably in the case of Bali's traditional irrigation (*subag*) system.[15] Even in areas such as Central Java, which have a history based more on 'hydraulic kingdoms' (Wittfogel, 1959) and central colonial control (Geertz, 1970), such associations find easy cultural acceptance. Water users' associations have also been found appropriate in urban *kampung* areas. Key factors in the effectiveness of such associations relate to honesty and efficiency of management, co-operation by local authorities, logistics of distribution, costs, and prices and, above all, popular understanding and the will to act co-operatively.

An example of a mainstream NGO taking the initiative in this area is LP3ES Klaten, which opened up a new water source in the hills, and set up a pipe system and public taps servicing twenty-three water user groups in the Wonogiri area of south Central Java, which commonly experiences severe shortage of household and drinking water during the dry season. Three local specialists are paid a fee to supervise the whole system, supported by six field officers and one administration staff. Otherwise, the programme operates on the basis of voluntary labour. Groups, which average around fifteen members each, are brought together to discuss feasibility, willingness to work, and division of tasks. The overall system is co-ordinated by a committee composed of representatives from each water users' group. Monthly routine meetings are held at both group and village levels. Water is rationed to cover only minimum household needs during the dry season, when there is an exodus from villages in search of work.

Lack of discipline has been a problem for some groups, which has threatened water supply to others, and so placed the overall system in jeopardy. As of February 1991, thirteen groups were reported to be effectively self-managing. LP3ES has operated a similar system in Kudus, East Java. It has also worked in a subcontracting role to the Dutch water consultants, IWACO, in West Java, with the aim of linking the formation of water user groups to income-generation programmes.

In the early 1980s, Bina Swadaya established a Farmer Water Users' Association (Perkumpulan Petani Pemanfaat Air—P3A), initially with six units in the Subang district of West Java, and subsequently with three in the neighbouring district of Indramayu, and five at Lebak, west of Jakarta.[16] In 1990, it came to an agreement with the provincial government to work in Indramayu and Purwakarta. P3A is the district-level apex structure linking units and sub-units. Local units are self-managing in day-to-day affairs, with financial and technical support from P3A. Sub-units, consisting of 20–50 families, elect P3A's management committee. Members' subscriptions vary with the size of land under irrigation. However, in contrast to the normal arrangement in Bina Swadaya's co-operative enterprises, which is based on one vote per family, each individual member of its irrigation sub-units has one vote. It is claimed that this procedure gives a greater say to women, as decisions on behalf of households tend mostly to be exercised by men. Initial capital came from USAID, Agro Action (Germany), the Ford Foundation, and other agencies on a revolving loan basis.

Overall, Bina Swadaya has established positive relations with the West Java provincial government (Utomo and Thamrin, 1989: 30). However, its experience illustrates both the need for and difficulty of establishing good relations with all levels of government simultaneously, without losing the confidence of the people. For example, Bina Swadaya set up an irrigation programme in 1980 in response to reports of a serious water shortage in a village in Karawang district (Utomo and Thamrin, 1989: 28). While obtaining authority from the village head, it failed to clear the programme with the district authorities, who evicted village-level staff after the scheme was already in operation. In Subang, Bina Swadaya took pains to cultivate good relations with the district head who wrote in glowing terms of the project's success. He particularly praised Bina Swadaya's evoking of popular participation and sense of ownership, which he considered would increase the chances that people would later maintain the facilities. However, the district head's support did not eliminate the negative attitudes towards the scheme by at least one sub-district head and several village heads (Utomo and Thamrin, 1989: 29–30).

In both the above programmes, initiative came from an LPSM recognizing a local need and, in effect, negotiating with the local authorities to provide a service which the latter were, for various reasons, unable to fulfil. Unlike health or education programmes, for example, which can be replicated independently across many localities with varying degrees of effectiveness, rural water supply requires flexible cross-community, village, and agency linkages which LSM/LPSMs are often well-placed to supply. However, their intervention also entails what may well appear to the authorities to be the creation of parallel structures, leading to the kind of tensions noted above in relation to Bina Swadaya.

Citanduy

The case of Citanduy in West Java provides a different model, where a non-government institution galvanized the governmental apparatus itself to mobilize the people. It also provides an example where environmental specialist groups have found it necessary to mobilize community co-operation and undertake rural development programmes beyond those immediately associated with the environment.

Around 1980, the Environmental Research Centre at the Bandung Institute of Technology (PPLH/ITB) became involved in a participatory research programme based at Cigaru village in the densely populated Citanduy River basin in Ciamis district.[17] This programme operated within the framework of the Citanduy II programme, established in 1980 by the Department of Agriculture, assisted by USAID, with the aim of improving watershed management. As 13 per cent of the land was classified as too degraded to sustain permanent staple agricultural crops, PPLH/ITB was asked by the Department of Population and Environment to undertake a policy review of approaches to upland development. The aim was to rehabilitate critical land and prevent further damage through appropriate soil and water management practices, using terracing systems adapted from earlier traditional practices. Whereas the Department of Agriculture sought to motivate farmers through incentives linked to a network of extension agents and demonstration plots, the PPLH/ITB team saw a need for closer working relationships with local communities.

Terracing requires active local co-operation, involving many workshops and mass meetings. According to PPLH/ITB's account, sub-village level groups were formed and joined together into *usaha bersama* at village level. Groups visited demonstration terraces in villages where the system was already installed. Domicile groups of 35–40 households co-operated in terrace-building, animal husbandry, intensification of house-gardens, cottage industries, and resettlement of homes formerly built on steep, erosion-prone slopes. Functional groups such as dry-land farmers, irrigation users, and sheep-pen groups were formed in liaison with domicile groups, with all groups linked together into a network of co-operative economic groups (Kelompok Usaha Bersama Ekonomi—KUBE).

As noted earlier, agricultural co-operatives can only operate legally at village level as government-sponsored Village Co-operative Units (Koperasi Unit Desa—KUD).[18] While informal arrangements can often be negotiated, these require personal goodwill and co-operation from local authorities. In Cigaru, the problem was resolved by the establishment of the Institute for Environmental Care (Yayasan Bina Lingkungan Hidup—YBLH) to link local co-operative economic groups. YBLH also served to provide an official legal umbrella, and to perform an intermediary role between sub-village authorities and relevant public and private institutions. Co-operation from local authorities varied. According to PPLH/ITB, least success was achieved in areas where village heads insisted on directly controlling the whole programme, thus discouraging open discussion at mass meetings.

YBLH has co-operated closely with the government from the outset, and is perceived by local people in this light. Its management board included a former chairman of the People's Regional Representative Assembly (Dewan Perwakilan Rakyat Daerah—DPRD) and the project manager for the Presidential Instruction (Instruksi Presiden—INPRES) rural development programme in the area, who was evidently disillusioned with official approaches to planning. His brother, who heads the Provincial Development Planning Board (Badan Perencanaan Pembangunan Daerah—BAPPEDA), played a key advisory role. Support from local Islamic leaders and teachers has enabled programmes to be disseminated through mosques and Islamic educational institutions. YBLH has also worked a good deal through established official village-level groups, such as the Association for Promoting Family Welfare (Pembinaan Kesejahteraan Keluarga—PKK), the Indonesian Farmers' Association (Himpunan Kerukunan Tani Indonesia—HKTI), or co-operatives associated with the official KUD system.

YBLH's close political relations with the government undoubtedly both reflect and influence a 90 per cent vote for GOLKAR in the Cigaru area. One manager, appointed in 1987, was removed after one year when his connection with one of the official political parties, the Development Unity Party (Partai Persatuan Pembangunan—PPP), became known (Nindyantoro, 1989: 8). YBLH's experience further illustrates that leadership from intellectuals and local influentials often lacks continuity. Key local leaders took up other work, causing the organization's development to languish (Nindyantoro, 1989: 3–4). YBLH failed to develop its own locally based analysis, and continued to look to PPLH/ITB for both environmental knowledge and funds (Nindyantoro, 1989: 5, 21–2). It also failed to see the importance of networking with other LPSMs. Women's activities appear to have relied a good deal on PKK and Dharma Wanita's styles of operation, which fail to reflect the growing economic strength and independence of a number of women's groups associated with YBLH.

According to a survey conducted in 1989, YBLH is seen locally as an environmental arm of the government, with PPLH acting as an intermediary at a higher level. However, this survey also considered that, although YBLH had failed to establish an independent identity for itself, it had succeeded in establishing effective and autonomous local units (Nindyantoro, 1989: 21–2). Earlier terracing work had provided the basis for the co-operative group's later success in non-agricultural as well as agricultural fields. The turnover from unit enterprises ranged from Rp200,000 to Rp6 million (Nindyantoro, 1989: 7). Groups were flexible in finding entry points and organizational forms were adapted to the situation of each group and locality. As indicated in earlier discussion, local leadership and a more stable organization often emerge once initial outside leadership has withdrawn.[19]

The strategy of basing many co-operative economic groups on existing organizations, such as the PKK or informal *arisan* groups, appears to have given them access to resources and a stamp of recognition, while still retaining a good deal of autonomy in day-to-day management. In practice, even officially based organizations can prove quite heterogeneous in character. For example, Koperasi PKK Sartika, based on the local PKK unit, covers several villages around Sukadana (Nindyantoro, 1989: 12–15). This co-operative was initiated by a schoolteacher who had gained experience elsewhere in a previous, unsuccessful venture run by women. Sartika was the name of a West Javanese heroine (*pahlawan*) during the national independence struggle, and a pioneer of women's education. Wives of village leaders play a leading role in this co-operative, which appears reasonably well-managed, achieving an 80 per cent loan recovery rate. Co-operative groups associated with the Institute for Environmental Care are not legally registered in their own right but through Village Co-operative Units. No payments are required, only an annual report. This arrangement proved possible because of the co-operative's standing as a PKK activity. Koperasi PKK Sartika, nevertheless, refused suggestions of becoming a sub-unit of the KUD.

Pelita Sukma, also located in Sukadana, is based on heads of families, including eleven widows (Nindyantoro, 1989: 16–18). One motivation for its foundation was to reduce and rationalize the burden of local tax collection by combining co-operative membership with payment of all sub-village taxes. In principle, this arrangement has also given Pelita Sukma power to determine its level of taxes, based on needs. In this case, the Neighbourhood Council head also acted as superintendent of Pelita Sukma.

The long-term viability of YBLH co-operative economic units is uncertain. Lack of group cohesion is indicated by reports that, once terracing operations have been undertaken co-operatively, agricultural and other activities tend increasingly to be carried out on an individual or competitive basis. The number of co-operative groups had declined sharply from a peak of around forty to fourteen by early 1991.[20] Lembaga Studi Pembangunan has been undertaking training in an attempt to arrest this decline though, according to Prof. Poerbo, the quality of available local leadership is affected by a brain drain from the area. Overall, it appears that such popular organization as has emerged has been largely the result of independent local initiatives rather than YBLH efforts.

An Overview of Environmental Mobilization

The full spectrum of action approaches is represented in the environmental field. At one end, the approach pursued in the Cigaru–Citanduy area seeks to use governmental structures as a means of gaining access to and stimulating community action among local groups. Bina Swadaya, as in other fields of activity, has sought co-operative relations with regional and local authorities. However, it has not drawn government personnel into the actual management of local water users' federations, concentrating rather on building independent local capability. At the opposite end of the spectrum, SKEPHI has adopted an essentially confrontationist stance towards the government, while distancing and differentiating itself from the main body of LSM/LPSMs.

WALHI, which embraces a wide diversity of environmental organizations and loosely structured groups, can be seen as occupying the middle ground between close co-operation with and opposition to the government. WALHI has also gone some way, both conceptually and in practice, towards bridging the gap between a professional and science-based understanding of Indonesian ecology and popular empowerment. It has also achieved a fairly dynamic balance between advocacy and local action. Communication problems between national, regional, and local contexts, and between groups pursuing different understandings and approaches, nevertheless remain considerable.

1. See Cribb (1988); Hardjono (1986; 1991), and YLBHI (1991c) for an overview of environmental issues in Indonesia.

2. *Wahana* literally means 'vehicle' for gathering and conveying ideas.

3. See WALHI (1990c: 2–6) and WALHI (1993) for information concerning WALHI's background and evolution.

4. WALHI sources.

5. See pp. 52–3.

6. Act of the Republic of Indonesia No. 4 of 1982 concerning 'Basic Provisions for the Management of the Living Environment'. For details and commentary, see Koesnadi (1987).

7. See p. 116.

8. In that context, the costs of EIA tend to be exaggerated, according to the World Bank, which has estimated the cost of producing and implementing an EIA at between 0–3 per cent of the capital cost of an average project (WALHI, 1987: 9–10).

9. PPLH/ITB sources.

10. See pp. 201–7.

11. See pp. 122–4.

12. This programme is part of a national programme for cleaning up Indonesia's rivers: Program Kali Bersih (PROKASIH) (YLBHI, 1991c: 251–6).

13. LPTP sources; interview February 1991.

14. See pp. 63–4.

15. Local government and water management systems were closely linked under traditional Balinese structures.

16. Bina Swadaya sources, January 1991.

17. Comments in this paragraph are based on interviews with Prof. Hasan Poerbo, director of PPLH/ITB, in January 1988 and January 1991. See also Terrant and Poerbo (c.1988: 172–82).

18. See pp. 68, 75–6.

19. See pp. 77–86 regarding local co-operatives fostered by Lembaga Studi Pembangunan.

20. Interview with Prof. Hasan Poerbo, January 1991.

8

Non-Government Organizations and the Mobilization of Women

EARLIER chapters have noted examples relating to the participation of women in the context of mainstream non-government organizations (NGOs). This chapter will focus on the role of independent women's organizations in Indonesia. All known groups in the Jakarta and Yogyakarta–Solo region at the time fieldwork was conducted in 1988 and 1991 have been included in this account, which has been supplemented by other documentary evidence. The Productive Women's Programme, initiated by the Social and Economic Research, Education, and Information Institute (Lembaga Penelitian, Pendidikan, dan Penerangan Ekonomi dan Sosial—LP3ES) in Klaten district, whose stated aim is to establish an independent federation of co-operatives owned and managed by women, is also included.

The chapter will look first at the goals of women's mobilization taken up by self-reliant community institutions (Lembaga Swadaya Masyarakat—LSM) and institutions for developing community self-reliance (Lembaga Pengembangan Swadaya Masyarakat—LPSM).[1] This is followed by a discussion of organizational contexts in which different women's groups have sought to establish a measure of independence from dominant government structures. Issues here are illustrated with reference to co-operatives—a form of organization favoured a good deal by women's groups. More detailed consideration is given to the impact of economic programmes by comparing LP3ES's Productive Women's Programme in Klaten with the East Java Women's Co-operatives' Centre (Pusat Koperasi Wanita Jawa Timur—PUSKOWANJATI), an independent federation of co-operatives managed at all levels by and for women. While LP3ES's programme seems better targeted towards poor women, both economic and non-economic benefits to participants are more apparent in the case of PUSKOWANJATI, which has placed special emphasis on developing the organization, confidence, and communication skills of women.

The remainder of the chapter covers individual organizations, with special reference to issues taken up, styles of mobilization, and ways of relating to the Indonesian government. Elements of all four models proposed in Chapter 2 are evident among the groups surveyed in this chapter. The blurred nature of distinctions between government and non-government spheres, in this as in other contexts, is illustrated by an account of the active links forged between the Women's Section of the All-Indonesia Workers' Union (Serikat Pekerja Seluruh Indonesia—SPSI), the labour section of the Foundation of Indonesian Legal Aid Institutions (Yayasan Lembaga Bantuan Hukum Indonesia—YLBHI), and some independent women's organizations. The chapter concludes with an assessment of the relative strength and unity of independent women's organizations.

Goals and Issues in Women's Mobilization

The mobilization of women in Indonesia, as in most other countries, has been directed towards raising their social and economic status. In practice, the economic aspects have received greatest emphasis. Both government and non-government programmes directed towards women have been primarily designed either to generate increased income or to focus on basic needs deficiencies considered particularly salient to women, such as water, nutrition, family planning, and health. Questions relating to the situation of women within the household, gender-based division of labour, and the construction of social roles have generally been considered too complex and sensitive to confront in any direct way. One major survey has argued strongly that many, perhaps most women, particularly in rural areas, are at this stage only willing to discuss such matters in strictly private contexts (Berninghausen and Kerstan, 1992). All but a few urban-based non-government organizations have adopted this view.

The reasons for such reticence derive, in part, from official government policies which seek to enhance women's contribution towards the fulfilment of national development goals, building on their traditional frameworks (Cooley, 1992). Approaches which might disturb these objectives, or cause social disharmony, are likely to incur heavy-handed government disapproval. Nevertheless, notions of social harmony and avoidance of conflict are widely accepted as representing deep-rooted values in Indonesian society, particularly among the Javanese. LSM/LPSMs working among women appear to accept this normative framework as a basis on which to build. Women activists in Indonesia, with some exceptions, mostly adopt the view that women's issues can best be addressed in the context of general societal problems, stressing partnership and solidarity between men and women in their solution. The implications of this outlook for action strategies point to low-profile, behind-the-scenes problem-solving and consensus-building rather than strident assertion of rights.

To some extent, there has been an assumption underlying many programmes in this field that improving the economic position of women will also raise their status within the family. Field studies cited provide some support for this proposition, but question whether there is any necessary correlation between them (Berninghausen and Kerstan, 1992: 225–7). It has been argued that further educational efforts are needed in order to improve women's confidence and capacity to participate in building their own organizations, for example, in speaking at meetings. Such consciousness-raising programmes should also seek to identify and support women's own interests, not just their contribution to household income. However, such ideas soon come into conflict with Javanese custom, which discourages the egoistic pursuit of personal wishes or the open discussion of intra-family issues.

The Institutional Context

Officially sponsored organizations, such as Dharma Wanita, representing the wives of civil servants, and the Association for Promoting Family Welfare (Pembinaan Kesejahteraan Keluarga—PKK), which has units in villages throughout Indonesia, have sought to monopolize the mobilization of women. While they have not entirely succeeded in this aim, their presence is pervasive and greatly inhibits the emergence of independent organizations which are democratically managed by and for women. These government-based bodies project an official image of the ideal Indonesian woman as active citizen and home-maker, as well as nurturer and supporter to her husband. While many extra tasks are imposed on women in the name of promoting national development, such new roles are subordinate to their primary domestic roles (Berninghausen and Kerstan, 1992: 225–7, 233–8). When the overall regulatory and political context confronting LSM/LPSMs in Indonesia is taken into account, those working with women thus suffer a double set of constraints in formulating local programmes.

Both Dharma Wanita and PKK replicate the functional role and position of husbands within the bureaucratic hierarchy, in accordance with instructions by the Minister for Home Affairs in 1984 (MENDAGRI, 1984). It has been claimed that 'the explicit function of local PKK units, according to the government's own official statements, remains a passive one of transmitting government directives and promoting state ideology to the mass of ordinary women' (Sullivan, 1983: 160; C. Warren, 1990: 8). One consequence at village level is that the village head's wife is automatically assigned responsibility for the family planning programme within the framework of the PKK programme. As Carol Warren has observed, the PKK 'assumes a subordinate political and economic position in the household and promotes an ideology of the family and women's role in it (as wife, mother, housekeeper and prime socialiser) which is more compatible with the state's interest in social control than with its stated economic objectives of expanded production and improved living standards'.[2] The simplest strategy for LSM/LPSMs in such circumstances is to include programmes for women as part of more general interventions in local development processes. As in other fields, organizations which directly challenge or seek to supersede official institutions or ideology cannot be sustained in rural areas, and only with great difficulty elsewhere.

The question of whether women's problems can be most effectively addressed by distinct organizations, or within more general organizational frameworks, represents a significant theme within the international literature on the status of women in developing countries.[3] There appear to be relatively few independent women's organizations in Indonesia, although their number has been growing slowly in recent years. Also, more women's units and groups can now be found at the grass-roots level, supported by local LSM/LPSMs. On the one hand, separate organizations give women more space to identify needs and concerns and develop their own styles and strategies. They also provide greater opportunity for female leadership to emerge. On the other hand, it is important for all-women's groups not to become marginalized, and to maintain access to a broad range of contacts and information of the kind available to larger mixed LSM/LPSMs. Correspondingly, as the organizational strength of independent women's groups grows, they are better able to deal with male groups on equal terms, and to gain opportunities to influence decision-making.

Co-operatives: Three Case-studies from Java

Some of these issues can be illustrated with reference to co-operatives, which many policy-makers have tended to see as representing a natural development for women's groups, as most Indonesian women already belong to strong informal networks (Berninghausen and Kerstan, 1992: 216–17). For example, in Java, the traditional *arisan* system is based on the norms of mutual help and obligation. As noted in Chapter 4, *arisan* have been developed into many kinds of productive small enterprise, and have also been converted to serve health and nutrition goals. Sexual division of labour in Java requires women to manage household finances, while the supposedly female qualities of thrift, conscientiousness, and reliability, and social and communication skills are seen as equipping them to manage co-operatives (Berninghausen and Kerstan, 1992: 217). In that context, the government has defined the role of women as contributing to national development through membership of co-operatives, as pioneers and motivators for co-operatives, and as contributors to household income through activity as both producers and consumers, particularly in the retail sector. Women's co-operatives can also contribute to charitable and educational work, according to the chairman of the Credit Union Co-ordinating Organization (CUCO) (Berninghausen and Kerstan, 1992: 217). However, these expanded roles should in no sense be seen as a challenge to women's primary role as wives and mothers.

Three operational models for women's co-operatives were identified by Berninghausen and Kerstan as (i) female auxiliary units of rural multi-purpose co-operatives; (ii) units of functional women's groups, and (iii) independent local or area co-operatives, or federations of co-operatives. In 1985, only 660 out of more than 28,000 (2.3 per cent) registered co-operatives throughout Indonesia were independent women's co-operatives. In Java, the figure was only 242 out of 13,280 (1.8 per cent).[4] Such data appears to conflict with women's evident preference to run their own organizations (Berninghausen and Kerstan, 1992: 216, fn. 65). The first two models nevertheless allow women a measure of autonomy at the level of day-to-day operation and management within the framework of larger, mixed organizations.

The Contact Board for Women's Co-operatives (Badan Kontak Wanita Koperasi—BKWK), which is a member of the Indonesian Council of Co-operatives (Dewan Koperasi Indonesia—DEKOPIN), supports the establishment of all-women's co-operatives as a medium-term strategy, with the ultimate aim of full women's participation in mixed co-operatives. This aim is in line with the strong policies of the International Labour Organization (ILO) and the International Co-operatives Association (ICA), though at this stage Indonesian practice leans strongly towards gender segregation in most kinds of organization. In 1979, BKWK initiated a project to upgrade the role of women in co-operatives, which resulted in the establishment of 108 new groups across Indonesia between 1979 and 1985. These consisted of thirty-nine pre-co-operatives,[5] thirty-two village co-operative units (Koperasi Unit Desa—KUD), and thirty-three independent groups in 1985 (Berning-hausen and Kerstan, 1992: 217, fn. 70 citing DEPKOP, 1985: 11).

The Productive Women's Programme, Klaten

Berninghausen and Kerstan have drawn out some issues relating to the cultural and organizational aspects of women's co-operatives through comparative field studies of LP3ES's Productive Women's Programme (PWP) in Klaten district of Central Java and PUSKOWANJATI.[6] By 1991, seventy-six women's groups had been formed across seven sub-districts in Klaten. Their activities covered poultry and goat rearing, small shops or stalls (*warung*), household crafts, food preparation, and sewing. In selecting members, LP3ES targeted women with a maximum daily income of Rp1,500. In reality, this figure was often exceeded, sometimes reaching Rp3,000 (Berninghausen and Kerstan, 1992: 223–4).

A principal justification of the programme has been that women's status would rise with income. Berninghausen and Kerstan (1992: 218) cite the LP3ES Klaten programme director, Mohammed Zainuddin, as stating that the PWP works on the assumption that it is legitimate for a woman to supplement her household income so long as she does not neglect her duties as wife and mother.[7] The survey's authors observe wryly that such an outlook is compatible with that of official national women's programmes, while the PWP displays little obvious difference in its implementation from PKK programmes.[8] How far such comments reflect a personal view, LP3ES's core values, or merely an ultra-cautious policy of non-confrontation deemed necessary in a still politically sensitive local environment, is open to question. It is more pertinent to question whether any causal relationship can be established between increased income contribution and women's status within the family. At the time of the Berninghausen and Kerstan survey, it was still uncertain whether incomes had risen sufficiently as a result of the programme to test for significant difference compared with non-participating women.

LP3ES Klaten commissioned a survey in 1990 (by Riawanti, Noviana, and Harun), which broadly reflected Berninghausen and Kerstan's earlier findings which had found no clear correlation between women's income-earning capacity and their status within the household. While observations by LP3ES female fieldworkers indicated some sharing of household tasks between men and women, in terms of minding children and undertaking housework,[9] both groups of researchers found that women enjoyed limited participation in household decision-making, especially in major economic and investment decisions. Women surveyed in Klaten also enjoyed more limited social contacts, interaction, and participation in community gatherings compared with men, and were consequently liable to be marginalized in community decision-making.

The PWP was also criticized for the narrowness of its training courses. These emphasized technical skills without confronting hierarchical Javanese structures and styles of communication.[10] The absence of literacy classes limited participation, which was mostly confined to motivators and other functionaries. As these latter gained more training in communication, the gap between them and average members tended to widen. More generally, it was urged that economic activity alone would not be sufficient 'for the PWP groups to develop into a functioning, cooperative organisation which effects a broadening of its members' economic and social sphere of activities'. Specific measures were also needed 'to foster the members' capacity for reflection, their general competence and their capability for democratic self-administration' (Berninghausen and Kerstan, 1992: 227).

Subsequently, a team led by Adriani Soemantri from Yayasan Anisa Swasti, an independent women's organization based in Yogyakarta, undertook a programme of consciousness-raising in line with these recommendations (Soemantri, Soehendera, and Widjajanti, 1988; Berninghausen and Kerstan, 1992: 227). Six women supervisors were recruited by LP3ES Klaten to support this work.[11] Each supervisor controls five 'motivators', who, in turn, cover 1–5 groups. The (female) supervisor meets sub-district team leaders once a month. All teams meet together monthly in Klaten to review achievements and problems, and to make future plans. LP3ES claims that one result has been that the customary prohibitions against women going out at night have been challenged by pointing to the social usefulness of meetings and classes. Women also became more active in collecting funds for public purposes, such as the neighbourhood watch, street lighting, and the repair of irrigation channels. Subsequently, women's representatives have been asked to give their opinions on these issues at village meetings.[12]

The marketing of products of local groups has constituted a significant problem for NGOs throughout the Third World, including Indonesia. Overcrowding and duplication, particularly in the handicrafts field, plus the distance and dispersion of their mostly urban and overseas markets, constitute key sources of difficulty. Various efforts to overcome such problems through networking have been attempted among groups of larger national LPSMs, though with limited success. One approach could be to involve women in marketing, particularly in identifying suitable products for local markets. This could enhance their skills in new ways, and bring wider contacts, confidence, and capacity to shape the overall functioning of their enterprises. While the lack of local purchasing power remains a limiting factor, that situation may be expected to improve, as Klaten is strategically located between Yogyakarta and Solo, in a region which continues to experience sustained and diversified economic growth.

The Islamic Education Foundation

One smaller attempt at empowerment of women through co-operative income-generation programmes may be noted in the case of the Islamic Education Foundation (Yayasan Pendidikan Islam) located in Tanjung Kawalu village, in the Tasikmalaya district of West Java.[13] This forms part of the development network around Pesantren Cipasung. The programme has combined Islamic education with skills training in machine embroidery. Women return to their villages and train others. The Foundation estimates that beginners would earn around Rp500 per day rising to Rp4,000–5,000 after one year. The Foundation established a co-operative to purchase sewing-machines. In 1988, there were 148 members, while nearly Rp3 million had been accumulated in capital, mostly from members, but partly from the Association for Pesantren and Community Development (Perkumpulan Pengembangan Pesantren dan Masyarakat—P3M) network. The produce is brought to the *pesantren* each year and further material purchased. Markets are mostly being found in the Middle East. The Department of Trade actively seeks markets, while the Department of Industry checks quality. Once export quality has been certified, registered co-operatives are eligible for credit at 9 per cent per year from the Indonesian Trading Bank (Bank Dagang Negara).

There is little evidence that the social or structural issues highlighted in Berninghausen and Kerstan's survey of the Islamic Education Foundation's programme have received attention. However, a focus on accumulating capital in addition to simply earning income could, over time, bring a measure of empowerment to the women concerned. As the programme is aimed particularly at school drop-outs, this could be important to young women otherwise doubly disadvantaged. The live-in nature of training programmes seems also likely to enhance their general, as well as religious, education. In a wider context, co-operatives are becoming more central to the strategies of Islamic social movements.

Active involvement by Muslim women in co-operatives would therefore seem a prerequisite to their exerting influence over the direction of these movements.

The Association of East Java Women's Co-operatives

The East Java Women's Co-operatives' Centre (Pusat Koperasi Wanita Jawa Timur—PUSKOWANJATI) is an independent, self-managing all-women's organization based in Malang, with membership open to all women in East Java. Its origins reach back to the pre-1965 period. A temporary set-back to its growth occurred in the early 1980s, when a male bookkeeper allegedly embezzled the co-operatives' joint funds.[14] However, by 1986 the organization had grown into a federation of 16,000 members based on twenty-nine member co-operatives. Accumulated net capital had reached Rp120 million (Berninghausen and Kerstan, 1992: 229). Some funding support was received from the Ford and Asia Foundations, Friedrich Ebert Stiftung, and USAID for training in technical, managerial, motivational, and counselling aspects.

Formal democratic structures have been set in place, with the executive accountable to the members' meeting, and composed of delegates from member co-operatives (Berninghausen and Kerstan, 1992: 228–31). Detailed management is in the hands of a five-person board of directors, elected for a three-year term, which controls office workers, teams, and trainers. Each co-operative elects its leaders for a two-year term. Co-operatives are divided into local groups of 10–25 women. Co-ordinators are appointed to maintain mutual links and support 8–10 groups in a given area. Group leaders meet monthly. Small group size is intended to maintain close communication and mutual support. It is claimed that strong reciprocal links and a sense of mutual obligation make for a strong ethic of repayment. A system known as *tanggung renteng* is in operation, whereby individual women may be provided with emergency support, either from local group funds or from the co-operative. Inter-lending between secondary and primary co-operatives is sometimes available to finance larger programmes.

By contrast with PWP Klaten, Berninghausen and Kerstan (1992: 228) identified PUSKOWANJATI as 'one of the only co-operatives which still calls women's traditional role into question and which has single-mindedly translated the theory of self-help into practise'. PUSKOWANJATI has been active in educating women in the processes of democratic group formation, and in training them in skills necessary for active participation, such as public speaking. However, the organization has avoided open confrontation with either the government or with traditional family norms and structures. In that context, both PUSKOWANJATI and PWP leaders see Western-style feminist language as counter-productive.

In summary, PUSKOWANJATI's emphasis on building an independent democratic movement of like-minded women reflects important elements of the popular empowerment model in terms of its relations with the government and approach to popular mobilization. While PUSKOWANJATI has been built up gradually from small groups, LP3ES Klaten's PWP represents an extension downwards from a large organization run predominantly by men in its higher echelons. For this reason, while it may be possible to mobilize women on specific issues, PWP's structures seem to have inhibited development of any real solidarity between LP3ES and local women.

Two independent women's organizations broadly representative of the empowerment approach are Yayasan Anisa Swasti and Kalayana-mitra.

Yayasan Anisa Swasti

Yayasan Anisa Swasti, popularly known as Yasanti, was started in 1982 by six young women friends in Yogyakarta, who, according to their own account, conducted a weekly discussion group while still at high school, from which the idea for an organization devoted entirely to women was born. One of the six, Sri Kusyuniati, became the director, while the other five comprised the board (WALHI, 1988: 10–11). Yasanti aims to work only with the poorest of the poor, but its work among typists and shop workers, for example, suggests that some of its target groups are one or two rungs above the bottom of the socio-economic ladder. Moreover, the promotion of small-scale co-operatives and enterprises requires some level of basic education, at least from group leaders. Nevertheless, Yasanti has made serious efforts to reach out to factory workers, and has been gradually extending its work in rural areas near Yogyakarta.

Yasanti runs training centres in Yogyakarta and Semarang. It operates savings and loans groups and informal co-operatives (*usaha bersama*), and also conducts general education and awareness-building programmes among women shop assistants in Yogyakarta and factory workers in Semarang. Yasanti's key philosophical aim is to develop an alternative to the PKK model, which it sees as seeking monopoly control of women's organizations, without regard to social and other differences among them. Essentially, Yasanti's strategy is one of empowerment by means of quiet education, rather than seeking to influence or challenge official policy through direct confrontation. Good relations are nevertheless cultivated with government agencies to the extent necessary to facilitate its work. It is also active in networking with other LSM/LPSMs, thus reflecting a combination of the second and third models in its overall relations with the authorities.

Yasanti's basic entry point is through skills training, in which women are brought together to identify and solve problems impinging on them in their workplace. Training programmes are supported by an informal environment, which provides opportunity for wider discussion and for the development of confidence to discuss rights. Specific legal education is undertaken in co-operation with the Yogyakarta Legal Aid Institute (Lembaga Bantuan Hukum Yogyakarta—LBHY) and some supportive academics. Popular theatre is also employed in co-operation with the Indonesian People's Theatre Institute (Yayasan Teater Rakyat Indonesia—YTRI). Yasanti claims that, as a result of its programmes, women sales assistants in large stores in Yogyakarta have become bolder in demanding overtime payments, leave, and other rights to which they are entitled under various kinds of legislation. A group of typists in Yogyakarta also successfully organized themselves to achieve higher wages and improved conditions through strike action (WALHI, 1988: 10–11).

The Women's Section of Indonesia's only officially recognized trade union, the SPSI, has been pressing for female supervisors in female-majority workplaces. Situations where claims for two-day menstruation leave entitlement have entailed checks by male supervisors, have proved particularly obnoxious to women workers. Non-co-operation tactics have even been encouraged in some instances. Use of such tactics in Yogyakarta succeeded in achieving the desired result in Toko Ramai and some other stores. Women workers are learning to read contracts, and to demand references on leaving employment. Yasanti has also indirectly confronted female beautification stereotypes by encouraging demands for employers to pay for the lipstick which they oblige store girls to wear. It also encouraged agricultural workers to protest at the fruit used for decoration purposes at Dharma Wanita and PKK functions, being subsequently thrown away.

In 1992, Yasanti held a review of its work over the past five years. It was decided, in principle, to concentrate its efforts on women textile workers around Yogyakarta. It is planned that other aspects of its work, such as research and publication, education, and training will be split off to form separate LSMs. It appears that Yasanti continues to face a number of internal organizational strains and tensions (Strintzos, 1991).

Kalyanamitra

Kalyanamitra, based in Jakarta, has similar aims to Yasanti, with whom it maintains close contact. However, it has avoided taking up action programmes of its own, concentrating rather on research, publications, and other support activities. It offers a meeting-place and resources, enabling women to share information and develop mutual support networks. Kalyanamitra is relatively unusual in its willingness to publicly raise questions about the status of women in the family, the gender-based division of labour, and the social portrayal of women. It has also not been afraid to discuss normally taboo issues, such as violence against women in both the domestic and workplace contexts. It publishes a popular-style magazine called *Dongbret*, which includes a lively cartoon section.

One catalyst for Kalyanamitra's foundation was the pressure being brought to bear by the elements within the government on the Women's Study Centre, which was linked to the University of Indonesia's Faculty of Social and Political Science, in relation to the receipt of foreign funds.

Reorganization as an NGO has enabled some of the Centre's more controversial work to be carried on in a more informal environment. Kalyanamitra's links with staff and students at the nearby University of Indonesia campus at Depok have remained strong. Kalyanamitra has also networked closely with the Women's Section of SPSI and the labour section of YLBHI, for example, assisting them with research and other kinds of informal support for programmes aimed at empowering domestic servants (Kalyanamitra, 1986).

Kalyanamitra has been strongly criticized by the Indonesian Network for Forest Conservation (Sekretariat Kerjasama Pelestarian Hutan Indonesia—SKEPHI) for refusing to join its campaigns, and for its supposedly intellectual and non-political analysis. Philosophically, the two groups represent opposite poles in the class versus gender debate. Whereas radicals emphasize class and structural factors as dominant causes of women's oppression, which is seen as part of a more general oppression, Kalyanamitra has focused on more gender-specific causes. It has also maintained its position as an all-women's organization. While radicals operate self-managing women's units, these are closely integrated within mixed-gender networks which take up joint issues. Like Yasanti, Kalyanamitra appears to fit the popular empowerment model in its avoidance of any close interaction with government authorities or official programmes, and in its emphasis on supporting independent groups. While Kalyanamitra's direct, hands on experience of women's situation at grass-roots levels appears limited, its knowledge base in this regard has been strengthened by contact with activists engaged more directly with working-class women in several fields.

The Legal Aid Consultative Institute for Women and Families

The Legal Aid Consultative Institute for Women and Families (Lembaga Konsultasi Bantuan Hukum Wanita dan Keluarga—LKBHWK) provides a more conservative example of an independent women's group, which combines elements of the first and second models in its approach to popular mobilization. It was established in 1979 as an offshoot of YLBHI, with the aim of more specifically targeting women's needs in this field. The major initiative came from a group of Muslim women professionals who aimed to improve the status of Muslim women within a framework of continuing commitment to Islam. The chairman of LKBHWK, Ibu Yani Yamin, had been actively involved with LBH in its early years.

LKBHWK has focused primarily on issues relating to marriage and family law. It operates information desks at religious courts in South and West Jakarta, with more planned in Central, North, and East Jakarta. Assistance has been provided by the Asia Foundation, as part of a more general project of research and education in Islamic religious (*Syariah*) law conducted in conjunction with Islamic, legal aid, and academic institutions. The organization's headquarters was initially located in the Mesjid Agung Al-Azhar in Kebayoran Baru, a largely middle-class area of Jakarta, but had to be moved in 1986 as a result of pressure from conservative and fundamentalist groups. Suspicions of LKBHWK's foreign and other high-level connections also appear to have been a factor. As a consequence, drop-in visits and contacts fell fairly sharply, while the enforced move also led to a severe rise in rental costs. Branches have been established in Bandung, Yogyakarta, Palembang, and Banda Aceh. Others are planned in Padang, Riau, and Semarang. In 1988, sixteen full-time staff were located in Jakarta, assisted by a team of volunteers, including several professionals. There were approximately forty staff in the regions at that time but only 5–6 were full-time.

Financial donations are canvassed from researchers and other visitors. Clients pay what they can. As a novel mode of fund-raising, fifty high-ranking women are named as 'first ladies' of the Institute, paying Rp500,000 for the honour. LKBHWK claims to raise about 60 per cent of its own income from these efforts, plus other consultancies. The rest comes mostly from the Ford Foundation (an important supporter of YLBHI) and the Asia Foundation.

LKBHWK's outlook towards government-sponsored women's organizations has been ambivalent. Generally, efforts have been made to influence rather than confront them. Ibu Yamin appears to have influential contacts in Dharma Wanita for whom she runs training courses. Cultivation of such contacts is justified in terms of building support for the organization. However, its impact on the empowerment of poor and average women whom LKBHWK aims to serve, appears more dubious and potentially counter-productive.

High-level contacts almost certainly provide informal support and protection for LKBHWK's work, indicating, at least in principle, an approach in line with the second model of popular mobilization. In an overall sense, however, LKBHWK projects a fairly upper middle-class ethos, while, in Jakarta at least, its enforced élite location has hindered its outreach to poorer groups. Consequently, LKBHWK has been in danger of sliding into a welfare role. A more promising alternative would be to develop a general advocacy role for the status of women within Islam and, over time, empower Muslim women to take up issues for themselves. LKBHWK appears well-placed to undertake such a task in terms of the education, background, and contacts of its leaders and members.

The All-Indonesia Workers' Union, Women's Section

Progressive elements within the Women's Section of SPSI have developed informal co-operation with a few women's groups and NGOs, notably YLBHI. SPSI's structure provides for a Central Council which oversees thirteen economic sectors and four more loosely structured institutions (*Lembaga*), including the Institute for Women and Teenagers (Lembaga Wanita dan Remaja—LWR). Such institutions or foundations have the potential for greater flexibility than sectoral structures. The Institute's mandate allows it to take up all problems of women and teenagers, including raising awareness about labour laws and women's status within labour unions.[15]

One Institute project, the Pondok Project for Working Women (Proyek Pondok Wanita Pekerja) has set up boarding-houses (*pondok*)-cum-informal meeting centres for working women. These provide an informal setting for discussion of labour issues and the conduct of practical activities covering sewing courses, nutrition and health education, small enterprises, and savings and loans groups. The aim of the programme is to develop a broad knowledge of the labour and related legal situation, linked to reflection on the causes of poverty. Formal demands arising from such discussion can later be channelled through the Women's Section at enterprise level, supported by other contacts within the official trade union structure.

The SPSI Women's Section has further sought to make input into both the formation of new enterprise units, and the compulsory training courses which precede the establishment of boards of management of these new units. As noted in relation to Yasanti, the SPSI Women's Section has conducted a strong campaign, including tactics of non-cooperation, to secure the appointment of women supervisors in predominantly female workplaces. They have highlighted unpleasant situations which can result, for example, in relation to menstruation leave where male supervisors are in charge. Only partial success has been achieved so far, while similar problems faced by women in male majority workplaces are yet to be addressed.

Domestic Servants

The SPSI has given indirect support to initiatives in organizing domestic servants (*pembantu rumah tangga*) in Jakarta and some other centres. These were begun around 1985 by a former chairwoman of the Institute for Women and Teenagers, who obtained funds from the Ford Foundation for a three-year pilot project under the umbrella of an NGO called Foundation for Development of Domestic Servants (Yayasan Pengembangan Pembantu Rumah Tangga). The Foundation aimed to test possible mechanisms for training and placing domestic servants, in particular, to raise workers' wage bargaining capacity by improving their skills and sense of professionalism. The foundation arrangement was not continued, for reasons which are unclear, but the work was maintained for a while in Jakarta and Salatiga on a voluntary basis. As the programme proved sensitive and inappropriate to conventional-style union organization, it was operated in very informal and *ad hoc* ways. It appears to have subsequently lapsed as a unified programme, due to officers going overseas to study and the pressure of other work affecting key personnel. Other non-government women's groups have begun work with domestic servants in various small ways, building on experience gained from this programme.

The basic aim of the programme was for employers in search of domestic help to register and to agree to (i) monthly home visits by fieldworkers, subject to advance notice; (ii) minimum wages and conditions—Rp30,000 per month plus three good meals; (iii) twelve days holiday and two sets of new clothes per year, and (iv) forty-eight hours of personal free time per month, plus free soap and cleaning materials. A registration fee of Rp30,000 was charged in return for obtaining a servant who had received some preliminary training. Wages were to rise to Rp35,000 after three months and to Rp40,000 after eight months. Time off was to be allowed for further training after one year. At the height of the programme, nearly 150 girls were undertaking full-time training, with others in part-time training.

Organizers reported that initial resistance to the programme had weakened as employers came to see the benefits of trained servants and that the scheme was honestly managed. Some householders who either could not afford or needed additional domestic help could offer training in their houses in lieu of paying wages, provided they attended orientation courses. Some householders have provided opportunities for half-day school attendance. Some serious problems facing young people, who are mostly from rural backgrounds and have limited education, were identified. These include emotional suffering resulting from long hours of isolation. In many cases, domestic servants enjoy little or no human communication except to receive orders. The situation of domestic servants can also foster unrealistic dreams of attaining luxurious lifestyles.

Despite the informal involvement of government employees, initiatives in this field fit loosely into the third, empowerment model of mobilization, though elements of the first are also evident in terms of the intermediary and advocacy roles played by supporting groups. Although the limitations of working within official trade union structures are obvious, the example of SPSI's women's wing illustrates the diverse nature of the Indonesian government structure, and the potential scope for co-operation between some official elements and NGOs. The relevant SPSI women officials appear to have sufficient influence to provide a measure of support and advocacy within the government on behalf of informal women's groups. Significant breakthroughs in the future, however, will be greatly facilitated by the development of more open trade union structures.

Radical Groups

Not surprisingly, radical groups retain an undifferentiated opposition to co-operation with the government in relation to women's issues, as in other fields. They are also opposed to what they consider the 'genderism' displayed by independent women's organizations of the kind discussed above. Tension between radical and other women's groups appears particularly sharp in Jakarta, notably between SKEPHI and Kalyanamitra, over the respective emphasis to be placed on class and gender aspects of women's exploitation. A new women's organization called Women's Solidarity Group (Kelompok Solidaritas Perempuan—KSP) was established, initially in association with SKEPHI. However, this group also became divided over these issues. As the Kalyanamitra group has informal links with several mainstream NGOs, this particular quarrel served to widen the more general rift which had opened up between them and the radicals, aggravated by tensions at a personal level.

Interestingly, in view of their determined 'anti-genderism' on other fronts, radical groups have attempted to seize some ideological high ground in their refusal to use the term *wanita*. Instead, they prefer *perempuan* as a general classifier in referring to women. It is claimed that *wanita* has Sanskrit origins, with associated connotations of female subordination, whereas *perempuan* supposedly implies independence and assertiveness. The etymological basis for such claims remains unclear.

The Yogyakarta Women's Discussion Forum

Forum Diskusi Perempuan Yogyakarta (Yogyakarta Women's Discussion Forum—FDPY) provides an example of an autonomous women's group which is actively involved in many radical campaigns and networks at both local and national level. FDPY emerged from the student movement following a workshop in April 1989. Two previous women's organizations in Yogyakarta had broken up. These were the Women's Consciousness Movement (Gerakan Kesadaran Perempuan), which was based in Salatiga but also had a group in Yogyakarta, and the Yogyakarta Women's Forum (Forum Perempuan Yogyakarta—FPY). Overlap existed between the two organizations, while FPY had experienced major divisions over its focus of action, operating style, and personalities. Younger students wanted a more radical organization of their own, and so set up FDPY.[16]

While FDPY has been very active since its inception, its support base among students appears limited. In February 1991, it had thirty-three members spread across branches in several city campuses, with others participating in specific campaigns and demonstrations. FDPY is, in any case, more focused on off-campus activities, although it holds small-group discussions on each campus every two weeks on a rotating basis. It also publishes comics and organizes public meetings both on- and off-campus, as the opportunity arises. The whole group meets once a month to review its plans. FDPY is self-supporting financially. Members pay Rp1,000 per month, with additional donations coming from friends, plus some income from the sale of posters and publications. FDPY's campus meetings cover broad issues relating to women's struggles, such as the position of domestic servants, equal wages, sexual harassment, unequal marriage laws, plus more general issues of history, politics, and economy.

FDPY resolves the class versus gender conflict by characterizing itself as pro-people as well as pro-women. This more positive formulation, compared with SKEPHI's negative rhetoric against 'genderism', perhaps reflects the different cultural ethos prevailing in Yogyakarta compared with Jakarta, which obliges even the most radical groups to avoid unduly sharp styles of personal confrontation.

Local off-campus campaigns by FDPY have included the celebration of Women's Day of Action (Hari Ibu), on 22 December 1990, in defiance of a government ban. Two issues were taken up. First, vegetable sellers at a new market (Beringharjo) off Jalan Malioboro, the main street in Yogyakarta, were forced to shift to the second floor when the first floor was allocated to textile sellers. Such arrangements were considered by the authorities as more pleasing to tourists. As a result, less fruit was sold and it became rotten after one day. The move also added to the women's workload. Five joint actions were undertaken without result, following which FDPY joined in direct action in front of the People's Regional Representative Assembly (Dewan Perwakilan Rakyat Daerah—DPRD). FDPY claimed that this was the first such occasion in Yogyakarta, under the Suharto government, at least. The military later surveyed FDPY's meeting-house but did not enter. Secondly, in March 1990, FDPY organized an exhibition in Yogyakarta of paintings by children from East Java, in co-operation with 'Consciousness-building through Art' (Seni Rupa Penyadaran). These were displayed on Indonesian national television. Earnings were split with the children.

FDPY has been involved in other campaigns in various parts of Indonesia, including:

(i) A farmers' land struggle at Badega, near Garut, West Java in which several farmers were gaoled and subsequently acquitted (SKEPHI, 1991: 34–7). A Badega Women's Solidarity Group (Kelompok Perempuan untuk Solidaritas Badega) was formed to support a gaoled woman farmer (Ibu Oom). This was followed by a supporting demonstration in Jakarta.

(ii) On 8 August 1990, students at the Bandung Institute of Technology demonstrated against Home Affairs Minister, General Rudini, which led to some being gaoled. In response, a new group was formed called the Women's Group Against Repression (Kelompok Perempuan Anti Kekerasan), networking between Jakarta, Yogyakarta, Bandung, and Bogor.

(iii) On 8 March 1990, to mark International Women's Day—for which celebrations are banned in Indonesia—various groups demonstrated against the Minister for Women's Affairs in relation to the Sulastri case, where a domestic servant was allegedly raped and burned by a hot iron on her back by her employer, who was also an official trade union leader and a member of the People's Representative Assembly (Dewan Perwakilan Rakyat—DPR). The case had been taken to court and dismissed. Women's groups demanded legislation to protect domestic servants. The groups also joined in solidarity with women from Sugapa Sianipar who had earlier demonstrated in Jakarta against the banning of local NGOs, which had supported their struggles against PT Inti Indorayon Utama and the regional government authorities in North Sumatra.[17] Women's groups involved in this action included the Indonesian Women's Awakening Group (Kelompok Kebangkitan

Perempuan Indonesia) and the Women's Solidarity Group (Kelompok Solidaritas Perempuan—KSP). Three demonstrations were held in front of the DPR concerning these issues.

An Overview of Women's Mobilization

From this brief survey it is evident that both mainstream and radical women's groups have opened up new fields of action during the past 5–10 years. However, sharp differences over ideology, strategy, and operating style have so far prevented the emergence of a unified, broad-based women's movement in Indonesia. Even within the radical camp, there are differences as to whether various sectoral and issue-based groups should merge into a more tight-knit political body. Both radical and moderate women have reservations on this score, based on fears that the specificity of women's issues would be submerged, while opportunities to build cross-group links could be lost.

The number of independent women's organizations remains relatively small at this stage, although many local all-women's groups sponsored by mainstream, mixed-gender NGOs are in evidence. However, mainstream NGO programmes directed towards women appear fairly *ad hoc* and not designed to address major issues concerning relations between men and women and the construction of women's roles. Networking between disparate women's groups has been weak, in view of the many differences between them, and this has diluted their potential impact. However, to the extent that at least some groups have forged an outlook somewhat independent from prescribed official ideology and organizational structures, they can be said to have embarked on a process of change, which may ultimately offer some alternative means of mobilization and awareness building among Indonesian women. Over time, such new approaches may serve to accelerate mainstreaming of gender issues in the day-to-day processes and programmes of LSM/LPSMs. Further research is needed into more general questions relating to the extent of women's participation in formulating agendas and strategies within the Indonesian NGO community, which have been covered only incidentally in this study.

1. See YLBHI (1989b: 71–6) and YLBHI (1991b) for a general discussion of women's issues in Indonesia. See also Staudt (1979), Rogers (1980), and Heyzer (1987) for comparative reading on issues relating to women's status, and social, economic, and political participation.

2. See C. Warren (1990: 8 and fn. 8) citing Staudt (1986: 325–33). Staudt argues a general case that there is an entrenched bureaucratic resistance to women's participation, based on the potential for redistribution of power which this could pose.

3. See Staudt (1979) for a general discussion of this issue. See also Locher-Scholten and Niehof (1987) for an Indonesian perspective.

4. Berninghausen and Kerstan (1992: 215 and Part III, fn. 64), citing figures from DEPKOP (1985: Appendix) and DEPKOP (1986).

5. See p. 68 for a discussion of pre-co-operatives. These have proved a popular legal method of preserving a measure of freedom from official control.

6. See Berninghausen and Kerstan (1987; 1992: 211–59). These accounts have been supplemented by interviews with senior (including female) LP3ES staff at Klaten in January 1988 and February 1991, and from independent surveys cited in the account of this programme in Chapter 5.

7. See also Berninghausen and Kerstan (1987) for a more detailed survey of the status of women participating in the Productive Women's Programme.

8. Participants could not identify specific characteristics of PWP, and had no knowledge of LP3ES's existence. This is arguably to LP3ES's credit in that its organization has not been obtrusive. A later report found some villagers had confused LP3ES with the Development Unity Party (Partai Persatuan Pembangunan—PPP), referred to in popular parlance as P3 (Riawanti, Noviana, and Harun, 1990: Bab VI, p. 1).

9. Interview with LP3ES Klaten, February 1991.

10. The relatively narrow technical and economic nature of LP3ES's approach, at least during the early years of the PWP, is evident from their internal report (LP3ES, 1987b).

11. LP3ES Klaten sources, February 1991.

12. Ibid.

13. Based on interviews with Yayasan Pendidikan Islam, January 1988.

14. Ford Foundation sources, Jakarta, August 1983.

15. See YLBHI (1991b) for an overview of the rights and status of women industrial workers in Indonesia.

16. FDPY sources, February 1991.

17. See pp. 116–17.

9
Religious Influences

FROM the evidence of this survey, self-reliant community institutions (Lembaga Swadaya Masyarakat—LSM) and institutions for developing community self-reliance (Lembaga Pengembangan Swadaya Masyarakat—LPSM) with Christian origins have tended to follow an approach broadly in line with the first of the four models proposed in Chapter 2, in so far as they (i) avoid conflict and, where possible, co-operate in their relations with the government and (ii) use the space thus afforded to develop a capacity for co-operation and organization among local groups. By contrast, LSM/LPSMs with Islamic links, which also place strong emphasis on forming local groups, have been more willing to adopt a stance of 'critical collaboration' in their dealings with the government, and have been generally less cautious in becoming involved in political interactions at higher levels. Muslim-based LSM/LPSMs have also been more inclined to use support generated through local mobilization as a means of exercising leverage with the authorities, in accordance with the second model proposed in Chapter 2.

While Islamic involvement in social and developmental fields has far earlier roots in Indonesia, organizational expression in the specific form of LSM/LPSMs only became evident on any substantial scale in the 1970s. By contrast, quite a few Christian-based foundations (*yayasan*) were active a decade or two earlier. Any general explanation of such differences can only be very tentative and speculative in the context of this work, since religious aspects have not provided any major focus for study. However, the later evolution of Islamic LSM/LPSMs can probably be attributed to the close integration between social, educational, and political activity within Nahdlatul Ulama and Muhammadiyah, the two major institutional networks representing Islam prior to 1965. This nexus was drastically weakened under the New Order by the enforced amalgamation of parties, and the effective depoliticization of mass movements. Such trends appear to have provided an impetus for developing new organizational forms capable of undertaking social and developmental work. A perceived need to counterbalance Christian organizations already established in the community development fields, together with the availability of foreign and other funds, provided an additional spur.

While core Islamic theology and ideology have been undergoing some reinterpretation during the course of the New Order, their basic thrust is still to require integration between personal, social, and political spheres of life (Hassan, 1982; Felderspiel, 1992). Demands for an Islamic state or, at least, a state with laws which broadly follow the teachings of Islam, have persisted with varying degrees of strength since the proclamation of national independence in 1945. However, since the 1970s, influential elements among modernist-minded Islamic intelligentsia have increasingly challenged such assumptions. Interestingly, such intellectuals have found greater affinity with the Nahdlatul Ulama, which is widely perceived as traditionalist, than with groups such as Muhammadiyah, which have been more obviously associated during most of the twentieth century with the cause of Islamic modernism. Nahdlatul Ulama's withdrawal from the formal political arena in response to the the 1985 Law on Social Organizations (Undang Undang Organisasi Kemasyarakatan— ORMAS), while no doubt partly tactical in motivation, has also provided an opportunity for leading Muslim intellectuals, such as Nurcholish Madjid, to openly question why the establishment of an Islamic state should necessarily be seen as a prerequisite for achieving change in a socially progressive direction (Hassan, 1982: 89–98, 216–33).

Christians have historically experienced great difficulties in determining the proper relationship between religious and political spheres. Although all major contemporary streams of Christian theology, in principle, assert some nexus between social and spiritual expressions of the Gospel, links between Church and State have, in most countries, been substantially dismantled, while Christian-based parties have proved increasingly unviable in secular, pluralist, and multi-faith contexts. There are now few calls for the revival of such parties in Indonesia, which at elections in 1955 and 1971 only polled around 5–6 per cent of the overall national vote. Given their minority status, Christians are bound to exercise a good deal of caution in political participation. Nevertheless, Indonesian Churches reflect trends in other parts of the world, among both conservative and radical Christians, towards broader social and political involvement, defined in a non-party sense.

Indonesian Christians agonized a good deal about whether or not the 1985 ORMAS legislation compromised the essentials of their faith. Eventually, they resorted to traditional forms of separation between spiritual and worldly aspects, whereby both Catholics and Protestants draw an explicit distinction between the Church as a spiritual body and social organizations established to work in the community. As part of this same strategy, heads of Churches' bodies were reorganized in only partially successful attempts to avoid their being classified as mass organizations.[1] By contrast, despite some avant-garde revisionism, mainstream Islamic theology denies the possibility of splitting spiritual and material, personal or political dimensions. Indonesian Muslims have, consequently, experienced far greater difficulty than most Christians in accepting the official ideology of Five Principles (Panca Sila) as the 'sole foundation' for their social organizations.

Christian representation in the non-government organization (NGO) community has been significant. A number of today's larger LSM/LPSM networks, particularly in the health and education fields, were initiated by individuals associated with either Protestant or Catholic Churches during the Sukarno period. As with other NGOs, it is necessary to distinguish between church-based charity and welfare organizations, and LSM/ LPSMs concerned with social and economic programmes aimed at enhancing the capacity of disadvantaged groups for co-operation and self-management. Those engaged in the latter kind of activity mostly take pains to establish organizational structures and identity distinct from any Church, while ensuring autonomy in their basic management and direction. To this end, they employ explicitly secular styles of outreach and discourse, and dissociate themselves from suggestions of 'missionizing'. Nevertheless, many Christian activists see social and even political involvement as a legitimate personal or, in the case of religious orders, corporate expression of their faith.

The Indonesian Catholic Church

The Catholic Church's diverse programmes, of which only a small sample is discussed in this section, should be understood in their specific context, as well as in their relation to the dominant theological and development orientations holding sway at the time of their inception. Compared with individual NGO programmes, which can usually be identified with particular ideological trends and time-periods, Catholic-based agencies tend to manifest a greater mixture of orientations in line with trends within the wider Catholic system.

Although these organizations are explicitly secular in their structure and operation, some Catholic individuals associated with Bina Swadaya, Yayasan Purba Danata, and the Indonesian Credit Co-operative Co-ordinating Board (Badan Koordinasi Koperasi Kredit Indonesia—BK3I),[2] have been specially active in promoting the credit union and informal co-operative (usaha bersama—UB) movements. As discussed in Chapters 4 and 5, the promotion of credit unions by NGOs surveyed accords with either the first or second model of popular mobilization in Chapter 2. The above organizations fall mostly into the first category, though the work of Yayasan Purba Danata, which minimizes groups' contact with the government in efforts to build entrepreneurial capacity, could perhaps be seen as a socially conservative variant of the third model.

As noted in Chapter 4, the Panca Sila Farmers' Association (Ikatan Tani Pancasila—ITP), which subsequently evolved into Bina Swadaya, was conceived by a core of Catholic social thinkers and activists based in Semarang (Central Java) and Yogyakarta.[3] The Church has operated a network of welfare services in both cities since the 1950s, supporting a diversity of 'at risk' and marginal groups, such as orphans, the homeless, and political prisoners and their families. These programmes evolved in a gradual and piecemeal fashion in a self-help direction, in line with a more general shift in development thinking among voluntary agencies during the 1960s and 1970s. At a later stage, the Catholic Church in Indonesia was influenced by 'liberation theology' ideas deriving from Latin America, although their expression has proved far milder and less doctrinally heavy than appears to have been the case in the neighbouring Philippines. For example, the work of Fr. Mangunwijaya in Kedung Pring, Gunung Kidul, and the Gondolayu *kampung* of Yogyakarta, noted earlier,[4] has combined a non-violent approach to popular empowerment with a high degree of sensitivity to local culture and contexts.

The Jesuit Order (Society of Jesus) made a significant intellectual and organizational input during the formative years of the credit and co-operative movement in several neighbouring countries, notably India, Malaysia, and the Philippines, as well as in Indonesia. This form of economic organization is acceptable to Catholic social activists on both theological and practical grounds, as broadly in line with Catholic social teaching. One important motivation here has been a rejection of class conflict as a solution to social problems, despite increasing acknowledgement of 'structural' causes of poverty. A related concern among Jesuits has been to keep Catholic people and others out of Marxist organizations. Within this general context, co-operatives and credit unions can be seen as representing a potential middle way between state-dominated collectivism and outright capitalist individualism. Islamic-oriented LSM/LPSMs operating in this field are motivated by a broadly similar outlook.

During the 1970s and 1980s, Jesuits in many parts of the Third World underwent an evolution in their understanding of economic and social development, from earlier paradigms of modernization dominant during the 1950s and early 1960s, to more radical methodologies of structural analysis. However, class-based paradigms have been softened by the approach of Paolo Freire (1970), which emphasized dialogue between oppressor and oppressed with a view to humanizing both. Freire also stressed the character of men and women as subjects rather than objects of development. Such thinking has led to a shift in priorities within the Jesuit Order, from promoting prestigious educational institutions to involvement with slum-dwellers, squatters, and labour and peasant organizations. Whether from reasons of conviction or prudence, focus on such struggles in Indonesia still appears to enjoy a low priority relative to the development of saving and loans and credit co-operatives.

Yayasan Sosial Soegyapranata

The resettlement of homeless people by Soegyapranata Social Institute (Yayasan Sosial Soegyapranata—YSS), based in Semarang, Central Java, represents an interesting combination of charity and the promotion of self-help. Social workers identify those in need, such as scavengers and people sleeping under bridges, and discuss with them the possibility of their contributing to the construction and ownership of their own accommodation. Those who agree to participate attend preparatory classes. Two or three transit houses are available for trainees. YSS liaises with the city authorities to identify available land, and checks possible sites with regard to the availability of health, water, education, transport, and other services, negotiating improvements where existing arrangements are inadequate.

A significant charitable element is also entailed in YSS's housing programme. Labour is contributed by beneficiaries on a voluntary basis, with skilled labour being employed. At Mangunharjo, on the outskirts of Semarang, which was surveyed briefly in January 1988, standard two-room houses had been constructed at a cost of Rp350,000 (at that time around US$210). This was to be repaid in instalments of Rp50 per day or Rp500 per month. Ten per cent of the purchasers had completed repayment, with overall recovery rates running at around 50–60 per cent. YSS discouraged very rapid rates of repayment, fearing that people would sell their land if pressed too hard, and judging that a contribution in line with their abilities would engender both a sense of ownership and a better all-round effort.

Prima-facie evidence supports such claims in the case of Mangunharjo, where in many cases the original house structure had been improved or extended with brick construction. Trees and small gardens were in evidence, roads had been asphalted, and bridges and drains constructed on the basis of voluntary community labour (*gotong royong*). A local unit of the Neighbourhood Watch System (Sistem Keamanan Lingkungan—SISKAMLING) was in operation, using a radio communications system installed and operated by the community. OXFAM had provided a well. Services provided by the authorities included a health post, a school at a distance of about 1 kilometre, and a bus service to the city. Electricity was soon to be installed. There was evidence of small enterprises beginning or at a trial stage in retailing, radio repairs, and tile-making. Housing repairs were conducted on a co-operative basis via an *arisan*.

Despite this positive picture, the future of many children and young people at Mangunharjo and other sites was uncertain, as houses could not be shared among them. YSS was offering assistance with transmigration as one option, providing training and general orientation to this end. It also undertook liaison with the diocese of the transmigration region concerning the availability of land and facilities. Fares plus four months' living allowance were provided for transmigrants under this scheme.

YSS's active and continuing intermediary role with government agencies is in broad alignment with the first model proposed in Chapter 2. However, there was little evidence of people being equipped to undertake their own direct negotiations. Realistically, YSS saw a need to act as a buffer against more heavy-handed forms of guidance by local authorities. As many participants lacked residence certificates prior to their resettlement, most would lack the strength and confidence to bargain on their own.

The provision of accommodation and living by YSS during the training and associated transition process, together with substantial subsidies provided towards the purchase of land and the construction and maintenance of buildings, represent a significant charitable component of the overall programme. YSS justifies this aspect in terms of getting severely disadvantaged persons to the starting-line. Although such persons' capacity for self-help increases dramatically, given reasonable opportunity, judging from the evidence of Mangunharjo, continuing long-term support is also needed. Conventional wisdom among mainstream NGOs, both in Indonesia and internationally, currently favours self-reliance and the withdrawal of outside support as soon as possible. However, in this author's view, sufficient information is accumulating, both on the ground and in the files of international agencies, to question how far such an outlook is realistic when applied to the poorest of the poor. Small enterprises and credit unions, widely favoured by NGOs, are less relevant to the poorest groups, who seem more interested in employment programmes.

Nevertheless, the sustainability and relative costs and benefits of YSS's programme are open to question on other grounds. For example, the process of land acquisition and negotiation is time-consuming. Costs have been kept down by identifying land considered unproductive. However, the availability of such land has decreased as the city has grown. YSS's success in opening up land and gaining new services has increased the attraction of such areas, and so contributed to rising land prices. YSS's housing programme began in 1965. By January 1988, 1,641 houses had been built across twelve sites, housing 7,594 persons from 1,766 families.[5] While the programme has brought solid gains for the families in question, such limited numbers can scarcely hope to make a dent in the overall housing needs in Semarang, unless other organizations come forward to replicate YSS's efforts. Despite YSS's pleas to this effect, the high costs involved and rising land prices have discouraged others from coming forward.

One other possible way forward might be to initiate a wider popular mobilization for low-cost housing, which would involve the recognition of the rights of the poor to adequate housing through pooling the resources of the government, NGOs, and the people. A Campaign for Housing Rights has been conducted in India along these lines since around 1988 (Lokayan, 1989). At the time of writing, no parallel movement seems to have emerged in Indonesia, apart from several *ad hoc* campaigns to defend urban *kampung* from demolition or other forms of development considered threatening by their inhabitants.[6] Any general campaign would entail comprehensive empowerment strategies, of which YSS's programmes have shown little indication, and which would now be difficult for YSS to initiate, given its extensive intermediary role *vis-à-vis* government agencies.

Indonesian Churches: Networking and External Links

Both Catholics and Protestants in Indonesia are linked to strong Asian regional and international networks, in the case of mainstream Protestant Churches via the Christian Conference of Asia (CCA), and on the Catholic side through the Asian Partnership for Human Development (APHD). The CCA and APHD have jointly established the Asian Committee for People's Organizations (ACPO). The ACPO appears to have experienced some communication difficulties within Indonesia due to duplication between official Church counterparts, with whom ecumenical bodies normally deal, and informal contacts who liaise in relation to particular programmes and struggles.

Indonesian Protestant Churches derive most of their external funds for social development programmes from denominational counterparts, particularly in the Netherlands. The Indonesian Communion of Churches (Persekutuan Gereja-Gereja Indonesia—PGI) has derived most support through bilateral partnerships with counterpart ecumenical bodies in Europe, North America, and Australasia, plus the World Council of Churches based in Geneva. The PGI operates its own development programmes through various regional networks. These are co-ordinated by its development arm responsible for promoting people's participation. Catholic links are particularly strong with Holland and Germany. However, significant assistance from the East Asian and Australasian region is channelled through the APHD. Indonesia is represented on the APHD by the Institute for Social Research and Development (Lembaga Penelitian dan Pembangunan Sosial—LPPS). LPPS acts as a clearinghouse for all Catholic funding agencies, both foreign and domestic, operating in the field of social and economic development in Indonesia, while also undertaking associated monitoring and evaluation roles. LPPS operates under the umbrella of, and reports to, the Conference (formerly Council) of Catholic Bishops, but is autonomous at management and operational levels.

The CCA and the APHD have both, at times, issued strong guidelines on the need for the Churches to support the poor and oppose injustice. They have also espoused participatory approaches to human development, in opposition to established, often repressive top–down development models. This stance has occasionally led to conflict with the Indonesian Council of Churches, which substantially downgraded its participation in the CCA for several years, overtly on the issue of East Timor,[7] but also due to pressure to adopt a more militant stance not considered by Indonesian Churches to be appropriate to their situation. Both Catholic and Protestant leaders were also unhappy with an educational resources package disseminated by the Asian regional Church bodies, which combined the teachings of Paolo Freire and Saul Alinsky (Alinsky, 1969, 1971; Freire, 1972). This package was later modified for local use.

Islam and Non-Government Organizations

Leading Islamic-based LPSMs, including those discussed in this survey, also operate along secular lines. However, they see themselves, to some extent, in rivalry with Christian-based agencies, which they consider to have disproportionate influence, and as being able to tap far larger resources through foreign assistance. In that context, they affect to perceive one of the largest and most influential NGOs, Bina Swadaya, as a quasi-Catholic organization. While accepting that many individual Christian social activists are uninvolved with missionary activity, they are unable to easily accept that the pattern of institutional structures outlined above can sustain the public–private, secular–religious distinctions offered as standard frames of reference by Christians.

While some among the groups surveyed, notably within the Social and Economic Research, Education, and Information Institute (Lembaga Penelitian, Pendidikan, dan Penerangan Ekonomi dan Sosial—LP3ES) network, are genuinely tolerant in outlook, the norm, even among more moderate Muslim activists, is to see social and political action as natural expressions of religious belief. In any case, questions of proselytization are considered as irrelevant, since the vast majority of Indonesians confess the Islamic faith. External links in this regard have also proved sensitive, with Western governments and NGOs accused, it would appear with little supporting evidence,[8] of bias in favour of Christian LSM/LPSMs. In any case, links between Indonesian Muslim groups and Islamic countries also invite scrutiny in terms of their political and societal implications.

Such problems derive essentially from the aspirations of most Muslims to integrate secular and sacred aspects. This core issue can be understood in greater depth through some further study of traditional religious educational institutions known as *pesantren*, referred to in earlier contexts.[9]

The Pesantren Programme

During the 1970s, LP3ES, together with other smaller modernist Islamic networks, most of whom had student activist backgrounds, conceived the idea of using traditional Islamic educational institutions known as *pesantren* as vehicles to reach rural people. Their longer-term aim was to democratize both *pesantren* and villages. Previously, *pesantren* had been associated with the more traditional stream of Islamic thinking. Most are linked with the Nahdlatul Ulama (NU) rather than the modernist Muhammadiyah. NU has its strongest support base in Java, and has historically proved more culturally accommodating towards Javanese culture. Both intellectually and theologically, NU appears to be more eclectic in theological borrowing across different traditions within Islam, and even from non-Islamic sources where appropriate.

Networking among *pesantren* leaders (*kyai*) through NU and other associations has provided a vehicle both for exchanging experience concerning the educational, religious, and social development of *pesantren*, and as a base for broader political mobilization. In that context, NU's withdrawal from formal party politics in 1984 greatly weakened the Islamic-based Development Unity Party (Partai Persatuan Pembangunan—PPP), reducing its national electoral strength from around 27 per cent to 15 per cent between 1982 and 1987, at the same time sharpening conflict between various elements of the former party. While NU declared its intention to concentrate on social and educational work, its decision also represented a tactical response to the 1985 Law on Social Organizations (Undang Undang Organisasi Kemasyarakatan—ORMAS) legislation.[10]

Major issues arising from the experience of *pesantren* develop-ment programmes may be summarized as: (i) the appropriateness of *pesantren* as vehicles for promoting participatory styles of grass-roots development; (ii) the implications for *pesantren* identity and structure; (iii) the impact on relations between *pesantren* and the government, and (iv) the impact on relations between *pesantren* and supporting NGOs.

To what extent can *pesantren* provide an appropriate vehicle for popular mobilization? Here, a major source of difficulty for *pesantren* has been in reconciling their established institutional interests with their proclaimed objective of building autonomous community structures. The problem has been aggravated, in many instances, by the social dominance of *pesantren* over their surrounding communities.

In recent times, *pesantren* have increasingly developed a social as well as religious orientation. Pesantren Gontor, East Java, has for many years sought to develop a systematic pedagogy in this regard (Saifullah, 1974). Pesantren Darul Falah, near Bogor, West Java, has for at least 20–5 years included social, particularly agricultural, programmes in its education of students (Widodo, 1974). While these are seen as a means of disseminating religious values among farmers, agricultural development is equally justified as a religious activity in its own right. The late Kyai Hamam Ja'afar of Pesantren Pabelan (where LP3ES's programme was first initiated) saw action programmes as a practical form of missionary work, reinforcing more traditional vocal dissemination of the Islamic message.[11]

In principle, Islamic and Christian organizations confront the same dilemmas in linking their social outreach and mission activities, particularly in relation to whether social programmes are to be undertaken solely for the benefit of the people, or primarily as a means of extending religious influence and control. At the same time, imbalance between the institutional strength and resources of both *pesantren* and Churches relative to local people can limit the empowerment and capacity for self-reliance of any base-level groups which they may form.

Many *kyai* and students (*santri*) refuse to acknowledge any distinction between *pesantren* and the surrounding society. Both are seen as part of the same community and religion, while distinctions between socio-economic and strictly religious forms of Islamic missionary activity (*dakwah*) are seen as equally invalid.[12] Yet, it cannot be assumed that local people necessarily view *pesantren* in the same light. In that context, some activists in the *pesantren* movement acknowledge that memories of political conflict in the pre-New Order period are still alive, and to some extent continue to hinder co-operation.[13]

The burgeoning internal movement for community outreach has also created tensions within the *pesantren* structure. On the one hand, there is no inherent conflict, and indeed a good deal of convergence between Islamic theology and social and economic development work among the masses. On the other hand, problems have arisen in defining the relationship between such work and the overall religious and educational life of the institutions, specifically in integrating the work of their community development units with the *pesantren* hierarchy. In that context, a former director of the Indonesian Association for Pesantren and Community Development (Perkumpulan Pengembangan Pesantren dan Masyarakat—P3M), Mansour Fakih, has argued that *pesantren* social programmes are aimed at enhancing their status, tradition, and identity in the eyes of the surrounding village community, which provides them with a crucial source of social and political support. Their relations with NGOs entail contradictions to the extent that *pesantren* interests conflict with NGO goals of promoting popular participation (Fakih, 1987).

While the vision underlying the *pesantren* movement is one of involving all elements in the *pesantren* in development processes which will ultimately democratize the *pesantren* itself, relations between *santri* and even the most enlightened *pesantren* leaders are traditionally deferential and hierarchical. Indeed, *kyai* are held in awe, bordering on reverence, by many students. Many *kyai* naturally fear that *pesantren* will lose their distinct character and links with the people. *Kyai* are mostly direct descendants of the founder of their institution, and often have close kinship ties with neighbouring *pesantren*. Consequently, they play a crucial role in balancing the religious and social roles of their *pesantren*. Kyai Hamam Ja'far commented that 'pesantren community development efforts ... appear to strengthen and preserve pesantren leadership', and claimed that as an informal leader he, more than any other local leader, is more often obeyed by the local community (Fakih, 1987). Evidence of such influence was provided in 1982 when the local *pesantren* organized the nomination and election of one of its graduates as village head, defeating a candidate nominated by the government network of the government-sponsored network of Functional Groups (Golongan Karya— GOLKAR) and favoured by local authorities.

While the extension of participatory styles of decision-making within the *pesantren* may threaten the position of the *kyai*, a failure to integrate community development ideals into the overall life and structures of the *pesantren* will render such ideals ineffective. However, if the *kyai* take the initiative to accept and legitimize new roles, change will occur quite rapidly in both *pesantren* and the local community. This is illustrated by comparing the experience of Cipasung, West Java, and An-Nuqayah, Madura (Sulaiman, 1985). Both *pesantren* participated in initial training programmes on appropriate technology conducted by LP3ES. But whereas An-Nuqayah sent representatives close to the founding *kyai*'s family and those of senior religious teachers, Cipasung sent only senior *santri* unconnected to the *kyai*'s family. This difference persisted in relation to other programmes, indicating the different priority placed on community outreach by the two institutions, and resulting in unequal levels of community support.

The relationship between specialized bureaux set up to promote community development and the overall *pesantren* decision-making structure can also cause problems. At An-Nuqayah, all *kyai* and religious teachers (*ustadz*) have been linked in a Foundation for the Development of Islamic Education (Yayasan Pengembangan Pendidikan Islam—YAPPI), which deliberates on all major issues, thus providing opportunity for outsider perspectives to be considered (Sulaiman, 1985). As this foundation predated the development bureau by over ten years, thinking about the social role of their *pesantren* had clearly reached a far more advanced stage than at Cipasung.

A different kind of problem arose in the case of Pesantren Haslakul Huda, Kajen, near Pati in northern Central Java. Here, the *pesantren*'s community development bureau enjoyed strong endorsement from Kyai Sahal Mahfudz, who was for many years chairman of the provincial structure of NU. This facilitated the extension of an active and high-profile programme in surrounding villages (Mudatsir, 1985). However, over time, Kyai Mahfudz's responsibilities within NU, together with other religious and teaching duties, precluded him from active personal involvement in development work. This is reported to have caused confusion in perceptions of the priority of social development activities relative to the traditional religious and educational role of the *pesantren*.

As noted earlier, P3M was established in 1983, with the aim of empowering *pesantren* participating in development work.[14] It was also considered that *pesantren* themselves would be best placed to integrate community development work with the life of *pesantren* as a whole. While grounds for such hopes have, in many respects, proved justified, it also appears that P3M's formation has led to subtle shifts in emphasis over time towards the development of *pesantren* relative to the development of the people. This was never the intention of either LP3ES or P3M, which have continued to co-operate closely through training programmes, forums, and the distribution of each other's literature. Yet goal displacement appears to have occurred in at least two ways.

First, P3M represents not a federation of development units and organizations, but of *pesantren* participating in development outreach. As we have seen, relationships between specialized development units and overall *pesantren* structures have been subject to some strain and uncertainty. The structure of P3M makes it even more difficult for base-level groups to develop direct links with each other, beyond the very local level, as these will need to be increasingly mediated through the entire *pesantren* structure, and not merely their development units.

Secondly, *Pesan* magazine was established by LP3ES with the aim of linking participating *pesantren* with news and views. P3M continued with the same objective when it took over the publication. However, P3M is becoming a significant generator of publications in its own right, covering very broad questions of Islamic theology, epistemology, political ideology, social analysis, and methodology.[15] Logically, all these matters are interconnected but, in practice, it appears that the weight of so much structure and theory is causing a loss of specific focus on the needs and problems of poor people. At the same time, P3M's location in Jakarta, despite strong regional and local links, inevitably draws it into NGO and Islamic politics at the national level.

The strategic intention underlying P3M's intellectual efforts is directed towards self-transformation of *pesantren* values and structures, which, in turn, is intended to have an impact on their conceptualization of the surrounding society. Yet, an internal seminar paper prepared by P3M staff claims that, after over a decade, visions of people-based development have taken only limited root among *kyai* and *santri* (Pesan, 1991). It was also claimed in this paper that Abdurrahman Wahid, chairman of NU, considers that *pesantren*, as educational institutions, are not appropriate as agents of economic development. Indeed, many activists see the *pesantren* movement as being at a crossroads, where it must choose whether to be on the side of the government or that of the people. Such comments are based on perceptions that some *kyai*, if they consider their *pesantren* to be in danger, will choose to defend its survival rather than oppose the government.

These issues have been confused by an attack by P3M on the role of LSM/LPSMs for allegedly seeking to use *pesantren* as agents for purveying their own development paradigms, and taking no real account of the nature of *pesantren* (Pesan, 1991). The hierarchical organization and lifestyles of LSM/LPSMs have also been portrayed as incompatible with their stated egalitarian and democratic values. Essentially, this attack is aimed at LP3ES, which P3M claims is seen by *pesantren* as composed of outside, urban-based intellectuals. By contrast, P3M is owned and managed by and for *pesantren*, with an accountable structure of annual general meetings, triennial elections, and so forth. P3M further claims to be concerned with both the development of the people via *pesantren* and the development of *pesantren* themselves, whereas LP3ES is depicted as being only concerned with the former. P3M can therefore be bolder in initiating discussion about the need to evaluate education programmes and practice, such as rote learning of the Koran, still prevalent in many *pesantren*. However, this logic seems to assume that internal educational and external developmental goals are always mutually compatible and supporting.

Reflection suggests that co-operation between LSM/LPSMs and *pesantren* will depend on recognition of their different goals and identity, and the more specific division of labour, based on mutual respect. *Pesantren* represent a special kind of Islamic community, seeking to consolidate its identity and preserve its autonomy from outside intervention. At this stage, institutional coherence is seen as depending on the maintenance of traditional patterns of hierarchical solidarity. In this context, *pesantren* perceive that the adoption of NGO-style ideology of bottom–up development and popular participation could prove counter-productive. Further, as the *pesantren* movement is well able to undertake its own advocacy and, indeed, political action where necessary, the role of LSM/LPSMs seems reduced to one of technical, management, and training support.

The most fundamental crisis faced by *pesantren* relates to their education system, which faces pressures from both the government and wider society to modernize its syllabus and pedagogy. Possibly, *pesantren* and supporting NGOs could co-operate to develop some new institutional model which might bridge the cognitive distance between modern scientific and village-based knowledge systems. Such institutions could, over time, develop into centres for social action and experiment.[16] An alternative tertiary education route is, in any case, much in demand by students denied entrance to state universities or higher education overseas. However, there is an equal likelihood that such a combination of pressures could oblige such institutions to imitate universities of the conventional kind, as is already occurring at secondary level.

Overall, while the attempt to change *pesantren* may be a worthwhile objective in its own right, one may question the appropriateness of using grass-roots groups as a vehicle for such an experiment, unless concrete developmental benefits can be shown as accruing to them. More fundamentally, aspirations held by some Islamic-based LSM/LPSM networks for the democratization both of *pesantren* and their surrounding communities are in basic conflict with the traditional identity of *pesantren*. However, as these institutions have become a kind of flagship for many Muslim urban, middle-class intellectuals, activists, and overseas supporters concerned to promote more just and participatory styles of development, there has been a curious unwillingness to recognize the realities of this situation.

1. On the Catholic side, the Council of Bishops (Majelis Agung Wali-Gereja Indonesia—MAWI) separated its various social and welfare bodies into formally autonomous bodies. MAWI was subsequently reorganized as an informal Forum of Catholic Bishops. The (Protestant) Indonesian Council of Churches (Dewan Gereja-Gereja Indonesia—DGI) became the Indonesian Communion of Churches (Persekutuan Gereja-Gereja Indonesia—PGI).

2. BK3I operates from the same building as Bina Swadaya. See pp. 72, 172 for further discussion of BK3I.

3. See pp. 66–8.

4. See pp. 125–6.

5. YSS sources.

6. OXFAM sources.

7. PGI was reported at one stage to have been placed under heavy pressure by the Indonesian military to gain recognition from the CCA of East Timor's incorporation into Indonesia.

8. For example, LP3ES, LSP, P3M, and several *pesantren* have received significant funding from Western agencies, such as the Ford and Asia Foundations, USAID, OXFAM, NOVIB, Friedrich Ebert Stiftung, plus assistance from Western volunteers.

9. See pp. 92–4.

10. See pp. 47–9.

11. Based on conversations with the late Kyai at Pesantren Pabelan in 1983 and 1988.

12. *Dakwah*, in a literal sense, means missionary activity. However, another common meaning refers to struggles to apply Islamic beliefs in every field of activity, linked to personal efforts to live a fully Islamic life.

13. Based on a seminar discussion on *pesantren* at LP3ES Jakarta on 15 February 1991.

14. See p. 193.

15. The journal *Pesantren* deals with these matters on a regular basis.

16. These issues were canvassed at the February 1991 P3M–LP3ES seminar cited earlier.

10
Networking, Scaling Up, and Coalition-building

NETWORKING has become a major issue among the non-government organization (NGO) community world-wide, driven in large measure by perceived needs to achieve wider social and political impact, and to articulate local needs on a broader regional, national, and international stage. Networks commonly exchange information and experience, undertake joint training programmes, and support campaigns and issues of common interest. Many such newer kinds of institution-building and advocacy roles are carried out by individual NGOs. However, the benefits of undertaking at least some of them co-operatively are becoming increasingly apparent. NGOs are also learning to share experience, both in shaping their internal strategies and programmes, and in developing common positions towards their governments and, to some extent, foreign donors.

At the same time, as we have seen, NGOs interact constructively with government agencies. The process of extending the scope of such co-operation has been described by Korten as scaling up—though the term will be used in this chapter in the more general sense of coalition-building by NGOs, and their operation across a wider institutional canvas (Korten, 1987; 1990: 113–32; Edwards and Hulme, 1992). According to Korten, scaling up begins when a local organization takes a request or issue to a higher level. As a next step, it is common for several groups to undertake joint lobbying or negotiation with a government agency. A further stage is reached when NGOs develop new systems and processes to link with government agencies in ways which more effectively enhance the capacity for self-management of base-level groups. Examples of scaling up in this more specific sense, discussed in this study, include water users' associations supported by the Social and Economic Research, Education, and Information Institute (Lembaga Penelitian, Pendidikan, dan Penerangan Ekonomi dan Sosial—LP3ES) and Bina Swadaya; local health cadres trained by Yayasan Indonesia Sejahtera (YIS) to link up with the system of integrated health service posts (Pos Pelayanan Terpadu—POSYANDU) and community health centres

(Pusat Kesehatan Masyarakat—PUSKESMAS), and informal sector co-operatives linked to credit systems from state banks and agencies.

  Networks of self-reliant community institutions (Lembaga Swadaya Masyarakat—LSM) and institutions for developing community self-reliance (Lembaga Pengembangan Swadaya Masyarakat—LPSM) in Indonesia may be categorized as territorial, at national, regional, or area levels. Alternatively, they may be based on common functional, sectoral, or other affinities. Often they spring up in quite random ways, for example, through common attendance at seminars or workshops. Foreign funding agencies sometimes initiate networking for particular purposes, which may then develop into more powerful groupings. Several larger LPSMs, as we have seen, promote and, in effect, build networks among clusters of smaller LSMs spread across Indonesia. This situation is in a constant state of flux as many of the latter gain strength, form new groupings, or merge with others. Furthermore, not all networking represents a scaling up from field experience. Often it is initiated by governments or other large agencies seeking convenient mechanisms to impose bureaucratic order on a diffuse, seemingly unmanageable local reality. Networking also gives scope for upward mobility by NGO professionals, including international travel. Foreign aid can also have a distorting effect in this, as in other fields.

Sectoral Networks

Some of the functional or sectoral networks in fields such as environment, labour, and human rights, have been discussed in earlier chapters. Other important national networks are found in the health, welfare, family planning, consumer rights, and credit union fields.

Health, Welfare, and Family Planning

The Indonesian Council for Social Welfare (Dewan Nasional Indonesia untuk Kesejahteraan Sosial—DNIKS) was established in July 1985. This apex body is composed of Social Welfare Co-ordinating Boards (Badan Koordinasi Kegiatan Kesejahteraan Sosial—BK3S) which, according to an instruction by the Minister for Home Affairs issued on 29 January 1985, are supposed to be established in all provinces (Aditjondro, 1987: 3–4). This instruction designates these BK3S as the only provincial co-ordinating bodies of NGO activities in social welfare in each province. DNIKS receives corresponding recognition at national level and, since 1967, has been accepted as the Indonesian chapter of the International Council on Social Welfare (Aditjondro, 1987: 5).

  DNIKS is clearly a government-initiated and -controlled network, although Mrs J. S. Nasution, appointed as the Council's chief, is reported to have fought a long rearguard action to minimize government control. Historically, the Department of Social Affairs (Departemen Sosial—DEPSOS) has proved more open to encouraging grass-roots initiatives, with a good deal of freedom allowed during President Sukarno's time for Village Community Institutions (Lembaga Sosial Desa—LSD) to operate independently from formal village structures. For this reason, DEPSOS's responsibilities in the field of community development were transferred to the Department of Home Affairs (Departemen Dalam Negeri), with DEPSOS's role confined to social welfare (Schulte-Nordholt, 1985). However, DEPSOS has shown itself equally expansion-minded, with the promulgation of Decree No. 58/1984 declaring DNIKS as the sole co-ordinating body of Indonesian NGOs, especially those which work in the field of social welfare (Aditjondro, 1987: 5). Ironically, bureaucratic conflicts between the Departments of Home Affairs and Social Affairs as to boundaries between social welfare (*kesejahteraan sosial*) and community development (*pengembangan/pembangunan masyarakat*) have created difficulties in defining social organizations, and so have weakened the government's capacity to exercise controls over them as originally intended in the 1985 Law on Social Organizations (Undang Undang Organisasi Kemasyarakatan—ORMAS).

More bottom–up style networks are in evidence in the health field, where both Protestant and Catholic health organizations have formed their own networks—the All-Indonesia Christian Health Service (Pelayanan Keristen Kesehatan Seluruh Indonesia—PELKESI) and the Indonesian Association of Voluntary Health Groups (Persatuan Karya Dharma Kesehatan Indonesia—PERDAKHI). These two networks have joined together with the health arm of NU and Muhammadiyah to form the Communication Forum for Religious-based LSMs (Forum Komunikasi LSM Beragama).

PERDAKHI was established on 2 February 1976. By 1991, it had thirty-one member organizations and eighteen regional offices, of which the most active are Palembang, Semarang, and Irian Jaya.[1] National meetings, with election of board members, presentation of accounts, and reports are held biannually. PERDAKHI performs standard network functions of advocacy and information exchange, but additionally supplies medicines at cost price by buying in bulk. It has co-operated with the Faculty of Pharmacology at the University of Indonesia, Jakarta, in preparing, storing, and distributing generic medicines. While air-conditioned storage is available for twenty-four hours a day in Jakarta, such facilities cannot be relied on in the regions. In Irian Jaya, where the Churches reportedly provide around 50 per cent of health care, an ecumenical system of supply has been worked out, with the government paying the cost of employing health cadres. As noted earlier, PERDAKHI has also tried to maintain the system of voluntary, community-based health insurance (Dana Sehat) pioneered by the Christian Foundation for Public Health (Yayasan Keristen untuk Kesehatan Umum—YAKKUM) and Yayasan Indonesia Sejahtera (YIS) in the Solo area during the 1970s.[2]

These non-government networks have developed independently, with a strong base among organizations which were providing services and reaching out to remote areas of Indonesia long before the government became actively involved. Their main interactions with the government relate to sharing facilities and providing services. PERDAKHI and

PELKESI have made joint representations with regard to regulations they consider irksome, such as the need to register with the Department of Trade, despite their non-profit operational basis, and the requirement for private hospitals to inform the Department of Manpower as to the employment of night staff.

By contrast, the Indonesian Family Planning Association (Perkumpulan Keluarga Berencana Indonesia—PKBI) has institutionalized links with the government due to its affiliation as the Indonesian arm of the International Planned Parenthood Federation. This latter is a semi-voluntary association sponsored by the United Nations, with informal links to the World Health Organization. The status of PKBI is correspondingly ambivalent, as agencies associated with the United Nations can only deal directly with governments at field level. On the other hand, PKBI was established in 1957, when the Indonesian government lacked any concept of family planning and refused to have a family planning policy.

Under President Suharto, formal responsibility for implementing family planning policy has rested with the National Family Planning Co-ordinating Board (Badan Koordinasi Keluarga Berencana Nasional—BKKBN). BKKBN leads a fairly independent existence outside the formal hierarchy of the Health Department, due to the urgency which the President has always attached to family planning. PKBI works closely with BKKBN, but operates along less hierarchical lines in its efforts to spread the family planning message more effectively. BKKBN also sponsors and co-operates with a variety of applied research programmes. It has branches at provincial and district levels, working through established village structures, such as the Village Community Resilience Institution (Lembaga Ketahanan Masyarakat Desa—LKMD) and the Association for Promoting Family Welfare (Pembinaan Kesejahteraan Keluarga—PKK), and through non-government organizations, to the extent that these are available. PKBI also undertakes a general education role in schools and among teenagers, in 1982 establishing the Indonesian Forum for Self-reliant Population Control (Forum Indonesia untuk Swadaya Kependudukan—FISKA). By 1988, FISKA had 110 affiliated organizations.[3]

Consumer Organizations

Advocacy in the field of consumer rights and standards was initiated from an urban, middle-class base. Primary initiative has come from the Indonesian Foundation of Consumers' Organizations (Yayasan Lembaga Konsumen Indonesia—YLKI). YLKI's focus has been mainly on products and practices in the modern retail sector, whereas most Indonesians look far more to village and informal sector markets in the cities for their needs. YLKI has no membership base of its own, working through established LSM/LPSMs and other social organizations in order to spread consumer consciousness. YLKI is, nevertheless, aware of the need to broaden its social base, and has tried such strategies as establishing clubs for women and teenagers. Fifteen *pesantren* in Lampung and fourteen in Lombok have consumer clubs.

YLKI has seen consumer issues as providing a potential catalyst for wider empowerment of women, who constitute the majority of its active support base. At this stage, however, YLKI's links with rural-based LSMs are not sufficiently strong to justify such a claim, which carries more force in the urban, middle-class context. Also, any overly narrow focus on consumer issues could unwittingly have the effect of reinforcing conventional perceptions of women's domestic role, for example, in relation to food preparation.

Progress in the consumer movement has been hindered by an imbalance in bargaining strength between producers and consumers (YLBHI, 1989c). Consumers lack systematic and reliable information in the face of rapid expansion of products and advertising. Control over safety and health aspects is still minimal in Indonesia (YLBHI, 1991d). Strategically, the consumer movement has yet to determine the model it intends to pursue. In Malaysia, a polarization has become apparent between those favouring a strictly product monitoring and consumer grievance adjudication role, as pursued by the Federal Union of Malaysian Consumer Organizations, or the more proactive stance adopted by the Consumers' Association of Penang, which has attempted to challenge the root causes of consumer exploitation, which it sees as deriving from the behaviour of multinational companies and a prevailing ethos of rapid growth, consumerism, and lack of environmental awareness (Eldridge, 1991: 8–12).

YLKI belongs broadly in the second stream of NGOs, in so far as it seeks to actively change policies and mobilize a support base, while supporting independent action by local groups. It was initiated independently and has maintained autonomy from the government, although public perceptions were clouded by the fact that Rachmat Witular, the husband of Erna Witular, YLKI's president for many years, was until 1992 a member of the People's Representative Assembly (Dewan Perwakilan Rakyat—DPR) and secretary-general of the government-sponsored network of Functional Groups (Golongan Karya—GOLKAR). Both are moderately outspoken reformists in their general social and political orientation. Erna Witular was the first director of the Indonesian Environment Network (Wahana Lingkungan Hidup Indonesia—WALHI) and has remained on its governing body. She has also held the position of president of the International Organization of Consumer Unions based in Penang. Rachmat Witular was not renominated by GOLKAR at the June 1992 elections. His appointment as Indonesian Ambassador to Russia, in July 1993, effectively removed his wife from any active role in the NGO community.

Credit Unions and Co-operatives

The Indonesian Credit Co-operative Co-ordinating Board (Badan Koordinasi Koperasi Kredit Indonesia—BK3I) originated from the Savings and Loans Consultative Bureau (Biro Konsultasi Simpan

Pinjam—BKSP) which had been established in 1970 in co-operation with the Credit Union International, based in the USA. By 1989, 1,489 credit co-operatives (*koperasi kredit—kopdit*) were affiliated with BK3I across Indonesia, with approximately 167,000 members holding savings around Rp16 billion.[4]

The overall goals and philosophy underlying the credit co-operative movement display a number of contradictions, reflecting philosophies in vogue at different times. The core of credit union activity is savings and loans, operated through small, self-managing groups. The education of group members is seen by all concerned as an essential precondition for effective group formation, as reflected in BK3I's basic slogan of 'no education, no credit union' (Utomo and Thamrin, 1989: 2). Educational content concentrates on such practical matters as auditing, bookkeeping, management, and entrepreneurship. Some of the motivation training reflects theories by the American social scientist, David McClelland, concerning the allegedly culturally determined nature of the need for achievement, popularized during the early New Order period as part of the general push for social and cultural modernization (McClelland, 1961).

Credit unions are commonly seen by their supporters as vehicles for social co-operation, linked to goals of material improvement and efficiency. More recently, BK3I has claimed that credit unions are vehicles for promoting goals of social solidarity and popular democracy in opposition to capitalism, which is based on individual accumulation. Neo-Marxist style reference to 'structural analysis' and 'core–periphery' characteristics in Indonesian development also began to feature in training programmes during the 1980s, as did more radical bottom–up interpretations of 'participation'. The language of self-reliance (*swadaya* and *kemandirian*) featured prominently during both phases, interpreted malleably in terms of both individual and co-operative meanings.

In early 1991, BK3I was divided into twenty regional credit co-operative co-ordinating boards (Badan Koordinasi Koperasi Kredit Daerah—BK3D). Regions are based on operational areas and not necessarily on provinces. Base-level groups belong to their respective regional body, which is, in turn, represented in the management structure of BK3I. Membership of co-operatives or credit unions may be based on local community, common place of work, occupation, social, recreational, or other affinity. BK3Ds must accept the norms and rules of BK3I, and not become members of any other co-operative network (Utomo and Thamrin, 1989: 13). Credit unions and co-operatives are combined into chapters (*perkumpulan*) of up to twenty units, based on areas of strength. Each unit sends a representative to the chapter which elects a board of management. Elections are held triannually, with accounts and reports presented each year. Regional bodies are based on chapters. In areas where there are no chapters, the regional body itself deals with base-level groups. It may also take initiatives to form new groups, first working through local contacts to find out local needs and problems.

BK3I is governed by a supreme council, elected by representatives of regional bodies at a members' meeting.[5] The council lays down overall policy with respect to membership and conduct of the organization, together with guidelines for base-level and intermediate groups. Two key committees are also elected by the members' meeting. These are (i) a credit committee, which lays down detailed guidelines for disbursal and recovery of loans, and effectively determines the volume and conditions of credit in circulation among groups at lower levels and (ii) an investigating board, responsible for investigating and dealing with mismanagement or fraud by individual co-operatives or intermediate bodies. Constitutional changes require a two-thirds majority of those present and voting at a members' meeting.

BK3I supports primary and secondary (area or regional) groups with training, instruction manuals, legal and management advice, insurance funds for death and disablement, and inter-lending. It may also provide additional capital for productive purposes (Utomo and Thamrin, 1989: 4). To that end, BK3I has encouraged inter-lending from strong to weak regions.[6] However, credit unions are essentially savings and loans (*simpan pinjam*) bodies in which, unlike co-operative enterprises (*usaha bersama*), loans are not only for productive purposes but may also cover school fees, medical costs, and other emergencies. In practice, the two aspects are frequently combined. National and regional bodies support area initiatives in forming new groups, for example, by offering basic training courses. Programmes of cross-visiting, cross-auditing, and cross-lending have been instituted at regional and area levels (Wiryosaputro and Muharram, 1989: 5).

The legal basis of credit unions is unclear, in so far as they cover only savings and loans. Registration as a credit co-operative must be undertaken with the Indonesian Council of Co-operatives (Dewan Koperasi Indonesia—DEKOPIN), whose regulations require at least twenty-five initial members (DEPKOP, *c.*1968). Registration also requires regular reporting to the Department of Co-operatives. Such conditions are insufficiently flexible for most groups which start with smaller numbers on a more informal basis. BK3I, like Bina Swadaya, sees group formation as an extended process, requiring much preliminary education and discussion. Consequently, only 60–70 groups affiliated with BK3I are formally registered as legal bodies (*badan hukum*).

Nevertheless, the existence and activities of BK3I are legitimized by Article 33 of Indonesia's 1945 Constitution, plus various other decrees (Utomo and Thamrin, 1989: 10). More specifically, in July 1971, the Savings and Loans Consultative Bureau was invited by the director-general of the Department of Co-operatives to foster the development of credit co-operatives. A more specific agreement was signed on 24 January 1983 with BK3I. The director-general of the Co-operatives Institute (Lembaga Koperasi) within DEPKOP wrote to regional and area offices on 24 December 1987 instructing them to co-operate with regional and area bodies of BK3I, accord them legal recognition, and provide the necessary facilities (Utomo and Thamrin, 1989: 10). BK3I interpreted this instruction as opening the door to competition with DEPKOP's own Village Co-operative Units (Koperasi Unit Desa—KUD). Nevertheless, the official status of BK3I's credit co-operatives remains ambivalent in that they are not acknowledged as rural co-operative organizations, for which monopoly status was accorded to KUDs in 1974 (INPRES, 1974). This restriction has been partly evaded by establishing new chapter secretariats on the edge of cities (Wiryo-saputro and Muharram, 1989: 3–4).

BK3I's admission to DEKOPIN has given it considerable leverage at local and district levels. Nevertheless, local groups have experienced both co-operation and some negative reactions in their relations with KUD officials. Some credit co-operative members buy from KUD with credit union funds, while their leaders are sometimes invited to sit on the management boards of local KUDs (Wiryosaputro and Muharram, 1989: 15). Some observers, consequently, see BK3I's work as comple-mentary and alternative to, rather than in rivalry with, the government. Its legal subordination to the government is made clear by requirements to provide annual reports to DEPKOP at both national and regional levels. Government officials are also regularly invited to be present, and even offer suggestions and opinions at co-operative meetings (Wiryo-saputro and Muharram, 1989: 11).

BK3I's close relations with the government have been illustrated in studies of two base-level credit co-operatives in the Bogor–Sukabumi region of West Java, namely, Kopdit Sejahtera at Cibinong, and Badan Kesejahteraan Karyawan Pendidikan (BKKP) at Cibadak. Kopdit Sejahtera sent reports every three months to the Co-operatives Office at the district headquarters in Bogor, although it operated sepa-rately from the KUD. Senior district and sub-district officials were co-opted on to the respective credit co-operative advisory and management boards (Wiryosaputro and Muharram, 1989: 10, 15).

In both cases, the main motivation for membership appeared to be in order to avoid moneylenders. Loan demands in BKKP regularly exceeded supply, while the main motive for repayment seemed to be in order to borrow again (Wiryosaputro and Muharram, 1989: 10, 15–16). The social composition of both organizations was predominantly middle class. In the case of Kopdit Sejahtera, just 0.2 per cent of members were farmers or agricultural workers, though 17.4 per cent were classified as workers. The remainder included traders and entrepreneurs (14.6 per cent), teachers (10.5 per cent), private business employees (16.2 per cent), drivers, students, and housewives (29 per cent). Most members of BKKP were teachers and government officials. The lack of farmers no doubt explains the lack of rivalry with the KUD. As BKKP was founded by a local teacher who attended a BK3I training course in Jakarta, this example raises doubts whether reaching out to poorer members of the commun-ity has represented any more than a rhetorical component of BK3I objectives, in this area of Indonesia at least.

BK3I exchanges information and managerial experience with the De-partment of Co-operatives to a modest extent. Nevertheless, in an attempt to counter government control over local co-operatives, and promote the cause of independent co-operatives, BK3I has been working with LP3ES, the Institute of Development Studies (Lembaga Studi Pembangunan—LSP), Pengembangan Agribusiness, and Bina Swadaya to establish a new Co-operatives Development Forum (Forum Pengembangan Koperasi). This was designed as an informal communications and information-sharing network in order to prevent umbrella control by DEKOPIN. The new forum established informal links with the Canadian Co-operative Association. BK3I has continued to exchange information and visits with other NGOs at national, regional, and credit co-operative levels, where possible working with established LSMs to link income-generation with savings and loans programmes (Wiryosaputro and Muharram, 1989: 7). BK3I claims to have encouraged LSMs to enter areas where none were active, citing the example of the Foster Parents' Plan in the Gunung Kidul region.[7] It is also a member of the Asian Conference of Credit Unions, which includes nine other countries—Thailand, Malaysia, Philippines, Korea, Hong Kong, Japan, India, Sri Lanka, and Bangladesh (Utomo and Thamrin, 1989: 10–11).

In some respects, BK3I could be described as an LPSM specializing in credit unions and small co-operatives, rather than a network designed to link together existing LSM/LPSMs. Moreover, as we have seen, several LPSMs undertake similar activity. However, BK3I has proved flexible in supporting existing local groups and in co-operating with other LSM/LPSMs. The establishment and operation of BK3I's credit co-operatives remain under the close scrutiny, if not detailed day-to-day control, of DEKOPIN and its various local arms. Unlike other spheres of LSM/LPSM operation, there appears to be less scope for taking advantage of inter-departmental rivalries in their dealings with the government.

To the extent that the two examples observed by Wiryosaputro and Muharram cited earlier are representative, they point to a lack of serious targeting towards the lowest socio-economic groups, or even towards farmers and agricultural labour in general. Nor do women appear to represent any special target group for BK3I, although some credit co-operatives have been established by women (Utomo and Thamrin, 1989: 3). While they probably contribute towards spreading economic opportunities and activities more widely, it seems unrealistic to expect that credit co-operatives can be a suitable vehicle to reach more seriously disadvantaged groups. In any case, there seems no basis for believing that the coming together of a random group of people to save and borrow money will significantly enhance social solidarity, although it may serve to introduce some small element of pluralism and competition within state-dominated structures. It may well be more realistic to see credit co-operatives as an intermediate step to capitalist development. Indeed, some commentators wish to speed up this process, and are inclined to see co-operatives and credit unions as an obstruction to the development of entrepreneurial capacity by individuals (Strand and Fakih, 1984). In any case, international experience suggests that since people seek to borrow at the lowest possible rates and lend at the highest rates, and since interest rates between institutions tend to even out, credit unions are reduced to competing for marginal advantages in service and access.

In principle, and to a significant extent in practice, BK3I appears to follow Schumacher's 'subsidiarity principle' (1974: 203–4) in devolving operational decisions to lower levels. However, rules, guidelines, and training programmes are laid down in considerable detail, leaving scope for extensive intervention from higher levels. The autonomy of middle levels may also need strengthening. For example, while regional credit co-operative co-ordinating bodies enjoy wide discretion in approving unit allocations and individual loans, they are obliged to report on a monthly basis to the national body. The national body has also pursued a strategy of establishing its own credit co-operatives in cities, with the aim of either strengthening existing regional and area bodies or developing new ones. Weak chapters are frequently absorbed into regional bodies, leaving only the strongest credit co-operatives represented at either level. On balance, the Indonesian Credit Co-operative Co-ordinating Board appears to be moving towards greater centralization, in the name of promoting greater solidarity, unity, and discipline.[8]

National Networks

The first major effort to establish a national network of LSM/LPSMs was through the establishment of the Indonesian Secretariat for the Development of Human Resources in Rural Areas (INDHRRA), which came to be known as Bina Desa. Bina Desa began in 1974 as an informal association between community development organizations and sympathetic intellectuals supporting programmes in rural areas targeted to the poorest groups. It should be noted that most participating organizations, including several of the currently most powerful LPSMs, were fairly small and still at a relatively formative stage at that time. Bina Desa was seen as a convenient forum for facilitating exchange between established organizations, while assisting the emergence of new organizations, particularly in obtaining funds and representing their interests to the authorities in the initial stages.

By the 1980s, moves to force social organizations to conform to the official state Five Principles (Panca Sila) ideology had replaced the relatively *laissez-faire* environment of the 1970s. With the emergence of the 1985 Societies Law (Witjes, 1986), the idea of developing Bina Desa as an apex organization for LSM/LPSMs was seen as too vulnerable to take over. Bina Desa survived for a while as a secretariat only, without member organizations. Its legal identity was later secured by the establishment of a foundation called Yayasan Sekretariat Bina Desa. This arrangement left the board of management not obviously accountable to anyone. Its functions were defined in equally vague terms, but seem to have centred on training, evaluation, research, publications, and consultancy. The rationale for networking based on Bina Desa appears to have been superseded by the emergence of more specialist networks in fields described earlier, and later by the emergence of the International NGO Forum on Indonesia (INGI). There have also been suggestions that Bina Desa could develop a role in fostering small groups outside Java where LSMs are still relatively thin on the ground. There appears to be little evidence that this has happened. Bina Desa has continued to handle substantial foreign funds,[9] giving it a potentially important inter-mediary role in dealings with the government. In any case, at this stage it would be more accurate to regard Bina Desa as an LPSM, rather than as a national-level network.

For a while, the Group of Thirteen (Kelompok Tigabelas—K-13) served as a partial substitute for Bina Desa. The Group of Thirteen con-sisted of a group of major LPSMs invited, around 1985–6, by the Canadian Embassy to explore the potential for co-operation between Indonesian and Canadian NGOs. Soon afterwards, the National Devel-opment Planning Board (Badan Perencanaan Pembangunan Nasional—BAPPENAS) persuaded the Group of Thirteen to establish a Scholarship Steering Committee, which would advise on suitable NGO candidates for study in the USA and Canada. The Group then continued operating as a loose network with no formal structure or regular meetings. How-ever, its mere existence reinforced the growing perception of many small LSMs of big NGOs (BINGOs) as wielding excessive powers of patronage through their role in distributing foreign funds. The ready access of BINGOs to the government, and their corresponding lack of account-ability, fuelled resentment at what was perceived as their growing tend-ency to speak on behalf of all NGOs (Aditjondro, 1987). In reality, the Group of Thirteen, as such, never became a significant force. It soon became subject to internal tensions, based partly on personal and reli-gious rivalries. More fundamental differences arose over strategy in handling relations with the government, particularly the potential dangers of participating in government-dominated umbrella organizations.

In the latter context, working groups established by the Department of Home Affairs on the role of NGOs in regional development, and the Cabinet Secretariat on foreign funding agencies, at one stage provided a cause of controversy within the Group of Thirteen. Adi Sasono, founder of LSP, was secretary of the first working group, while LP3ES co-ordinated research for the second. Bina Desa was represented on both. Several academic supporters of NGOs served on the regional develop-ment study group. Both groups encountered strong criticism as being Java-centric, unwieldy, and strongly penetrated by bureaucratic interests (Aditjondro, 1987). Some reports were critical of regional and local authorities as well as some collaborating NGOs, as for example in the case of the Foundation for Social and Economic Development (Yayasan Pembangunan dan Pengembangan Sosial Ekonomi—YPPSE) in Banjar-negara. As these reports were not publicly released, it is difficult to assess the balance of advantage to LSM/LPSMs from participating in official working groups, though this may have served to neutralize government efforts to control NGOs more tightly following the ORMAS legislation.

The International NGO Forum on Indonesia

These earlier efforts to establish national-level networking among LSM/ LPSMs were largely superseded by the formation of the International NGO Forum on Indonesia (INGI). INGI was set up in 1984–5 with the aim of fostering co-operation among Indonesian and associated overseas NGOs in member countries of the Inter-Governmental Group for Indonesia (IGGI), the annual consortium meeting which, until 1992, co-ordinated official aid to Indonesia (INGI, 1991a: 1–3). The INGI Statute laid down that the INGI Conference 'will be held at a point in time largely preceding the IGGI Conference, so that policy-makers and other people concerned will be able to inform themselves about and to make pronouncements on the results of the INGI Conference' (INGI, 1991a: 8). IGGI, and its successor, the Consultative Group for Indonesia (CGI), have thus represented both a framework and target for INGI mobilization.[10] This has not prevented INGI from co-ordinating strategies and advocacy across an increasingly broad front.

INGI's organization is divided into domestic and overseas groupings which function independently but in parallel, coming together to make joint decisions. This structure has the dual advantage of preserving the autonomy of Indonesian NGOs, while providing them with a vehicle for internal co-operation. INGI's overseas component has also rendered co-option by the Indonesian government more difficult. The INGI Conference is the supreme governing body for the whole organization. Indonesian NGOs elect an Indonesian steering committee at their own separate forum. This committee can range from seven to fifteen members, with a requirement to seek balance in terms of region, field of activity, orientation, gender, and so forth. There is no separate conference for international members, who are represented by a steering committee elected by non-Indonesian member organizations at the INGI Conference. The INGI secretariat acts on the mandate of the Conference. Secretariat offices have been located in Jakarta and The Hague. Since the winding up of IGGI in 1992, consideration has been given to replacing The Hague with offices in either Brussels, Washington, or possibly both.

The Indonesian Forum decides on issues to be raised at the Conference, which has adopted a convention of not raising issues publicly before they have been cleared with Indonesian representatives. Decisions are taken on the basis of consensus to the greatest extent possible, but voting is employed where necessary. The INGI Statute provides that the Conference Committee will decide whether a voting procedure will be implemented. A 75 per cent majority is required to change the Statute. Any member organization may propose new members, but such nominees must be approved by both steering committees. Members must endorse the INGI Statute and be active in shaping and implementing decisions. Admission to the INGI Conference is controlled by the two steering committees. The Conference is closed to the media, although its policy statements are made public.

Though INGI is open to all LSM/LPSMs which accept its rules and guidelines, and has attracted membership from all LPSMs active in earlier networks,[11] legal rights and environmental networks appear to have provided the driving force. The Foundation of Indonesian Legal Aid Institutions (Yayasan Lembaga Bantuan Hukum Indonesia—YLBHI) and WALHI have been particularly active. However, the more radical Indonesian Network for Forest Conservation (Sekretariat Kerjasama Pelestarian Hutan Indonesia—SKEPHI) and the Indonesian Front for the Defence of Human Rights (INFIGHT) have refused to join INGI. As discussed in earlier chapters, both YLBHI and WALHI have been moving strongly since the late 1980s towards greater emphasis on advocacy, particularly in relation to land, labour, and environmental issues. In defining human rights, YLBHI's own activities have generally emphasized legal and democratic rights relative to the promotion of economic development. By contrast, the INFIGHT–SKEPHI network sees these as instrumental to more general political and economic struggles, rather than as ends in themselves.

Recognizing the need to harmonize these two aspects, YLBHI has sought co-operation with LSM/LPSMs, which have provided a vehicle to channel its messages to the grass roots. Many NGOs, oriented primarily towards community development work, have become more willing to take political and legal aspects more seriously, although they still tend to view them in an essentially instrumental light. In any case, the IGGI-centred rationale for INGI's establishment has led to a strong focus on developmental issues. Potential contradictions here have been addressed through efforts to formulate paradigms emphasizing participatory and sustainable development, linked to broader democratic advocacy.

The aide-memoire from the Eighth INGI Conference held from 21 to 23 March 1992 at Odawara, Japan, claims that:

Without full democratisation, economic deregulation will not benefit the majority of the Indonesian people.... Democratisation in Indonesia should involve respect for the basic freedoms of expression, assembly and association; that is an "openness" not just tolerated but gradually institutionalised in the form of independent organisations, unrestricted publications and speech, and academic freedom (INGI, 1992: 1).

Such democratic openness should lead to mutual independence of the executive, legislative, and judicial branches of government, equal access to justice by women and minorities, a reduction in the role of the military in government, and less reliance on force and coercion. This statement can be read as demanding a return to full political democracy, although the formation of political parties is not specified. As will be discussed in the Conclusion,[12] this point was made more explicit in a Joint Declaration on Human Rights by NGOs for Democracy, a broad coalition of mainstream NGO and radical networks.

INGI's 1992 statement went on to affirm its belief that

these principles of democratisation must be applied no less vigorously in the economic than in the political sphere in Indonesia, if economic de-regulation is to result in equitable and sustainable development. As a principle, INGI asserts that economic liberalisation should in all cases be subordinated to respect for the environment and provision of a sustainable livelihood for local communities (INGI, 1992: 2).

Here one may surmise that NGOs have been seeking to take advantage of the push towards economic deregulation by advocating its extension into the social and political spheres. If so, it may be difficult for them to attack the economic consequences of deregulation too vigorously. INGI seems to have been motivated by pressure from radicals to put social, economic, legal, and political aspects of human rights on an equal footing. This can be seen as part of a wider strategy by regional and international NGOs to counter attempts by Asian governments seeking to reduce the universal nature of human rights to a relative category, as was attempted at the Asian Preparatory Meeting for the World Conference on Human Rights at Bangkok, from 28 March to 2 April 1993, attended by fifteen Asian governments (United Nations, 1993a).

The final Declaration at the Bangkok conference stated, among other things, that 'while human rights are universal in nature, they must be considered in the context of a dynamic and evolving process of international norm-setting, bearing in mind the significance of national and regional particularities and various historical, cultural and religious backgrounds' (United Nations, 1993b: 3—Article 8). The Declaration further asserted that 'States have the primary responsibility for the promotion and protection of human rights through appropriate infrastructure and mechanisms, and also recognize that remedies must be sought and provided primarily through such mechanisms and procedures' (United Nations, 1993b: 3— Article 9). In an attempt to counter this kind of special pleading by their governments, more than forty international and Asian regional NGOs attended a counter-conference, held parallel to the official conference, which reasserted the indivisibility and universality of all kinds of human rights (FEER, 1993; United Nations, 1993a).

INGI has further strengthened the nexus between economic and legal-political advocacy by a strong focus on land rights and environmental issues. It has lobbied hard against projects which require alienation of land until the status of the traditional land, the processes for determining categories of land, the conditions for its release, compensation, and the rehabilitation of those displaced have been adequately determined. Other demands have included more equal terms and assistance for small entrepreneurs; support for independent village-level co-operatives; a decentralized, community-based approach to forestry, and more appropriate small-scale energy and technology approaches. Finally, in the wake of the Dili massacre in November 1991, the Eighth INGI Conference issued a statement on East Timor which fell just short of calling for outright self-determination.

INGI's overall strategic stance has required a fine balance between action in the international and domestic spheres. On the one hand, the Indonesian government depends on assistance and goodwill from Western governments, Japan, and various international agencies, particularly the World Bank and its regional affiliate, the Asian Development Bank. It is therefore vulnerable to public pressure in IGGI/CGI member countries to place conditions on, or to reduce aid allocations. Lower oil prices since the mid-1980s have further reduced Indonesia's financial independence. On the other hand, overly strong public criticism of the Indonesian government by INGI in the international arena is likely to invite retaliation, as indeed occurred in 1989 and 1992.

INGI has relied mainly on informal dealings with IGGI/CGI governments and the World Bank, supported by public statements designed to arouse pressure from public opinion in donor countries. Dealings with the World Bank have proved difficult, because the Bank prepares joint recommendations with the Indonesian government to IGGI/CGI. These may often result from difficult negotiations, requiring strict confidentiality. In any case, World Bank rules prohibit the release of documents without permission from the government concerned. Therefore, INGI has been unable to obtain key country and other reports. Nor has it succeeded in being granted observer status at IGGI/CGI meetings, even though most countries have expressed agreement, due mainly to the World Bank's insistence that the proposal must receive approval from the Indonesian government. There is a further problem in that INGI might have to reciprocate by conceding observer status to IGGI/CGI at INGI conferences.

In many ways, 1989 proved to be a watershed year for INGI. The Fifth INGI Conference in Belgium, on 24–26 April 1989, highlighted the environmental damage resulting from mining and energy policies pursued by the Indonesian government with World Bank support. Particular criticism was directed against the Kedung Ombo project and failure to provide adequate compensation.[13] The conference further demanded social impact surveys before projects like Kedung Ombo were implemented. Interviews were conducted with every donor government and the World Bank on this point.[14] The death of internationally known human rights activist, Yap Thiem Hien, in Belgium in May 1989, further increased the spotlight on INGI, while also attracting favourable domestic press coverage.

INGI's relations with the Indonesian government deteriorated sharply in July 1989, following Cabinet discussion which concluded that the April INGI Conference had resulted in several European countries announcing, at the subsequent IGGI meeting, their intention to withdraw funds from dam programmes. General Try Sutrisno issued various statements about the importance of not harming Indonesia when abroad, while the Minister for Population and Environment, Prof. Emil Salim, warned environmental activists against playing politics. A major meeting resulted between leading NGOs, the Minister for Home Affairs,

General Rudini, the State Intelligence Co-ordinating Board (Badan Koor-dinasi Intelijens Negara—BAKIN), and the State Secretariat (Sekret-ariat Negara—SEKNEG). The Convenor of Forum for Democracy, Abdurrahman Wahid, also attended. Rudini, though evidently under pressure from military sources, adopted a relatively soft line. He sought clarification as to the causes of discontent, and urged that his door was always open to LSM/LPSMs to assist in solving problems. However, in their dealings with foreigners they should adopt an approach of 'right or wrong my country' [*sic*].

NGOs conceded very little, explaining that INGI was attempting to complement the role of IGGI from an NGO perspective. Rudini pro-posed ongoing dialogue. The NGOs expressed willingness, in principle, but were at pains to avoid institutionalizing any such dialogue forum—although it appears that Aswab Mahasin, then director of LP3ES, later co-ordinated a small team to research the idea. It should be recalled, in this general context, that INGI leaders have come under attack from radical groups as well as the Indonesian government. On balance, this has probably assisted them in bargaining with their government by painting INGI in a more moderate light.

Undeterred by government pressures, INGI leaders attended an International NGO Forum on World Bank and International Monetary Fund (IMF) Lending, held in parallel with the annual meeting of the boards of governors of the World Bank and the International Monetary Fund in Washington, DC, from 26 to 28 September 1989. The Indo-nesian delegation, which included a local Kedung Ombo activist, worked closely with leading US NGOs and international environmental networks in preparing statements. These were presented and discussed with Indonesian and Asian regional desk staff of the World Bank (Van Tuijl, 1989: 6). Kedung Ombo was selected as one of four cases to be put to the US Congressional Human Rights Caucus as examples of forced resettlement supported by World Bank lending. However, in view of the sensitivity of this matter, it was determined that a non-Indonesian representative would present the case for INGI (Van Tuijl, 1989: 8).

It became clear in meetings with the US government and a 'staffer' from the Congressional Subcommittee on Asian and Pacific Affairs, chaired by Senator Stephen Solarz, that the Indonesian government's response to INGI's actions *vis-à-vis* the IGGI meeting earlier in 1989, including the summoning of NGO leaders to meet with Rudini, had been duly monitored in Washington. These officials indicated the inten-tion of the US government and Congress to continue supporting the autonomy of Indonesian NGOs.

In a further meeting with INGI, World Bank representatives strongly questioned the basis of the submission to the Congressional represent-atives two days earlier, painting it as inaccurate, negative, and failing to take account of joint efforts to improve the situation by the Indonesian government and the Bank. INGI representatives vigorously defended the accuracy of their testimony with further supporting evidence and recent photographs, stressing the care with which it had been collected.

They further contrasted the on-the-spot nature of their own information with the remoteness of the Bank's sources (Van Tuijl, 1989: 9–10). The Bank indicated that its discussions with NGOs were inevitably constrained, as it had no option but to work with governments as its main counterpart. Therefore, while NGOs could provide useful grass-roots information, it was unhelpful for them to do this by public statements or letters. For its part, the Bank claimed to have learned from the Kedung Ombo experience, but was unable to identify any specific lessons (Van Tuijl, 1989: 10).

INGI was again in the centre of conflict in 1992, when the Indonesian government responded to high-profile international advocacy at the Eighth INGI Conference held in Odawara, Japan, from 21 to 23 March 1992, by refusing to accept further Dutch government aid. According to INGI and other sources, pressure on this occasion, as in 1989, came from the State Secretariat. Swift action in banning all aid from Dutch government sources temporarily threw NGO leaders off balance. The Indonesian government cited allegedly unacceptable demands by the Dutch government in relation to East Timor and the implementation of development and human rights policies. The Dutch Minister for Overseas Development, Jan Pronk, was portrayed as behaving like a colonial Inspector-General. INGI itself was a clear target of the government's attacks. However, Indonesian NGOs considered it prudent to accept the government's nationalist rhetoric without demur, only querying its implementation, even though it appears that several of them had encouraged Pronk in adopting a critical line. The weakness of Indonesian NGOs in this matter may have discouraged other international supporters. In the event, other IGGI members immediately accepted, without protest, the restructuring of IGGI into a new consortium excluding the Netherlands.

INGI has since worked quietly to rebuild international support, repairing the flow of funds by means of the strategies outlined earlier.[15] INGI itself will need some restructuring following the demise of IGGI.[16] The World Bank, which chairs the new aid consortium for Indonesia, will, in terms of its structures and rules, be less accessible to INGI advocacy than member governments. Donor government support for NGO participation in development programmes remains fairly strong, although the World Bank has shown signs of shifting its priorities back to economic performance. Indonesia's external exchange situation has become more stable, with access to international capital markets correspondingly more assured. It is therefore important for NGOs to demonstrate their continuing usefulness in terms of an effective delivery of public services and benefits (Korten, 1987). On the other hand, signs were emerging during 1993 of a stronger commitment by both Japan and the Clinton administration in the USA, to strengthening links between economic aid and human rights performance.[17]

There have been continuing pressures from sections of the government to bring LSM/LPSMs under tighter forms of control. Since around 1991, proposals have been floated for a code of ethics.

These appear to emanate from the State Secretariat, although Bina Swadaya may have proposed the actual term in the context of earlier discussions about possible NGO–government co-operation. However, an interdepartmental seminar set up to look at this question was unable to agree on any basic concept, or even to define 'Lembaga Swadaya Masyarakat'. Interestingly, INGI was asked to provide a suitable definition, though it is hard to see why it should feel motivated to perform such a task.

Overall, INGI has provided the most successful example of national-level networking among Indonesian LSM/LPSMs. Several reasons can be suggested for such success. According to INGI leaders, its international links have served to embolden its members and other non-affiliated LSM/LPSMs to take up issues which they see as carrying weight with Western governments and NGOs. INGI has carefully avoided taking up direct operational roles and has concentrated on advocacy. Similarly, it has sought to utilize and encourage the research necessary to support such advocacy, without itself undertaking it. INGI has also been careful to avoid speaking on behalf of anyone other than its member organizations, or on other than commonly agreed matters. Nor has it claimed any monopoly in networking within Indonesia. In terms of broad philosophy, INGI has proved capable of synthesizing understandings of participatory and sustainable development with broader concerns for democracy and human rights within the NGO community, and in communicating these to wider domestic and international audiences. However, INGI leaders acknowledge that they still have some way to go in formulating an overall ideology, strategy, and programmes which could effectively challenge official policies.

Strategically, INGI has sought to maintain a balance between challenging and co-operating with the Indonesian government. So far it has survived attacks from its own government by 'going to ground' when necessary. At the same time, INGI has mobilized international support without alienating domestic constituencies, while the Indonesian government and radical hard-liners may each, at times, mobilize nationalist and anti-imperialist rhetoric against it. INGI has effectively occupied the middle ground between them. In all these respects, INGI is attracting interest as a potential model for other countries. Yet, the need for greater internal cohesion and solidarity will grow as the advocacy role of INGI, or any body which may replace it, strengthens and deepens, as its influence extends, and as the organization becomes correspondingly more vulnerable to counter-attack.

Regional Forums

INGI does not itself have regional forums and operates entirely through member organizations. As these are predominantly larger LPSMs, INGI relies on LPSM networks for contact with smaller LSMs. A patchwork quilt of networking between larger and smaller groups is in evidence at regional and sub-regional levels.

Yogyakarta

Networking in the Yogyakarta Special Region (Daerah Istimewa Yogyakarta—DIY) has been facilitated by proximity within a small geographical area based on one city of around 1 million people, which is relatively close-knit in social and cultural terms. The strength and variety of educational and religious institutions have provided a strong ethical and intellectual base for many kinds of social service, developmental, and awareness-building activities. The special historical and cultural role of Yogyakarta within the life of the Indonesian nation may also have given such activities a measure of protection against harsher forms of political control from Jakarta, though the price of such élite protection is no doubt felt in other forms of social constraint on activism. Economic and social disparities within the Yogyakarta region are very wide, not only between urban and rural areas, but between the fertile, well irrigated areas near to the city and the dry, hilly region of Gunung Kidul to the south, plus some upland pockets below Mount Merapi. NGO coverage is still fairly thin in these less-favoured areas, although the major LPSMs based in Yogyakarta also operate outside, as well as inside, the provincial boundary.

Yogyakarta has a long tradition of social and educational activity, notably with the Taman Siswa educational movement, which arose as part of Indonesia's independence struggle. It also has a strong concentration of Church and Islamic institutions, although their activities, until around the late 1960s, were mainly of the conventional welfare and educational kind. Local initiatives from Asrama Realino, Yayasan Dian Desa, Christian hospitals, individual intellectuals, and religious leaders, plus some longer-established NGOs like Bina Swadaya, were swelled in number and variety by the entry of newer national LPSMs which found Yogyakarta to be a relatively accessible point for outreach further afield.

Prior to its formal establishment in 1986, when fifteen organizations came together to establish the Yogyakarta Forum, there had been several years of informal exchange between key organizations. Apart from a desire to strengthen co-operation, there was a felt need to co-ordinate approaches to foreign funding agencies, and thereby achieve greater joint bargaining power. There was also concern that the government might initiate its own NGO Forum, as partially occurred in Central Java. A steering committee of nine NGOs, plus two government representatives, was established. In order to avoid government control, the Forum did not set up a formal legal structure, but has nevertheless maintained a reasonably democratic structure, kept records and accounts, and held annual elections.

The Yogyakarta Forum has developed training programmes for small LSMs. These began with initial training of ten days to which the participating LSM had to bring a leading village activist and a representative of the LKMD. This was followed by one month in the respective villages identifying problems and needs, with a final coming together for one week to sharpen up each other's project designs. The original plan was for foreign funding agencies to attend, but all declined. It was then agreed to submit proposals to funding agencies via the Forum's standing committee. This scheme represented a conscious attempt to overcome perceptions that large NGOs and associated networking structures are used as a buffer by foreign funding agencies, and as vehicles for patronage in relations with small LSMs.

Six such courses had been held by early 1991, by which time it became clear that attempts to reform the foreign funding process had become stalemated on the issue of monitoring. Overseas agencies clearly do not wish to undertake this task, and claim they are unable to deal directly with numerous small LSMs. The Forum for its part, in view of all the sensitivities surrounding the issue of big and small NGOs, also does not wish to play this role, for which it lacks time and resources. The Forum has therefore determined that it will only undertake information-sharing, training, and networking roles. One possible solution could be to extend training to cover self-evaluation or mutual evaluation by LSMs themselves, with results sent to foreign funding agencies. Even so, it is hard to see how funding agencies can avoid all obligations to visit the field. Furthermore, evaluation for self-learning, as distinct from gaining funding approval, is subject to quite different dynamics.

In terms of national links, Bina Desa initially gave some funds to the Forum, but communication between them was generally poor. The Forum refused to accept designation as the regional arm of Bina Desa, or the latter's perceived claim to represent NGOs on a nation-wide basis. Both Bina Desa and the Group of Thirteen were perceived by Forum leaders as having failed to provide follow-up support, after showing some initial interest, or to develop effective co-operative links. There has also been conflict in relations with the Jakarta office of WALHI which, according to Forum leaders, allocated Rp20 million to the Forum for village-level action programmes and training. After hearing that Rp60 million had been allocated by donors, Forum leaders say they unsuccessfully sought discussions with WALHI, and thereafter withdrew from the programme.

Relations with the Yogyakarta provincial government have been mediated a good deal through the Regional Development Planning Board (Badan Perencanaan Pembangunan Daerah—BAPPEDA). This agency has had a close working relationship with Gadjah Mada University, and is relatively open in its attitude to community organizations. This did not prevent initial conflict with the government, which sought to exclude both Yogyakarta's main legal aid and education groups, the Yogyakarta Legal Aid Institute (Lembaga Bantuan Hukum Yogyakarta—LBHY) and the Legal Aid Study Group (Kelompok Studi untuk Bantuan Hukum—KSBH), from the Forum, which nevertheless successfully insisted on their inclusion. Pembangunan Desa (BANGDES), the community development arm of the Department of Home Affairs (Departemen Dalam Negeri), was initially represented on the management committee. Since 1989, BAPPEDA and the Department of Population and Environment have taken the two government places. An important tactical consideration here has been that while BANGDES is omnipresent in villages, the other two agencies have far less outreach. In general, however, Forum leaders say there is still a problem of socializing the authorities at regional level to understand and accept the role of NGOs in social and economic development.

The Forum has worked through the Village Consultative Institution (Lembaga Musyawarah Desa—LMD), an officially recognized village consultative structure, rather than with the LKMD, which tends to be dominated by BANGDES. Forum leaders have claimed that this strategy gives them fairly direct access to informal village leaders. The Forum was also unable to agree with BANGDES on the use of aid money, believing that the correct sequence should be one of local identification of problems, planning from below, programme design, implementation, evaluation, and monitoring, whereas they see BANGDES's approach as one of dropping packets from above. Forum leaders consider that BANGDES officials became more assertive towards NGOs following the summoning of NGO leaders by Home Affairs Minister, Rudini, in July 1989.

Overall, the Forum's attempts to work directly in villages have not been very successful. For example, it became involved in the World Bank financed Mbangun Deso (Village Development) programme initiated in 1980. A report by an Australian anthropologist, Lea Jellinek, had strongly recommended NGO involvement. This view was reinforced when the LKMD system proved either unwilling, or unable, to take on a sufficiently proactive role due to inadequate resources and structures. The Forum was then approached around 1988, and adopted a strategy of jointly identifying projects in conjunction with local authorities in Kulon Progo. This approach changed in favour of village-initiated projects approved within the framework of the Mbangun Deso programme by the district government and BAPPEDA, with relevant government service and agencies supplying technical assistance. The Forum undertook a joint training programme with BAPPEDA in Kulon Progo. This led to identification of joint programmes in three villages, to be implemented by mobilizing local cadres. In the event, programmes were not followed through. After initial enthusiasm, everyone became involved in their own work, as NGOs experienced a period of expansion. As one Forum leader remarked, 'NGOs suffer from high levels of amnesia'.

Differences have emerged as to the feasibility and wisdom of co-operating with the government in this way. Grounds for such doubts include, first, the large number of villages involved and the resulting limitation of resources from the NGO side and, secondly, the legitimacy of working with either the government or the World Bank. A decision whether or not to participate was therefore left to individual LSM/LPSMs. A steering committee of groups still interested in participating was established, which others who might wish to join later could contact. By early 1991, four organizations had joined and a fifth was interested in doing so.

The Forum's internal working has never been entirely satisfactory.

Member organizations appear to enjoy limited interaction with and knowledge of each other's work, particularly in the case of smaller groups (Siregar, 1987: 83). Member organizations interviewed by the author all saw merit in the principle of networking, particularly the aspect of information exchange. However, the Forum was seen as relatively inactive after an initial burst of activity, which appears to have reached a peak around 1988. The initial convenor, Imam Yudotomo, resigned following the disagreements with Bina Desa and WALHI noted above. Participation subsequently dropped sharply. In 1991, out of nine representatives on the Forum's board of management, two were studying in the Philippines and one was absent in Bandung. A heavy responsibility thus fell on the secretary, who combined this task with the positions of secretary of Yasanti, co-ordinator of the WALHI Yogyakarta Regional Forum, and deputy director of PKBI. Reportedly, the board continued to meet every two months, but mostly to hear lectures from various notables, with relatively little sharing of experience after the first Forum meeting in 1988.

Central Java

As discussed in Chapter 7, WALHI has developed an active regional network with effective links at local level in several areas of Central Java. The WALHI Forum has been co-ordinated from the office of the Rural Technology Development Institute (Lembaga Pengembangan Teknologi Pedesaan—LPTP) based in Solo. LPTP has also provided the secretariat for the general Regional Forum, which has been closely linked by cross-membership with the WALHI Forum. The Central Java Regional Forum[18] is governed by an Open Forum, which is supposed to meet annually. However, this seems to depend on the initiative of the organization charged with responsibility for convening the Forum. Thus, the meeting in 1989 was convened by LP3ES Klaten, but was not called in 1990 when YPPSE Banjarnegara was responsible. (As discussed earlier, YPPSE is a quasi-government agency which has claimed NGO status.)[19] The Forum was supposed to work out a joint programme, but so far this does not appear to have happened.

The Central Java Forum has experienced somewhat sensitive relations with the government, after a premature initiative by BAPPEDA to establish a consultative grouping. LSM/LPSMs thereafter established their own network, but feel obliged to hold periodic formal consultations with the government about possibilities for co-operation. This apparently did not proceed beyond identifying potential areas of work, deciding on the division of labour, advocating the cause of NGOs, and attempting to remove misunderstandings of their role. At the same time, the call from some NGOs to clarify the respective roles of the government and NGOs may well carry potential dangers for them, in the sense of defining their role too tightly. However, they cannot avoid the appearance of attempting to co-operate. According to one source, the Forum was involved, to some extent, in negotiations relating to the 1990 instructions concerning LSM/LPSMs.[20] According to another, more actively involved organization, the Forum was supposed to meet government representatives for further discussions on interpretation of these instructions in February 1990, but apparently this never happened. NGO leaders expressed concern at the lack of clear meaning of terms like 'guidance' (*pembinaan*) used frequently in these instructions, although recognition of the role of LSM/LPSMs was seen as a positive outcome.

West Java

By contrast with Yogyakarta and Central Java, there appears to have been less systematic effort in West Java to bring together the various sectoral, functional, and other groupings into area networks which could exchange experience, confront differences, and present a common front in dealings with provincial and district authorities.

In early 1991, two major networks of LSM/LPSMs could be identified in West Java. One was affiliated with WALHI, and the other was clustered around the Bandung Legal Aid Institute. A third, very loose network existed between Yayasan Mandiri, Yayasan Bina Karya, and several *pesantren* in West Java. This grouping extended to some organizations in Central and East Java, such as the Legal Aid Study Group in Yogyakarta, and Pesantren Guluk-Guluk in Madura. The common link in the latter case appears to be an interest in appropriate technology, either as an entry point to more general social development and awareness-building, or to diversify existing skills. Yayasan Mandiri has also developed its own expertise in the environmental field.

Overlapping membership between these networks indicates that they were essentially set up as *ad hoc* groupings for particular purposes. They amount to little more than clusters around the three large organizations, which are sectorally and functionally, rather than territorially, organized. Good relations and co-operation exist between the three networks at a personal level, with many common ties in terms of their social, educational, religious, and earlier activist background. However, the major organizations concerned are all expanding their activities a good deal and, with limited resources and time, exchange between them has tended to be irregular. In retrospect, the high watermark of enthusiasm for networking in West Java was probably reached around 1988–9. Since then, while groups have maintained some loose contact, with small clusters coming together on specific issues, as in Yogyakarta and Central Java forums, the pressure of work on NGOs has largely caused them to operate separately.

The Bandung Legal Aid Institute (Lembaga Bantuan Hukum—LBH) is an autonomous affiliate of its national counterpart, YLBHI. In this context, it can perhaps be best classified as an LPSM which forms part of a national network. As we have seen, LBH Bandung has active links with many groups. In addition to its normal legal support and advocacy work, it has offered support by way of information, advice, and education for many kinds of struggle relating to scavengers, *becak* drivers, small traders, environmental pollution, and land tenure and alienation. With relatively few resources, it relies a good deal on voluntary labour, which it has successfully recruited from the large number of activist-minded students in the Bandung area. Ease of communications with the YLBHI national office in Jakarta, only 3–4 hours distant by road, has facilitated strong mutual support and the co-ordination of resources and strategies. Nevertheless, LBH Bandung appears to have adopted a somewhat more radical stance with regard to land and labour disputes.

As indicated in Chapter 7, WALHI West Java Forum has tended to be dominated by a few organizations and individuals, while relations between WALHI West Java and Jakarta have been strained. Funds were only available to employ a part-time co-ordinator who was unable to travel between the scattered 65–70 groups nominally affiliated with the Forum.[21] Nevertheless, the Forum co-operated with the LBH network in several joint activities and training programmes. Some successes have been claimed in improving communications, alternative tourism, and market information. Given the reluctance of most Forum members to concern themselves beyond local issues, network development in the longer term will depend on building skills and awareness relevant to each group's local context, which may, in time, lead to wider awareness. However, without a regular staff or budget, future progress is likely to be slow and uneven.

Conclusion

Networking and other kinds of scaling up have become increasingly important, since LSM/LPSMs cannot avoid dealing with government agencies concerning policy matters affecting their own and their members' interests, as well as matters of more general public concern. Given the recent rapid growth in NGO numbers, it is not feasible for government agencies to deal with most of them individually, other than at very problem-specific operational levels. However, as indicated from case-studies in earlier chapters, several larger LPSMs have manoeuvred themselves into positions of influence in various policy fields. Even here, those with long experience of the process consider that NGOs have achieved only an incremental impact in improving programme design and implementation, as the government tends to apply models mechanically, without regard to local and regional differences. This is seen as an inevitable result of inadequate popular participation.[22] It appears that major shifts in direction will only be achieved through sustained networking and advocacy as, for example, in the ongoing interaction between WALHI and the Department of Population and Environment (Departemen Kependudukan dan Lingkungan Hidup—KLH).

Both sectoral and geographical networks are needed, the first in order to concentrate specialized experience, and the second to bring diverse skills together for the purposes of integrated problem-solving and general advocacy. The two kinds of network also reflect the structure of the

Indonesian government, which is organized along both functional and territorial lines. The importance of provincial, district, and sub-district levels of government is not yet matched by a corresponding depth in NGO networking at these levels. However, networking should not be designed solely in order to deal with government agencies, but for broader educational and communication purposes, both within the NGO community and in the general society. Networks can also play parallel roles in relations with foreign funding agencies, as the case of INGI has shown. To the extent that networking is focused solely on relations with the government, many LSM/LPSMs are likely to keep their distance for fear of losing autonomy or, at the very least, becoming embroiled in bureaucratic politics.

Despite the potential advantages of networking, this survey has revealed some considerable difficulties entailed in this process. George Aditjondro, an intellectual and activist with many years experience in Irian Jaya, has queried the rationale and motivation underlying the sudden explosion of networking which occurred during the 1980s, particularly around the time of ORMAS (Aditjondro, 1987). Aditjondro noted two fundamental problems with networking as experienced in the contemporary Indonesian context. The first concerned the dangers of facilitating government control over LSM/LPSMs. The second related to the diversion of time and energy from direct action and problem-solving at field level, relative to the benefits to people at the grass roots. To these may be added a concern as to whether networking assists or weakens democratic processes and accountability within the NGO movement itself. Relatedly, large LPSMs dominate both sectoral and territorial networks.

The evidence supporting Aditjondro's first argument is rather mixed. Certainly, sectoral networks tend to create structures paralleling government programmes, which are consequently subject to government penetration. This is most obvious in government-initiated networks such as DNIKS and PKBI, although their counterpart government agencies have proved among the more flexible within the bureaucratic apparatus. The field of credit co-operatives is a more borderline case, with initiatives from both the government and LSM/LPSMs at each level. By contrast, networks in the health, consumer rights, legal and human rights, and environment fields have all originated from the voluntary sector, although the nature of their work constantly obliges them to interact with relevant authorities.

Similar conclusions are justified in relation to geographically based networks, though with some qualifications, particularly at the regional level. At the national level, following some uncertainty about the role of Bina Desa and working groups initiated by the government in conjunction with some leading LPSMs, the emergence of INGI as a strong advocate of NGO autonomy and popular democratic rights has gone a long way to reducing fears of government co-option. Probably the best evidence for this has been the strong pressure brought against INGI, even at some risk to the Indonesian government's international standing, in 1989 and 1992. INGI's domestic support base is strongest among environmental, legal, and human rights groups. Consequently, its public advocacy stance could be described as left of centre across the spectrum of LSM/LPSMs. INGI's outreach to the regions is indirect via supporting organizations. The impact of such advocacy within regional forums, as indicated earlier in this chapter, is rather limited and uneven. Regional forums themselves face difficulties in their relations with regional and local authorities, which have a limited understanding of the role of LSM/LPSMs. Nevertheless, the establishment of joint consultative processes and structures does not appear, so far, to have led to co-option or control by the government.

Networking is a costly process in terms of human and other resources. Either grass-roots workers must be taken away from the field, or additional staff brought in to undertake the new communication and administrative tasks which networking demands. In the first case, performance of both field and networking tasks is likely to suffer in terms of quality. In the second case, differences in experience and lifestyle between the staff of urban-based LPSMs and villagers may be still further widened. Nevertheless, evidence in this chapter suggests that some such process is unavoidable, while only effective networking among NGOs has any prospect of achieving widespread transformation (Wirosardjono, 1987). Yet, such efforts face contradictions in so far as they appear bound to entail significant centralization of information, while shifting discussion and decision-making away from specific points of interaction with local people.

Contradictions entailed in networking from above can be partly offset by emphasizing information-sharing, highlighting the autonomy of affiliated organizations, establishing forums, and basing advocacy as closely as possible on field-based experience and regular interaction with grass-roots groups. However, as even the organizational processes of radical groups indicate, it is hard to avoid informal styles of democratic centralism or core-group oligarchy emerging in one form or another. In principle, such contradictions could be overcome by base-level groups themselves forming federations on which networks could ultimately be built. None of the networks identified in this chapter remotely resembles such a model, though some more local networks, such as the co-operative federations supported by LSP, bear some of these characteristics.[23]

The survey of networks in this chapter, together with evidence in earlier chapters, have indicated a serious effort by at least some larger LPSMs to confront accusations that they are using foreign funds as vehicles to exercise patronage and control over smaller LSMs. Several LPSMs, as well as the Yogyakarta Forum, have developed deliberate strategies to empower small groups to develop their own project proposals, linked to greater skills in self-evaluation and programme and project design. Unfortunately, a stalemate has emerged, with foreign funding agencies proving unwilling, or unable, to process applications from large numbers of small groups, and LPSMs unwilling to act as conduits. The most feasible compromise at this stage seems to be one of submitting projects formulated by LSMs *en bloc*, following open discussion. Networks established by LPSMs for such purposes have further strengthened LSMs by enabling them to visit and evaluate each other's programmes.

Both functionally and geographically based networks confront the problem of how far they have a right to speak on behalf of LSM/LPSMs within their respective constituencies. The necessity of not establishing formal structures in order to neutralize potential dangers of co-option by government agencies, has aggravated this problem. For their part, network leaders claim that they do not see themselves as holding a mandate to represent the NGO community in any extensive way. Rather, they see their role as a more limited one of acting as a buffer between NGOs and the government. Even this stance lays them open to accusations of paternalism, although many smaller groups would accept that, at this stage, this is a necessary role, which network leaders are strategically placed to play.

Overall, democratization of relations within NGO networks, and in relations between LSM/LPSMs and their various grass-roots groups, could be greatly facilitated by more general democratization in relations between state and society in Indonesia. Specifically, the establishment of a clear legal right to organize by social and other NGOs could greatly reduce the need for urban-based networks to undertake protective and intermediary roles. This, in turn, could facilitate the evolution of more broad-based popular coalitions.

1. PERDAKHI sources.

2. See pp. 59–60.

3. PKBI sources, January 1988.

4. Utomo and Thamrin (1989: 9) and BK3I sources.

5. See Utomo and Thamrin (1989: 14–18) for details of BK3I's organizational structure.

6. According to BK3I sources (Jakarta, February 1991), the strongest BK3Ds in terms of management and financial capacity are the North Sumatra, South Sumatra, Yogyakarta, and Bogor–Banten–Bandung regional groups.

7. BK3I sources. Such claims are clearly unfounded, as YIS, Yayasan Dian Desa, Bina Swadaya, and many other NGOs, especially Church-related groups based in Yogyakarta, have operated in the Gunung Kidul over the past 20–30 years.

8. Utomo and Thamrin (1989: 6) quote from BK3I's Five-Year Plan (1986–90), from which the following translation has been extracted: 'The growth of credit co-operatives must be systematically oriented towards a system in which individual enterprises, regional and national credit associations become *integrated* into a single management structure, in a way which will be profitable in business terms and *consolidate* potential for social and economic self-reliance. This will be achieved by *fostering discipline* in developing co-operative credit' (author's italics).

9. US$500 million was received in 1987, according to Bina Desa sources, of which 88 per cent was channelled to small LSMs.

10. This strategy has been disrupted a good deal since June 1992, when the Indonesian government forced the winding up of IGGI and its replacement by the CGI. The

Netherlands, which until then had acted as host country, was excluded from the new body. CGI is co-ordinated and chaired by the World Bank.

11. One exception is Lembaga Studi Pembangunan (LSP), which was active initially but later withdrew, apparently due to INGI's alleged inactivity in relation to human rights abuses in Aceh.

12. See pp. 212–14.

13. WALHI had earlier written an open letter to the World Bank critical of its transmigration policies (WALHI, 1987: 7–8).

14. INGI Secretariat (Jakarta) sources.

15. See pp. 51, 56 fn. 7.

16. This process appears to have been set in train with the establishment, in mid-1993, of the International NGO Forum for Indonesian Development (INFID).

17. Evidence relates to the stance adopted by Japan at the Asian Regional Conference on Human Rights at Bangkok in April 1993 and the Clinton administration's stance on East Timor. However, delinking of trade and human rights issues in the US decision in June 1994 to continue China's 'Most Favoured Nation' status will clearly make it more difficult to link them in the case of Indonesia.

18. See Central Java Forum (1989) for background information on the Forum.

19. See pp. 33–5.

20. See pp. 49–50.

21. The Forum co-ordinator, interviewed in Bandung in February 1991, expressed considerable scepticism about the lack of professionalism or any systematic approach by many people engaged in NGO activities.

22. Based on discussions with the former director of YIS Jakarta, Dr Lukas Hendrata.

23. See pp. 77–86.

Conclusion: Future Prospects

Emerging Trends in Human Rights Debates

FIELDWORK for this book was conducted between 1983 and 1991, although both earlier historical and more recent evidence has been taken into account. In some ways, the parameters of debate among the main actors have shifted during the past two years, with evidence of some potentially significant realignments in 1993. While deepening intra-élite conflict provides the background context and, to some extent, the opportunity for greater boldness by non-government organizations (NGOs), conferences on human rights in 1993 sponsored by the United Nations in Bangkok and Vienna, preceded by an Asian regional workshop in Jakarta, appear to have provided a catalyst for, what may turn out to be, a significant reshaping of mainstream NGO ideology.

A Joint Declaration on Human Rights by Indonesian NGOs for Democracy, in June 1993, has provided evidence of an emerging convergence between radical groups and several mainstream NGO networks clustered around the International NGO Forum on Indonesia (INGI), concentrated particularly in the legal rights, labour, and environmental fields (IN-DEMO, 1993). In retrospect, the ground had been prepared by co-operation in the labour field and, to a lesser extent, in relation to land and environmental struggles. However, the catalyst for the joint statement was provided by the push by several Asian governments to amend the substance, or at least the interpretation and implementation, of the United Nations Charter on Human Rights, in order to take account of specific historical, cultural, and societal factors, and the necessities of economic development. Western countries, led by the USA under the Clinton administration, interpreted this as an attack on the universal nature of the Charter. Many Asian NGOs took a similar position. These issues were thrashed out in United Nations-sponsored conferences on human rights held in Bangkok (United Nations, 1993b) and Vienna (United Nations, 1993c; FEER, 1993) in April and June 1993.[1] The final statement achieved a synthesis, at least at a rhetorical level.

President Suharto, in opening a three-day UN workshop of Asian–Pacific countries on human rights in Jakarta in January 1993, emphasized the importance of culture and national sovereignty in determining how each country interprets and implements human rights. In response, the Foundation of Indonesian Legal Aid Institutions (Yayasan Lembaga Bantuan Hukum Indonesia—YLBHI) branded the Indonesian government as a major violator of human rights (Manoharan, 1993). The momentum for the joint declaration by Indonesian NGOs was given further impetus by a five-day counter-conference of Asian NGOs immediately prior to the Regional Meeting for Asia of the World Conference on Human Rights, held in Bangkok from 29 March to 2 April 1993. Asian NGOs stressed the universality and indivisibility of political, civil, economic, social, and cultural rights[2]—a theme repeated in the Indonesian NGOs statement in June 1993.

Perhaps most significantly, in terms of this study, the Indonesian NGO signatories declared that

It is necessary to pass laws at the national level which can guarantee, promote and accelerate the implementation of the rights to freedom of association, organization and expression. It is also necessary to guarantee by law, the freedom of the press from political censorship and *the guarantee of elections which are free, honest and just and which involve all section[s] of society and representative Organisations in [the] electoral process* (author's italics) (IN-DEMO, 1993: 4).

While calls for open and honest elections are not new, it is hard to see how representative organizations in the electoral process can mean anything other than freedom for political parties to operate within a framework of competitive elections.

For most of the period covered by this survey, it would not have been feasible for self-reliant community institutions (Lembaga Swadaya Masyarakat—LSM) and institutions for developing community self-reliance (Lembaga Pengembangan Swadaya Masyarakat—LPSM) to directly support such a proposition. It has been argued that most are primarily interested in pursuing social and economic goals in their respective fields. Scaling up of local concerns has largely taken the form of policy input, management, or consultancy roles in relation to official programmes, or public advocacy of policy changes. Since around 1988–90, entry points into debates among urban and intellectual élites about democratic reforms of the political structure have come via demands for greater freedom to organize, and for greater legal certainty arising from involvement in popular struggles in relation to issues such as land, labour rights, the urban informal sector, and the environment. While such demands can be legitimized within the framework of Panca Sila democracy, this is less clear in relation to statements concerning electoral processes in the NGOs' June 1993 Declaration.

An analysis of the fifty-two organizational signatories indicates thirteen in the field of legal and human rights, five oriented towards the environment, three women's organizations, four or five oriented towards citizens and democratic rights (notably the Forum for Democracy), and six social study groups. The Solidarity Forum for Labour (Forum Solidaritas untuk Buruh—FORSOL), the West Java Farmers' Association (Serikat Petani Jawa Barat—SPJB), and the Indonesian Scavengers'

Association (Ikatan Pemulung Indonesia—IPI) were more directly representative of workers and peasants. Key national network signatories were the International NGO Forum on Indonesia (INGI), YLBHI, the Indonesian Environment Network (Wahana Lingkungan Hidup Indonesia—WALHI), the Indonesian Foundation of Consumers' Organizations (Yayasan Lembaga Konsumen Indonesia—YLKI), and the Indonesian Inter-Religion Forum for Human Rights (Forum Agama-Agama untuk Hak Asasi Manusia—FAHAMI).

Regional forums and affiliates in the fields of environment, legal, and human rights were well represented, particularly from Yogyakarta and West Java, whose provincial NGO forums were also signatories. Key radical signatories were the Institute for Defence of Human Rights (Lembaga Pembela Hak-Hak Asasi Manusia—LPHAM), the Indonesian Front for the Defence of Human Rights (INFIGHT), and the Women's Solidarity Group (Kelompok Solidaritas Perempuan—KSP). The Indonesian Network for Forest Conservation (Sekretariat Kerjasama Pelestarian Hutan Indonesia—SKEPHI) was a notable absentee. It is also noteworthy that among the LSM/LPSMs covered in this survey, signatories have been overwhelmingly by networks rather than individual organizations. The extent to which they would each wish to be identified with the Declaration is therefore not clear at this stage.

Non-Government Organizations and Democratic Values

Indonesian NGOs have clearly come far during the past two decades, growing in numbers, diversity of roles, and capacity to act together across an increasing range of policy fields and action fronts. In attempting to pinpoint their contribution to Indonesian political life, it is necessary to distinguish between advocacy and policy input in specific fields, and efforts to bring about changes in the overall political system, whether in a limited constitutional or more far-reaching structural sense. This study has provided many examples of the first kind of activity. However, evidence of the second is largely confined to the most recent period.[3] There has also been a proliferation of study groups and forums promoting citizen and democratic participation since around 1990–1, after the main bulk of fieldwork for this study was completed. This process accelerated during 1993.

This new trend may be in the process of changing the overall ideological balance within the NGO community. At this stage, however, the urban, particularly Jakarta-based and middle-class nature of many new groups is apparent. While this is also true of many longer-established LSM/LPSMs, they can claim to have achieved a significant nation-wide outreach to the rural and urban poor. Unless the new groups follow a similar path, their impact on either policy-making or the overall political process will be limited. In that context, many students and others involved in the wave of reformist activism from 1973 to 1978 concluded that their efforts to achieve change at that time had been frustrated by lack of grass-roots links. While there is now a broader constituency for change across Indonesian society, there is a tendency for new organizations to adopt expansive names and objectives, but to lack substantive links.

Of the groups covered in this survey, the legal aid network has fought actively over many years to establish due process and rule of law in the conduct of the judiciary and governmental apparatus generally. YLBHI has had modest success in disseminating legal awareness at provincial and, to some extent, sub-district and village levels, working mainly through regional and local LSM/LPSMs. It has also formed significant co-operative links with other public advocacy networks relating to labour, women's, consumer, and environmental issues. Legal and environmental networks have been particularly active in developing the INGI Forum.

INGI has represented the most credible attempt to form a national forum so far, and projects an increasingly radical and reformist cutting edge for Indonesia's NGO community. It has partly achieved this position by applying a skilful strategy of using international forums to raise domestic issues, thereby encouraging greater boldness by local groups. Its stance has probably been more radical than most of its nominal affiliates. However, evidence has emerged recently of differences within INGI as to whether its overall approach is appropriate or feasible (Mas'oed, c.1992: 8–14). Particular anxiety has been expressed about INGI's overseas-oriented strategic emphasis, and the Indonesian government's hostile reaction. For these reasons, despite the recent NGOs' joint declaration on human rights, it is not clear how far the INGI network will carry any campaign for political democratization. At the time of writing, INGI has yet to formulate any detailed proposals for reform of the political structure. While this does not deny the possibility, or even likelihood, that many NGO personnel would welcome general reform along democratic lines, it is questionable whether demands for such change will be taken up in any systematic fashion by the NGO community in the near future.

By contrast, a number of radical groups and networks, which have become increasingly bold in their actions, criticisms, and demands, have emerged during the past 3–5 years. Rhetorically, at least, these latter express demands, not merely for specific legal and political reforms, but for more structural change. Ironically, more sweeping radical demands are likely to be seen as less threatening by the Indonesian government, due to their non-specific and rhetorical nature. More concretely, they have been balanced by joint mobilization with workers and peasants in local struggles, in ways calculated to generate pressures within the state apparatus at both national and regional levels. During 1993, identification of NGOs by radicals with hegemonistic state structures had extended to a section of the NGO community itself (INDECO DE UNIE, 1993).

Four broad categories were employed to define the approaches of LSM/LPSMs and radical groups in shaping their relations with the Indonesian government, and strategies of popular mobilization. Over and above judgements about the relative success achieved by each approach, the more basic values and objectives underlying them remain open to speculation. While there has been no shortage of statements among groups surveyed about the ideals of participation and self-reliance, linked to aspirations towards a just and prosperous society, most have had little to say about the overall social and political system which they would like to see in place.

It is appreciated that formulation of these categories is open to potential confusion between structure and ideology, in so far as the organization and activities of NGOs may not reflect stated values. Both may reflect caution and constraints, rather than actual beliefs. Essentially, the method of investigation followed has been to compare stated objectives with practice, and infer more general orientations. Whether such inferences have been too optimistic or pessimistic as to the likelihood of various approaches achieving change, is left to the reader's judgement.

In attempting to pinpoint major ideological streams of thought among Indonesian NGOs, there are obvious dangers in a study of this nature of projecting some kind of *ex post facto* 'plan rationality' on such a motley array of groups. Also, those who have survived for any length of time have experienced substantial change, both internally and in the external environment in which they operate. After initially pursuing only limited and immediate goals, many have found that, in the process, new problems and opportunities have opened up, while interaction and networking with other groups have brought broader issues into perspective. Certainly, there are some strategic thinkers within the NGO community, particularly within the second stream identified in Chapter 2, who may well have foreseen the kind of opening out of public agendas that NGOs have since achieved. There are also key actors within the first stream who have a clear grasp of their role in influencing policy formulation and implementation. For most LSM/LPSMs, however, it seems to have been more a case of opening up space as opportunities have arisen, and of following their intuition, rather than pursuing any deep laid strategy.

Despite these qualifications, some broad conclusions about NGO values do emerge from this study. Here, the June 1993 Declaration on Human Rights by Indonesian NGOs for Democracy provides a useful starting-point. While this statement may have gone further in a politically liberal direction than most LSM/LPSMs are willing to travel at this stage, it does highlight an underlying synthesis of ideals, supportive of democratic participation in both developmental and socio-political contexts. Any attempt to understand NGO values must link these two arenas of action and ideology. However, identifying NGO values in relation to political change is more difficult compared with developmental goals. In part, this can be explained in terms of the culture of silence surrounding political discourse, which has persisted throughout the New Order period. The macro political arena also lacks immediacy, and is perceived by most LSM/LPSMs as beyond their control or influence. Finally, for reasons explained at various points in this study, LSM/LPSMs' insistence on their non-political identity represents more than a tactic, and remains an important part of their identity. While an advance guard of

NGOs may assist in opening up the necessary social and political space, the battle for freedom of political party association will ultimately have to be fought out by those who wish to establish and operate directly in the political sphere.

Self-reliance, Participation, and Democracy

NGO concepts of self-reliance, participation, and democracy must be looked at together in attempting to understand their ideology. As we have seen, each of these three concepts is open to different, even conflicting, interpretations. However, the values of community and co-operation clearly predominate in the overall orientation and practice of Indonesian NGOs. Thus, their emphasis is on groups becoming self-reliant within a framework of co-operation, both with other like-minded groups and the wider society. Participation has mostly been interpreted in inclusive rather than exclusive ways, to the extent that the focus on the most disadvantaged groups has tended to become diluted in most contexts surveyed. Both the orientation of NGOs towards conflict avoidance, and the integrated nature of community structures at village and neighbourhood levels, militate against any too exclusive targeting towards the poorest of the poor. In order to gain the support of village hierarchies, it is usually necessary to demonstrate more general benefits in designing programmes targeted towards the poor. Such strategies can draw on still extant, though declining, traditional norms of shared poverty, with the aim of ensuring minimum subsistence and inclusion in community functions of least-advantaged groups.

Indonesian LSM/LPSMs have been criticized from many quarters for their hierarchical and essentially undemocratic internal structures. As we have seen, these, to a considerable extent, have been necessitated by the various legal and executive constraints placed upon them. While government control has mostly been contained at arm's length, this has been achieved through the adoption of informal strategies and operating styles which weaken formal accountability to base-level groups. However, this argument should not be carried too far. The experience of groups associated with LSP, for example, has shown that legal registration can serve not only to enhance benefits to members, but also to gain increased leverage.[4] On the other hand, NGOs operating in more sensitive fields of advocacy, such as labour rights and political prisoners, are more likely to attract adverse attention from the government. As discussed in Chapter 10, networking structures are also vulnerable to co-option.

It was suggested in Chapter 1 that Indonesian NGOs were more naturally oriented towards Panca Sila than Western liberal or social-democratic concepts of democracy, in view of their emphasis on co-operative values and group solidarity. In some ways, NGOs can be seen as keeping alive basic needs and social solidarity-type values from the earlier Sukarno period, and employing them in struggles to extend areas of independent social space. For example, Setia Kawan trade union, at its foundation in 1990, affirmed that the organization was based on Panca Sila 'according to its meaning ... in the preambule [*sic*] of the 1945 Constitution and ... the 1945 Constitution and its exposition'. Articles 27, 28, and 33 of the 1945 Constitution were invoked, alongside goals of building solidarity among workers to struggle for their rights as part of a harmonious and just society (Setia Kawan, 1990: 15). Article 27 refers to the equal application of Indonesia's laws, Article 28 to freedom of speech and association, and Article 33 to the use of Indonesia's resources for the common good, based on family principles of economic management.

There are grounds for arguing that, although there is no evidence of any formal alignment with this group, the ideological outlook of many LSM/LPSMs seems compatible with more open, pluralist, and less corporatist versions of Panca Sila of the kind proposed by the Petition of Fifty group. It will also be recalled that the key point made by that group in its original declaration centred on rejection of government claims to monopolize the interpretation of Panca Sila. However, most Indonesian NGOs have indicated their willingness to work within the value framework of Panca Sila. Other things being equal, the two major LSM/ LPSM streams have proved willing to co-operate with government agencies in relation to policy advice, training, and the implementation of programmes. All but the radicals have operated, as far as possible, on the basis of avoiding conflict with the government.

Nevertheless, Indonesian NGOs clearly value some key elements of liberal democratic ideology, notably freedom of speech and association, together with less arbitrary, more accountable structures of law and government. Logically, such principles imply freedom to operate political parties and fully democratic electoral and parliamentary processes. Since the mid-1980s, hopes have been expressed in several quarters that economic deregulation will be accompanied by political deregulation. Such sentiments have struck a chord among NGOs, though mostly their concerns have been more narrowly concentrated on ensuring the freedom to organize and conduct their own affairs.

To some extent, the unwillingness to openly espouse liberal democracy stems from justifiable caution in challenging one of the Suharto government's basic ideological tenets. To do so could also be seen as incompatible with core NGO values and praxis in several important ways, in that competitive values of liberal democracy conflict with their emphasis on co-operation and mutual benefit. These values direct their primary energies towards building social cohesion within and between groups. The examples of India and the Philippines show that NGOs can survive, and even flourish, in an environment of competitive party politics. However, political parties in those countries represent a constant source of conflict, and a rival focus of popular mobilization, in which the ethos of self-help, which NGOs seek to foster, is always liable to be undermined by the propensity of politicians to enhance dependence through patronage, and the tendency of state structures to seek ways of weakening independent forms of popular association (Kothari, 1988). Finally, even the most ardent advocates, such as

YLBHI, of subjecting governmental systems to the rule of law, have been at pains to emphasize links between legal and economic rights. It is not unreasonable to interpret this as meaning that forms of political democracy which fail to provide for the basic material needs of the masses will not gain legitimacy.

At this point, the dangers of streaming philosophical ideas about legal and political rights and democratic reforms, as against practical matters of basic needs pursued by grass-roots activists, into distinct analytical categories, need to be acknowledged. Many Indonesian activists engaged on these fronts find little conceptual difficulty in integrating the two aspects within broad notions of human rights. In practice, however, limited time and resources necessitate a division of labour, which, in turn, can lead to communication difficulties between groups pursuing different emphases. The majority of LSM/LPSMs are engaged in day-to-day programmes which pursue self-improvement by local groups through income-generation, small co-operatives and credit unions, primary health, training, and literacy. The public advocacy and policy advisory roles which they undertake are drawn from field experience, as the necessity and opportunity may arise. By contrast, groups such as YLBHI specialize in education and awareness of legal rights. Even though their programmes are linked through other LSM/LPSMs with grass-roots struggles over land, labour, and environmental issues, they do not undertake such programmes or campaigns directly themselves.

While most LSM/LPSMs seek to extend their own freedom and that of groups they support in organizing and managing their own affairs, notions of reforming Indonesia's political and governmental structures in a wider sense appear remote to them, even if they were to prove feasible. Increased participation by LSM/LPSMs in public statements provides evidence that efforts by YLBHI and INGI to spread a general awareness of legal and human rights may be bearing fruit. However, initiative for such statements appears to come from a relatively small core of activists in these fields, with most LSM/LPSMs concentrating on building strong independent groups at grass-roots level, outside the arena of formal politics.

Radical Groups and Democratic Values

At the other end of the spectrum, radical groups have shown a willingness to confront the political and governmental system and demand change. Their participation in local struggles has been linked to this larger objective. This does not necessarily imply using people as objects of externally imposed agendas. Discerning the truth here can be difficult, since in cases when radicals and NGOs have both become involved in a local issue, mutual accusations of claiming credit have tended to fly thick and fast. Demonstrations are also more photogenic than quiet discussion and work in small groups. Nevertheless, the wholeheartedness of radical student, women's, and other groups' involvement in pursuing justice in many kinds of struggle, alongside industrial workers, farmers, and land-

less people, is hard to deny and contrasts sharply with the seeming iner-
tia of many more conventional organizations. At the same time, the radicals have sought to highlight the broader structural causes of local
exploitation, and to encourage people to carry their struggles to a political level.

Judging from their literature, public statements, and general stance,
the overall analysis of Indonesian radicals appears to be guided by a form
of populist neo-Marxism (also known as dependency theory) in which
Third World governments play subordinate roles to multinational
companies, Western governments, and international agencies such as
the World Bank and the International Monetary Fund. More recently, a
Gramscian perspective has emerged. The limitations of the dependency
approach, from both liberal and classical Marxist perspectives, have
been exposed in both the general literature on international development
theory (W. Warren, 1980; Higgott, 1983: 45–73) and in relation to
Indonesia (Robison, 1986). These two perspectives converge in seeing
the evolution of capitalism as the next logical stage in Indonesia's development, although views within these schools of thought differ as to
whether associated political change will take the form of liberal democracy or some more pluralistic form of corporatism (MacIntyre, 1990:
258–62).

Clearly, liberal democracy arouses little enthusiasm among the new
radical groups discussed in this survey, which associate this concept
closely with Western-style capitalism. This is not surprising, since the
major push for reform in that direction has come from the professional
and business middle class. However, radicals appear willing to use the
legal tools of liberal constitutionalism to serve the aims of wider economic and societal transformation. They also seek to exploit intra-élite
divisions.

The wholesale rejection of the Indonesian government's structures
and developmental strategies by radicals should logically lead to the rejection of its central ideology. In practice, radicals make little reference
to Panca Sila. Nor have they yet articulated any comprehensive political
goals of their own, as distinct from short-term strategies designed to
open up space for further mobilization. The radicals' preference for
direct mass action, rather than intermediary styles of advocacy, may be
inferred from their patterns of commentary and action. Yet, without
some clearly articulated political aims and ideology, mobilization is in
danger of becoming an end in itself. In any case, demonstrations organized by radicals in Jakarta and other major cities tend to attract fairly
small crowds.

The Social and Developmental Role of Non-Government
Organizations

To concentrate on NGOs' still limited contribution to any direct transformation of Indonesia's political structures would be to miss their more
extensive impact at the societal level, and in influencing the agenda and

ethos of public policy in many contexts. While only qualitative evidence has been offered, examples provided in this work indicate that such impact has been pervasive. However, this study never sought to evaluate the social or economic impact of NGO programmes in any formal cost-benefit terms. It is therefore necessary to remain agnostic about constantly repeated NGO claims to offer low-cost alternatives and more effective delivery of programmes at local level through the mobilization of local resources and people's participation. Anecdotal evidence from this survey indicates a rather mixed performance in relation to mobilizing participation, though, on balance, the picture appears more positive than negative.

The only substantial study of the economic performance of LSM/LPSMs of which this author is aware, relating to West Java,[5] has been cited in relation to various organizations discussed in this book. Major findings from that study (Utrecht, 1990: 57–63) indicate that:

(i) Target groups for both productive and savings and loan programmes tend to be among the low to middle socio-economic strata, rather than the very poor. This is less the case in resource-poor areas where most of the population are equally poor.

(ii) The small-scale productive programmes of NGOs, which are commonly based on co-operative units of 10–20 families, have had only limited outreach. While savings and loan programmes reach larger numbers of people, around 70–90 per cent of credit was used to meet immediate family needs, including children's education, rather than for productive purposes.

(iii) NGOs, with one or two exceptions, have been ineffective in marketing. Reasons for this include the uneven quality of their products, a lack of market information, and inadequate co-operation between LSM/LPSMs, and greater capital, resources, and, in most cases, efficiency by private business. Trends towards privatization are likely to accentuate these problems.

(iv) The problems of women, whether in social, economic, or cultural contexts, tended to be marginalized among NGOs in the West Java survey. The role of women staff at decision-making level within NGOs was seen as minimal.

(v) The somewhat limited economic performance of LSM/LPSMs has been balanced by their increasingly significant contribution in the field of policy advocacy, which has been scaled up from local and regional to national and international levels. However, while development consultancies, through which such policy advice is mostly mediated, may have some moderate incremental impact, structural problems remain untouched.

(vi) LSM/LPSMs are increasingly understanding their role as being part of a more general movement for democratization. However, the goals of building strong groups to this end are contradicted by the individualistic spirit of many economic programmes, which commonly include heavy doses of entrepreneurship training.

(vii) There is a tendency for LSM/LPSMs to fill gaps in services and infrastructure and to target groups not covered by government programmes. As government programmes expand, this has placed them in an increasingly subordinate role. This argument can be linked to objections heard in government quarters to NGO claims to have special skills in mobilizing popular participation and delivering low-cost alternatives to official programmes at local level. NGOs, it is argued, are in a position to concentrate resources in selected localities. By contrast, the government has a responsibility to deliver services across the whole country, and must therefore spread its resources far more thinly.

While conceding the force of many of these arguments, other perspectives can be brought to bear. For example, the author's own observation of co-operative federations in Jakarta and Yogyakarta indicated wider membership and outreach than were found in the West Java study. In general, NGOs in the Yogyakarta–Solo region are mostly longer established, with correspondingly wider outreach than in West Java, and enjoy a more supportive cultural and intellectual infrastructure. Fostering of individual skills and mutual self-help are not necessarily in conflict. While the West Java study's findings concerning women reflect many observations in the author's own study, observations about their lack of participation appear too sweeping. In any case, the problem is more complex in terms of self-perceptions and aspirations of Indonesian women.[6] Regional and religious factors are also important and likely to render uniform approaches ineffective. Overall, there is little strategic clarity among either Indonesian NGOs or their critics as to whether to pursue special programmes for women, or to integrate them more fully into general activities.

Findings concerning the subordinate, gap-filling role of NGOs require closer scrutiny. For example, the support role from NGOs required by the Indonesian government has grown, rather than diminished. While much of such demand can be attributed to the oil price slump since the mid-1980s, the search for low-cost alternatives has become more urgent in order to meet the demands of a growing labour force and a more aware population. To some extent, as for example in the push for integrated health service posts (Pos Pelayanan Terpadu—POSYANDU) linked to the recruitment of local health cadres, government agencies have attempted to replicate NGO initiatives. The community development role of the Foundation for Social and Economic Development (Yayasan Pembangunan dan Pengembangan Sosial Ekonomi—YPPSE) in Banjarnegara, and the work of Bina Swadaya, Yayasan Dian Desa, and the Social and Economic Research, Education, and Information Institute (Lembaga Penelitian, Pendidikan, dan Penerangan Ekonomi dan Sosial—LP3ES) in organizing water supply projects, indicate a capacity to develop infrastructure on a significant scale at district and sub-district levels. In the late 1980s, it was suggested in some sections of the government that NGOs could become responsible for implementing a majority of government development programmes during the next five years (Johnson, 1990: 78). Such euphoria has receded somewhat at the time of writing, as the problems of governments replicating locally pioneered innovations come to be better understood.

Pressure for NGO participation in official programmes from the World Bank and several Western governments indicates that their claims have carried weight in those quarters also. Yet, while overseas support has given Indonesian LSM/LPSMs some leverage in their dealings with the government, support from local people remains their only continuing basis for survival. Such support will only be forthcoming if their performance, whether in service delivery, training, organization, or advocacy, is considered appropriate to people's needs. The relatively easy acceptance which they have gained in many local contexts indicates that they are so perceived at this stage. However, their favourable reception by the authorities, while no doubt reassuring to poor people, may also indicate some differences of expectation at government and popular levels. Nor can it be assumed that villagers' perceptions of NGOs correspond with the messages the latter think they are conveying. Traditionally, rural people in Indonesia, as elsewhere in Asia, look for patrons and protectors. Urban-based NGOs may appear to them as playing new, if slightly eccentric, variants of familiar roles.

The influence on many programmes which LSM/LPSMs have undoubtedly exerted, does not mean that they are yet in a position to play a dominant role in shaping Indonesia's development strategies. These continue to reflect orthodox paradigms of economic growth and modernization, mediated by some trickle down of benefits to the masses. However, LSM/LPSMs have established a presence in virtually all fields of development activity by pioneering and advocating alternative approaches. They have, to some extent, succeeded in modifying top–down approaches through selective and critical collaboration with the government. Indeed, if the notion of loyal opposition was legitimate in Indonesian political culture, it would nicely summarize the role played by LSM/LPSMs—except that they have no aim or strategy to become an alternative government. Yet, if there is no change, either in dominant paradigms of development or in LSM/LPSM strategy *vis-à-vis* the political structure, the more likely outcome for them could well be one of permanent opposition.

Networking and Coalition-building

As indicated throughout this work, Indonesian NGOs play both political and developmental roles, even though they have been slow to acknowledge the former. Reconciliation between these two roles may eventually be found through an enhanced understanding among LSM/LPSMs of their core values of self-reliance and popular participation. However, their capacity to be effective in either context will depend increasingly on their capacity to co-operate and build coalitions between like-minded groups and movements. This aspect was explored in a limited way in relation to networking among LSM/LPSMs. Such analysis needs to be broadened to embrace social, labour, women's, cultural, religious, and educational movements, a number of which have been identified in this study, together with the growth in forums, associations, and study groups supporting democratic reform in the political arena. Student and other youth-based movements, though more volatile and less stable in duration, can, at times, contribute in dynamic ways in shaping this over-all equation.

The survey of networking among LSM/LPSMs in Chapter 10 indic-ated increased co-operation between them in a significant range of contexts. However, trends in this direction may have peaked around 1988–90, since when problems of workload and the constant energy required to maintain communication have caused the pace to slacken or, at least, become more uneven. It was also around this time that emer-ging radical groups launched blistering public attacks on NGOs generally, particularly larger LPSMs. While most did not accept the overall radical critique, the issue of small versus big NGOs struck a chord among many mainstream LSM/LPSMs. National-level networks were very much in the firing-line of radical polemic. To some extent, these criticisms also mirrored concerns which already existed in relation to the potential for the government to co-opt such networks.

INGI has played an increasingly crucial role in bringing Indonesian and overseas NGOs together in efforts to shift the direction and imple-mentation of development and human rights policies. Its corner-stone strategy of lobbying Western governments and international agencies to exert pressure on the Indonesian government has achieved a good deal of success, both in a direct sense and more indirectly by emboldening local activists to take up issues which they perceive as gaining interna-tional support. INGI's dual Indonesian and overseas-based organiza-tional structure has, in some ways, protected it from co-option by the Indonesian government. Such internationally oriented strategies have, nevertheless, proved vulnerable to counter-attack by an Indonesian gov-ernment increasingly able to attract external capital from a variety of private and governmental sources. In the medium or even short term, therefore, it is important for LSM/LPSMs and other social activists to reduce external dependence, and to enhance their legitimacy at home by mobilizing more resources of all kinds from within Indonesia.

If freedom of political association were to be achieved during the next 5–10 years, Indonesian NGOs could face difficult problems in adapting to a new environment. Many radical groups would probably see little difficulty in merging with new parties. The same would probably apply to some newer NGOs concerned primarily with reform in the political arena. Conversely, those whose orientation is clearly social and develop-mental would remain largely outside the sphere of party politics. How-ever, a significant number of LSM/LPSMs of the Model Two variety could well find themselves living in 'interesting times', in so far as the present patterns of commuting between 'political' and 'non-political' arenas would become more difficult.

Relevant considerations here are that (i) political parties exist first and foremost to achieve electoral success, while LSM/LPSMs are concerned with more multiple societal goals; (ii) parties are more eclectic and opportunist in gaining support, while the commitment of LSM/LPSMs to their base-level groups is generally more single-minded, and (iii) parties see capture and redirection of the state as their prime goal, while LSM/LPSMs, to a significant extent, seek to limit and avoid the state as well as to redirect its policies and practices.[7]

The extent of co-operation with other mass organizations will need to be negotiated. Even if these prove to be independent from political parties, the convergence of aims and philosophies cannot necessarily be assumed. The aims of such organizations, whether in the cultural, religious, economic, or ideological spheres, can often prove to be one-dimensional. Their notions of participation may or may not prove to be democratic, while concerns expressed for the uplift of disadvantaged groups may often be secondary or instrumental, as in the case of the *pesantren* movement. On the other hand, the experience of co-operation between LSM/LPSMs and emerging independent labour associations in recent years, has indicated the potential for mutual benefit.

Hopes that NGOs might provide a cutting edge in struggles for greater political democratization represent a form of scaling up of social and political awareness among professionals and activists, who were originally attracted by their potential to pioneer more relevant grass-roots development models. The link between democracy and development is provided by the NGOs' ideology of participatory decision-making and self-management. However, it appears that this link cannot bear the weight of expectation that NGOs will suddenly shift their centre of gravity from local problem-solving and struggles, and merge into some mass-based quasi-party movement to restructure Indonesia's political system.

Recognizing the necessity for division of labour in these diverse contexts will be essential during any future transition process, whether towards greater freedom of association, or some new protracted period of struggle. The severe limitations placed by the Suharto government on freedom of association have, to a considerable extent, created a distorted understanding of NGO roles and false expectations of what they might reasonably be expected to achieve in the political sphere. Conversely, there are dangers that when this point is fully understood, it may lead to a negative reaction, which could detract from the range of positive roles which NGOs can and do play. From another perspective, notions that NGO/LSMs have been merely playing a crisis role, and holding the fort in the absence of parties and mass organizations, as suggested by Arief Budiman (E. Sutrisno, 1992: 24–6), indicate limited appreciation of their potential contribution in empowering weaker groups outside the formal arena of politics.

Emerging Scenarios and Options

As discussed, LSM/LPSMs have benefited both from the liberalizing ethos surrounding policies of economic deregulation since 1985–6, and support from overseas aid agencies in pressing for greater community participation in development programmes. Future opportunities for LSM/LPSMs will be strongly influenced by changing configurations of power and interest within the Indonesian élite. Since these have depended heavily on Western countries and the World Bank exerting leverage on the Indonesian government, their views and interests are also important.

While intra-élite conflict remains intense, the composition of the new Cabinet installed in March 1993 has shown a shift in favour of economic interventionists, notably in the appointment of Dr B. J. Habibie as Minister for Technology and Research, at the expense of economic liberals and rationalists. In so far as the former group sees the state as the prime mover in national development, conflicts of interest may arise with LSM/LPSMs. There are also contradictory signs on the external front. On the one hand, the US Congress and Administration have shown some inclination to use trade preferences as a vehicle to force improvements in the situation of Indonesian workers. Even allowing that American economic interests play a part here, restrictions on arms supply to Indonesia, due to human rights violations in East Timor, also suggest some ideological shift in the US. On the other hand, the World Bank and other donors have proved meekly compliant with Indonesia's expulsion of the Netherlands from IGGI, and the latter's replacement with a new body, following Dutch efforts to make its aid conditional on improvements in Indonesia's human rights performance.

World Bank ideology has undergone various twists and turns since the 1970s, linked to internal factional battles. Generally, strategies of 'structural adjustment' linked to economic deregulation have been pursued.[8] While the philosophy of 'basic needs'[9], which it replaced, was generally more in accord with NGO ideals, the reduced role for the state implicit in structural adjustment has, as has been shown, opened up new opportunities for them. Attempts by the Indonesian government to reverse this strategy in favour of more statist approaches are likely to bring disapproval from Western countries and the World Bank, although it may be able to ride out such disapproval with private capital from a variety of sources, particularly East Asia.

It would be wrong, however, to explain the whole development of Indonesian NGOs to date and their future evolution as merely derivative from the interplay of macro-level forces or, alternatively, as a reflection of external ideological fashions. For example, Mas'oed (c.1992: 8) sees the growth of alternative theories of development, particularly basic needs, linked to 'transnational organization of relations among human communities as causing a "baby boom" of NGOs in Indonesia'. Yet, evidence offered in this study indicates that popular mobilization through a combination of LSM/LPSM and more radical strategies has continued to grow during the past two decades, irrespective of whether or not the domestic, external, economic, or ideological environment has been favourable. Indeed, several examples have been cited of groups which were initiated by former student activists who turned to social mobilization through NGOs in response to restrictions on political activity which intensified from 1977 to 1978, reaching a peak around 1984–5.

While the autonomy of any sphere of civil society from the state is always a relative matter in Indonesia, the country has enjoyed a tradition of social mobilization since the early twentieth century, in which NGOs interact with, but take initiatives independently from, the state. 'Integralist' theories of the state, which deny any autonomous existence of the civil sphere, have always been subject to challenge, not only by political actors such as Mohammed Hatta, or by liberal intellectuals, but in less obtrusive ways by the pluralism of social, cultural, religious, and economic organization at village and sub-regional levels, of which LSM/LPSMs are merely one expression. When necessity and opportunity converge, such institutions can coalesce quite rapidly to press initiatives or resist threats from the state sphere. At other times, they are adept at 'going to ground', concentrating on local tasks, adapting dominant ideology and discourse to their own ends, dissolving and re-forming, and generally surviving until better times return. It should also be noted that the reported increase in militant action by farmers, industrial workers, and others appears to have been occurring independently of any formal organization.[10]

Predictions as to even the short- to medium-term future of Indonesian NGOs, or the political and economic environment within which they will operate, are subject to considerable uncertainty. In any case, their evolution is unlikely to be either smooth or unilinear. Comparisons with the 1973–8 period may prove relevant in assessing prospects for democratization. Sustained pressure and demonstrations in urban centres for reform at that time failed to make any headway, and were followed by severe restrictions and a renewed drive towards corporatism. The government, faced with growing challenges and pressures arising from the process of succession relating to President Suharto's eventual retirement, may well respond in similar fashion. However, the situation in the 1990s is different from the earlier period in one crucial respect, in that the process of group formation, independent from both the state and political parties, is now more extensive and deep-rooted within Indonesian society. In so far as such group formation represents a necessary, if not sufficient, condition for the emergence of any broadbased representative democracy, Indonesia can be said to have reached the stage where democratization in the political sphere is a genuine prospect. Indonesian NGOs can claim a good deal of credit on this score.

Nevertheless, the processes of coalition-building will cause both practical and ideological dilemmas for Indonesian NGOs in the period immediately ahead. The June 1993 Joint Declaration on Human Rights, cited earlier, asserted the indivisibility of legal, civil, political, social, cultural, and economic rights. In practice, the democratization and development agendas envisaged in that document may prove to be in conflict on various fronts if policies of structural adjustment and export-oriented industrialization remain in place (Lambert, 1993: 22–4)). That would create a situation where workers considered themselves exploited by such policies, but NGOs found themselves relying on Western governments and the World Bank, both of which are responsible for promoting such policies, to contain the power of the Indonesian state. Both export-oriented industrialization and economic nationalist approaches contain potential threats to the environment, such that domestic coalitions and ideological coherence could only be maintained by campaigning against both.

Indonesian NGOs may judge that, in such circumstances, their external alliance strategies need to be scaled down. They may further consider that, by scaling down their democratization rhetoric, they may gain support from elements within the government who would be willing, in return, to concede a greater measure of 'openness', devolution, and participation in development, and even to scale up social justice aspects within an overall ideological framework based on Panca Sila. Such a stance could gain a significant cross-section of support from elements within the government afraid of ceding too much power to private business interests, yet still prove broadly compatible with many NGOs' core institutional interests and ideology.

An indicator of such trends is provided by the formation, in 1993, of the Participatory Development Forum (PDF) established under the National Development Planning Board (Badan Perencanaan Pembangunan Nasional—BAPPENAS), with the blessing of the newly appointed State Minister for National Development Planning, Ginandjar Kartasasmita. PDF is chaired by Kardinah Roestam, the wife of a former Minister of Home Affairs. Ibu Roestam is also active in the government-sponsored Association for Promoting Family Welfare (Pembinaan Kesejahteraan Keluarga—PKK). Major LPSMs involved include Bina Desa, the Institute of Development Studies (Lembaga Studi Pembangunan—LSP), LP3ES, and the Irian Jaya Rural Community Development Foundation (Yayasan Pengembangan Masyarakat Desa—YPMD). At the time of writing, WALHI and YLBHI appear to have been excluded. The new Forum has been making a strong push for foreign funds. PDF's orientation is clearly developmental, with suggestions that the NGOs' agendas have been 'hijacked' by an activist radical minority (Participatory Development Forum, 1993: 8). Not surprisingly, PDF has been opposed by the emerging radical networks.

Given the recent uncertainty surrounding the situation of INGI, there are dangers of polarization between radical and development-oriented networks, with the strong advocacy-cum-critical collaboration profile built up through INGI becoming weaker.[11] However, the new PDF strategy has clear limits. Sustainable co-operation between the Indonesian government and LSM/LPSMs will depend eventually on legal recognition of their right to organize, which all see as basic to their identity and survival. As yet, the government appears unable to concede this principle, fearing a return to free-fight liberalism. For these reasons, informal arrangements of the kind described in this study may continue for a while.

In the wider context of potential democratization in Indonesia, strategies of 'enlarged pluralism' will probably be pursued in the short term (MacIntyre, 1990: 258–62). However, these are unlikely, in the longer term, to provide any workable mechanisms for selecting representatives or establishing proportionality between them, other than by the present system of government nomination (Bourchier, 1993: 3–4). The present system also has no institutionalized arrangements for determining accountability or mediating disputes. Once this point becomes clear to them, Indonesian NGOs are likely to see the urgency for more extensive coalition-building, and will then find the means to interact more wholeheartedly with the political process, both in order to defend what they have already gained, and to enlarge the bases of popular participation. However, they would then need to remain alert to the increased danger that, in becoming more involved in macro-level agendas, they could lose touch with grass-roots realities and popular aspirations and needs. These provide the only viable basis for the continuing legitimacy and existence of NGOs.

1. See especially Sidney Jones, 'The Organic Growth: Asian NGOs Have Come Into Their Own' (FEER, 1993: 23).

2. See United Nations (1993a) for an account of both official and NGO statements.

3. YLBHI and associated groups may claim that their constantly expressed concern for the rule of law has always implied democratic reform. Students who were politically active in the 1960s and 1970s, and later initiated LSM/LPSMs, may also claim that they have always maintained their concern to achieve political change. The author's judgements in this context are, nevertheless, based on the stated goals of organizations and their activities.

4. See pp. 75, 77–86.

5. Utrecht (1990). For more comparative studies of NGOs' performance in other countries, see Riddell (1990); Robinson (1991); S. C. White (1991). These studies indicate rather mixed outcomes from NGO programmes.

6. See Berninghausen and Kerstan (1992), especially Part 3 relating to 'Women's Self-Help Organisations and Cooperatives'.

7. Some of these issues were canvassed in Eldridge (1985).

8. See Higgott and Robison (1987: 1–15) for a general overview of World Bank strategies of structural adjustment, with special reference to South-East Asia.

9. See, for example, Streeten et al. (1981).

10. Based, for example, on reports from *Inside Indonesia* and *Asia Watch*.

11. INGI itself appears to have recognized the danger by adopting a change of name in late 1993 to International NGO Forum for Indonesian Development (INFID). Nevertheless, a substantially similar structure and definition of objectives have been retained.

Bibliography

Aditjondro, G. (1987), 'Networking to Promote or to Control Indonesian NGOs? Questions Concerning the Networking and Coordinating Rush among Jakarta-Based NGOs, Ministries and Donor Agencies', YPMD–IRJA Working Paper for the 3rd Inter-NGO Conference on IGGI Matters, Zeist, The Netherlands, 27–29 April.

_____ (1990), 'Dampak Sistemik dan Kritik Kultural Yang Terlupakan: Suatu Refleksi Terhadap Kampanye Kedung Ombo Yang Lalu', *Kritis*, 4(3): 44–52.

_____ (1991), 'Aksi Massa dan Pendidikan Masyarakat Hanyalah Dua Aspek Gerakan Kaum Terpelajar Di Indonesia', *Kritis*, 3(5): 87–104.

Akhmad, F. (1989), 'The Indonesian Student Movement, 1920–1989: A Force for Radical Social Change?', *Prisma*, 47: 83–95.

Alinsky, S. D. (1969), *Reveille for Radicals*, New York: Vintage Books.

_____ (1971), *Rules for Radicals: A Practical Primer for Realistic Radicals*, New York: Random House.

Anderson, B. O'G. (1972), *Java in a Time of Revolution: Occupation and Resistance 1944–46*, Ithaca, NY: Cornell University Press.

Asia Watch (1990), *News from Asia Watch*, (15 October).

_____ (1992), 'Petition Before the U.S. Trade Representative on Labor Rights in Indonesia', (June).

_____ (1993a), 'Indonesia: Charges and Rebuttals Over Labor Rights Practices' (Analysis of Submissions to the US Trade Representative), *News from Asia Watch*, 5(2).

_____ (1993b), *Asia Watch Press Release*, 5(3).

_____ (1993c), 'More Worker Restrictions', *News from Asia Watch*, 5(12).

Aspinall, E. (1993), 'Student Dissent in Indonesia in the 1980s', Working Paper No. 79, Clayton, Vic.: Centre of Southeast Asian Studies, Monash University.

Bank Indonesia et al. (1987), 'Konsep Achir Laporan Penelitian Survey of Self Help Groups in Indonesia—Kasus: LPSM Jawa Tengah dan DI Yogyakarta, Kerjasama Antara Bank Indonesia, Jakarta, Dengan Pusat Penelitian Pembangunan Pedesaan dan Kawasan, Universitas Gadjah Mada, Yogyakarta', Jakarta (Unpublished report).

Bank Rakyat Indonesia (1987), 'Model Hubungan Keuangan Antara Lembaga Swadaya Masyarakat Dengan Bank', Seminar Nasional Pengembangan Hubungan Perbankan Dengan Lembaga Swadaya Masyarakat, Jakarta, 22–24 July (Unpublished report).

Baturaden Statement (1990), 'Pernyataan Keprihatinan' (Pertemuan Reflektif Aktivis LSM/LPSM Indonesia) (19 December), Baturaden.

Berita Nasional (1990a), '115 Calon Pelanggan Listrik Karangtengah Gelisah', *Berita Nasional* (13 January).

_____ (1990b), 'Unjuk Rasa Akibat Listrik Masuk Desa Belum Menyala', *Berita Nasional* (28 March).

_____ (1990c), 'Gara2 Belum Musyawarah Pelebaran Jalan Ditinjau Lagi', *Berita Nasional* (11 April).

Berninghausen, J. and Kerstan, B. (1987), 'The Change of Role Definition of Javanese Women through Their Participation in Formal and Informal Women's Self-Help Groups', Klaten: LP3ES (Unpublished report).

_____ (1992), *Forging New Paths: Feminist Social Methodology and Rural Women in Java*, trans. Barbara A. Reeves, London: Zed Books.

Billah, M.; Busyari, M. A.; and Ali, H. (1993), 'Visi, Masalah Posisi dan Para-digma ORNOP Di Indonesia Serta Upaya Untuk Mengatasinya', Jakarta: Centre for Participatory and Social Management (Unpublished paper).

Bina Desa (1981), *Katalog Bina Desa Edisi ke Tiga 1981: Profil Lembaga-lembaga Swasta Pengembangan Swadaya Masyarakat*, Jakarta: Sekretariat Bina Desa.

Bobbio, N. (1979), *Gramsci and Marxist Theory*, London: Routledge and Kegan Paul.

Bourchier, D. (1987), 'The "Petition of 50": Who and What are They?', *Inside Indonesia*, 10: 7–10.

_____ (1992), 'Setia Kawan: The New Order's First Free Trade Union', Clayton, Vic.: Centre of Southeast Asian Studies, Monash University, Annual Winter Lecture Series on 'Indonesia's Emerging Proletariat—Workers and their Struggles', 5 August.

_____ (1993), 'Contradictions in the Dominant Paradigm of State Organisation in Indonesia', Paper presented at the Conference on Indonesia Paradigms for the Future, Asia Research Centre on Social, Political and Economic Change, Murdoch University, Western Australia, July.

_____ (1995), 'Totalitarianism and the "National Personality": Recent Contro-versy about the Philosophical Basis of the Indonesian State', in Jim Schiller and Barbara Martin-Schiller (eds.), *Imagining Modern Indonesian Culture*, Athens: Ohio University Press (forthcoming).

Bourchier, D. and Legge, J. D. (eds.) (1994), *Indonesian Democracy: 1950s and 1990s*, Clayton, Vic.: Centre of Southeast Asian Studies, Monash University.

Budiman, A. (1988), 'Democratisation is Possible', *Inside Indonesia*, 17: 2–4.

_____ (1990a), 'Gerakan Mahasiswa dan LSM: Ke Arah Sebuah Reunifikasi', *Kritis*, 4(3): 53–9.

_____ (ed.) (1990b), *The State and Civil Society in Indonesia*, Monash Papers on Southeast Asia No. 22, Clayton, Vic.: Centre of Southeast Asian Studies, Monash University.

Byesouth, K. (1986), 'The Non-Governmental Organisations', in P. Eldridge, D. Forbes, and D. Porter (eds.), *Australia's Overseas Aid Program*, Sydney: Croom Helm, pp. 211–26.

Central Java Forum (1989), 'Forum LSM/LPSM Jawa Tengah: Pelaporan Temu Muka IV LSM/LPSM Se Jawa Tengah 8–30 Desember, 1989', Solo: LPTP and Klaten: LP3ES (Internal documents).

Cooley, L. (1992), 'Maintaining Rukun for Javanese Households and for the State', in Sita van Bemmelen et al. (eds.), *Women and Mediation in Indonesia*, Leiden: KITLV Press.

Cotton, J. (1991), *State Determination and State Autonomy in Theories of Regime Maintenance and Regime Change*, Discussion Paper Series No. 2, Canberra:

Department of Political and Social Change, Research School of Pacific Studies, Australian National University.

Cribb, R. (1988), *The Politics of Environmental Protection in Indonesia*, Clayton, Vic.: Centre of Southeast Asian Studies, Monash University.

Crick, B. (1992), *In Defence of Politics*, 4th edn., Ringwood, Vic.: Penguin Books.

Crouch, H. (1979), 'Patrimonialism and Military Rule in Indonesia', *World Politics*, 31(4): 571–87.

_____ (1986), 'The Missing Bourgeoisie: Approaches to Indonesia's New Order', in D. Chandler and M. Ricklefs (eds.), *Nineteenth and Twentieth Century Indonesia: Essays in Honour of Professor J. D. Legge*, Clayton, Vic.: Centre of Southeast Asian Studies, Monash University, pp. 41–56.

DEPKOP (Departemen Perdagangan dan Koperasi) (c.1968), 'Undang-Undang No. 12 Tahun 1967 Tentang Pokok-Pokok Perkoperasian', Jakarta.

_____ (1983), *Tunas Niaga*, 2, Proyek Pembinaan Pedagang Golongan Ekonomi Lemah, Jakarta.

_____ (1985), 'Laporan Proyek Peningkatan Peranan Wanita di Bidang Pekoperasian Tahun 1984/85', Jakarta (Unpublished report).

_____ (1986), 'Laporan Proyek Peningkatan Peranan Wanita di Bidang Pekoperasian Tahun 1985/86', Jakarta (Unpublished report).

Dhofier, Z. (1982), *Tradisi Pesantren: Studi tentang Pandangan Hidup Kyai*, Jakarta: LP3ES.

Drabek, A. G. (ed.) (1987), 'Development Alternatives: The Challenge for NGOs', *World Development*, 15 (Supplement).

Edwards, M. and Hulme, D. (eds.) (1992), *Making a Difference: NGOs and Development in a Changing World*, London: Earthscan Publications.

Eldridge, P. (1979), *Indonesia and Australia: The Politics of Aid and Development since 1966*, Monograph No. 18, Canberra: Development Studies Centre, Australian National University.

_____ (1985), 'The Political Role of Community Action Groups in India and Indonesia: In Search of a General Theory', *Alternatives*, 10(3): 401–34.

_____ (1990a), 'NGOs and the State in Indonesia', in A. Budiman (ed.), *The State and Civil Society in Indonesia*, Monash Papers on Southeast Asia No. 22, Clayton, Vic.: Centre of Southeast Asian Studies, Monash University, pp. 503–38.

_____ (1990b), 'NGOs and the State in Indonesia: Popular Movement or Arm of Government?', Working Paper No. 55, Clayton, Vic.: Centre of Southeast Asian Studies, Monash University.

_____ (1991), 'Reflections on Non-Government Organisations and Social Movements in Malaysia', Paper presented at the Seventh Malaysia Society Colloquium, University of Melbourne, 4–6 October.

Emmerson, D. K. (1983), 'Understanding the New Order: Bureaucratic Pluralism in Indonesia', *Asian Survey*, 23(11): 1220–41.

Esman, M. et al. (1980), *Paraprofessionals in Rural Development*, Ithaca, NY: Center for International Studies, Cornell University.

Fakih, Mansour (1987), 'Community Development in Pesantren: Issues and Problems', *Pesantren's Linkage*, 3(2): 5–8, Jakarta: P3M.

FEER (1993), 'Rights Thinking', 'Vienna Showdown', and other articles, *Far Eastern Economic Review* (17 June), pp. 5, 16–28.

_____ (1994), 'High Anxiety', *Far Eastern Economic Review* (29 September), p. 32.

Feith, H. (1962), *The Decline of Constitutional Democracy in Indonesia*, Ithaca, NY: Cornell University Press.

Felderspiel, H. M. (1992), *Muslim Intellectuals and Development in Indonesia*, New York: Nova Science Publishers.

Fernandes W. (ed.) (1985), *Social Activists and People's Movements*, New Delhi: Indian Social Institute.

Frank, A. G. (1971), *Capitalism and Underdevelopment in Latin America*, Harmondsworth: Penguin.

Freire, P. (1970), *Pedagogy of the Oppressed*, New York: Herder and Herder.

―――― (1972), *Cultural Action for Freedom*, Harmondsworth: Penguin.

Geertz, C. (1960), *The Religion of Java*, London: Collier-Macmillan.

―――― (1970), *Agricultural Involution: The Processes of Ecological Change in Indonesia*, Berkeley: University of California Press.

Guinness, P. (1986), *Harmony and Hierarchy in a Javanese Kampung*, Singapore: Oxford University Press.

Hardjono, J. (1986), 'Environmental Crisis in Java', *Prisma*, 39: 3–13.

―――― (ed.) (1991), *Indonesia: Resources, Ecology, and Environment*, Singapore: Oxford University Press.

Hassan, M. H. (1982), *Muslim Intellectual Responses to 'New Order' Modernization in Indonesia*, Kuala Lumpur: Dewan Bahasa dan Pustaka.

Hewison, K.; Robison, R.; and Rodan, G. (1993), *Southeast Asia in the 1990s: Authoritarianism, Democracy and Capitalism*, Sydney: Allen and Unwin.

Heyzer, N. (ed.) (1987), *Women Farmers and Rural Change in Asia: Towards Equal Access and Participation*, Kuala Lumpur: Asian and Pacific Development Centre.

Higgott, R. (1983), *Political Development Theory*, Canberra: Croom Helm.

Higgott, R. and Robison, R. (eds.) (1987), *Southeast Asia Essays in the 1980s: The Politics of Economic Crisis*, Sydney: Allen and Unwin.

Hill, H. (1992), 'The Economy 1991/92', in H. Crouch and H. Hill (eds.), *Indonesia Assessment 1992: Political Perspectives on the 1990s*, Canberra: Department of Political and Social Change, Research School of Pacific Studies, Australian National University.

ILO (International Labour Organization) (1951), *Record of Proceedings, International Labour Conference, 32nd Session 1949* (Appendix XVIII: Authentic Texts), Geneva.

INDECO DE UNIE (1993), 'Laporan Diskusi: Studi tentang LSM', Jakarta (Unpublished papers).

IN-DEMO (Indonesian NGOs for Democracy) (1993), 'Joint Declaration on Human Rights' (June), Jakarta.

INDOC (Indonesian Documentation and Information Centre) (1986), *Indonesian Workers and Their Right to Organise* (May), Leiden.

INFIGHT (Indonesian Front for the Defence of Human Rights) (1990), 'Other Voices from Indonesia: Some Notes for the 33rd Session of IGGI', Presented at the People's Forum with the Chairman of IGGI (Inter-Governmental Group for Indonesia), Mr J. P. Pronk, Jakarta, 13 April, Indocumenta 1990/01, Leiden.

INGI (International NGO Forum on Indonesia) (1991a), 'International NGO Forum on Indonesia (INGI) Statute' (May), Jakarta (Internal document).

―――― (1991b), 'Labour Rights and Wrongs', *Inside Indonesia*, 27: 2–9.

―――― (1992), 'International NGO Forum on Indonesia (INGI), Eighth INGI Conference, 21–23 March 1992, Odawara, Japan, Aide Memoire', Jakarta (Internal document).

Ingleson, J. (1986), *In Search of Justice: Workers and Unions in Colonial Java, 1908–1926*, Singapore: Oxford University Press.

INPRES (Presidential Instruction) (1974), 'Instruksi Presiden (INPRES) No. 4', Jakarta: Departemen Dalam Negeri.

Ismawan, Bambang (1990), 'Profile Bina Swadaya: Community Self-Reliance Development Agency', Jakarta: Bina Swadaya (Unpublished Report).

Jackson, K. D. (1978), 'Bureaucratic Polity: A Theoretical Framework for the Analysis of Power and Communications in Indonesia', in K. D. Jackson and L. W. Pye (eds.), *Political Power and Communications in Indonesia*, Berkeley: University of California Press, pp. 3–22.

Jellinek, L. (1991), *The Wheel of Fortune: The History of a Poor Community in Jakarta*, Sydney: Allen and Unwin.

Johnson, M. (1990), 'Non-Government Organisations at the Crossroads in Indonesia', in R. C. Rice (ed.), *Indonesian Economic Development: Approaches, Technology, Small-Scale Textiles, Urban Infrastructure and NGOs*, Clayton, Vic.: Centre of Southeast Asian Studies, Monash University, pp. 77–92.

Kahin, G. McT. (1952), *Nationalism and Revolution in Indonesia*, Ithaca, NY: Cornell University Press.

Kalyanamitra (1986), 'Pembantu Rumah Tangga', *Dongbret*, 2 (April), Jakarta.

Kedaulatan Rakyat (1990), 'Penduduk Karangtengah Tuntut Nyalanya Neonisasi', *Kedaulatan Rakyat* (5 April).

Kelompok Pinggiran (1988), 'Mosi Tidak Percaya Beberapa NGO-Indonesia', *Potensi*, 22(2): 13–16.

King, D. (1982), 'Indonesia's New Order as a Bureaucratic Polity, a Neopatrimonial Regime or Bureaucratic Authoritarian Regime: What Difference Does it Make?', in B. Anderson and A. Kahin (eds.), *Interpreting Indonesian Politics: Thirteen Contributions to the Debate*, Interim Reports Series (Publication No. 62), Ithaca, NY: Cornell Modern Indonesia Project, Cornell University, pp. 104–16.

Koentjaraningrat (1985), *Javanese Culture*, Singapore: Oxford University Press.

Koesnadi, Hardjasoemantri (1986a), *Aspek Hukum Peran Serta Masyarakat Dalam Pengelolaan Lingkungan Hidup*, Yogyakarta: Gadjah Mada University Press.

_____ (1986b), *Hukum Tata Lingkungan*, Yogyakarta: Gadjah Mada University Press.

_____ (1987), *Environmental Legislation in Indonesia*, Yogyakarta: Gadjah Mada University Press.

Korten, D. (1987), 'Third Generation NGO Strategies: A Key to People-Centred Development', in A. G. Drabek (ed.), 'Development Alternatives: The Challenge for NGOs', *World Development*, 15 (Supplement): 145–60.

_____ (1990), *Getting to the 21st Century: Voluntary Action and the Global Agenda*, West Hartford, Conn.: Kumarian Press.

Kothari, R. (1984), 'The Non-Party Political Process', in H. Sethi and S. Kothari (eds.), *The Non-Party Political Process: Uncertain Alternatives*, Delhi: Lokayan, pp. 18–46.

_____ (1988), *State Against Democracy: In Search of Humane Governance*, Delhi: Ajanta Publications.

KSBH (Kelompok Studi Bantuan Hukum) (c.1981a), *Hak Anda Dalam Pencabutan Hak Atas Tanah*, Yogyakarta.

_____ (c.1981b), *Hak-Hak Atas Tanah dan Pendaftaran Tanah*, Yogyakarta.

_____ (1987), *Nawala*, 4(8): 1–12.

Lambert, R. (1993), 'Authoritarian State Unionism in New Order Indonesia', Working Paper No. 25, Murdoch, WA: Asia Research Centre on Social, Political and Economic Change, Murdoch University.

Lane, M. (1991), 'Openness', Political Discontent and Succession in Indonesia: Political Developments in Indonesia, 1989–91, Australia–Asia Paper No. 56, Nathan, Qld: Centre for the Study of Australia–Asia Relations, Griffith University.

Laporan (1993), 'Laporan Workshop dan Paradigma-Paradigma Perubahan Sosial Salatiga, 6–7 Maret 1993', Salatiga (Unpublished papers).

Lev, D. S. (1987), 'Legal Aid in Indonesia', Working Paper No. 44, Clayton, Vic.: Centre of Southeast Asian Studies, Monash University.

Liddle, R. W. (1985), 'Soeharto's Indonesia: Personal Rule and Political Institutions', Pacific Affairs, 58(1): 68–90.

_____ (1987), 'The Politics of Shared Growth: Some Indonesian Cases', Comparative Politics, 19(2): 127–46.

Lipton, M. (1977), Why Poor People Stay Poor: Urban Bias in World Development, London: Temple Smith.

Locher-Scholten, E. and Niehof, A. (eds.) (1987), Indonesian Women in Focus: Past and Present Notions, Dordrecht, Holland: Foris Publications.

Lokayan (1989), 'Towards a Political Economy of Housing Policy', Lokayan Bulletin, 7(2): 7–33.

LP3ES (Lembaga Penelitian, Pendidikan, dan Penerangan Ekonomi dan Sosial) (1983), Prisma, 12(4): 3–69 (Series of articles on LSM/LPSMs).

_____ (1987a), 'Refleksi Aksi Budaya Lokal', Alternatif: Jaringan Kominkasi dan Pengembangan Riset Aksi, 8 (June–July), Jakarta.

_____ (1987b), 'Pelaporan Akhir Proyek Pembinaan Wanita Produktif (PWP) Klaten September 1984–Augustus 1987', Klaten (Internal report).

LSP (Lembaga Studi Pembangunan) (1983), Galang (Informal Sector Series), 1(1), Jakarta.

_____ (1986a), 'Informal Sector Development', Jakarta (Unpublished paper).

_____ (1986b), 'Labour Cooperative Movement', Jakarta (Unpublished paper).

_____ (c.1987), 'Labour Community Development', Grassroots, 3(3–5), Jakarta.

Lucas, A. (1990), One Soul One Struggle: Region and Revolution in Indonesia, Sydney: Allen and Unwin.

_____ (1992), 'Land Disputes in Indonesia: Some Current Perspectives', Indonesia, 53 (April): 79–92.

MacAndrews, C. (ed.) (1986), Central Government and Local Development in Indonesia, Singapore: Oxford University Press.

McClelland, D. (1961), The Achieving Society, Princeton, NJ: Van Nostrand.

MacIntyre, A. (1990), Business and Politics in Indonesia, Sydney: Allen and Unwin.

Macuja, J. P. (1992), 'The Mass Movement and the 1992 Elections', ed. Steven Rood, Paper No. 2, Baguio City: Cordillera Studies Center Issue Paper.

Majelis Luhur Persatuan Tamansiswa (1982), Buku Peringatan Tamansiswa 60 Tahun 1922–1982, Yogyakarta.

Manning, C. (1988), The Green Revolution, Employment and Economic Change in Rural Java: A Reassessment of Trends under the New Order, Singapore: Institute of Southeast Asian Studies.

_____ (1989), 'Employment Trends in Indonesia in the 1970s and 1980s', Paper presented at the Conference on Indonesia's New Order: Past, Present and Future, Australian National University, Canberra, 4–8 December.

Manoharan, M. (1993), 'Asia Supports National Human Rights Commissions', Reuter (27 January), Jakarta.

Mas'oed, Mohtar (c.1992), 'INGI and the Politics of Development in Indonesia', Yogyakarta: Gadjah Mada University (Unpublished paper).

Media Indonesia (1993), 'Turbulence with the US', *Media Indonesia* (14 August), editorial.

MENDAGRI (Menteri Dalam Negeri) (1984), 'Keputusan Menteri Dalam Negeri No. 28 Tahun 1984 tentang Pembinaan Kesejahteraan Keluarga (PKK)', Jakarta.

_____ (1990), 'Instruksi Menteri Dalam Negeri Nomor 8 Tahun 1990 tentang Pembinaan Lembaga Swadaya Masyarakat', Jakarta.

Minister of State (1982), 'Act No. 4 1982 of the Republic of Indonesia: Basic Provisions for the Management of the Living Environment (Elucidating Guidelines)', Jakarta.

Mortimer, R. (1974), *Indonesian Communism Under Sukarno: Ideology and Politics, 1959–1965*, Ithaca, NY: Cornell University Press.

Mudatsir, A. (1985), 'Kajen Desa Pesantren', in Dawam Rahardjo (ed.), *Pergulatan Dunia Pesantren—Membangun Dari Bawah*, Jakarta: P3M, pp. 197–218.

Mulder, N. (1978), *Mysticism and Everyday Life in Contemporary Java*, Singapore: Institute of Southeast Asian Studies.

Nindyantoro (1989), 'Penelitian Peranan LPSM Dalam Peningkatan Peluang Usaha dan Kerja Di Sektor Non Pertanian Di Jawa Barat: Kasus Yayasan Bina Lingkungan Hidup (YBLH), Kabupaten Ciamis (Laporan Sementara)', Bandung: Institut Teknologi Bandung; Bogor: Institut Pertanian Bogor; and The Hague: Institute of Social Studies (Unpublished report).

Nugroho, Bambang Isti (1991), 'Memerjuangkan Demokrasi dan Hak-Hak Asasi Manusia Di Indonesia', Forum Komunikasi Mahasiswa Yogyakarta, August.

Ostergaard, G. (1985), *Non-Violent Revolution in India: Sarvodaya, Vinobha Bhave and the Total Revolution of Jayaprakash Narayan*, New Delhi: Gandhi Peace Foundation.

OXFAM (Oxford Committee for Famine Relief) (1987), 'SISTIM KRING Yayasan Pembangunan dan Pengembangan Sosial Ekonomi (YPPSE) Kabupaten Banjarnegara, Jawa Tengah: Sebuah Penelitian tentang Latarbelakang dan Pembinaan, serta Rekomendasi dan Tindakan-Tindakan Alternatif yang Disarankan (21 Augustus–31 Oktober 1987)', Semarang (Unpublished report).

Participatory Development Forum (1993), 'NGO Self-Management', *People-Centered Development New Forum*, 1(2): 8–10.

Pesan (1987a), 'Rekapitulasi Kegiatan Pengembangan Masyarakat Sekitar Desa Kajen', *Pesan*, 2: 16–21.

_____ (1987b), 'BPPM, TPM dan Dukungan Pamong', *Pesan*, 2: 21–3.

_____ (1991), 'Kerangka Acuan Diskusi Majalah Pesan "Meninjau Ulang Konsep Pengembangan Masyarakat Di Pesantren" 1991', Paper presented at a seminar, LP3ES, Jakarta, 15 February.

PPERT (Proyek Peringkatan Ekonomi Rumah Tangga) (1986), 'Laporan Pelaksanaan Proyek Peningkatan Ekonomi Rumah Tangga (PPERT) Bagi Masyarakat Miskin Di Pedesaan Klaten Tahun 1986', Klaten: LP3ES; Semarang: OXFAM; and Jakarta: Asia Foundation (Unpublished report).

Princen [H. J.] (1992), 'Years of Living Dangerously: The Memoirs of Princen', *Inside Indonesia*, 30: 7–9; 31: 15–16; 32: 13–14.

Qureshi, M. A. (1988), 'Bank Dunia dan LSM: Sebuah Pendekatan Baru', *Potensi*, 13(2): 30–6.

Rahardjo, Dawam (*c*.1990), 'LSM dan Program Pengembangan Masyarakat', Jakarta: LP3ES (Unpublished paper).

Reeve, D. (1985), *Golkar of Indonesia: An Alternative to the Party System*, Singapore: Oxford University Press.

Riawanti, S.; Noviana; and Harun, H. (1990), 'Kedudukan dan Peranan Perempuan Di Dalam dan Di Sektor Produktif LP3ES Klaten', Jakarta: LP3ES (Unpublished report).

Richards, D. C. (1986), 'Report on LP3ES' Small Industries Development Project (PIK) Klaten, Central Java (P10/T 398-0249-3)', Undertaken for the Office of Employment and Enterprise Development, Washington DC (Unpublished report).

Riddell, R. (1990), 'Judging Success: Evaluating Approaches to Alleviating Poverty in Developing Countries', Working Paper No. 37, London: Overseas Development Institute.

Riker, J. V. (1990), 'Contending Perspectives for Interpreting Government–NGO Relations in South and Southeast Asia: Constraints, Challenges and the Search for Common Ground in Rural Development', Paper prepared for the Joint Project on the Role of NGOs in Development, 6 December, Ithaca, NY: Department of Government, Cornell University (Unpublished paper).

Riwanto, Tirtosudarmo (c.1991), 'Mampukah LSM menjadi "Counter Hegemonic Movement"?: Komentar atas Tulisan George J. Aditjondro (GJA) dan Arieff Budiman (AB) dalam Kritis no. 3, tahun 5, 1990', Kritis, 5(3): 105–8.

Robinson, M. A. (1991), 'Evaluating the Impact of NGOs in Rural Poverty Alleviation: India Country Study', Working Paper No. 49, London: Overseas Development Institute.

Robison, R. (1986), Indonesia: The Rise of Capital, Sydney: Allen and Unwin.

_____ (1987), 'After the Gold Rush: The Politics of Economic Restructuring in Indonesia in the 1980s', in R. Higgott and R. Robison (eds.), Southeast Asia Essays in the 1980s: The Politics of Economic Crisis, Sydney: Allen and Unwin, pp. 16–51.

Rogers, B. (1980), The Domestication of Women: Discrimination in Developing Societies, London: Tavistock.

Saifullah, Ali (1974), 'Darussalaam, Pondok Modern Gontor', in Dawam Rahardjo (ed.), Pesantren dan Pembaharuan, Jakarta: LP3ES, pp. 134–54.

Sartono, Kartodirdjo (1973), Protest Movements in Rural Java: A Study of Agrarian Unrest in the Nineteenth and Early Twentieth Centuries, Kuala Lumpur: Oxford University Press.

Sartori, G. (1965), Democratic Theory, London: F. A. Praeger.

Schulte-Nordholt, N. (1985), 'From LSD to LKMD: Participation at the Village Level', Working Paper No. 25, The Netherlands: University of Twente Technology and Development Group.

Schumacher, E. F. (1974), Small is Beautiful: Economics as if People Mattered, London: Sphere Books.

Sethi, H. (1984), 'Groups in a New Politics of Transformation', Economic and Political Weekly, 14(7): 305–16.

Setia Kawan (1990), 'First Congress Setia Kawan Free Trade Union, December 15–16', Jakarta (Internal document).

Sidin, Fasbir HM Noor (1989), 'Peranan LPSM Dalam Peningkatan Penghasilan Di Sektor Non Pertanian Di Jawa Barat: Kasus Yayasan Mandiri—Bandung' (Februari–April), Bandung: Institut Teknologi Bandung; Bogor: Institut Pertanian Bogor; and The Hague: Institute of Social Studies (Unpublished report).

Simunjuntak, Marsillam (1992), 'Konstitutionalism dan Demokrasi di Indonesia', Detik, 565 (30 November).

Siregar, Amir Effendi (1987),'The Communication Patterns Among Indo-nesian Non-Government Organisations in Yogyakarta: A Pilot Study', MA (Journalism) thesis, University of Iowa.

Sjaifudian, Hetifah (1989), 'Laporan Studi LPSM Besar (BINGO): Kasus Lembaga Studi Pembangunan (LSP)', Bandung: Institut Teknologi Bandung; Bogor: Institut Pertanian Bogor; and The Hague: Institute of Social Studies (Unpublished report).

Sjaifudian, Hetifah and Thamrin, Juni (1989), 'Laporan Sementara—Penelitian Peranan LPSM Dalam Peningkatan Peluang dan Kerja Di Sektor Non Pertanian Di Jawa Barat: Kasus BINA KARYA' (October), Bandung: Institut Teknologi Bandung; Bogor: Institut Pertanian Bogor; and The Hague: Institute of Social Studies (Unpublished report).

SKEPHI (Jaringan Kerjasama Pelestarian Hutan Indonesia) (1989), 'The Cibodas Golf Course Controversy', *Setiakawan*, 2 (September–October), Jakarta.

——— (c.1990), 'The History of SKEPHI', Jakarta.

——— (1991), *Setiakawan*, (July), Jakarta.

Soemantri, Adriani S.; Soehendera, Djaka; and Widjajanti, Dra (1988), 'Pem-binaan Wanita Produktif: Sebuah Studi Evaluasi', Jakarta: LP3ES (Unpub-lished report).

Soepardjo, Rustam (1987), 'Pemerintah Tetap Mondorong Peran LPSM', *Bulletin Setia Kawan*, Jakarta: Bina Swadaya.

Soeratman, Ki (1982), *Pemahaman dan Penghayatan Asas-Asas Tamansiswa 1922*, Yogyakarta: Majelis Luhur Persatuan Tamansiswa.

Staudt, K. (1979), *Women and Participation in Rural Development: A Framework for Project Design and Policy-Oriented Research*, Ithaca, NY: Center for Inter-national Studies, Cornell University.

——— (1986), 'Women, Development and the State: On the Theoretical Impasse', *Development and Change*, 17(2): 325–33.

Straits Times (1993), *The Straits Times* (10 February), Singapore.

Strand, J. W. and Fakih, M. (1984), 'An Assessment of Indonesian NGO Small Enterprise Development Programs', Jakarta: USAID (Unpublished report).

Streeten, P. et al. (1981), *First Things First: Meeting Basic Human Needs in Developing Countries*, New York: Oxford University Press.

Strintzos, M. (1991), 'Australian Volunteer Work in Indonesia: A Personal Ac-count', in H. da Costa (ed.), *Australian Aid to Indonesia*, Clayton, Vic.: Centre of Southeast Asian Studies, Monash University, pp. 45–58.

Sulaiman, Irchamni (1985), 'Pesantren Mengembangkan Teknologi Tepat Guna Ke Desa', in Dawam Rahardjo (ed.), *Pergulatan Dunia Pesantren: Membangun Dari Bawah*, Jakarta: P3M, pp. 245–53.

Sullivan, N. (1983), 'Indonesian Women in Development: State Theory and Urban Kampung Practice', in L. Manderson (ed.), *Women's Work and Women's Roles: Economics and Everyday Life in Indonesia, Malaysia and Singapore*, Monograph No. 32, Canberra: Development Studies Centre, Australian Na-tional University.

Sutrisno, Erry (1992), 'Penundaan UULAJ Langkah Kecil Ke Arah Demo-kratisasi', *Kritis*, 36: 17–27.

Sutrisno, Loekman et al. (c.1986), 'Laporan Evaluasi Proyek PPERT Di Daerah Tingkat II Klaten, Kerjasama Antara OXFAM Dengan P3PK, Gajah Mada University', Yogyakarta: Gadjah Mada University Press and Semarang: OXFAM (Unpublished report).

Tanter, R. and Young, K. (eds.) (1990), *The Politics of Middle Class Indonesia*,

Monash Papers on Southeast Asia No. 19, Clayton, Vic.: Centre of Southeast Asian Studies, Monash University.

Tapol (1988), *Tapol Bulletin*, 85 (February), London.

Terrant, J. F. and Poerbo, H. (*c.*1988), 'Strengthening Community-Based Technology Management Systems', in D. C. Korten (ed.), *Interventions to Empower*, West Hartford: Kumarian Press.

Thamrin, Juni (1989), 'Peranan BINGO Dalam Peningkatan Pendapatan dan Kesempatan Kerja Di Sektor Non-Pertanian Jawa Barat (Kasus LP3ES—Jakarta)', Bandung: Institut Teknologi Bandung; Bogor: Institut Pertanian Bogor; and The Hague: Institute of Social Studies (Unpublished report).

Thompson, E. (1993), 'Practising What You Preach', *Inside Indonesia*, 36: 7–9.

Tjondronegoro, S. (1984), *Social Organization and Planned Development in Rural Java*, Singapore: Oxford University Press.

Uhlin, A. (1993), 'Indonesian Democracy Discourse in a Global Context: The Transnational Diffusion of Democratic Ideas', Working Paper No. 79, Clayton, Vic.: Centre of Southeast Asian Studies, Monash University.

United Nations (1993a), 'Asian Preparatory Meeting for the World Conference on Human Rights Opens in Bangkok', Press Release No. G/10/93 (29 March), Bangkok: United Nations Information Service.

—— (1993b), 'Final Declaration of the Regional Meeting for Asia of the World Conference on Human Rights: Report of the Regional Meeting for Asia of the World Conference on Human Rights, Bangkok, 29 March–2 April, 1993' (7 April), Bangkok: United Nations Information Service.

—— (1993c), 'Vienna Declaration and Programme of Action 25 June 1993', New York: United Nations.

Uphoff, N. et al. (eds.) (1979), *Feasibility and Application of Rural Development Participation: A State-of-the-Art Paper*, Ithaca, NY: Center for International Studies, Cornell University.

UPI (United Press International) (1993) (23 August), Jakarta.

US Trade Representative (1992), 'Statement of the Government of Indonesia before the Office of United States Trade Representative' (16 November), Washington, DC: Trade Policy Staff Committee, Generalized System of Preferences Subcommittee.

Utomo, Bambang S. (1989), 'Peranan BINGO Dalam Peningkatan dan Kesempatan Kerja Di Sektor Non-Pertanian Jawa Barat (Kasus Badan Koordinasi Koperasi Kredit Indonesia—BK3I Jakarta)', Bandung: Institut Teknologi Bandung; Bogor: Institut Pertanian Bogor; and The Hague: Institute of Social Studies (Unpublished report).

Utomo, Bambang S. and Thamrin, Juni (1989), 'Peranan BINGO Dalam Peningkatan Pendapatan Kerja Di Sektor Non-Pertanian Jawa Barat (Kasus Bina Swadaya—Jakarta)', Bandung: Institut Teknologi Bandung; Bogor: Institut Pertanian Bogor; and The Hague: Institute of Social Studies (Unpublished report).

Utrecht, Artien (ed.) (1990), 'Peranan LPSM di Sektor Non Pertanian Pedesaan Jawa Barat', Bandung: Institut Teknologi Bandung; Bogor: Institut Pertanian Bogor; and The Hague: Institute of Social Studies (Unpublished report).

Van de Laar, A. (1980), *The World Bank and the Poor*, Boston: M. Nijhoff.

Van Tuijl, P. (1989), 'International NGO Forum on Indonesia (INGI): Report on a Duty Tour to the United States of America 23 September–3 October, 1989', The Hague: INGI Secretariat (Unpublished report).

WALHI (Wahana Lingkungan Hidup Indonesia) (1987), *Environesia*, 1(2).

—— (1988), *Environesia*, 2(3).

_____ (1989), 'Indonesia's Watersheds Struggle for Survival', *Environesia*, 3(4): 1.

_____ (1990a), *Development Refugees: An Indonesian Study with Twelve Case Studies*, Presented at the Southeast Asia Regional Consultation on People's Participation in Environmentally Sustainable Development, Puncak Pass, 20–22 March.

_____ (1990b), *Environesia*, 4(2).

_____ (1990c), *Environesia* (September/December) (WALHI's Tenth Anniversary Double Issue).

_____ (1990d), 'NGO Joint Statement on the Indonesia(n) TFAP (Tropical Forestry Action Plan) Process' (16 November).

_____ (1991), *Environesia*, 2.

_____ (1993), *Environesia*, 7(1).

Warren, C. (1990), 'The Bureaucratisation of Local Government in Indonesia', Working Paper No. 66, Clayton, Vic.: Centre of Southeast Asian Studies, Monash University.

Warren, W. (1980), *Imperialism: Pioneer of Capitalism*, London: Verso.

Weber, M. (1930), *The Protestant Ethic and the Spirit of Capitalism*, trans. Talcott Parsons, London: Unwin.

Werner, D. (1980), *Where There Is No Doctor: A Village Health Care Handbook*, New Delhi: Voluntary Health Association of India.

White, B. (1989), 'International Experiences with NGOs Active in Developing Countries', Paper presented at the Experts' Forum on Non-Governmental Participation in Development, Jakarta, 1 May, The Hague: Institute of Social Studies.

White, S. C. (1991), 'Evaluating the Impact of NGOs in Rural Poverty Alleviation: Bangladesh Country Study', Working Paper No. 50, London: Overseas Development Institute.

Widodo M. S. (1974), 'Pesantren Darul Falah: Eksperimen Pesantren Pertanian', in Dawam Rahardjo (ed.), *Pesantren dan Pembaharuan*, Jakarta: LP3ES, pp. 121–33.

Wirosardjono, Soecipto (1987), 'Peranserta LPSM: Peluang dan Tantangan', Jakarta (Unpublished report).

Wiryosaputro, K. and Muharram, A. (1989), 'Peranan LPSM dalam Peningkatan Penghasilan di Sektor Non Pertanian Jawa Barat (Kasus Badan Koordinasi Koperasi Kredit Daerah (BK3D) Bogor–Sukabumi)', Bandung: Institut Teknologi Bandung; Bogor: Institut Pertanian Bogor; The Hague: Institute of Social Studies (Unpublished report).

Witjes, B. (1986), 'The Indonesian Law on Social Organisations', Nijmegen: NOVIB (Internal report).

Wittfogel, K. A. (1959), *Oriental Despotism: A Comparative Study of Total Power*, New Haven: Yale University Press.

World Bank (1986), *World Development Report 1986*, Washington, DC: Oxford University Press.

_____ (1992), *World Development Report 1992*, Washington, DC: Oxford University Press.

YIS (Yayasan Indonesia Sejahtera) (1991), *Vibro*, 69 (December).

YLBHI (Yayasan Lembaga Bantuan Hukum Indonesia) (1989a), 'Hak Atas Lingkungan', *Laporan Keadaan Hak Asasi Manusia di Indonesia 1989*, pp. 31–48.

_____ (1989b), 'Hak Asasi Manusia, Bagaimana dengan Hak-Hak Wanita?', *Laporan Keadaan Hak Asasi Manusia di Indonesia 1989*, pp. 71–6.

_____ (1989c), 'Hak-Hak Konsumen: Menggapai Bintang Di Langit', *Laporan Keadaan Hak Asasi Manusia di Indonesia 1989*, pp. 115–28.

_____ (1990), *Laporan Kasus (Cases Report) Cimerak, Badega, Pulau Panggung*, 1, Jakarta: YLBHI and JARIM (People's Information Network).

_____ (1991a), 'Tatanan Perekonomian Rakyat Dalam Kekuasaan', *Demokrasi Masih Terbenam: Catatan Keadaan Hak-Hak Asas Manusia Di Indonesia 1991*, pp. 73–103.

_____ (1991b), 'Hak-Hak Perempuan Dalam Hubungan Kerja: Studi Tentang Buruh Perempuan Industri Pengolahan', *Demokrasi Masih Terbenam: Catatan Keadaan Hak-Hak Asas Manusia Di Indonesia 1991*, pp. 209–41.

_____ (1991c), 'Hak Rakyat Atas Lingkungan (Sebuah Tinjauan Kritis)', *Demokrasi Masih Terbenam: Catatan Keadaan Hak-Hak Asas Manusia Di Indonesia 1991*, pp. 243–63.

_____ (1991d), 'Realitas Hak-Hak Konsumen Di Indonesia', *Demokrasi Masih Terbenam: Catatan Keadaan Hak-Hak Asas Manusia Di Indonesia 1991*, pp. 265–92.

_____ (1992), 'Reports on Human Rights Violations', *Indonesian Human Rights Forum*, 4 (April–June): 18–25.

YPPSE (Yayasan Pembangunan dan Pengembangan Sosial Ekonomi) (1986), 'Final Report for the Workshop on Encouraging People's Participation in Regional Development, 4–7 December', Banjarnegara, Central Java (Unpublished report).

Yunanto, Haris (1989), 'Kelompok Hobi Lembaga Swadaya Masyarakat Sebagai Wadah dan Bentuk Peran Serta Masyarakat Dalam Pengelolaan Lingkungan Hidup', BL dissertation, Yogyakarta: Gadjah Mada University.

Index